THE KIDS WILL BE ALL RIGHT

'This book has it all. No topic is shied away from. Robyn and Molly share their unique style and deliver an insightful, inclusive and incredibly current view of parenting and childhood. A must-read!'
— Nathan Wallis, Neuroscience Educator

'*The Kids Will Be All Right* is a timely and important read for parents in Aotearoa. Specifically, Robyn's chapter on porn and youth offers refreshing, shame-free and relevant tools for parents to help educate, equip and encourage young people as they navigate the rapidly changing online landscape.'
— Nikki Denholm, Director of The Light Project

'Robyn and Molly have taken on the unique quest of supporting parents and caregivers through the many tough conversations they need to have with their teens. It is so important for us to have books like these based in the New Zealand context. Thank you to you both.'
— Miriam Gioia Sessa, Sexual Violence Prevention Specialist

'This book offers parents of today an insight into their teens' world, providing a platform to empower parents in communicating with their teens. The easy-to-read style allows you to focus on the chapters that are pertinent to you or read it from cover to cover. There are links to research and more resources if you want to delve further into a particular topic. A big plus is the involvement of teens in the development and writing of this book. It's a great resource for parents who want to keep the channels of communication open with their teen and it offers real-life examples of how to do this.'
— Cassandra Woollett, National Clinical Supervisor at Natural Fertility NZ, Fertility Educator and Registered Nurse

A GUIDE TO RAISING TEENS IN A COMPLEX WORLD

THE KIDS WILL BE ALL RIGHT

Robyn Fausett and Molly Fausett

ALLEN&UNWIN
SYDNEY • MELBOURNE • AUCKLAND • LONDON

Disclaimer: This book does not contain medical advice.
The contents are intended for informational and educational
purposes only and are not intended to substitute for
professional medical advice, diagnosis or treatment.

First published in 2022

Allen & Unwin
Level 2, 10 College Hill, Freemans Bay
Auckland 1011, New Zealand
Phone: (64 9) 377 3800
Email: auckland@allenandunwin.com
Web: www.allenandunwin.co.nz

83 Alexander Street
Crows Nest NSW 2065, Australia
Phone: (61 2) 8425 0100

A catalogue record for this book is available from the National
Library of New Zealand.

ISBN 978 1 98854 756 5

Design and illustration by Megan van Staden
Set in Adobe Caslon Pro 12/16
Printed and bound in Australia by Griffin Press, part of Ovato

10 9 8 7 6 5 4 3 2 1

MIX
Paper from
responsible sources
FSC
www.fsc.org
FSC® C009448

The paper in this book is FSC® certified.
FSC® promotes environmentally responsible,
socially beneficial and economically viable
management of the world's forests.

CONTENTS

FIRST THINGS FIRST

HOME

GROWING IN INDEPENDENCE

WORLD

LAST WORD

PREFACE

As I started to write this book, I felt a keen need to consult with my own children. In their early and mid-twenties they aren't so far away from being teenagers that they don't remember what it was like, and I thought I'd better, at the very least, seek their comments before publishing. As a parent, through their teens I certainly felt as though I learned more from my mistakes than my successes. Well, they seem to have overlooked or forgiven whichever blunders I made. My son concluded that he is thriving — which, considering his teens, is definitely an achievement — and gave his blessing. My stepdaughter, who has special needs, communicated in her own way that she was happy for me to go ahead; and my daughter Molly watched with interest, as is her way, as I began the initial stages of drafting. That interest grew, and soon enough she became my co-author.

Writing this brought up many stories and memories of what went well and what challenged us over the years. It has reminded me of the scary bits — that sometimes loosening boundaries felt a little as though things were out of control. It also reminded me how important it was to trust yourself and trust them; to allow for some wobbles along the way; to give teens space to develop, try stuff out, experience success and failure while still within the safety of the whānau.

And then there's the indisputable and wonderful knowledge that your young person is absolutely and wholly themselves. They will forge their own path and that's how it needs to be. They won't always do it your way — but you may find that you learn an amazing amount from watching them do things their way. A full-on time.

This is my first book. My route to becoming an author was not a direct one. After a career in nursing and with a particular interest in health and wellbeing in the community, I set up a social enterprise. Nest Consulting was born in 2008 and now provides New Zealand-wide in-school education on topics related to healthy relationships, sense of self, body image and sexuality. Nest also runs parent and whānau information evenings on all things tweens and teens. In addition, Nest presents community and corporate health and wellbeing events, including peri-menopause talks and 'well women' workshops, as well as providing professional development for teachers and medical professionals. Nest's recent work has included consultation and reporting to the Ministry of Education on issues such as period poverty in schools.

Molly has been involved in various capacities since the organisation's very beginnings, initially spending weekends putting together resources, and later playing a more integral role reflecting the youth voice and assisting in the development of programmes. Since leaving school she has moved out of home (and back in, and left again, as they do), studied at uni, and been on her big OE — thank goodness, just before Covid-19 hit — and not all in the order I might have foreseen or even wanted, but it's all worked out in the end, as it tends to do. She is now busy navigating this whole 'adulting' thing and has recently gained a degree in cultural anthropology and sociology with a focus on gender studies and sexuality. Her involvement in the book gave me an invaluable perspective on the topic areas covered. Her experiences, thoughts and ideas have been captured in the 'kōrero' sections throughout. We hope you find them enjoyable and insightful.

Kōrero with Molly

I am so honoured that my lovely mum decided to include me as co-author — not that I gave her much choice! We have worked together on projects like this since I was old enough to contribute, and we have created some incredible resources to share with the young people of Aotearoa New Zealand. I am very proud of her and I'm grateful to have the opportunity to participate in such rewarding work. I remember when my mum was driving me to some after-school activity I was doing (her favourite place for a chat! You'll learn why very soon . . .), and she told me about how she was going to start a business and hopefully help teach young kids about growing up. I think my first reaction was fear that she might not be around to help me with homework as often! She included me in much of the process, and I was lucky enough not only to watch it grow into the successful business it is today, but also to be a part of it. Thank you, Mum, for being the strong, smart and wonderful woman I've had the privilege of looking up to.

INTRODUCTION:
LET'S GET TALKING

Nau mai ki enei kōrerorero / Welcome to the conversation. And what a conversation it is! Keeping on the same page with your teen is all about communication.

This is not a rule book (if only there were one . . .). There aren't any universally applicable guidelines to growing our teens; every teen is different and every parent is different, and as a result every relationship between a teen and their parent will be unique. What works for one child may not work for another, even within the same family. Ultimately, though, as your children mature, you will begin to give one another a little room so that, no matter what their opinions and yours, you can continue to enjoy being around one another.

Nobody can be an authority on everything. In some ways it doesn't matter if you don't know a Snapchat from a TikTok, or what every letter stands for when talking about LGBTQIA+ (although we will tell you in Chapter 10). Our aim instead is to give you an insight into a few 'hot topics' that may well be resonating with your teen. Being more in the picture gives you a framework within which to operate when your teen reaches out for your understanding, support and direction. Upskilling yourself will hopefully give you a chance to feel out where topics sit within your own family values. Discussions should not become a competition: empathy is key here since at times you (and they) may find the areas covered challenging or uncomfortable. Your teen is going to hear this stuff regardless, and your perspective is important. At the same time, they are going to want to start making their own decisions.

We have enquired, listened, researched, and then collated material so that we can share an overview of current learnings and resources.

The overarching focus of this book is to provide information rather than opinion — to create a platform that empowers you to start (and partake in) conversations, and a roadmap to help you understand where your teen might be coming from. They need skills to cope with what's going on around them, and you have an exciting opportunity to support them and find new ways to stay connected as you watch them thrive.

> *'Parents can only give good advice*
> *or put them on the right paths,*
> *but the final forming of a person's*
> *character lies in their own hands.'*
> — ANNE FRANK

HOW THIS BOOK WORKS

We have arranged information in a format that you will, we hope, find easy to use. Some issues may feel more relevant to you than others, so it may make sense to read the chapters in the order that best meets your current needs. At the same time, however you choose to read this book, we strongly recommend you begin with Chapter 1, 'The Teenage Brain: Communication and Teens'.

There's a lot to talk about! Though we can't cover every teen topic in full detail, we've tried to be as comprehensive as possible. After the chapter on communication, we concentrate on issues close to home — such as school, relationships, health and wellbeing. The focus then shifts to practical issues — such as money management — as you help your teen prepare to fly the nest. Later we take a broader world view as your teen looks to understand their local and global impact on society. The chapters sometimes have elements that overlap, so you might find a topic mentioned briefly in one and examined more thoroughly in another. Cross-references are provided to help you find your way around the content. Most chapters follow the same format:

Hashtags

Our media-savvy teens may understand the language of '#' better than we do. These hashtags can be a helpful way to search for more information on a topic — and they were all content appropriate at the time of going to press.

Kōrero with Molly

For parents, the teenage years can feel like a lifetime ago, whereas Molly is somewhat nearer that age. Her thoughts may act as a gentle reminder of how you, too, felt then. And how your teens might be feeling now.

What do you mean by that? /
He aha te tikanga o tāu kōrero?

This section outlines the topic, giving an overview and brief rundown of why it might be important for your teen.

Tell me more . . . / Kōrero mai anō . . .

This section will go into more detail to give you some confidence about the subject. It's a bit of a deep dive, including some user-friendly research and statistics. Wherever possible, we have incorporated Australasian data.

How can I have this conversation? /
Me pēhea tēnei matakahi?

It's important to be able to engage with your teen. The aim of this section is to provide you with some suggestions as to how you can keep talking. It's about trying to understand their perspective and trying to get them to understand yours.

Talking box questions

These conversation starters (Nest resources) are related to the topics discussed in each chapter. The idea is that they can be cut out and put into a 'box'. When you have the family together (over an evening meal, for example), you randomly select one or more of the questions from the box for the whānau to discuss. Try to make sure that everyone listens and is listened to — use a timer or some kind of 'talking stick' if you find it useful.

This exercise can sometimes be met with a groan, but give it five minutes and the teens are usually fully involved and actually enjoying themselves. It can:

- help to open debate and sound out ideas,
- let you know what your teen thinks on topical issues,
- help them articulate their opinions and respond to alternative views, and
- improve listening skills and encourage tolerance of other people's ideas.

If you don't wish to cut the questions out of this book you can download them here: nestconsulting.nz/books-products/talking-box-questions-download

Resources / Rauemi

You may want to delve further into topics that are of particular interest to you or your teen — to help you do this, resources are included at the end of each chapter.

A word on terminology

- Individual families might use different terms to refer to their young people (for example, 'child', 'kid', 'teen', 'adolescent' and 'young adult'). For the sake of continuity, we have chosen 'teen' (this is not intended to exclude those who are a little older or a little younger).
- We celebrate all whānau and communities: we have used the word 'parent' to refer to parents, guardians and caregivers in general. We recognise that your teen may be your child by birth, your stepchild, another relative, or adopted or fostered.
- We have made every effort to use the appropriate abbreviations (such as LGBTQIA+) consistently.

FIRST
THINGS
FIRST

1. THE TEENAGE BRAIN: COMMUNICATION AND TEENS

#teenagebrain #teentalk #pickyourbattles

*'Communication works for
those who work at it.'*
— JOHN POWELL

Kōrero with Molly

Being a teenager definitely wasn't all smooth sailing, and there were times when I felt misunderstood. Commiserating with my friends really helped. We could compare notes and support one another when it felt like the world was working against us. Retrospectively, emotions were high and things felt harder to control or regulate. I often struggled to differentiate between what I was 'thinking' and what I was 'feeling'. It was helpful to find a shoulder to cry on, loud angry music to dance to or some pages to scribble on.

The part in this chapter about having some of the more serious chats with your teen in the car is such a big memory for me. Looking back, I'm grateful that my parents occasionally chose this way to communicate with us. With no pressure for eye contact, it provided a more peaceful atmosphere to get into the nitty-gritty — there were also no means of escape! I still recall the many birds and bees (and everything in between) chats we had on the way to the supermarket. Weirdly, this conversation style has stuck, even now that I've moved out of home. I frequently pop my phone on speaker and have a chat with my parents about literally anything and everything on my way home from work.

What do you mean by that? /
He aha te tikanga o tāu kōrero?

Your teen is incredibly important to you — you wouldn't be reading this book if they weren't. You want to have a good relationship with them, and being able to talk to each other is a fundamental part of that, yet it can sometimes feel like they are speaking a different language. In many ways they are, with all the latest hashtags, slang and apps. Even the content of some of the topics they are discussing can feel strange and unfamiliar. It all might seem a little overwhelming.

The aim of this book is to help you stay in each other's orbit. As well as giving you a background to some of the issues that teens face, we also want to help you have open and ongoing conversations with your teen, because one without the other can be frustratingly fruitless. As they progress from the primary school years into adulthood, you will want to maintain a healthy connection with them. Teens are much more likely to listen to you if they feel you have listened to them and, even better, if they feel you've understood them (or at least shown willingness to).

The world has changed. Yes, to be fair, over time things have always changed. But in the last decade or two, the speed of this seems to have accelerated exponentially and a lot of us feel we are having a hard time keeping up. Our teens are immersed in the advances of technology and have grown up with the rise of the Internet. With so many new ways to keep in touch, all sorts of concerns are raised around, for example, privacy, dating, bullying and safety. There may even be moments when we wonder if, as parents, we are equipped to support them. And yet our teens need us — they always have and always will.

So we have a responsibility to keep the conversation going. Let them know they can talk about anything; that they have a safe forum at home where they won't be judged. Be patient, as sometimes it can take a while for them to get their heads around what they want to say. Don't second-guess what it is that they are trying to tell you: if you leap in with advice or solutions, your teen is less likely to confide in you in the future. Give them some space to process their thoughts and work things through. They will come to value using you as a sounding board. Don't be afraid that they might know more than you about some topics. After all, you can't be expected to speak with authority on absolutely everything. And it can be fun for you both if the usual roles are reversed and they are sometimes able to teach you.

Any relationship is built on a bit of **give and take**. We need to figure out how we can engage with our teens, which oftentimes is not the easiest thing to do. It is, however, essential. Up until now, you may have been used to setting boundaries and expecting your offspring to follow the rules that have been laid down. Teens tend to challenge the status quo: you may remember doing the same yourself. To accommodate this, give them a little more wriggle room and think about whether there are **different ways to frame things**. It's a question of moving from, for instance, 'Your bedtime is 8 p.m. because you have school tomorrow' to 'What time do you need to go to bed tonight? You said that you have an exam in the morning.' This enables them to start to think things through for themselves, so that they take a bit more responsibility for their actions (and any consequences!).

Teenagers tend to feel the world in a way that's really quite intense: you are with them or you are against them. And if you don't agree with them, then you are obviously against them. Sometimes when a teen is struggling, it's easy for them to focus on the downside. Try to **interrupt their negative spiral**, so that you don't get caught up in this too. Concentrate their attention on any positives.

If they feel that whatever they do, they are going to be met with a wall of criticism, it becomes harder for them to even want to engage. Yes, they were back half an hour after curfew, but this time they remembered to text; yes, they did chip that plate, but they were at least loading the dishwasher. Try to always assume that the glass is at least half full, and they will get the message that you see them, and that you see they are trying.

As they change their perspective, you may need to re-evaluate yours. In some ways, communication may be as much to do with what you don't say as what you do say. This is sometimes called **reflective parenting**, and an example might be:

Teen: 'I was so embarrassed. Tess handed out some tickets to that gig this weekend. I was standing right there and she didn't give one to me. I'd thought she was my friend . . .'

Parent: 'I'm sorry that happened. That must have been really hard. I'm hearing how left out you felt. That's really tough . . .'

You can acknowledge and validate your teen's feelings without giving specific advice. It helps to let them know that you're always available if they want to talk more about things, in their own time, in their own way.

Sometimes you might wish you could protect them: if they could only learn from the mistakes you made at a similar age . . . but they have to go through the process themselves. We can at least let them know we have their back and that we love them.

This type of **positive reinforcement** can become a habit — even if it starts out in the 'fake it till you make it' vein. What's more, it can give your teen a template for better communication, not only with you but also with others. Remember: sometimes teens say things they don't really mean, because they feel cornered or because they need to let off steam, and you're the only place that they can safely do this. It's not personal. In fact, take it as a compliment that they feel their connection with you is solid enough to push against in this way. Ignore comments such as 'I hate you', 'it's not fair' and 'what do you know about anything?'. When they shout at you that you don't understand, reply that you might not yet — but you really want to.

Tell me more . . . / Kōrero mai anō . . .

It's perfectly natural for your teen to push limits; they are testing and seeking out where the boundaries are. You may remember being a similar age: there's a maelstrom of thoughts battling for attention in your head, and the connection between your brain and the words that spill out of your mouth isn't always what it could be.

Your teen will be:

- starting to get to know themselves,
- deciding how they want to present themselves,
- contemplating where they fit in with others,
- wondering how they see themselves in the world, and
- figuring out **what they value**.

Nudge, don't nag

Your teen will begin to want to take the reins more, which enables them to further develop their confidence and self-worth. This in turn will impact positively on their wellbeing and mental health (see Chapter 8). As their parent, allowing your teen to take more control of their own life is not always easy. They might need you to respect their increasing independence, but they still need to be clear on where their boundaries are; for example, they can't stay up late on a school night. Let them know why you feel a particular rule is important. There will be times when you need to be flexible (for example, if it's their school concert). However, being consistent with your bottom line lets them know you care for them. No, they can't go clubbing until 3 a.m. on a Wednesday, because they are only 14. Think of it as them feeling out their futures in a safe environment before any mistakes might have larger consequences. Interact with them on the assumption that they are able to reason. Throughout all this, they really need you to hear them. They will (eventually) start to listen, too. Bear in mind that you may at times find them a brick wall . . . but ask yourself: would they say the same about you?

It's a good idea to **pick your battles**. If you fight with your teen over every mundane thing you will find you're always at loggerheads. Constant lecturing will begin to feel like 'white noise' to a teen. So, if they are not listening, find a different way to get your message across, instead of becoming irritated by what is, after all, archetypal teen behaviour. One tool at your disposal is nudge theory, coined a few years back by American scholars Richard Thaler and Cass Sunstein; the premise is that, by shaping someone's environment, you can influence their decisions. Note that 'influence' does not mean 'control'. 'A key factor of Nudge Theory is the ability for an individual to maintain freedom of choice and to feel in control of the decisions they make.'[1]

Ultimately, don't forget that you are your teen's cheerleader. Sometimes when they feel like you're getting at them it's worth reminding them that you're proud of them and you are on their side.

Start with the science: The developing brain

The brain grows extremely rapidly in size during the pre-school years, but after about nine years of age its physical dimensions don't really change. Nonetheless, research shows that the development in the different centres of the brain as each bit wires up and becomes functional continues until a person is in their twenties. This is neatly summarised by Stanford Children's Health:

> *The rational part of a teen's brain isn't fully developed and won't be until age 25 or so.*
>
> *In fact, recent research has found that adult and teen brains work differently. Adults think with the prefrontal cortex, the brain's rational part. This is the part of the brain that responds to situations with good judgment and an awareness of long-term consequences. Teens process information with the amygdala. This is the emotional part.*
>
> *In teens' brains, the connections between the emotional part of the brain and the decision-making center are still developing — and not always at the same rate. That's why when teens have overwhelming emotional input, they can't explain later what they were thinking. They weren't thinking as much as they were feeling.*[2]

The natural processes of brain development affect teens' behaviour. They are more liable to misread social or emotional cues, are prone to acting impulsively, and often don't take a moment in order to process potential consequences. As a result this can lead them into fights, accidents or other risky or inappropriate behaviour.[3]

So it's not just hormones that might make a teen seem a little bit all over the place on occasion (see pages 213–218).

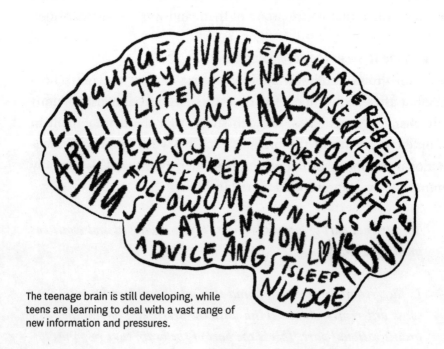

The teenage brain is still developing, while teens are learning to deal with a vast range of new information and pressures.

Try to remember being a teenager. Remember feeling misunderstood, misinterpreted, hard done by and harshly judged. Remember how hard it was to get your head around the well-meaning practical suggestions offered by your parents, which in retrospect now may feel fairly reasonable, but at the time felt like an unwarranted intrusion on your personal space. Empathise with your teen that sometimes life can feel confusing and hard to manage. This is not, however, to say that they get a free pass to behave selfishly or inconsiderately; they've been around long enough to know what is and isn't acceptable behaviour towards you and others.

As children turn into tweens and then teens, they may find it harder to control their head and body at the same time. When the big emotions do hit, most teens know the three rules — 'you can't hurt yourself, you can't hurt other people and you can't damage property'.[4] Get them to talk things through so they can start to anticipate their mood swings and learn how to pre-empt them (by going on a run, or playing the drums, for example). When they make a mistake, taking responsibility for their involvement in it is all part of becoming an adult, as is apologising and making amends.

Sleep — the teenage brain needs lots of it

The teenage brain needs plenty of sleep in order to develop, so it is ironic that changes in teens' daily rhythms mean they can often still feel wide awake at their ideal bedtime, delaying the onset of sleep. As clinical psychologist Dougal Sutherland explains, 'Their body and their brain are both undergoing a lot of development, and you need sleep to help with that.'[5]

There's an obvious tension here: teens need their sleep to be able to function, but the sleep pattern that they might naturally gravitate towards is at odds with the time frame imposed on them by school hours. It is recommended teens get 8–10 hours' sleep a night in order to be able to rest, recuperate, recharge, and assimilate the day. Some downtime and a good pre-bedtime routine — perhaps including a milky hot drink or a herbal tea — will do wonders for their ability to regulate their mood (but encourage them to avoid caffeine). Poor sleep patterns can adversely affect mental health (see page 200). Discuss with your teen the value of winding down for sleep without tech in the bedroom (see page 103). If they are using their phone as an alarm clock, think about purchasing the old-fashioned kind so there isn't an excuse for having their phone in their room overnight.

Introspection

As you're winding up for the night it's useful to think back on how your interactions went with your teen that day. Don't use this moment of introspection to beat yourself up if you don't think things went well — for example, jumping to a conclusion in a way that didn't give them the opportunity to respond and offer their explanation of events. Thankfully there's another day tomorrow. Everyone needs a little time to process things and understand where we might have gone wrong. Showing your teen that you, too, can make mistakes is powerful. We are all human. Acknowledging this, following up with apologies and putting things right sets an excellent example. It actually takes a strong person, not a weak one, to admit to being at fault. Teens also benefit from having space: space to think, to disagree and to reflect. They might be finishing their day feeling that they, too, could have handled things better.

It's important to realise that you are continually setting an example to your teen in the way you speak to others, especially when angry or upset. They are always watching, even when they don't want you to think they are. We've all got history, and living with your teen may strike a chord with something in your past or the way you were parented. You may decide you don't want to repeat some of these patterns, yet are unsure how to move forward. Being vulnerable at times is okay, and help is out there.

Different types of communication

If your teen doesn't feel heard, the reality is they'll switch off and likewise not hear what you are saying. The mechanics of communication involves listening to them, talking with them, being curious about their lives, exchanging opinions with them, negotiating situations and guiding them. In addition, communication doesn't just mean talking or body language. It also includes actions, such as being present at sports games they're playing in or watching their favourite TV programme with them. These are all ways to communicate non-verbally that you want to spend time with them and that you care about them very much.

Recognise that there are different communication styles (see box opposite), and that different individuals use different approaches. In general, the healthiest way to interact is to use assertive communication wherever possible.

The four styles of communication

A helpful resource from the UK Violence Intervention and Prevention Centre sums up the four basic styles of communication as follows, and gives examples of the things each communication type might say.

Passive Communication is a style in which individuals have developed a pattern of avoiding expressing their opinions or feelings, protecting their rights, and identifying and meeting their needs. As a result, passive individuals do not respond overtly to hurtful or anger-inducing situations. Instead, they allow grievances and annoyances to mount, usually unaware of the build-up. But once they have reached their high tolerance threshold for unacceptable behaviour, they are prone to explosive outbursts, which are usually out of proportion to the triggering incident. After the outburst, however, they may feel shame, guilt, and confusion, so they return to being passive.

For example: 'People never consider my feelings.'

Aggressive Communication is a style in which individuals express their feelings and opinions and advocate for their needs in a way that violates the rights of others. Thus, aggressive communicators are verbally and/or physically abusive.

For example: 'I'm superior and right and you're inferior and wrong,' and 'I'm entitled.'

Passive-Aggressive Communication is a style in which individuals appear passive on the surface but are really acting out anger in a subtle, indirect, or behind-the-scenes way. People who develop a pattern of passive-aggressive communication usually feel powerless, stuck, and resentful — in other words, they feel incapable of dealing directly with the object of their resentments. Instead, they express their anger by subtly undermining the object (real or imagined) of their resentments.

For example: 'I will appear cooperative but I'm not.'

__Assertive Communication__ is a style in which individuals clearly state their opinions and feelings . . . [They] value themselves, their time, and their emotional, spiritual, and physical needs and are strong advocates for themselves while being very respectful of the rights of others.

For example: 'We are equally entitled to express ourselves respectfully to one another,' and 'I can't control others but I can control myself.'[6]

Active listening

How to listen is just as important in communication as how to speak.

> **'When people talk, listen completely.**
> **Most people never listen.'**
> **— ERNEST HEMINGWAY**

Active listening is an art. Have you ever asked someone's name, and yet moments later you have no idea what it is? That's because you weren't really paying attention. Active listening involves:

- having an open mind (not immediately judging what you are hearing),
- being attentive and present (fully absorbing and not rushing the conversation),
- showing through body language that you are engaged (e.g., nodding), and

- checking that you've understood by paraphrasing back and seeking clarification.[7]

Conflict resolution and management

There will be times when you fall out with your teen: there will be stand-up rows, stony silences, flounces, slammed doors and unreasonable behaviour. On occasion it can feel as if you are treading on eggshells around them in order not to 'set them off'. If you can remain reasonable and consistent, then your teen will know that once they've calmed down there is a way forward where both sides get to be heard. Have some strategies in place so that they understand disagreements are not a competition. Conflict resolution is not about one side 'winning' and the other 'losing'; rather, a healthy debate is one in which both sides end up feeling as though they've been listened to, and their needs are met.

Remember, too, that your teen will also take their cues from how you handle yourself. It's about acknowledging that you will clash with each other sometimes, but then demonstrating how to work through this without getting angry or resorting to threats. If you can role-model coping with disagreements, you will be teaching them an invaluable life skill.

Fight fair with your words

Middle Earth, an American youth counselling service, provides the following practical tips you could share with your teen:

Remain calm. If you can't stay calm, take a break for a few minutes.

Be respectful. Treat the other person the way you want to be treated.

Be specific about what is bothering you or what you need.

Do not attack the other person. No name calling, yelling, hitting, accusing, or threatening.

Use 'I' statements rather than 'you' statements, for example, 'I feel hurt when . . .' instead of 'you are so mean when you . . .'

Don't generalize. Avoid words like 'never' or 'always'.

Avoid exaggerating. Stick with the facts and your honest feelings.

Stay in the present. Don't bring up other problems you have had in the past.

Avoid clamming up. Positive results can only be attained with two-way communication.[8]

Competing with a screen

Who hasn't messaged their teen to come for dinner when they're only a few metres away? It may seem like the only way to get their attention sometimes, given how glued most teens are to their phones (see page 102). We can use tech to bring them back into the real world on occasion, so that they learn how to value **face-to-face contact**. Sitting together for a family meal, eating and chatting, is one of the best communication opportunities there is. It might be just a few times a week, or even once in a while, but it'll still make a difference. Your teen has grown up with screens all around them, pretty much all of the time. It's the way they talk to their peers, and it informs the way they interpret the world. Keep with it, and ignore all the groans as you ask them to **switch off** in order to enjoy their company. Maybe find a little **humour** in the situation too:

Teen: Mum! What's the WiFi password?
Mum: Clean your room first.

[30 minutes later]

Teen: Mum, I've cleaned my room, what's the WiFi password?

Mum: It's cleanyourroomfirst in lowercase and no spaces.

A word on words

Remember when your parents didn't know what you were talking about? Well, now it's your turn. Every generation has its own vernacular. As social worker Amy Morin puts it, teens use slang 'to exert independence, sound cool, and/or to fit in with their peers. They seek to differentiate themselves from their parents and want to feel unique, free, and even revolutionary. Using slang helps teens do that while also bonding with friends.'[9] You could ask your teen what their slang means, although this doesn't always go down well. These days, at least, if we don't understand what our teens are talking about we can look it up on the Internet.

By now your teen is old enough to know that the swear words they are exploring with their peers are not necessarily appropriate at a family barbecue. What they also need to understand is that when we are talking face to face with someone, a lot of our messaging comes from our body language, facial expression and tone of voice. So it's not just what we say that matters, but **how we say it**. Texting and other types of digital messaging cut out a lot of this non-verbal communication, which can lead to misunderstandings and problems. Using emojis such as smiley faces, or acronyms such as 'imho' (in my humble opinion), or adding your feelings in brackets (seriously) can help others understand what you are really trying to say.

> ### 'Words are the source of misunderstandings.'
> — ANTOINE DE SAINT-EXUPÉRY, *THE LITTLE PRINCE*

Encourage your teen to be straightforward and kind in their interactions on social media. Saying something snarky but then adding 'haha' or 'jk' (just kidding) can feel a little less than honest. It may also not reflect particularly well on them.

If you are co-parenting

There are different reasons why you may be co-parenting; whatever they might be, it certainly adds another dimension to bringing up teens. Co-parenting is not always easy, as not everyone will necessarily be on the same page. Alternative approaches and agendas may mean that the house rules in your teen's other home are not even within the ballpark of your own. Whatever the stresses and strains, try to be as consistent as possible. Aim for respectful and direct communication, primarily focusing on your teen's needs, and try to avoid using them as an intermediary. It's all the better when your teen is able to see the adults involved working together to ensure their best interests and wellbeing are at heart.

How can I have this conversation? / Me pēhea tēnei matakahi?

How you communicate with your teen now will act as a building block for your future connections with them. You are there as their backstop: to listen, to support, to proffer the occasional bit of advice, and to help pick up the pieces. Not everything happens at the time, or in the manner that you (or they) might prefer or expect. Try to have an open mind, keep positive and think in terms of the long game.

**This is why we need to have the conversation,
and primarily the message here is to
set patterns for the future.**

It is worth considering **when** and **where** you might be able to talk with your teen. Pick your moment in the same way that you might pick your battles. This does not mean lying in wait for them as they come back late from a party — if they feel ambushed, they will almost certainly clam up altogether.

Though it's easier said than done, try to find a calm time and space to interact. If one or other of you isn't a morning person, probably avoid such times and keep breakfast for breakfast. Likewise, avoid such talks if you're in a rush or under pressure. We've all had experiences where we've pushed on with a conversation that should have been left to another time and regretted it.

As a family, you may have more time over an evening meal where everyone is beginning to wind down for the day. This could be when you try out some of the Talking box conversation starters included within each chapter.

Another useful opportunity for a chat is when you have your teen in the car. Keep this as a safe space to talk, free from judgement (otherwise they may start seeking out alternative transport options). There's something about the lack of direct eye contact that facilitates the conversations that don't seem to happen elsewhere (you will be amazed at how important the road becomes . . .).

Figure out when works best for you and your teen to get some dedicated one-to-one time to talk things through: over a flat white or a milkshake (at home or at a favourite cafe); sitting outside watching the sunset; on a walk (with or without a dog); doing a favourite activity together (such as going to the cinema, having a pedicure, or shooting hoops). Bear in mind that *how* you talk may be just as important as the content of what you are saying (and that less is often more).

Points to keep the conversation going

If you and your teen find yourselves drying up, or if the chat tends to be one-sided, here are some suggestions for keeping dialogue flowing:

- Encourage your teen to come up with their **own solutions** to issues before you jump in with ideas. If they are struggling, ask: 'Would you like to **brainstorm** ideas for how to handle this?'
- Your teen may sometimes want to use a less direct way to let you know that they need to talk things through. Decide on a word ('chat . . .?'), activity (eating ice cream) or neutral space (on the stairs) that serves as an open invitation to spend a bit of time together. Always try to **make space** for this if they have asked for your attention.

- If you find that your teen is on transmit mode rather than receive mode most of the time:
  - Point out how many people are involved in the conversation and get them to work out the amount of time each would be speaking if split equally.
  - Ask your teen if they ever find themselves silent only because they are thinking of the next thing to say instead of listening to others' contributions.
  - Point out that talk is organic: sometimes conversations will move on without time for their input, meaning what they want to say is no longer relevant — but there will be space for them to talk this through another time, or in another context, or with other people.
- Ask your teen how they think you might react in different challenging situations – for example, if they found themselves in trouble (crashed the car, perhaps, or got stood down from school). There is a balance to be had here: poor behaviour has consequences, but this type of conversation gives you the chance to reassure them that **you are on their side** (even though they still might get grounded).
- When emotions run high — which they inevitably will — remember that it might be okay to postpone discussions about a problem. For example, there's no point in trying to deal with an issue if tempers are frayed. By sitting on it for a short time they (and you) may find that the big feelings have dissipated, enabling a more **constructive solution**.
- You know your teen well, and will almost certainly be aware of what **triggers** them and the first signs that they are getting frustrated. Agree on a subtle cue, such as a small (polite!) hand gesture, which allows you to communicate, in company, that they might need to take a minute. Don't be offended if they use it on you when they sense you are becoming irate . . .

Talking box questions

In what ways do an adult brain and a teenage brain function differently?

See if you can explain this quote: 'I know that you believe you understand what you think I said, but I'm not sure you realise that what you heard is not what I meant.' — Robert McCloskey

Think of different ways to apologise. How do you most appreciate someone apologising to you?

Resources / Rauemi

ONLINE	Short clips explaining brain development, including how it works and why it matters: classificationoffice.govt.nz/news/latest-news/brain-development-how-it-works-why-it-matters Resource hub for parents, including information on adolescent brain development and more: brainwave.org.nz Whānau pack with information on understanding the teenage brain and how to engage with your teens: hqsc.govt.nz/assets/Consumer-Engagement/Resources/NDHB-whanau-pack-Feb-2014.pdf Information and short video clips with tips for co-parenting effectively: justice.govt.nz/family/care-of-children/parenting-through-a-break-up/putting-your-children-first

HOME

2. LEARNING AND LOOKING TO THE FUTURE

#gradesdontdefineyou #futurepathways

'Everybody is a genius. But if you judge a fish by its ability to climb a tree, it will live its whole life believing that it is stupid.'
— ALBERT EINSTEIN

Kōrero with Molly

High school felt like it went on forever and yet somehow, at the same time, went by in a heartbeat. I don't think I or any of my friends got through without at least some moments of what felt like disaster (in fact, it felt like the end of the world at the time). I'll never forget that frantic energy buzzing around as we waited to head in for an exam! Had I studied enough? Did I practise enough? Will my pen run out? I remember there being a lot of pressure to get the best results I could. We all dealt with those feelings in various ways, some of us better than others. Amazingly, we somehow came out the other side ready for the next adventure. I know the connections I made with a few good teachers and guidance counsellors made all the difference to me, and many of my friends, in getting through high school. My experience since school has taught me that there is something out there for everyone and it doesn't have to be academic. Some of my friends went straight into full-time work, others have started families, and some of us are still studying in various places around the country. The majority are doing really well. Those bizarre cliques we were trying to fit into at high school seem so irrelevant now (thank goodness). In the course of life, we've all met many new and diverse people who have helped us to widen our world view and grow into our authentic selves.

What do you mean by that? /
He aha te tikanga o tāu kōrero?

Teens will all walk their own paths through high school/kura (and beyond, into tertiary education, the workplace or whatever stage they next choose). Some will find school easier than others. Even the most academic don't normally excel at every subject, and actually your teen may love a subject that they don't score highly in. Alternatively, they might prefer sport or extracurricular activities where success isn't measured that way. Some will feel happier and more confident than others whatever their academic achievement.

What we do know is that school takes up a huge portion of your teen's world. It's all about them, as individuals, and finding out what fits for them. They will require your support, your wisdom and your understanding. Your job is to really get behind your teen and practise encouragement.

Most parents have been through the schooling system themselves. You may have loved your school days and have the same expectation for your teen. On the other hand you could have had a difficult experience, in which case you will certainly be wanting better for them. It may be that you, and your parents before you, placed a higher or lower value on schooling and further education, which may, in turn, influence your perspective. Some might feel that schooling now is so far from what they experienced that they don't know how to guide their teens within it.

A 'productive' journey through school looks different for each of our teens. For some parents, though, their vision of the 'very best' is heavily reliant on a stream of successes: their teen achieving the highest grades, ideally being nominated head prefect, taking part in several extracurricular activities, winning a few awards, securing a couple of scholarships (at least) and enrolling in university, where they end up with a double major. Then comes the well-paying and prestigious career. Perfect, and job done — right?

Well, no, not necessarily. Schooling is about so much more than grades. Some parents may prioritise academic results above anything else, yet teens develop at different speeds, have different abilities and work to different agendas. With the vast array of opportunities now available, their future is incredibly bright whether they be academic or not. There's a fine line between supporting your teen to excel at school and unintentionally sapping their confidence, which could increase their anxiety, taking up the space they need to develop self-motivation. There's also a boundary between living vicariously through your teen by holding them to your expectations, instead of nurturing their abilities.

An American research paper points out the importance of all those other skills learned at school:

> *School performance is a complex phenomenon, shaped by a wide variety of factors intrinsic to students and in their external environment. In addition to content knowledge and academic skills, students must develop sets of behaviors, skills, attitudes, and strategies that are crucial to academic performance in their classes, but that may not be reflected in their scores on cognitive tests.*[1]

Let your teen know there are many ways of being smart. A school test isn't going to show how good a friend, how reliable, how creative and talented, or what an awesome human being they are. Exams don't measure kindness, thoughtfulness or bravery. Neither do they always assess how hard a student is trying. If your teen is working as best they can, setting their own targets, and is generally happy and relaxed (allowing for the hormones), they'll be on the right path. Your guidance can help them to learn perseverance and take on more independence. During this time their problem-solving skills, initiative and autonomy will grow, excellent exam marks or not. As further discussed later, failing means developing resilience, and it's not unheard of for those who do sail through school to miss out on this crucial life skill and struggle a bit more later.

And we shouldn't forget the massive social side that goes on at school/kura, which can be equally or more difficult for your teen to navigate: which group they'll hang out with, popularity, the horrible thought of bullying, relationships that develop and potentially end, balls and other social events. All of that, plus the delights of puberty, means the school years can be a rollercoaster. Academics, at times, might be the least of their worries. Most of these topics are covered in other chapters but it seemed neglectful not to at least mention them.

So, if your teen is relatively happy and functional at school, great. But what if your teen is not? They may be struggling with additional learning needs, they may be showing signs of being 'gifted' or, as discussed within other chapters, bullying may be in the mix or mental health issues may be showing up. And if nothing becomes obvious, as a parent you can start to feel quite helpless, scared and hopeless. It's often said that a parent is only as happy as their least happy child, and in such circumstances it is entirely natural for you to feel protective and defensive. Ironically, however, these feelings are not always useful to your teen. There's a lot to unpack here, and your own experience and residual feelings from school may also be acting as a trigger.

It may even be that the school your teen is attending is not a good fit for them. Moving them to another school (if available) can have its own negative impacts, but if you feel you have explored all other avenues, it is worth thinking about. The issue could be the school and not your teen. It was the case for Melbourne parent Amy Kelly:

> *It was a good lesson for me that if you look after a kid's mental health, then learning looks after itself . . . The decision to move schools is an emotional one. Just like workplaces, each school has its unique culture, which may suit some kids, and not others. Ideally, as parents we make the right decision about the right school for our kids first time around. However, it is often not until [our] child is attending a school that we can fully gauge the culture.*
>
> *The right school environment/fit has immeasurable psychological and academic effects on your children. For my family, I look back on the decision we made with great relief. Whilst often thought to be a*

'last resort', and unlikely to solve all your problems straight away, moving schools is sometimes the best option available.[2]

Some families opt for home-schooling or online schooling (such as the state-funded Te Kura — formerly known as the Correspondence School — which, according to its website, has over 23,000 students every year). There are also private online options — for example, the Crimson Global Academy. About 1 per cent of children in New Zealand are currently schooled at home.[3] However, we all know more about schooling from home since the pandemic!

As a parent, with a wider viewpoint on life, you may justifiably look on school/kura as just a stage to pass through. For your teen, however, it is all-consuming. Moreover, school will later feed into their world of jobs or careers, further education or apprenticeships. It may form their views on travel, relationships and possibly parenting. Some will take the academic route, while others will head straight for a job; some will prioritise adventures such as their overseas experience (OE), and others will focus on what they want from their home life, fitting any work or study around this. All of these choices are valid. If you are able to be accepting of your teen's many talents and understand where their particular challenges lie, together you can find realistic goals and expectations. There's no need to narrow them down too quickly. If you can do this without imposing your own personal realities, without it needing to be on your terms and without shutting down their dreams, you might just see them reaching for their own stars. It can be better to identify their strengths than to identify their careers. Push passion rather than prestige.

Over the last few decades, life expectancy has increased dramatically. In 1952, Kiwi men could expect on average to reach 67 years and women 71; by 2019, those figures were 79 and 83,[4] and the trajectory looks likely to continue. Our teens will be living longer, and probably working longer too. They may well work in several places and have more than one career. Indeed, they may do several jobs at once. They'll need to be flexible and embrace opportunity, and lifelong learning is one of the ways they can do this. We need to remember that they have time on their side. There's no need to rush, and their first choices don't have to be their only ones.

Tell me more . . . / Kōrero mai anō . . .

Your teen needs you in a different way than they did through their primary school, so your involvement will be different too. No longer are you at the school gate. Up until recently this might have been a big part of your life. You are moving from being behind them as wicketkeeper to taking your place in the field. Trusting that your teen will be okay with this new distance is a learning in itself.

On the other hand, parents have never had more access to information about their teens' schooling. There are league tables that allow comparisons between schools and may even compare individual students. Online portals enable you to continually monitor results. Sometimes it's difficult to drag yourself away from the constant checking. Being in the loop and keeping up with what's going on at school is a good idea. Making sure your teen knows that their schooling is important to you and that you are interested is also useful. So do keep an eye on the school website and attend school events and parent/teacher conferences (preferably with your teen), but try not to add to their pressures or make them feel they are under a microscope, which is not healthy for you or for them. Allow your teen to develop to be their 'best self' by recognising and nurturing their strengths, alongside recognising and supporting their weaknesses. You don't want your teen to feel as if their best is not good enough or that they can't succeed.

Let's have a deeper look at some of the issues they may be facing.

School stressors

A short-term focus on a deadline where your teen reaches their goals is a useful life experience. A music exam can push and motivate them to practise their guitar when they'd rather be hanging with friends.

41

A bit of extra adrenaline isn't a bad thing in the right circumstances. But chronic stress is different.

Constantly piling on the pressure can create anxiety and interfere with your teen's ability to learn. This could become a self-defeating cycle for both you and them. In some worst-case scenarios it can even lead to issues with substance abuse. If you think back to when you were a teen and trying to manage stress, you may remember that it sometimes had unintended consequences — for example, avoiding tasks, situations or even people — when in fact you just didn't know how to deal with things. You may even have been accused of being disinterested, lazy or uncaring.

Ways to recognise your teen may be struggling include:

- poor sleep patterns,
- issues around food,
- excessive worry and increased anxiety,
- cheating (this can occur for a multitude of reasons and in a number of different ways), and
- becoming socially withdrawn.

These points are explored in more detail in Chapter 8. Take advantage of school holidays to make sure your teen has a complete break for at least some of this time.

Failing

Failure is a stepping-stone to success. From time to time we are all guilty of wanting to rescue our teens, unable to bear watching them fail. We may find ourselves doing their projects for them and delivering their forgotten swim kits to school, attempting to keep them from the consequences. If we are constantly saving them, we are doing them a disservice. Failing a test because they didn't study for it will teach them something, and your reaction to this failure will teach them even more.

Failure at some point is guaranteed, and a little practice while still at school does a lot to help them develop coping strategies and resilience, through which they can overcome any fear of failure; this helps set them up for success later in life.

> *'All of old. Nothing else ever.*
> *Ever tried. Ever failed. No matter.*
> *Try again. Fail again. Fail better.'*
> — SAMUEL BECKETT, 'WORSTWARD HO'

The dreaded homework

Sometimes the amount of work sent home can appear intense. It can definitely have an impact not only on your teen's academic results but also on their performance overall. Different teens approach homework differently: some tend to avoid doing it, while others may be constantly tired from staying up half the night to meet deadlines. Either way, it can interfere with the entire family. There needs to be a balance between having some downtime and getting school work completed. This balance is something that needs to be practised, and starting young is going to prepare your teens to learn routines that work for them as they grow.

It may be worth exploring with your teen if any homework problems are down to their time management or the level at which the work is pitched, or if there's just too much of it. You could ask another parent with a similar-aged teen about their experiences to get a clearer picture of what might be going on.

Make sure that your teen takes responsibility for when they have messed up: they need to do enough work for a test, they need not to stay out until all hours on a school night, they need to help with chores, or they may have a Saturday job to fit in. However, it's equally important to give them a pat on the back when they do well. If you can create an environment where they feel able to communicate with you about their school work — good or bad — you'll be better able to support them.

Here are some practical ideas to take into consideration:

- Negotiate with your teen what works best for them. If they can take ownership around when homework happens, when gaming happens and when going out happens, and their homework is getting completed — no problem. If not, they might find 'to do' lists helpful. Many phones or laptops have these inbuilt, and some schools have their own apps; alternatively, there are plenty of free versions available, such as Trello.
- Ensure your teen has a quiet, well-lit space in an area where they won't be distracted.
- If possible, purchase a 'white light' bulb — 'cool' light has been found to improve learning and academic performance.[5]
- Provide a desk that is at the right height, and a comfortable office chair (preferably one without wheels) if possible.
- If you have the space, get your teen a whiteboard for visual planning. Using a permanent marker, break it up into the days of the week and also include spaces for urgent tasks and weekly tasks. Then provide them with awesome coloured whiteboard markers.
- Check in with your teen regularly and bring snacks . . .
- Think outside the box and try to make study more fun and engaging — if your teen doesn't get on with reading, give them a graphic novel. Use crosswords to help with spelling and extending their vocabulary.
- Encourage and help your teen, if required, to access additional academic support. Some subjects or some aspects of the syllabus may just be particularly tricky, and asking for help is not a sign of failure. Often there's a lot on offer at school and there is also the option of working with tutors, even if just for a short time, like the run-up to exams.
- Remind your teen to make use of the local library — not only is it (unsurprisingly) full of books, but it also has quiet spaces, free Internet and other useful resources.

Specific support

Some students, including those who aren't neurotypical, will need to access learning support. A substantial amount of the additional resources recommended for their use are actually super-helpful to all teens, such as the whiteboards mentioned previously. It's worth remembering that, for these teens, a school day can be extra exhausting. They may have been running to catch up all day and spending a lot of energy concentrating and fitting in, so some time out after school is essential. When they come home, they need space to process the last few hours. Without this, discussions around homework can get messy quickly.

It may be that your teen would benefit from being fully assessed for any extra needs if they are showing signs of distractibility, or if they have difficulty concentrating or focusing; writing at the speed of the rest of the class; processing, hearing and retaining information; or with balance and coordination. This may also be true if you notice a disparity between how bright and articulate they are in general and what appears on the written page.

It's not always the easiest process, but speaking with the school is a good start. It certainly doesn't hurt to get their feedback and share your concerns. Ideally discuss this with your teen first. They may be fully aware of feeling different to their peers and appreciate you being on side. In addition, they may qualify for assistance that could make their life so much easier, such as the use of a computer or reader/writer, a little extra time to complete tasks and exam papers, and better understanding from teachers.

It may be that your teen has been recognised or will be recognised as 'gifted' (roughly 5 per cent of students are classified as such).[6] This has its own minefield of delights and challenges, and you may find some of the material published by Te Kete Ipurangi useful. Their website gifted.tki.org.nz (see Resources/Rauemi, page 57) also contains information specifically directed at those of Māori or Pasifika heritage.

Here are a few guidelines on gifted children:

- Giftedness comes from natural ability and cannot be learned.
- Giftedness can cause problems for the gifted teen, based largely on difference. Because their emotional development can lag behind their intellectual development, they may have different interests from their peers and may struggle to fit in — some even deliberately underachieving in order to do so.
- Gifted teens can easily grow bored with school work, and their need for greater challenges, often exhibited by asking more questions, can disrupt the class.
- You can help gifted teens by seeking and providing the right support.

So what comes after school?

When your teen is approaching the end of their high-school days, what comes next? Is it straight to work, maybe through training via a modern apprenticeship? Do they take a gap year? Go into the military? Move on to tertiary education? There are so many choices.

The last few years at school may include trying to pick the 'appropriate' topics to study to pave the way for a specific job or career. Generally this goes better when the choices are your teen's own, rather than those strongly influenced by you.

All schools nowadays offer more than just preparation for NCEA or Cambridge exams. Some have academies, such as military or hospitality, for students in their senior years who choose to target these sectors for their future. Others have courses that offer day-release and work placements. Your teen may also have a part-time job while at school that gives them some direction, even if that direction is to want something more fulfilling. Saturday jobs not only give teens more money in their pocket, but also skills they can't learn at school. Programmes for voluntary work teach them about the importance of community, and may also help them to uncover their passion (the Duke of Edinburgh's Hillary Award scheme is an example of this).

Hopefully they've had some career guidance from school as well as home and are feeling they have some sort of way forward; certainly, career guidance can help them think critically about how their educational choices affect their future. They may require your help in navigating the paperwork required when applying for apprenticeships, jobs or uni. They'll need only direction; it's important they do the work themselves. Whatever their decision, it is certainly a crossroads for your teen and can feel daunting.

Kōrero with Molly

I worked hard in school and feel like I got a lot of recognition for this. However, I don't think I necessarily left with the resilience I needed to tackle university and the real world. After taking myself so seriously throughout high school, upon entering university, I got a bit lost. It was nothing like the movies said it would be! It was also very different from high school, and neither my peers nor I were prepared for that. Everyone has such a different path to travel and a lot of us had no idea what we were doing. To be honest, though, the messy bits are the best bits.

Modern career planning

As we look to the changing work environment in the modern world, we realise that things will be different for our teens. So how do we future-proof them?

Research tells us that, worldwide, students are leaving school and uni more highly qualified than the generations that went before them. The issue, it seems, is whether the graduates are then able to match their skills and interests with a position in the workforce. With this in mind it's worth taking the time to consider modern career planning.

Advances in technology offer us exciting new ways of working, and the pandemic has thrown this into sharp relief. Some jobs are supported by tech in a way that was unimaginable even a decade ago, whereas others are becoming almost totally automated. It's not easy to predict the life choices our teens might aspire to. There was a time when careers such as law, engineering, architecture and medicine were perceived by many as the 'top rung', attracting both kudos and monetary gains.

Today, though, for those students taking three sciences and maths, there's a shift away from traditional medicine and towards STEM (science, technology, engineering and mathematics), for example. There are roles, too, that value insight and communication skills. Apprenticeships are gaining in popularity as an alternative to uni; when qualified, many tradespeople are earning just as highly as uni graduates.

Entirely new jobs are materialising, too. Only 15–20 years ago, the following job titles didn't exist:

- social media manager,
- search engine optimisation,
- influencer,
- app designer/developer,
- carpool driver,
- driverless car engineer,
- podcast producer,
- telemedicine physician,
- cloud computing specialist,
- drone operator.

It's therefore fair to assume that some of the jobs our teens will be doing in 15–20 years also don't yet exist. So how do we plan for that? We may wonder whether our schools even provide the skills our teens will need in the years ahead. Skills we were told were vital (such as spelling and other types of rote learning and memorising) aren't now prioritised in the same way. Most teens are dependent on tech for their learning. They have a spell-checker, and access to all the information they could ever need at the touch of a button, though clearly they need the skills that allow them to know *what* to Google, and enough spelling and word recognition to use a spell-checker at all.

Perhaps the brainpower no longer needed to store information can instead be channelled towards more creative and innovative thinking. In the decades ahead it may be that the following skill types and attributes will be the ones sought after:

- problem solving,
- critical thinking,
- communication,
- conflict management, and
- resilience and flexibility.

If your teen has these competencies on their CV they will have access to any number of job markets. Changes are already afoot: we are seeing some well-known organisations such as finance company PwC providing innovative options by employing (and training) students straight from high school instead of after uni, preferring to 'hire the skills of the future, not the degrees of the future'.[7]

A word on the gig economy

If you've not come across it before, the gig economy offers a new way of making a living, and it's on the rise. According to Investopedia's definition, it's a system in which 'companies tend to hire independent contractors and freelancers instead of full-time employees', with the result that large numbers of people work in part-time or temporary positions or as independent contractors. The result of a gig economy is cheaper, more efficient services, such as Uber or Airbnb, for those who use them.[8]

There are positives and negatives to this new approach, and it's not always the 'employee' that benefits. Investopedia again: 'A gig economy undermines the traditional economy of full-time workers who often focus on their career development.' Also, 'People who don't use technological services such as the Internet may be left behind by the benefits of the gig economy.'[9]

Flexibility with your skills, time and property can be seen as a real plus, but zero-hour contracts and no sick or holiday pay can make the workplace for a contractor feel somewhat fragile. This is in stark contrast to recent legislative additions designed to safeguard employment rights. There are diametrically opposed messages being sent to our teens about their career choices: freedom versus security.

Travel

While still at school, your teen may have been able to take advantage of international trips or exchanges. You may have been in the lucky position to have gone overseas during your own studies. Your teen may be excited about the life experiences that could be gained while on an OE — considered by many as a rite of passage — or working abroad on a visa, or charity work in another country. All of these things may influence their views on how they want to organise their next few years. Around 70 per cent of Kiwis hold passports, which is a lot compared to some other countries. As we write, the pandemic is curtailing almost everyone's freedom of movement; however, even with borders shut, the online world means the workforce can still interact internationally. (This is especially true of the tech sector, where New Zealand is well on its way to becoming a key global technology hub. With a healthy 'median salary of $95,000' and endless opportunities, this will be appealing information to the growing number of teens who see themselves moving into the industry.)[10]

How can I have this conversation? / Me pēhea tēnei matakahi?

It's tricky to know if you are getting it right for your teen when it comes to their schooling and what follows, and that can make things stressful. Are you too involved? Are you not involved enough? Did you miss something serious? Have you advised them well? Can they do better if you have more input, or will that stress them out and have the opposite effect?

This is why we need to have the conversation, and primarily the message here is that they'll be okay.

You are almost definitely not going to get it 100 per cent right — even if there is a 'right'. And what's working one day may not work the next. Here are a few conversation points to help you along the way:

- **Find out how they learn.** There are several online tools if your teen's school/kura doesn't cover this. Have some fun with your teen by taking a 'learning style' quiz together (see Resources/Rauemi, page 57).
- **Understand their passions.** Chat with your teen about what they're interested in and encourage them to look for outlets locally. This gives you something to talk about that may not be specifically school-related. It's a point of contact and connection.
- **Sympathise with them** if they are finding school difficult. Offer your support, and, if required, help your teen find additional supports.
- **Discuss the limits of your involvement.** To ensure you don't hover like a helicopter parent, constantly giving directions, you and your teen may want to agree on some boundaries. Make it clear that you intend to respect these boundaries, but also that you reserve the right to cross them if you feel they are at risk or they stop communicating with you.
- **Teach them by example to accept failure.** Even the most dedicated academic can flub a test, the most talented actor can sometimes be given only a minor role and the most sporty can score an own goal. And even the most well-intentioned parent can accidentally make a situation worse.
- **Don't force attributes upon them.** You may be wanting your teen to seize opportunities you didn't have or, alternatively, follow precisely in your footsteps, but it's better they find their own way and develop motivation from within. Ask, don't tell.
- **Celebrate them for who they are.** If your teen needs it, help

them find their people, whether it be a group outside of school or within it. Remember: nerds are cool now! For example, doing an evening judo or chess class might lead them to meet others (perhaps even in a different age group) with similar interests, which can otherwise be tricky at school for some. You will obviously tell them that they're wonderful, but sometimes they will need that extra boost from among their peers.

In doing these things you are creating conversations and a non-judgemental environment. Giving your teen space means that they're more likely to raise something that's bothering your teen, which may not be the same thing that is bothering you. On the other hand, you may be surprised to find you are both looking at the same problem, just from different angles. For example, you may be worrying about their grades starting to fall off without realising that your teen is deliberately not doing as well because they have been labelled a swot and are feeling socially ostracised.

Points to keep the conversation going

- Talk with your teen about **breakfast**. This doesn't necessarily mean talking with them *at* breakfast. (Breakfast probably isn't the time to have a conversation about career planning.) It's more that if they're not fuelled up before school/kura, then they're not ready for learning. You may be the sort of person who has only coffee before 11 a.m., which could send them a mixed message of 'do as I say, not as I do'. Teachers would be the first to agree; breakfast is essential in order for your teen to have energy and motivation. Your teen's attention span, concentration and memory will be greatly enhanced if they have consumed something, hopefully nourishing, before they leave the house. Teens may well be making their own breakfast, but if they're running late it's handy to have bananas and muesli bars on hand for them to grab and run (unless they can access a breakfast at school). This same point applies to **lunch**.

- Talk to them about **sleep**. As noted in the last chapter, growing teens ideally need 8–10 hours, which can be tricky when you factor in travel, homework, social life and relaxation. According to American academics Jennifer Heissel and Samuel Norris, 'Important memory formation and consolidation processes occur overnight, as the brain replays patterns of activity exhibited during learning. Insufficient sleep also reduces alertness and attention levels the next morning, which likely affects students' ability to learn.'[11] There's some interesting research that talks of teens' brains being designed to stay up later and therefore sleep in longer, and that students aged 13–16 'who started their school day at 10 a.m. had improved health. The study found that student absence due to illnesses dropped by over 50 per cent with a 10 a.m. school start.'[12] Schools, however, have yet to alter their timetables to accommodate this! Either way, a fairly regular routine of winding down to bedtime will be helpful to your teen.
- Talk with them about **scheduling and planning**. Juggling assignments and prioritising means time management, and that's another skill that, at first, your teen may need assistance with, particularly if they are involved in extracurricular activities. For example, start a conversation by saying, 'Awesome to see you putting so much into your rugby team. I love your commitment and I see your skills growing. I remember struggling to fit my sport in with my academics when I was at school. How do you think you can find a way to balance it out a bit more?'
- Sometimes teens need a little time away from things to get the world back into perspective. Many workplaces now recognise the need for 'mental health days' and offer this in addition to sick time. Allowing teens to take time out for a breather can illustrate the importance of valuing themselves.[13] Pre-agree some ground rules should your teen need the very occasional **day to recharge** — for example,

this should ideally not be on a day when they have a test at school.

- Talk with them about **discovering their strengths** and how they might integrate these into their future. Perhaps recommend your teen take a career personality test — this could be helpful even if they are already fairly sure what they would like to do. Schools may offer these, but if not, there are various online options (note there may be a cost attached to some of these), such as the Myers-Briggs Strong Interest Inventory® tool. Many careers sites also have a tick-the-box process to help identify what your teen's interests and passions may be aligned with. Again, it might be fun for them if you do the test at the same time. Also talk with your teen about, and direct them to, the huge amount of **resources** designed to assist them in deciding what they are working towards and what comes next — most schools have career departments. There are also excellent websites for career information.

- Talk with them about their **view of the workforce** and foster a connection to the world of employment. Try to allow this conversation to happen organically: some teens will be raring to go and others may find the whole topic daunting. Discuss your own work ethics and what's involved in your job, including the ups and downs of your week. Give them permission to express what they see as positive and negative without taking what they say too personally. As your teen gets older, talk about CVs, cover letters, salaries and general work expectations (for example, most jobs do still involve a 40-hour week).

'Your time is limited, so don't waste it living someone else's life. Don't be trapped by dogma — which is living with the results of other people's thinking. Don't let the noise of others' opinions drown out your own inner voice. And most important, have the courage to follow your heart and intuition. They somehow already know what you truly want to become. Everything else is secondary.'
— STEVE JOBS

Kōrero with Molly

After primary (which I loved), I felt a bit lost at my next school. My self-confidence was low, I felt a bit stifled creatively, and the student culture felt competitive and unsupportive. I had many long discussions with my parents, and together we decided it was best to move to the high school across the street — it was the best decision we ever made. It was a diverse community of people that wanted to support their students, no matter what their situation. We had an incredible special-needs unit offering extra care to students with a variety of disabilities (important to me because my stepsister and other family members have additional needs), so that everyone had equal opportunity and access to getting some sort of experience or qualification. I loved that they provided options for everyone, whether they got good grades, had a passion for sport or building things or taking photos, or a combination. Whatever you were passionate about, they wanted to help connect you to take it further.

Talking box questions

If you could be anything in the world, what would it be? Why?

Imagine a career/job that doesn't exist yet but will in 10 years' time.

Name a job that you would have been interested in doing that no longer exists.

Resources / Rauemi

ONLINE FOR WHĀNAU	Take this quiz to assess your teen's learning style: how-to-study.com/learning-style-assessment/quiz-item.asp
	Take this quiz to see if you and your teen share the same expectations — plus get some tips on making life easier during their final year of school: parents.au.reachout.com/common-concerns/everyday-issues/ things-to-try-exam-stress/reflecting-on-your-expectations
	Information about identifying gifted students: gifted.tki.org.nz
	Support for whānau and their gifted and talented children: nzagc.wildapricot.org parents.education.govt.nz/learning-support/learning-support-needs/support-for-gifted-and-talented-students
ONLINE FOR TEENS	Ten tips for dealing with academic stress: oconnorpg.com/10-tips-deal-academic-stress
	Take these quizzes for some fun and easy ways to explore job ideas: careers.govt.nz/tools/careerquest sortyourfuture.com oecd.org/education/dream-jobs-teenagers-career-aspirations-and-the-future-of-work.htm
	A guide for New Zealand students (and parents and whānau) thinking about university: thinkingaboutuni.nz
	Information for teens interested in pursuing an apprenticeship: www.govt.nz/browse/education/training-and-apprenticeships/ apprenticeships
	A resource hub for independent travelling: bootsnall.com

3. FRIENDSHIPS AND FRENEMIES

#kindness #BFF #mytribe

'Anything is possible when you have the right people there to support you.'
— MISTY COPELAND

Kōrero with Molly

I remember the groups and cliques in high school: some seemed more fun than others and some were considered popular or nerdy (I was definitely one of the nerdy theatre kids). I noticed a few of my peers found themselves floating in and out of several different groups throughout their time at school, while others stuck with one or two close friends. There were a couple of my peers that seemed content simply in their own company.

In high school I was typically drawn to those people and groups with similar goals and values to myself, but as I got a little older I found I was developing friendships with people who had completely different interests and world views.

With some of those I had known for a long time, we sometimes needed to step back to allow space for each other to grow, and to redefine our friendship — we weren't always spending as much time together but I knew we could still rely on each other.

Looking back, I now see how much things were always changing. Relationships end, people move away and we meet new friends. Although this is normal, at the time it can feel unsettling and scary. It's easy to think when things are good, or bad, that it will stay that way forever, but I've learned that's not the case. It's a bit like a TV show: there are different seasons in your life with a regular cast, plus characters that get introduced or move on, as well as plot twists, new locations, and stories that drive the plot forward. A new episode is around the corner and things will inevitably change, so I'm learning to embrace it.

What do you mean by that? / He aha te tikanga o tāu kōrero?

We can all remember the highs and lows of our teenage social life — from chatting into the small hours at a sleepover, to feeling like you are the only person not invited to a party. Connecting with others, and forming accepting and supportive relationships, is one way in which teens can begin growing into independent young people. This can be true of all relationships, from platonic through to romantic. Intimate connections obviously include additional dynamics, and these are covered in the chapter on safe relationships (Chapter 12).

The advent of social media has changed the way we interact with others. Current parents of teenagers would likely have already built up a network of friends before the Internet became such a focus (remember Friends Reunited trying to get us all up to speed and online with everyone?). By contrast, your teen will have grown up with social media at the forefront of their world, a world that can be tricky to navigate. At the same time, most teens continue to find that solid friendships in 'the real world' are still very important. Do your best to encourage this type of contact — an afternoon at the cinema with some mates is a healthy break from fishing for likes on Instagram.

US research suggests that 98 per cent of teens would say that they have at least one close friend, 78 per cent would claim between one and five, but only 20 per cent would say they have six or more.[1] Perhaps you yourself met a best friend at school and still call them your best friend today. Friends can last a lifetime. They can be our safe space, a shoulder to cry on, our biggest cheerleaders and someone we can trust to honestly give their opinion while holding our best interests at heart. They can end up being closer than family. Or they may be part of the family. Friends also rely on us in the same way, which can feel just as good: to be valued for our opinion, to be someone's 'go to' ('you're my person', as they say in *Grey's Anatomy*). Being a part of a true friendship just makes things a little easier and life a little brighter.

Whether or not this is your own experience, it is almost certainly what you would wish for your teen, given that research tells us 'social connectedness is a predictor of good mental health'.[2]

> *"'Pooh!" he whispered.*
> *"Yes, Piglet?"*
> *"Nothing," said Piglet, taking Pooh's paw.*
> *"I just wanted to be sure of you."'*
> — A. A. MILNE

Even the closest friendships can have their ups and downs. Sometimes these wobbles can make connections stronger. The teenage years are a journey where individuals are searching for their identities, and as individual identities grow and change, friendships are made and remade — and some fall by the wayside. It's also okay for friends to outgrow each other. Sometimes a friendship reaches a natural crossroads, where either a person has some new life direction or additional interests, or heads off to a different school, making it harder to communicate with their previous cohort. Some friendships just have their own intense moment in time — for example, while working on a summer project together. This can be particularly important where your teen has interests that don't overlap with their usual peer groups. The real positive of social media is that it's now much easier for teens to keep people like this in their lives, which can enable these connections to blossom and consolidate.

Other friendships may be less positive. Where this is the case, your teen needs to learn strategies to protect themselves — which becomes easier as they mature and grow surer of themself. Given that friendships are so important, it's understandably distressing when the wheels come off. To deter your teen from catastrophising, get them to think about why someone else might be behaving in a particular way.

Sometimes, with the best will in the world, your teen may find themselves in a situation where they are used as social collateral damage by those-they-think-of-as-friends. Coping with this may mean giving a certain relationship a little bit of space to find ways to later reconnect, or it may be that they need to distance themselves on a longer-term basis. Without hindsight, it is not always possible to know what is going on for another teen — for example, tension from their home life may be spilling out into their behaviour towards others. Alternatively, behaviours like excluding or trolling, if left unchallenged, can escalate into bullying (see Chapter 4).

The teenage years see teens moving closer to their peer group as they increase their independence from parents. Don't think they are not continuing to look to you, though, particularly in how they are shaping themselves and laying down their own moral code and integrity. It's just that they tend to look to their friends for the more immediate choices such as clothing, activities, music and what's trending, for example. A teen requires many relationships to become a strong, resilient adult. Bear in mind, though, that not all teens are at their most self-confident during this time, and some struggle to make or keep friends. As a parent, you may occasionally need to steer your teen in the right direction: not everything is like an American teen drama where it all comes right in the end. You still need to keep the communication channels open — **because they need you too**.

To be able to form close and healthy friendships, it helps for your teen to have good examples to reflect on — they may model their behaviour on yours, so be aware of your baggage. Try not to assume people will necessarily behave towards your teen as others did towards you at that age. In addition, your teen may want to make very different choices to the ones that you might have made in a similar situation. In order to maintain your credibility with them you need to listen, and respond non-judgementally, to their current circumstances.

It's worth letting your teen know that even though their social circle (or lack of it) feels enormously important at the moment, their current opportunities for getting to know people are in fact rather narrow. Most teens get a chance to mix only with others who are of a similar age to them. (This will be the only time in their lives it will be this way.) On occasion they may feel a little socially isolated; that's natural and normal — pretty much everyone feels this way sometimes. Encourage them with the knowledge that, as they move on from school, their world will open up and there's a tribe out there for everyone. When they are having a wobble, remind them that although they may not yet see this, you are their champion for a very good reason: you can see all their positives and know that other people will too.

Tell me more . . . / Kōrero mai anō . . .

Child development expert Nathan Wallis states: 'Human beings are an interdependent species. They are not designed to be by themselves: the whole brain function is designed to be interacting with others.'[3] Your teen's social circle may range from one or two best friends, to several close friends, to groups that hang out together. Usually their social life will be a mixture of all three.

For some teens, friendships start when they mingle with people they identify with the most — for example, by being members of the same sports team, or rainbow, religious or cultural groups. How they get to know people will also vary, from those who are family or friends of family, to those they know from school, to those who live nearby, to those who share interests or experiences. Whichever way they gravitate towards others, it's important to encourage them to be as inclusive as possible and try to overlook differences such as social backgrounds, abilities or political perspectives. By being kind and inclusive, they may find their closest friends end up having very little in common with them on paper, but are the best support network they could hope for in reality.

The way that your teen will spend time with their friends will depend on whether they prefer contact in person or online, on the geography of where they are based, and on the amount of free time they have. Your teen may be a social butterfly who exudes confidence and charisma with hordes of friends, or shy and socially awkward, or perhaps somewhere in between. Understanding where your teen sits on this scale will help you provide any support and encouragement they may need. They are who they are, and good friendships will allow them space to develop into the 'best version' of themselves.

Classifying your teen as an introvert or an extrovert can be helpful, but it's worth remembering that this definition is on a spectrum and it's rarely useful to box people. For example, although some introverts would shudder at the thought of a large get-together, others do love to socialise, as long as they can then take some alone time to recharge.

Your teen finding their tribe

So, whether your teen is the life and soul of any party or prefers not to take centre stage, it's important to use opportunities to discuss with them their ideas about what makes a good friend. What sort of behaviour would prompt them to call the friendship into question? Are there situations when they would acknowledge that maybe they haven't been a particularly good friend themselves? Can they recognise the difference between a friend and an acquaintance? If your teen is actively looking for company, their eagerness can sometimes lead them to misread the realities of a social connection. By being needy and trying to get too close too soon, they may be oversharing and a little intense, which can also leave them vulnerable or feeling abandoned. Friendships can take a while to form, even if there's that initial 'click', and it's wise to chat with your teen about not confusing someone being friendly, polite and inclusive with a friend they can rely on.

Most of us know the qualities and benefits of a good friend. These include someone who:

- can be relied upon, is trustworthy and kind, and has your back,
- is prepared to listen and, when necessary, extend some of their wisdom,

- laughs with you in the good times and is there for you in the bad times,
- brings out the very best in you and has the confidence to respectfully call you out, and
- values you for just being yourself.

The endorsement that your teen will get from realising their peers think they are a good friend will give them an invaluable sense of belonging and confidence. If your teen is comfortable in their own skin, they are more likely to attract friends. In saying that, being a part of a friendship group may well help them reach that place.

GOOD FRIENDS BUILD CONFIDENCE ⟷ CONFIDENCE BUILDS GOOD FRIENDS

And remind them: when it comes to friends, it really is quality and not quantity.

Some teens may be struggling to find their friendship group or have had to start again due to a move or other life event. Obviously no teenager is going to appreciate you attempting to choose their friends for them. School gates and play dates are things of the past, as are the opportunities to actively guide them on how to 'play well with others'. It's also often the case that you don't know the other parents as you might have in your teen's younger days to help nudge things along. Now you have to sit back and watch without interfering too much, but there are a few things you can do to help.

Assist in creating opportunities for your teen to meet like-minded peers, such as suggesting various extracurricular activities and encouraging them to host and attend get-togethers. Involving the school is a tricky one: most teens would be mortified if they thought you had asked their teachers to intervene and, unless bullying is an issue (see Chapter 4), they will probably build more resilience if they can find their own way through. Good communication skills (see pages 24–28) also go a long way, and this is something that you could help them practise.

Being alone: Loners and loneliness

It's also important to differentiate between your teen being an introvert, who is generally happy and finds renewed energy from their own company, and actually being lonely. And that's not to say that extroverted teens can't also be lonely, as epidemiologist Dr Amanda Kvalsvig notes: '[F]eeling isolated from others is strongly associated with symptoms of depression, anxiety and other forms of mental distress, and also with lower levels of life satisfaction.'[4]

Loneliness and social isolation are generally not life choices, and they can impact your teen negatively, as the statistics bear out. For instance, in New Zealand a recent social report for the Ministry of Social Development found loneliness to be highest among youths aged 15–24, with females (16 per cent) more likely than males (12 per cent) to report feeling lonely[5] (although some research suggests men are simply more reluctant than women to admit such feelings).[6] Lockdowns during the pandemic haven't helped, either, causing young New Zealanders to feel more isolated, stressed, anxious and depressed.[7]

There are some tell-tale signs that can indicate your teen is lonely:

- They spend long periods of time in their room.
- You find they are talking to you more than usual, and spending less time with friends — they may even stop hanging out with friends altogether after school hours.
- They seem to feel low a lot of the time, and talk about themselves in negative terms.[8]

They may not wish to discuss how lonely they are feeling with you: they may feel embarrassed or they may think that you cannot help them. They may not even recognise loneliness for what it is. Seeing your teen being excluded can be heart-wrenching. Try to get the message across to them that they are worthwhile, and that sometimes other teens just take a while to figure that out; that this sort of thing happens to most people at some point. Assist them to make choices, so they don't feel that you are making the choices for them — this will help them develop positive strategies for the future. If things get worse, and/or the situation continues without resolution, consider seeking some more formalised help (see Resources/Rauemi, page 204; the school counsellor, your GP or a youth hub may also have useful resources).

It can be tempting to blame loneliness and social isolation on your teen spending too much time sitting in front of a computer, but this may not be the case. For some teens, making connections online can help ease loneliness. As long as it's not to the exclusion of all else and there is balance, this resource may even be the start of solving any loneliness. This includes multi-player gaming (see page 113), which not only allows teens to connect with new people from all parts of the world, but can also enhance existing friendships. In one recent study, 78 per cent of teen gamers reported that playing online strengthened existing friendships.[9]

Navigating friendships

Good friendships give your teen a solid platform to help them understand and further develop their identity, their values, their image and their opinions. But what if things aren't going so well? Do you get the feeling that your teen's friends are always letting them down, or call them only when they want something? Do they seem to treat the friendship as a power struggle, and are never really happy when something goes right for your teen, or are otherwise a bad influence? When they have been in contact with any particular friend, does your teen seem to be more withdrawn or unhappy?[10] These are all signs of someone who is not really the most positive type of friend. In this case, if your teen decides to take a step back from an individual, or takes a break from socialising, it can actually be an emotionally intelligent move.

Falling out and fixing things

Misunderstandings are par for the course in most relationships, and not all arguments mean the end of a friendship. The important thing here is that your teen has seen examples of conflict resolution and knows that it is absolutely possible to fall out with friends and fall back in with them again. If this is a true friendship and means something to them, recognise that emotions will be running high. Communication is key, so encourage them to use their active listening skills (see page 26). Some friendships are all the stronger for finding a way through disagreements and learning the art of compromise.

If your teen does bring this type of situation to you, let them talk it out with as few interruptions as possible. It's important to them, so try to give it the time it deserves. The falling out may well have something to do with broken trust, not feeling accepted for who they are, or not being respected for their views and opinions. You'll want to validate your teen's perspective while giving them a chance to understand the context of what has happened. This may also make it easier for them to understand their friend's point of view and opinions.

Competition and jealousy can also create distance within even the best friendships. This can make it hard for teens to celebrate one another's achievements — for example, where one has been offered a coveted lead role in a school performance or a place on a sports team. But your teen needs to be able to celebrate others' successes and want the best for people. They are also entitled to hope that their friends will reciprocate. It may be that your teen is struggling with their friends' successes as they feel that they are being left behind. If this is the case, be sympathetic, but suggest to them that instead of seeing this only as a negative, they could use it as a springboard to explore avenues where they too can find validation.

Where a friendship is still really floundering, draw attention to the fact that people are not perfect and mistakes happen, but that it is possible to fix things and give the friendship another chance. Your teen can be assertive about their needs within a framework of fairness and kindness. They alone can decide if any fracture is irreparable.

Toxic friendships and frenemies

Sad as it is when your teen can't find their way back to a friend, sometimes they need to recognise that the friendship they had wasn't healthy. The term 'frenemy' was invented for exactly such connections.

Frenemies vs Friends

Sherri Gordon, a bullying prevention advocate in the US, sums up the friend/frenemy divide as follows.

Frenemy
- *Wants power over friends and to make the decisions*
- *Excludes others, forms cliques, controls who their friends are friends with*
- *Belittles, shames, and gossips about others*
- *Pursues popularity at the expense of others*
- *May spread lies and twist facts*
- *Is emotionally manipulative*
- *Talks about friends behind their backs*

Good friend
- *Collaborates as an equal in the friendship*
- *Is open, inclusive, welcoming of more friends*
- *Respects others and shows kindness*
- *Values friends more than popularity*
- *Tells the truth and takes responsibility*
- *Respects boundaries, is supportive*
- *Keeps friends' personal information private* [11]

Sour friendships, or friendships gone sour, are exhausting and destructive. In addition to the points listed in the box opposite, think about whether your teen is dreading checking their phone, is embarrassed by a friend's behaviour towards others, or even doesn't really know why they're friends with a person they spend time with.[12] It can be really hard (not to say explosive) to bring your concerns to your teen's attention, so tread carefully. Get them to discuss what a good friendship looks like, and give them space to work out whether or not their 'frenemy' meets these criteria. Try not to make negative personal comments about any of the parties involved. Your teen may be able to work out for themselves if they have a friend who is toxic. Let them know that they have a choice to remove themselves from unhealthy connections. Bear in mind that if you are having an open discussion (see page 17) with your teen about friendships, you need also to be prepared for them to challenge you about your choices. Acknowledge that it's a real life skill to be able to recognise when a so-called friendship almost certainly isn't a friendship at all. It's also a skill that will stand your teen in good stead for making decisions around more intimate relationships.

Groups, cliques and peer pressure

Birds of a feather flock together, and it can be empowering to be part of a friendship group. Some groups are flexible and open to new 'members'. Some are happy for members to be connected to more than one group. When it comes to groups and cliques, it's important that the feel is more *High School Musical* than *Lord of the Flies*. Ironically, while attempting to gain their identity and independence, some teens feel a definite need not to stick out and their individuality can consequently seem a bit lost for a time — even to the point of wanting to dress in the same way as their peers (remember the T-Birds or the Pink Ladies in *Grease*, or the Plastics in *Mean Girls*?).

Within any group there could be some who are closer than others. Perhaps new friends have come on board and there's a shuffle within the group. It can be challenging for your teen if they feel things are changing, especially if they're happy with the status quo, and they may feel a little excluded. Remind them that change can be a positive thing: sometimes things happen organically, giving them space to find their own new BFF or maybe even several BFFs.

At other times, such a group can morph into something not so fun, with rules on how to behave, meaning that others are excluded or not welcomed. Groups or cliques of this kind can be really restrictive and a stress for teens. They may feel they have to go along with behaviour they wouldn't normally endorse (such as gossiping, or spreading rumours), because they fear being rejected if they don't conform to the group's expectations. The peer pressure can feel overwhelming. They may find themselves egging on someone else's questionable behaviour, or 'throwing someone under the bus', to avoid being excluded from the group themselves.

It's really useful to check in with your teen on occasion about their social scene: whether there any new faces at school, what their friends are up to and so on. This gives them space to raise any concerns they might have about their current friendship group. You may find the box below a useful schema for this type of discussion.

Find your friendship group

Here are a few suggestions from KidsHealth for your teen on how to find the group that works for them:

- *Find the right fit — don't just fit in.*
- *Stick to your likes.*
- *Keep social circles open and diverse.*
- *Speak out and stand up.*
- *Take responsibility for your own actions.*[13]

Try to get your teen to use their own examples so you are not overly steering the conversation. This can give them a moment to reflect on their own values without you having to say too much more. Leave the door open for them to chat further once they've had a think.

Bear in mind, not all peer pressure is negative. Positive messaging from those with your teen's best interests at heart can encourage and challenge them, meaning that they are supported in achieving their goals, whether they be sporting, academic, personal or otherwise.

Kōrero with Molly

Loneliness is uncomfortable, but a toxic friendship can feel much worse. I think most of us have been there at some point... It can be hard to see it at first, but eventually we find ourselves having to let go of friendships that aren't serving the people involved.

I remember navigating friendships, cliques and fallings-out as a big part of high school. At the time, it felt like my whole world! I met some incredible people throughout my schooling years who I went on to flat and travel with. They are still my best friends as a young adult. The friends that I value in my life give me the space to be who I am. They encourage me and hold me accountable, and I do the same for them. Sometimes they even push me out of my comfort zone — for example, motivating me to do a 2-kilometre extreme off-road run through the New Zealand bush and big muddy puddles (trust me, this is really not my thing, but boy was I proud that I did it!).

Disengaging from a friendship or group

It's horrible to fall out with people. And it's really horrible to watch your teen go through this, particularly if they seem to be getting the raw end of the deal. Sometimes they may need to be a little more proactive in disengaging from a particular person or group; at the same time, try to encourage them to 'create distance with dignity'.[14] There will inevitably be a lot of feelings, but they should avoid bad-mouthing any of those involved — either face to face or online — even if they are experiencing this kind of treatment themselves. If you can see that your teen is having a hard time, try to give them a boost — it's important that any social isolation doesn't impact on their wellbeing and mental health (for example, on their eating or sleeping patterns; see also Chapter 8).

A word on friendships in a pandemic

Covid-19 meant changes worldwide, with most countries sensibly mandating lockdowns and social distancing, and cancelling larger gatherings and events. With sporadic and continued school closures, many teens missed out on some pretty important events that would have been part of their usual rites of passage, such as their end-of-year ball/prom or school graduation. It was also a tricky time for those who were in the process of making new friends, since some of the natural opportunities to do so had been removed. This kind of life-changing event can cause anxiety; as professor of psychology Catherine Bagwell points out, 'Social distancing contradicts much of what being a teenager is all about.'[15] American research on young people's health and habits during the pandemic found three-quarters of parents reporting negative effects on their teens' social connections.[16] The world over, teens struggled with the reality of not being able to connect with their friends for support. Unsurprisingly, social screen time increased — when hanging out in person is not an option, safe online communication then becomes even more important.

How can I have this conversation? / Me pēhea tēnei matakahi?

After spending so much of your life feeding, watering and nurturing your offspring, it can feel a little disorienting when they blossom into teens and suddenly it's as if their friends are their first and only priority. Nonetheless, it's completely age appropriate for them to start to define their own identity by extending their social circle.

**<u>This is why we need to have the conversation,
and primarily the message here is that
they want to find their tribe.</u>**

You will always be there for them, and, safe in this knowledge, they can begin to spread their wings.

Points to keep the conversation going

- Chat with your teen about the **differences between people** when it comes to friends: some have just one or two, whereas others have many. Help them find out what works best for them. Brainstorm some opening conversations and give them some **ice breakers** if they feel nervous about approaching new people.
- Use **teachable moments** to think together about what a **good friendship looks and feels like**: there are plenty of opportunities when watching a movie or a TV series, or in celebrity news. Talk with your teen about your own friendship experiences from when you were their age. Discuss the challenges and positives from various friendship types. In sharing, you can support them in **developing their own judgement**.
- Does your teen feel that their groups are **inclusive**? Ask them what they would do if there was a new kid at school, and get them to imagine how they would want to be treated if they were the new kid.
- Explain that it's crucial to be able to feel you belong and make connections with **people who understand you**. Encourage your teen's **social connections**, whether these are school-related or extracurricular events, or something more specific to their needs for support — for example, a rainbow youth group.
- Ask them how their **friends stand by one another**, and how they would react if one of them was having a hard time and needed help.
- Create an environment where they are **comfortable chatting about their friends** and the current highlights and dramas,

and try to be non-judgemental (where they have fallen out with someone, they may be BFFs again the next day). Give them the space to come up with their own plan. Encourage them to see situations from all sides — and to empathise if and when appropriate. By offering your opinion only when requested or via open questions, you may encourage your teen to **keep you in the loop.**

- If you have concerns about whether your teen is being treated well by their friends, ask them **why they like them.** Try to focus any conversation on the outcomes, rather than point a finger at a particular person. You could comment that when they spend time with this friend or friendship group you notice they aren't quite themselves. Remember that they need your support, not your criticism — they may feel that they have only limited friendship options available to them.

- Let your teen know it **takes skills both to start and to end a friendship.** It may not feel the most natural thing in the world to start talking to someone you don't know. Equally, it can feel unimaginable to stop being close to someone who has been a special part of your life. It's okay to talk things through.

- **Check in regularly** as to how your teen is doing in times when they are unable to see their friendship groups, whether this be due to a lockdown, illness or moving away. If they have a sibling at home, perhaps set them tasks around the house that require a bit of teamwork: the interaction may initially feel a bit forced, but it can improve sibling bonding and encourage friendship skills, as well as help fill the gap left by absence.

Talking box questions

What do you look for in a friend?

Can you think of a fictional friendship that you would want to emulate and why?

Resources / Rauemi

ONLINE	Resource hub with tips and advice on friendship: whatsup.co.nz/teens/friendships
	How to identify and handle your frenemies: tearaway.co.nz/how-to-identify-and-handle-your-frenemies
	A guide to supporting your teen with friendship issues: kidspot.co.nz/tweens-to-teens/helping-teenager-with-friendship-problems

4. BULLIED, BULLYING AND BYSTANDERS

#pinkshirtday #speakupstandtogether #antibullying #choosekindness

'We explain when someone is cruel or acts like a bully, you do not stoop to their level. Our motto is when they go low, you go high.'
— MICHELLE OBAMA

Kōrero with Molly

Everyone I know has been, directly or indirectly, impacted by bullying throughout their schooling experience, some of us worse than others. Some of my peers were particularly competitive, catty, judgemental and fond of spreading rumours. Before I found my close tribe, and with no one in my corner, I really struggled. When I did find them, and felt a little more confident in who I was, bullying behaviour seemed to wash off me. One particular incident that has stuck with me was when a group of popular boys decided to tease me one afternoon about my weight. I was hesitant to talk to a teacher about it, but eventually I did. The teacher's input did contribute to resolving the situation and helped my peers see how their actions and words can hurt (and the boys were asked to apologise). Despite their embarrassment about a joke gone wrong, I think they took that lesson with them as well. There were people in my classes and in my friend groups, however, who continued to struggle and became easy targets for the more intimidating among us. It was important to me that I supported those people after having experienced bullying behaviours myself. Some of my friends had it a lot worse than I'd thought, and it wasn't until we were a bit older that they had the courage to talk about it.

What do you mean by that? /
He aha te tikanga o tāu kōrero?

Bullying is a perennial problem. It takes place in many different forms and in a wide variety of settings that aren't exclusive to teens: within the home, relationships, friendships, the workplace and online. This chapter focuses primarily on what your teen may experience within their peer group, at school, in any activities outside school and now also in cyberspace. It explores three distinct perspectives: your teen **being bullied**, your teen **being the one who bullies**, and your teen **being in a situation where there is bullying going on**. As a parent, it is important to know how to recognise when this happens, give the appropriate support to those involved and, where required, seek assistance.

The last thing you want to hear is that your precious teen is being bullied or hurt in any way. What's more, if you find out about it indirectly, it can be particularly tricky to know how to deal with it. Broaching the subject with them and getting them to open up isn't always easy. This news can bring up intense feelings in parents, and you could be bringing your own baggage to this, so it's good to be alert to your own triggers and any past experiences. Mama and Papa Bear rage is understandable, but it's not useful in tackling the problem. Be aware of instant or knee-jerk reactions. You may even be tempted to take the matter into your own hands, but this rarely fixes the problem, nor does it model good coping mechanisms to your teen. Ultimately the bullying needs to be resolved, with your teen coming away feeling empowered and gaining skills for themselves. You are on their side and they need to see you as part of their team: if you cause further damage it may take a long time for them to trust you enough to reach out again. You can let them know that nobody has all the answers while **helping them find their strategies**. What you can tell them for certain is that no one deserves to be bullied and that includes them.

If you hear that your child is the one doing the bullying, it will undoubtedly bring up strong feelings. Here the response does need to be immediate. They need to know clearly that their behaviour is unacceptable and has to stop straight away. It may be that they need some support in order to take responsibility for their actions and to change their ways. If you understand the context of their bullying behaviour, although not excusable it may be explainable. If a teen is bullying, they need as much appropriate, multifaceted help as possible in order to stop straight away.

We know that bullying occurs way too often and that even if your teen has not been bullied, they will probably be aware at some point of others in this situation. Some safe steps to tackle bullying are discussed below; as a parent you will need to know how to convey these messages. It is also important to check in with yourself and the whānau/family to ensure that behaviour at home isn't in any way inadvertently or overtly bullying.

Tell me more . . . / Kōrero mai anō . . .

As the United Nations acknowledges, 'School-related violence in all its forms is an infringement of children's and adolescents' rights to education and to health and well-being. No country can achieve inclusive and equitable quality education for all if learners experience violence and bullying in school.'[1]

So how can you recognise bullying? How do you determine if the situation is more than just a bad day, or friends being a bit off? There is a nuance here: there are bullying behaviours and unpleasant instances that do not constitute a pattern of bullying. That's not to say these occurrences aren't serious in themselves. Most widely accepted definitions of bullying are based on four elements: it is **deliberate and intentional**; there is a **misuse of power** in a relationship; it is **repetitive**; it is behaviour that **causes harm**.[2] Broadly speaking, this pattern of behaviour rests under four headings: **verbal** bullying involves hurting a person by means of saying or writing mean things; **physical** bullying involves hurting a person's body or their possessions in some way; **social** bullying centres on the damage to a person's relationships or reputation, including being socially excluded; **cyberbullying** involves the use of digital technology to deliberately harass or humiliate.[3]

Bullying, as defined above, is serious, and the statistics give us an insight into its prevalence:

- A 2007 estimate put the worldwide number of children and youth being bullied by their peers at any one time at 200 million.[4] (Sadly, there is no reason to believe this number has reduced.)
- Fifteen-year-olds in New Zealand reported the second-highest rate of bullying out of 51 countries.[5]
- One in two New Zealand children are reported to have been bullied.[6]
- In one study of New Zealand students, 8 per cent reported being threatened, 7 per cent said they had been hit or pushed around by other students, and 6 per cent said other students took or destroyed things that belonged to them.[7]
- In another survey, 25 per cent of New Zealand parents or caregivers indicated that their child had been a victim of cyberbullying at some point in their lives.[8]
- In a 2013 survey, 94 per cent of New Zealand teachers said bullying occurred at their school, with around 45 per cent saying verbal and social bullying was brought to their attention once a week, while 25 per cent heard of physical bullying once a week.[9]

Bullying is harmful and can have deep and lasting psychological effects. Being bullied can impact on your teen's sense of safety, diminish their self-esteem, limit their ability to study, and be detrimental to their wider experience both inside and outside of school. An American study found that students who were bullied have more negative feelings: about themselves (27 per cent), their relationships with friends and family (19 per cent), their school work (19 per cent) and their physical health (14 per cent).[10] Victims of bullying tend to find it difficult to forge friendships or settle at school. They can even feel suicidal.

There are also repercussions for the one doing the bullying, and for others who witness what is going on; one study found that bystanders often report feelings of guilt or helplessness for not confronting the bully and/or supporting the victim.[11]

Being bullied

Bullying certainly says more about the person bullying than about the people they target. Bullies are usually focused on people they see as vulnerable in some way, or whom they consider easy to intimidate. While bullying can occur across the spectrum, it seems some groups are more vulnerable than others, including rainbow youth, those with disabilities or special needs, and socially isolated youth.[12]

In saying that, being bullied can amount to no more than being in the wrong place at the wrong time, and no teen is necessarily immune from being targeted. No matter what, **it is never the fault of the teen being bullied**; rather, it is always the person bullying who is making the wrong choice. They are misusing their power in a repeated pattern of intentional, harmful behaviour, and it's they who need to change. A UK research project found the following perspectives from respondents aged 12–18 years who had been bullied within the previous 12 months:

Who bullied you?
- a classmate (62 per cent)
- somebody at school I don't know (37 per cent)
- an ex-friend (34 per cent)
- an enemy (30 per cent)
- a close friend (30 per cent)
- an ex-romantic partner (10 per cent)
- a current romantic partner (4 per cent)
- my brother/sister (9 per cent)
- a family member (6 per cent)
- a teacher (7 per cent)
- I don't know who they are (10 per cent)
- someone I know only online (10 per cent)

Why?
- my appearance (47 per cent)
- the clothes I wear (17 per cent)
- my mannerisms (11 per cent)
- my sexuality (11 per cent)
- gender identity (4 per cent)
- people misunderstanding my sexuality (22 per cent)
- a health condition I have (8 per cent)
- a disability I have (7 per cent)
- my race (6 per cent)
- my culture (5 per cent)
- my religion (5 per cent)
- something I did (24 per cent)
- the things I do online (8 per cent)
- my interests or hobbies (30 per cent)
- my high grades (13 per cent)
- my low grades (11 per cent)
- my low household income (8 per cent)
- my high household income (6 per cent)[13]

If your teen is being bullied, they may tell you directly or you may find out from someone else. There are also several signs that may indicate they are in this situation, although these can be attributable to a number of causes, so it's important to try not to make assumptions. At the same time, if they're repeatedly demonstrating a number of symptoms from the list below, it's clear that they may be unhappy:

- Physical injuries and frequently missing gear or money (including lunch, which may show in how hungry they are upon returning home) are harder to miss. More subtle alerts include communication changes such as stuttering, being unwilling to talk about things, and increasingly seeming to be alone and miserable.
- Fear can manifest as not wanting to attend school or trying

to find a new way to get there. You may even hear from their homeroom teacher if there are concerns about behaviour changes at school, whether academically or socially.

- Other generalised observations are discussed more thoroughly in Chapter 8, including issues with eating, sleeping and mood.

You can help relieve the stress and pain caused by bullying.[14] Start off by giving your teen some space in a supportive and non-judgemental environment to let you know what is happening. See if you can establish how long it has been going on — and, if possible, why it started. This is not to imply that they are in any way responsible for being bullied, but rather that it may help in finding a solution. Your teen may feel embarrassed, helpless or fearful. They may also be worried that if you get involved it might exacerbate the problem. Once you've listened to them, show them you are calm and that you believe what they are saying. You can then reassure them and begin to work together to find solutions. Ask them how they think you can help and try to find a way through that is safe for them and won't make matters worse.

Dealing with this should be thought of as a process: it's not a one-off conversation, so check in with your teen regularly as to how they are doing and how things are going. The following suggestions may help:

- Initial strategies can include some role-playing and rehearsed responses, which may help to guard against your teen reacting to being bullied with anger or fear. If they can be successful in just walking away and not engaging, great; however, if this isn't working, some short phrases, well-placed humour and training in eye contact can move things on. Their response should avoid escalating the situation and ideally should even de-escalate things. The message that needs to be sent to the bully is that their pattern of behaviour will not be successful.
- A frequent aspect of bullying is isolation, so another step may

be to encourage your teen to have their friends around them: there's strength in numbers. If this is problematic for your teen, some schools have peer support systems in place. Showing that they have allies helps to challenge the intimidating behaviour. It's not, however, about becoming intimidating themselves.

- If things are not improving and your teen feels comfortable to do so, encourage them to speak with a teacher they respect and/or the school counsellor, who should be able to help with more strategies or implement a plan if required. Let your teen know there's a difference between 'narking' or 'telling on' peers and protecting themselves. Also, by challenging bullying behaviour it might interrupt the person bullying, which in turn will undoubtedly protect others.

- You may get to the point where you feel you need to approach the school yourself. It should have policies in place designed to address bullying and to protect your teen. Book an appointment with your teen's dean or the school counsellor. Provide them with any evidence you have. Ensure your teen is informed, involved and reassured throughout.

- If you feel the school is not taking the situation seriously, then you have the right to contact the Ministry of Education or the Office of the Children's Commissioner.[15]

A whole-school approach is key when tackling bullying — whether it's done in-house, or via one of the specifically designed programmes available. The holistic approach looks to: increase understanding of the potentially catastrophic outcomes of bullying; explore strategies for both those experiencing bullying and those who witness it; encourage empathy; teach skills around how to stick up for others; provide processes to deal with bullying behaviours; and suggest reparation methods. If this is not already happening within your teen's school, you may want to suggest that they consider implementing a proactive response. As a parent you also need to know what support there is for you (see Resources/Rauemi, page 98).

Obviously bullying can occur outside of the immediate school environment — for example, at extracurricular activities and clubs (which may also be attended by those that are home-schooled). Another context for bullying might be the school bus. If the strategies discussed above are unsuccessful, you could approach the leaders of any group or the bus company. What's more, if you do so, it's a good idea to let your teen's school know what's going on. In many cases those doing the bullying may also be connected to the school. Alerting the school to the fact that there is a bullying problem gives them a chance to support your teen and, where appropriate, instigate a broader response. It's about creating a safer environment all round, with an atmosphere where teens know it's not cool to bully, where they celebrate diversity, stick up for one another, and safely action incidents they see and hear that aren't okay. If bullying is seen as being a dysfunctional behaviour, then hopefully over time fewer people will want to be seen as dysfunctional.

Remember, you have the final option of removing your teen from any situation where you feel they are unsafe. Uninterrupted, bullying can escalate, and there will be occasions when it becomes serious enough for the police to be involved, in which case contact your local station immediately. See also the Resources/Rauemi section on page 98 for organisations and online support, as well as the list of helplines on page 393.

Cyberbullying

Cyberbullying refers to bullying that takes place online, and in an era when almost all teens have online access, it's a growing and worrying problem. In a 2020 survey of more than 6000 10–18-year-olds across 11 European countries, about half of the subjects had experienced at least one kind of cyberbullying in their lifetime, and 44 per cent of those who had been cyberbullied before lockdown reported an increase during lockdown.[16]

British educator Emily Marbaix identifies several types of cyber-bullying, including:

- **exclusion** — where a group online removes or excludes the person who is being bullied;
- **harassment** — where the person is targeted with offensive or abusive messages/images either directly or via a group post;
- **flaming** — similar to harassment, but two-way, in that the initial abusive post is responded to and a cyber 'fight' ensues;
- **masquerading** — which involves creating fake social media accounts or fake user profiles with the intention to abuse others online, including pretending to be the person who is being bullied;
- **trolling** — when people deliberately post negative comments with the intention of getting a rise out of others, often doing this behind a fake account; and
- **outing** (also known as **doxing**) — where someone shares private information designed to upset or humiliate the person it's written about.[17]

Cyberbullying is insidious. It can affect teens 24/7, and as most have some sort of Internet-capable device on them at all times, it is difficult for them to get away from it. It is certainly difficult to monitor as it's often completely out of sight from parents. Your teen may be reading a bunch of negative comments on their media platforms. These words and images are there for them to revisit and possibly available for their peer group to see. It's hurtful enough when negative comments come directly out of someone else's mouth — but at least then there is a chance to disassociate from what is being said. There is an additional impact when your teen is reading these words in their own inner voice: it's almost as though they are saying these horrible things about themselves to themselves, which makes it so much harder to disregard them.

One study reported that over a quarter of teens deleted their media profile as a result of bullying.[18]

THINK

BEFORE YOU POST

Is it **T**RUE?

Is it **H**ELPFUL?

Is it **I**NSPIRING?

Is it **N**ECESSARY?

Is it **K**IND?

An acronym for the key features of positive online behaviour.

If you can have ongoing conversations with your teen about digital citizenship and cyber safety, they will know there are expectations of how they should conduct themselves online (see page 104) and therefore also recognise when others are behaving in ways that are unacceptable.

You have to establish positive channels of communication with your teen, not least because research suggests that currently 'only about 38 per cent of [teens] who've been bullied online seek parental guidance'.[19] Always take note if your teen's behaviour changes immediately after having spent time online.

If your teen is being bullied in this way, one practical approach you can use is to take a screenshot of relevant interactions and store it on your own phone, so your teen no longer need have it on their device. You'll also have evidence for the school or any other authorities that might become involved. In addition, you should seriously consider reporting bullying to those running the relevant social platforms or the cell phone service provider.

You may be tempted to protect your teen by taking away their technology. Don't, as this might also have the effect of removing their supports and will discourage them from opening up to you. The possible exception to this would be overnight to ensure that they get a break (and, hopefully, some sleep). Instead, it's better to work with your teen to find a solution that holds them at the centre of the plan.

Countries around the world are recognising the dangers of cyber-bullying and many are working through how to legislate against it.[20]

Being the one who bullies

As New Zealand mother Kasey Edwards reported, the thought of learning that your own child is the bully is very hard to swallow:

> 'I hope she doesn't get bullied,' I confided to my husband on our daughter's first day of school. 'I hope she doesn't bully,' my husband replied. The thought that my darling angel could bully another child had never once entered my head. And when I did think about it I dismissed it immediately. I suspect I'm not alone because two years later, and after countless conversations with parents, I've heard many stories about children being bullied. But I'm struggling to think of even one time a parent told me that their child had bullied.[21]

There are only limited statistics on the number of teens who bully: it's not as if someone who bullies is likely to put their hand up. They may not even recognise that they are being intimidating to others. With that in mind, it is perhaps not surprising that a piece of US research found that more than twice as many students were categorised as bullies via peer nomination (11 per cent) as compared to self-reporting (5 per cent).[22]

What we do know is that there are some common features found in those who bully. These include poor self-esteem, often displayed in an inability to fit in with peers. As a consequence of this they may not be able to forge healthy long-term friendships. In addition, their behaviours can show signs of stretching boundaries, anger, and acting out without a true understanding of consequences.

If you are made aware of concerns that your teen's behaviour is bullying, be prepared to openly and approachably ask, 'What did they do?' Try to listen in a receptive way and be prepared to act on what you hear. You will also need to give your teen space to say what happened in their own words. See if they can understand the situation from the perspective of the person who feels bullied. They may need help in order to do this. It takes some longer than others to truly put themselves in another's shoes. Empathy is a skill. Your teen needs to learn that bullying is an unacceptable behaviour, and that it has consequences for them. They need to understand the impact of their actions, and to regret having caused distress or pain. Otherwise, they will see themselves as having been 'picked on' because they got into trouble for what they did. Separate them from the negative behaviour, but hold them accountable for what they have done in order to bring about effective change. Once a bully, not necessarily always a bully.

Help your teen find out what they can do to make things better. If you need support, there are options available (see Resources/Rauemi, page 98).

Why teens bully

Teens bully for a variety of reasons, and discovering what is behind their motivation in order to address it is imperative to break this pattern. They may bully because:

- they do not fully grasp the concept of empathy and how their behaviour is making the victim feel,[23]
- they have low self-esteem and want to take (perceived) power from others to feel better about themselves,[24]
- a group of friends is picking on one classmate,[25] and they want to fit in with the clique, perhaps for fear of otherwise becoming the one bullied,[26]
- they believe they need to pick on others in order to climb the social ladder,[27]

- they are seeking attention from teachers, parents or classmates, particularly if they've failed to get it in other ways,[28]
- they misguidedly believe they are defending themselves, if they have a tendency to perceive the behaviour of other kids as hostile even when it is not,[29]
- they are driven by prejudice against someone, or because they feel threatened by difference,[30] or
- they want to feel power and control over their own environment if they are experiencing bullying themselves.[31]

It can be hard to think your teen would behave in such a way. If your teen has bullied, you may be justifiably furious with them, but obviously you can't just berate them as this would not demonstrate the positive patterns you want to instil in them. You may also be worried, or feel guilt or shame, about how the situation may reflect on you and your parenting; you may also feel disappointed in your teen. This is quite normal.[32] The best parenting you can do here is have them take responsibility for their actions and model the behaviour you want to see in them.

Ensure your teen knows you have zero tolerance for harming others. There are some practical steps you can take to interrupt their online bullying, such as restricting their unsupervised access to the Internet, or monitoring their social media usage for a period of time. A multifaceted approach may be required as the causes of their behaviour may be deep-seated. It is a huge parenting choice to report your teen if you think that they have been bullying, but doing so may open new avenues for help; it may for example, give them access to the school counsellor.

Being in a situation where there is bullying going on

If your teen is neither being bullied nor bullying, that's not the end of the story. Should they find themselves observing a negative situation, they are still involved in what is happening to a degree,[33] and their response can play out in a variety of ways. They might exacerbate the problem (be a **colluder**), they could choose to do nothing (be a **bystander**), or they could assist in the solution (be an active bystander, sometimes referred to as an **upstander**).

Intervention can be key, with one study showing that stepping in halted more than half (57 per cent) of bullying situations.[34] This is by no means straightforward. As one US research team noted, 'Some bystanders are plagued by uncertainty. They see the bullying and know in their heart that it is wrong, but they have no idea what to do.'[35] As a parent you will undoubtedly want your teen to do the right thing; however, you will also be wanting them to make decisions that keep them safe. It might be a helpful exercise to discuss their role as a possible upstander so that they can be informed and prepared — one useful tool is the 5Ds schema developed by Green Dot and advanced by Hollaback!:[36]

- **Distract** — your teen could take an indirect or subtle approach to **draw the attention away** from the scene. In this approach they should ignore the person who is bullying, and talk instead to the person being bullied — for example, by asking an unrelated innocuous question, such as what time it is, or creating a distraction, such as spilling a drink.
- **Delegate** — if your teen is not comfortable with intervening, or it is not safe for them to do so, they could find a **third party** to help. This may be a teacher, the bus driver or even another friend. With someone else involved, your teen may then be able to check in on the person being bullied to see if they are okay.
- **Document** — if someone else is already assisting, it can be extremely useful to **record a harassment event**, though only if it is safe to do so. Smartphones make this relatively straightforward. If videoing, it can be helpful to say the date and time, and feature a street sign or other landmark. The record may be used as evidence, should the situation warrant it, and your teen should not share or post it online — certainly not without permission from the person being bullied.

- **Delay** — if your teen is **unable to act in the moment,** they could step up later, when there is no further danger, to ensure the person being bullied is okay and offer any support needed. If appropriate, they could offer to document or be a witness.
- **Direct** — it is problematic to advise someone to directly intervene in a situation where a person is being bullied. If your teen has assessed the situation and determined they could safely **call the person out** without risk to themselves, they should keep any conversation direct and to the point, for example by saying, 'Leave them alone,' or, 'That's homophobic — just stop.' They should not engage in discussions or make themselves into a target.

A word on Pink Shirt Day

Pink Shirt Day began in Berwick in Nova Scotia, Canada, in 2007. It was instigated by two students who witnessed the homophobic bullying of a fellow student who was being harassed for wearing pink clothing. In an effort to address this, they encouraged as many classmates as possible to wear pink the following day. After the message went viral on social media, a large number of students arrived wearing pink, many from top to toe. This peer support made such an impact that it soon turned into an annual event across Nova Scotia, and then went global.

New Zealand joined this activism for the first time in 2009 and now many schools and groups celebrate Pink Shirt Day Aotearoa with various activities and, of course, students wearing pink. The aim is to raise awareness about bullying prevention, supporting one another, celebrating diversity, and ensuring all spaces are inclusive and safe for all people. The support of the LGBTQIA+ community remains a particular focus alongside broader targets of bullying. Pink Shirt Day Aotearoa, which is funded by donations and run by the Mental Health Foundation, is usually on the Friday of Bullying-Free New Zealand Week in May.

Kōrero Mai, Kōrero Atu, Mauri Tū, Mauri Ora

Pink Shirt Day Aotearoa's tagline is 'Kōrero Mai, Kōrero Atu, Mauri Tū, Mauri Ora — Speak Up, Stand Together, Stop Bullying'. In the words of the organisers:

> 'Speak Up' refers to having conversations with your friends, whānau, children, kaiako/teachers, tauira/students and wider communities to come up with ideas and strategies to address bullying. 'Speak Up' is also about asking for help when you need it. This can be scary, and sometimes the first person you ask can't or won't do anything to help you. Keep asking. Pink Shirt Day shows there are many people who care about supporting you.
>
> . . .
>
> 'Mauri Tū, Mauri Ora' means to stand together in life and wellness. 'Stand Together' refers to how bullying behaviour is influenced by the actions and values of friends, whānau, schools, kura, workplaces and whole communities. Real change happens when we Stand Together, sending a strong message that there is no place for bullying in Aotearoa. Bullying often makes people feel alone, but Pink Shirt Day shows that many people care. Many people want to play their part in making Aotearoa a safe, welcoming and respectful place for everyone, regardless of age, sex, gender identity, sexual orientation, ability, or cultural background.[37]

'Don't turn your face away.
Once you've seen, you can no longer
act like you don't know.
Open your eyes to the truth.
It's all around you.
Don't deny what the eyes to your
soul have revealed to you.

Now that you know,
you cannot feign ignorance.
Now that you're aware of the problem,
you cannot pretend you don't care.
To be concerned is to be human.
To act is to care.'
— VASHTI QUIROZ-VEGA

How can I have this conversation? / Me pēhea tēnei matakahi?

Being bullied can be very isolating and scary. It's important that your teen knows they are not alone and that they will be protected. It's also important that any response to their disclosure is coordinated and frequently followed up on. Bullying is a real problem with potentially significant and ongoing consequences for all involved.

This is why we need to have the conversation, and primarily the message here is to take it seriously.

There are two levels to the dialogue here. Firstly (as touched on above), you can have more individualised discussions about:

- forming strategies as to what to do if your teen is bullied,
- how to interrupt any negative behaviours on their part, and
- how they can be a good ally and safely support others.

Secondly, you will need to have ongoing conversations, so that:

- your teen understands what bullying is,
- they know they can bring this kind of issue to you, and
- they develop **zero tolerance** for harmful behaviour.

Points to keep the conversation going

- Remember, your teen may well be **modelling their behaviour on you,** consciously or subconsciously. Find ways to underscore the following vital messages: be kind and respectful; celebrate difference and diversity; value others; and reach out to those needing support. In this they will understand your whānau/family has zero tolerance for putting people down, aggression and harmful behaviours such as bullying.
- Consider, if you do not have one already, **introducing a whānau/family motto**: a word or phrase that all family members can embrace and aspire to. This motto could encompass a set of values or be one word to talk from (such as integrity, generosity, kindness or equality). You could come up with it together, discussing what you want to include and why — or even use Michelle Obama's quote from the start of this chapter on page 76.
- If you feel your teen is lacking in **confidence and social skills,** work with them to build these attributes. Involve the school; this might mean tapping into a peer support system. Perhaps suggest a sport where individuality is respected (martial arts or parkour, for example), or a club where supporting others is a highlight (e.g., Scouts, Air Training Corps or Guides). Encourage them to find activities they might enjoy where they will meet other people who share their interests (such as music, art or the environment).
- Ask them what the word 'bullying' means to them and provide them with **factual information** if required (for instance, that it can affect anyone, that it can be subtle or overt, that it can be

by one person or a group, that it can be face to face or via a cell phone or other digital device).

- **Actively talk about the topic** of bullying with your teen. This may open a discussion around their own experiences and give you further insight into their world. Ask if they have ever encountered a situation where there was bullying, either directly or indirectly. What did they do, how did they feel and what were their observations of how others responded? In hindsight would they now behave differently and, if so, why? If they have not had this experience, encourage them to imagine it and then answer the same questions. Don't press them too hard if things are a bit raw for them — **leave them space to come to you.**

- Praise your teen when you see them being really supportive to someone they know who has been having a bad time — take the opportunity to have a conversation about what they think **being a good friend** means. This could branch out into what values they want to see in their friends' behaviours and also get them thinking about how they themselves are behaving.

- Use **role-playing scenarios** to help your teen explore empathy. For example, ask how they might respond to a younger sibling or cousin who disclosed to them that they were being bullied. This gives them a different and more invested perspective. Respond to their suggestions by saying things like, 'I can see that this makes you feel really emotional,' or, 'I know you like to stick up for people.' This will help them understand the mixture of emotions felt in these situations, and in turn help them take a step back to assess how best to act if required.

- Share your knowledge of the **5Ds** (see page 90) so your teen is prepared should they find themselves being around someone bullying others; again, role-play if they are willing to.

- It's hard to feel pity for bullies, especially if it's your teen who is being bullied. And yet if you can help your teen understand the bully's context, and what their motivation is, it can provide a different perspective; it's about your teen knowing that **they are not the problem** here.

- Access to the Internet means that schoolground bullying now doesn't finish at the last bell and can be 24/7. Make sure your teen has a **bully-free space**. Their room should be their haven, and it's important they have uninterrupted sleep. Perhaps consider a family pact of leaving all electronics charging in the lounge overnight (see page 103), even if that means purchasing alarm clocks. This may not stop ongoing cyberbullying, but it does give your teen a break while they are potentially at their most vulnerable. And it gives them space to realise that they don't have to interact with it or put up with it.

- Ensure your teen knows what your expectations are with regard to **digital citizenship and media manners** (see page 104) — talk about some of the 'discussions' that find their way into the comments sections after an online article. They will then hopefully start to recognise when someone else's behaviour is unacceptable.

- Discuss examples of well-known and successful people — such as Lady Gaga, Elon Musk and Rihanna[38] — who have shared their own experiences of being bullied. Knowing that other people have been through something similar but have gone on to be inspiring people in later life may be reassuring if your teen is struggling with their current feelings.

- Highlight any actions you hear about on the news or radio where people have recognised and stood up to injustice (such as the Black Lives Matter and #metoo movements; see Chapters 10, 11 and 15). See if they can identify other examples of bullying in a historical context.

- Encourage your teen to **be an activist in challenging prejudice and hate** — for example, talk with them about the background of Pink Shirt Day (see page 91).

'If you are neutral in situations of injustice,
you have chosen the side of the oppressor.
If an elephant has its foot on the tail of a
mouse, and you say that you are neutral, the
mouse will not appreciate your neutrality.'
— DESMOND TUTU

Talking box questions

What is a safe way to intervene if your friend is being bullied?

Why would someone bully?

Resources / Rauemi

ONLINE	Resource hub with information on bullying and support: bullyingfree.nz
	Information pack for whānau dealing with bullying: bullyingfree.nz/assets/Uploads/Tackling-Bullying-A-guide-for-parents-and-whanau.pdf
	More information about cyberbullying: keepitrealonline.govt.nz/parents/online-bullying
	A quiz for teens to see if they are displaying bullying behaviours: pacerteensagainstbullying.org/advocacy-for-self/do-you-bully
	Information about bystanders: ihollaback.org/app/uploads/2016/11/Show-Up_CUPxHollaback.pdf ditchthelabel.org/why-do-people-bully
	Bullying, cyberbullying and New Zealand law: legislation.govt.nz/act/public/2015/0063/latest/whole.html

5. TEENS AND TECH

#DeviceFreeDinner #MediaManners #GamingCommunity

*'We are all now connected by the Internet,
like neurons in a giant brain.'*
— STEPHEN HAWKING

Kōrero with Molly

I remember feeling like I was missing a limb when I left my phone at home. Having access to the Internet was (and is) important to me for many reasons: homework, connecting with friends near and far, booking appointments, directions and so much more... Not to mention attending university during the pandemic!

Now that I'm a little older, I can appreciate those wonderful things and balance them against the not-so-wonderful things, including cyberbullying, unhealthy comparisons, misinformation and forgetting to spend time in the 'real world'. I love taking a day off from my phone once in a while. Having a balance between screen time and putting the phone down is super important for my mental health, and the people in my life really appreciate getting my full attention when I'm with them.

What do you mean by that? / He aha te tikanga o tāu kōrero?

Our teens have grown up with Google at their fingertips. Some of them may have learned to use a touch-screen long before they could read. Smartphones are ubiquitous and most schools have a laptop or tablet as part of their stationery list. And then there's the hugely popular pastime of gaming, which today even enables people from different countries to play online together. Access to the Internet is now pretty much an integral part of everything teens do. It is important to their daily existence: for relaxation and recreation, for making and keeping up with friendships, for studying, and even for future job opportunities. However, for many parents there is a residual nervousness associated with their teen having access to the World Wide Web, including questions such as:

- Will this ever-changing technology affect our teen's ability to communicate in real life (or, as they now say, 'IRL')?
- Will they end up with issues around sociability?
- Will gaming promote violent behaviour?
- Will they be exposed to unsavoury content or people?

These are some serious concerns. As parents we may freely admit we're not as computer-savvy as our teens; but we should, at the very least, gain an overview of the current digital landscape. We need to, in order to keep them safe.

Throughout history, there have been times where advances in technology have felt threatening to the status quo. These days it may feel like technology is moving *really* fast, and it can be a little scary to find ways to keep up, even for the most tech-savvy among us. Current-day teens have grown up online and are finding their own ways of interacting with the digital world. For example, TikTok is not targeted at the middle-aged. There's an expectation of immediacy in any material that might interest teens, and they are in general not overwhelmed by the wealth of opportunities or possibilities of available information that might still leave us reeling like rabbits in the headlights. Concepts such as streaming on their phone, sharing memes and cloud-based gaming are water off a duck's back. Technological developments should perhaps be seen as an opportunity, not a threat. Statistics show us that the majority of our teens are not only using IT, but also embracing it. Pre-pandemic statistics on New Zealand teens found that:

- New Zealand's 15-year-olds spent more time on the Internet than their peers in all countries except Denmark, Sweden and Chile.[1]
- One-third of New Zealand teens (33 per cent) spent four or more hours online on an average day.[2]
- Four in 10 use five or more social media platforms.[3]
- Teens regarded themselves as confident technology users. More than four in 10 rarely or never seek support regarding an online or technical problem.[4]
- One in four reported they would be 'devastated' if they had no access to digital technologies for a month.[5]
- One-third of children under 14 years use social media; TikTok, which did not exist in 2014, is now the most popular social media platform.[6]

Additionally, research by CensusAtSchool found that nearly half (49 per cent) of high school students with a phone said that they would 'always or often check for messages and notifications as soon as they wake up in the morning', and that half said 'a weekend without their phone would make them feel angry, anxious, frustrated, sad, or lonely'.[7]

Unsurprisingly, new routines in the wake of the pandemic saw an exponential rise in the use of apps such as WhatsApp, Zoom and Houseparty, and we all learned about this tech pretty quickly (even though some of us still forgot either to turn the camera on or unmute . . .). Social media and other platforms allowed us to connect in a way that helped to fight isolation through this time. Initial research about lockdowns found that 'adolescents generally . . . increased their use of social media sites and streaming services'[8] and that 'eighty per cent [of parents] . . . relaxed the rules around social media use'.[9]

Whatever the circumstances, however, it's still important to have rules that keep your teen safe within their digital world. What's more, if your teen has some input into setting parameters, you may find them easier to enforce.

Tell me more . . . / Kōrero mai anō . . .

From apps to zettabytes (one billion terabytes), technology is a universal feature of teenage life in a way that would have been unimaginable for us at the same age. Teens embrace the fun that can be had by innovative use of different platforms, which peak and wane in their popularity. Yesterday's email and Facebook are today's Snapchat and Instagram.[10] Who knows what tomorrow's will be.

Phones

A handset with a connected earpiece and mouthpiece is still used today when indicating 'voice calls' — think of the WhatsApp icon, for example (pictured). Now try to get your teen to imagine this handset being connected to a phone with a rotary dial in a draughty hallway by a coiled cable . . . and this being the only phone in the house! Your teen may be tired of hearing you reminisce about having to pull that cable as far away from its base as possible in order to find an element of privacy when trying to chat to your friends.

Nowadays, almost everyone in every household will have a cellular device of their own. A lot of homes won't even have a landline. And today's smartphones look like something from *Star Trek* in comparison to the cell phone 'bricks' of yesteryear: a handheld computer that can be used to plan your day, book stuff, buy stuff, surf the net, take amazing photos, message your friends, play games — oh yes, and it can also still make telephone calls. Over two-thirds of global Internet traffic is via cell phones, and this proportion is likely to be even higher for teens.[11] Today, almost two-thirds of New Zealand children have their own phone by age 11, and by their final year of high school this figure is at 98 per cent.[12] Almost all of these will be smartphones, and this is also the most common way for teens to access the Internet.

All of this means that if you want to successfully establish some ground rules about your teen's cell phone use, it will have to be a collaborative process. For instance:

- The main reason you will want your teen to have a phone is for **security** — so that you can be in touch with each other in case of emergencies. Discuss whether they want to have a ringtone reserved just for you (they may even have done this already . . .). Explain that they need to get back to you within an agreed period of time following, for example, your 6 p.m. text asking why they aren't back from school. Apps like 'Find my phone' can provide useful reassurance for all parties when teens are becoming more independent.
- Particularly with younger teens, you may want to **build up trust around their phone use** — for example, their asking permission before downloading a new app, sharing their passwords with you, and letting you have access to their social media.
- Have agreed **code words or phrases** so that you know when they need your assistance. The traffic light system can work well: 'green' for 'all's good', 'amber' for 'let's keep in touch' and 'red' for 'come and get me now'. A portable charger may also be helpful if your teen is out and about.
- Get them to **take responsibility for charging their phone.** Think about whether there is a place at home where your teen can do this overnight that is not in their room, so that they are not tempted to check their social media at bedtime. Some evidence indicates that if cell phones (and other screens) are used close to bedtime they can adversely affect sleep. (Blue light in particular tends to wake us up, and some devices enable the screen to be switched to a more soothing colour.)
- Perhaps have a basket into which everyone can drop their phones over meal times, and on other occasions when you have **tech-free family time** (see page 28). Teens are not usually fans of 'do as I say, not as I do', so they will also be monitoring how you handle phone etiquette. If you are constantly distracted by buzzes indicating notifications, you may well find that they are as well. Be gracious if they call you out.
- Make sure they understand any **school rules on phone usage**

in and around the classroom. If they breach these rules they will need to deal with the consequences — for example, confiscation until home time.

- **Taking care of their phone** needs to be implicit in the agreement to their having one. Think about who pays for any repairs or replacements in advance of any damage or loss. Allow for the fact that this may be a steeper learning curve for some teens than others. And remember that screen protectors and tough phone cases are your friends.

- For many teens, it will be their parents who pick up the bill for any prepay arrangement or plan. Different families work within different budgets and have different boundaries with regard to phone use. It may be that you want your teen to work within their existing plan — and once it's gone for the month, it's gone. Or if they would like a more generous **data allowance**, you may want them to contribute some money from a part-time job or do some extra chores around the home. It may be worth looking at family share plans to see what works best for your household.

As time has gone on, a whole language around texting has developed. We may have caught up with LOL ('laugh out loud' — or was that 'lots of love'?), but you may also want to check one of the abbreviation guides available online (see Resources/Rauemi, page 123). There are some that might raise concerns — for example, KPC ('keeping parents clueless') or ASL ('age/sex/location') — and this is also true of some emojis, many of which have become laden with subtext.

Internet and digital citizenship
Around 94 per cent of the population in New Zealand were active Internet users in 2021.[13] Like all of us, teens have to identify and manage risk in cyberspace. According to Netsafe, the non-profit online safety organisation, an overall seven in 10 teens in New Zealand 'have experienced at least one type of unwanted digital communication in the past year. Not all these resulted in harm or distress.' These

unwanted communications commonly involved 'being contacted by a stranger' and 'accidentally seeing inappropriate content online'. Netsafe also quotes teens as saying 'they most commonly encounter unwanted digital communications through social media'.[14]

There are two sides to everything: how people will potentially behave towards your teen, and vice versa. The first is difficult to control, so your teen needs an understanding of risk and strategies; for the second, they need to cultivate media manners. Both are covered by the concept of being a good digital citizen.

Issues to consider

Practising good etiquette

Sometimes it is difficult to express subtleties digitally in the way you can when you see someone face to face. You can't hear the tone of voice or see the facial expressions and actions that contribute to your understanding, and this may lead to misinterpretation. Luckily, most teens are fluent in emoji, and know WHEN NOT TO USE CAPS (as that seems like you are shouting). However, there are a few other points that they should also bear in mind when posting. Again, over to Netsafe:

> *Keep it positive. Always respect others online and communicate in a constructive way. Do not create or publish content that is indecent, threatening or offensive.*

> *Check consent. Before downloading software to the school network or onto devices, seek permission. Interfering with the school systems, digital technologies, equipment/network or the online security of another person is never okay at any time.*

> *Recognise others' work. Follow copyright and intellectual property requirements by attributing references, images, text, audio and video appropriately.*

Respect the rights of others. Only record and share video, photo or audio content if the people in it know it has been taken and have provided their consent.[15]

If your teen is changing their relationship status, it is always better to touch base with anyone else involved first. If they are cross or upset about something, it is always better to wait a few hours, rather than post when they are still angry or hurting. Make sure that they have reviewed any tagging options on their apps, as this enables them to decide the extent to which content other people have shared appears on their profile. If they are using a public computer, make sure that they are posting from their own account rather than unintentionally from someone else's.

Screen time and socialising

Most parents have at least questioned their teen's amount of screen time and worried that it might be too much. This can also be true of teens themselves: CensusAtSchool found that 'one in three high-school students felt that their use of social media was excessive. This was highest among girls, with 40% [feeling like they spent] too much time on social media, compared with just 20% for boys.'[16] Establish with your teen some parameters around the amount of time spent online, and the time of day that's acceptable (acknowledging that much of this will be via their phone). Sharing Spotify playlists can be fun, but not at the expense of homework, for example. Make sure they have other activities aside from looking at a screen. When they get together with friends, encourage them to be fully present, rather than being in one room but each actually in parallel virtual worlds. Remind them that being with friends is not just about staging the next Instagram 'moment'.

Age limits and accessibility

A net nanny can act as a firewall for younger children, and browsers will record their surfing history so that you can check whether it is age appropriate. As children become teens, we should rely instead on education and explanation, and get them to critically analyse how they access and interact with the Internet (in any event, they often know how to get around firewalls and delete their histories). Most social media platforms require age eligibility in order to join (although teens will often get around this, too). Get to know the age limits for different apps, and set ground rules with your teen (see Resources/ Rauemi, page 123). Just saying 'no' without explanation can make things even more enticing, and you do not want your teen having to go underground and then be unable to approach you for help.

Privacy

Have your teen consider their digital footprint. One way to do this is to Google themselves, as this can inform them (and you) of what's already freely available about them. They need to protect their profile. Once content is out in the ether, removing it can be tricky, and that's if it hasn't already been shared. Posts they are happy with now might not sit so well in a few years' time. Ask them to think about curating their online presence so that if, say, a future employer were to look at it, they would not be put off. As an example of this, an international cricketer in his late twenties was recently suspended from the England team due to some inappropriate comments he tweeted as a teenager. This is now the first thing that you see when you search his name.[17]

Check in with your teen about the security and privacy settings on each and every app they run, turning off any location data that isn't necessary (check you have done this too!). Ensure they know to have passwords that mix numbers and cases and include special characters, and to be sure not to use the same password for every app. It may be teaching them to suck eggs, but remind them never to disclose these to anyone (except you!).

Identity theft

Our teens should understand the importance of protecting their identity, because it can be stolen and reproduced by someone else. If they have any issues with purchases or bank credit, or start receiving random invoices, tax and money-related letters (via text, email or regular mail), you might be wary that a less-than-reputable organisation has acquired their details.

Discourage them from doing online quizzes that ask them, for example, for their favourite colour, their mother's maiden name or the name of their first pet: these are often the types of security question used to retrieve forgotten passwords. It's good to be mindful of your own behaviour as well, in case you accidentally reveal details about your teen by 'sharenting' — your social media can inadvertently leak birthday dates, favourite sports teams, or times when your child might have been in a particular place.[18] What's more, research has suggested that '85 per cent of parents hadn't checked their privacy settings in over a year, while only 10 per cent were even confident of knowing how to do so'.[19]

Catfishing is another form of identity theft in which someone sets up a false online identity in order to lure someone into a relationship.[20] Their intentions may be to scam, troll, harass or otherwise abuse a person — or they may simply be lonely. One way to check another's identity is to use Google's reverse image search function: when you upload a photo it will alert you to other sites where the image exists. This allows you to check out if a profile picture is in several places with different information. Reverse searching is also useful if your teen suspects that their accounts have been hacked and their photos are being used in this way. If you discover a fake profile on a site or app, **report it to the platform and ask for it to be removed.** Also contact Netsafe and give them the URL.

Scams

Differentiating content from clickbait can be an invaluable skill. Scammers are finding ever more sophisticated ways to fool people into parting with their money or identity. Cell phone messages from unknown numbers saying you have won a prize (but first need to send your bank details so that it can be paid into your account), cloned websites that look official, phone calls from a bank asking for your passwords . . . the list grows continually. Many apps collect personal data and pass it on. If there is an option to switch off tracking, tell your teen to use it, and remind them to regularly remove cookies from all their devices. They should routinely ask themselves whether any site they visit is credible; one way to check this is by looking at reputable online reviews. Our teens sometimes receive fake adverts and misleading information, and everyone makes mistakes and clicks on a dodgy link sometimes. Reassure them that you are not going to judge them if this happens to them. Remind them of the old adage: if it looks too good to be true, it almost certainly is too good to be true (much as it would be wonderful if they had won a million dollars . . .).

Online shopping

If your teen is shopping online they should take security seriously. They may be more minded to do this if they are using their own money (see pages 339–341) via a debit card, Apple Pay, PayPal — or cryptocurrency! Teach them to keep an eye on their account for unexplained transactions that may indicate unauthorised access. They need to check, too, that shopping sites use secure technology — for instance, at the checkout screen the URL should begin with 'https' and be preceded by the tiny padlock symbol (which indicates a secure connection to the site, if not the site's bona fide intentions). And by reading a site's privacy policy, they can find out how it protects the personal information it collects.[21] Tell your teen to make it a habit to log out of a site or app that links to their (or your!) financial information once they have finished, particularly if using a shared computer or space. Consider installing a VPN (virtual private network) on your home computer: this encrypts your data and conceals your Internet history from others.[22]

Inappropriate people

As already indicated, not everyone online is who they say they are. This concept may well be familiar to your teen, since it is a fundamental lesson in all school programmes about Internet safety. The danger is that they might agree to meet someone in person whom they may not be able to trust. Talk to them in an age-appropriate way about the potential dangers of online grooming or predators. If they are affected by these issues, there are places that you can both go to for support (see Resources/Rauemi, page 123).

Inappropriate material

The World Wide Web provides access to a vast range of content and much of it is not age appropriate, reliable or accurate. From pro-ana YouTubers (promoting anorexia and eating disordered behaviour online) to sexually explicit messages (see Chapter 13), hate blogs and radicalisation sites, it can feel like they are all just a pop-up ad away. Let your teen know they are not to blame when an Internet search leads them to a part of the web where they would rather not be. Instead, advise them to block the site and report any URL to Netsafe.

Do we really know what our teens are up to online?

As much as all of the above information is designed to keep your teen alert and safe, there are occasions when it is your teen doing the misbehaving online: sharing photos without permission, spreading rumours or confidential information, posting anonymously and bullying, trolling people on social media, impersonating others, sexting and sending nudes, downloading material illegally (such as films), sharing others' passwords, accessing others' information, accessing accounts or making purchases using finances they shouldn't, or even being involved in identity fraud and scams.

While some of these behaviours are at worst insensitive, others may damage people's mental health and some are actually illegal. Any conduct along these lines needs to be challenged, so your teen knows in no uncertain terms that their actions need to stop immediately. At the same time, as mentioned in Chapter 4, it's also important to try to establish the underlying issue(s) leading them into this misbehaviour. It's useful to encourage empathy, having them consider it from their victim's perspective, and there will need to be consequences and possibly reparations. If you feel you need more help or support, see the Resources/Rauemi section (page 123).

A word on trolls and haters

'A troll', according to help site Bullies Out, 'is a term for a person, usually anonymous, who deliberately starts an argument or posts inflammatory or aggressive comments with the aim of provoking either an individual or a group into reacting. The phrase was coined after a fishing term meaning that basically they (the troll) attach their bait (their comment) and wait for others to bite.'[23] Teens will come across the good, the bad and the ugly in all corners of cyberspace. Some people seem to delight in going online simply to create drama. Perhaps they find that any attention is better than no attention, or maybe they thrive on the sensationalism of pushing radical suggestions and making others uncomfortable. They may just be bigots.

Some platforms are slower to react to and remove unpleasant posts or ban particular users. Here, the overwhelming advice seems to be to ignore trolls, and where possible to delete their comments and block them from your accounts. They don't want to be reasoned with. By engaging, you are putting the spotlight on them, which is what they thrive on. 'Haters gonna hate', so leave them to it. On other social sites, your teen may find that positive interactions are encouraged. Fair, challenging, useful and constructive conversation is appreciated and pushed to the top of any thread. Haters are quickly pushed out of the chain of chat. This is an interesting alternative approach, not without its own problems, but better than feeding the trolls.

Gaming

Were you an eighties kid and still have an abiding love of Pac-Man? Do you recall when the Sega game console was first on the scene? Did you own a first-edition Game Boy with its variety of games on little plastic disks? Gaming isn't a new phenomenon, but it has certainly come a long way. It's now possible to compete in *Fortnite's* multiplayer platform against someone who is in a completely different part of Oceania. These days it's not unusual for teens to spend roughly half their free time gaming, and more often than not it's with a mic and headphones in place, or possibly a VR headset. Gaming is now a multi-billion-dollar industry played by all ages and genders, bringing in more revenue than the movies.

It can be easy to assume gaming is predominantly taken up by younger, mostly male players. However, reports show that 73 per cent of players are aged over 18 years, and that nearly half are female (although in the 15–24 age bracket boys spend twice as long gaming has girls).[24] Seventy per cent of parents think video gaming has a positive influence on their child's life,[25] and over 50 per cent game with them.[26] Reassuringly, the majority of parents appear both to be familiar with family controls, and to talk with their child about safety online while playing.

If your teen likes gaming, how you manage it can depend on your background. Perhaps gaming is a pastime that you, too, grew up with and still enjoy. It can be a way to connect with your teen. Interactive quizzes and competitive games such as SingStar make for fun family times, and VR games can be incredibly active and a good way for teens to get some exercise. Alternatively, you may be rolling your eyes at the thought of joining in. There is conflicting evidence as to whether gaming can harm or help a young person's development, so it's difficult to know whether there is any actual reason for concern. It's also important to look at the authenticity of any studies and who funded them (in case it's the game producer). Some studies show gaming can improve memory and increase fine motor skills, for example, whereas others state that gaming can lead to emotional addiction.[27]

Whatever the research, you can certainly understand why many teens enjoy playing: it's an easy way for them to engage with others on a joint mission, experience an exciting and challenging virtual adventure with measurable goals but no real ongoing pressures, really see themselves achieve targets, and relax into another world for a bit.

And then there's the dopamine hit.

Reaching a high

Another reason people enjoy gaming is for its effect on the brain, courtesy of dopamine, our natural 'happy drug'. As licensed clinical social worker Katie Hurley explains:

> *Gaming triggers the brain's reward centre, which releases dopamine, sometimes referred to as one of the 'feel good hormones'. Dopamine is associated with feelings of euphoria, bliss, concentration, and motivation. When a video game gives a [teen] a thrill by allowing them to reach a new high score or take down an opponent, dopamine can surge. This results in a temporary feeling of bliss.*[28]

Perhaps the goal should be 'everything in moderation' — although this is easier said than done, given that games are often designed to keep players playing. This can make it tricky for teens to find a healthy balance between their virtual world and the rest of what life offers, particularly when things aren't feeling so great IRL. There are some games that might make you worry your teen could become desensitised to risky behaviours (we've all seen young drivers overtake like they think they are in *Grand Theft Auto* and not on an actual road). However, there are those that are also more educational, providing a wealth of factual information within the game itself. An iconic example of this is *Civilization*: the player builds empires and at the same time learns about cultures and ancient history.

Multiplayer versus single-player gaming

Multiple player options mean your teen can play online with their friends and people they haven't met. There is also often the added feature of being able to communicate directly with other players. It's worth being wary, though, that this doesn't open the door to people misusing any chat facilities.

Inside a multiplayer game there could be an age range and many different personalities. The intensity of some games means that it's not difficult to imagine a few temper tantrums, with hyped-up hormonal teens venting at the expense of others. Unfortunately, this can also spill over into abusive language (either on screen or verbal if using in-game chat) and bullying. It is known in gaming speak as 'flaming' and 'game rage' and is, sadly, well recognised as part of the experience. This can be exacerbated where players are allowed to remain anonymous. 'Griefing' is when players start to disrupt and annoy other players on purpose. This can involve cheating, stealing other players' swag, team kills, and generally causing as much grief to other players as they can.[29] This sort of activity can be reported to game moderators and admin teams. Although there are already some repercussions in these situations (such as being 'stood down' or banned), many gamers are calling for increased in-game monitoring of negative behaviour, and for penalties to be more strictly enforced.

Chat rooms can be made private, which means that your teen can restrict the people with whom they interact in this way. For any teens who are vulnerable, it's really important to ensure they are playing only with friends and not in a toxic environment.

Violent games
Aotearoa classifies all video games according to the Office of Film and Literature Classification (OFLC).[30] For example, *Grand Theft Auto* (*GTA*) is rated 18, and includes 'high-impact themes, drug use, violence and sex'; *Call of Duty* (*COD*) is a 16, and includes 'graphic violence, offensive language and cruelty'. These classifications will be displayed on the front of any packaging. There are concerns that constant exposure to — and immersion in — violent games (as opposed to watching it on television, for example) may drive aggressive behaviours in real life. Again, the research here is lacking and what is available is somewhat contradictory. It's interesting to note that in the US and New Zealand statistics show that violent crimes have actually decreased since the 1990s — the same time span during which games sales have increased exponentially.[31] You know your teen best and will be aware of their behaviour and any impact playing video games seems to have on them. You also probably don't want them watching

and interacting with shocking content, so it's a good idea to check the OFLC rating against their age and maturity level.

'Healthy gaming'

It's important to build healthy habits into the gaming experience:

- Establish **parameters** with your teen around when they can play and for how long. Some games have sequences in them (like the 20-minute battle times in *Fortnite*, for example). Try to set time limits that don't drag your teen away just when they've got to the important part of the action, as they may not always be able to save their game at that point. They can, however, agree to stop before they go on to the next level. Older teens should be able to take responsibility and figure things out for themselves. If dinner prep starts at 6 p.m., they shouldn't be picking up their controller at 5.50 p.m. . . .

- Work with any built-in breaks. Content within many games is **'time gated'**, meaning the adventure can be continued only after a break (this interval is characterised within the game as needing to 'fuel up', for example, and the wait may vary from a few minutes to a few days before players are able to recommence). This can be interpreted in different ways: as enforcing a useful breather from a game, as a method to encourage players to return again and again for the next instalment, or — as many of these time gates can be cut short with a monetary transaction — as another method of extracting real-life funds. You may already be familiar with this if your teen has harassed you for an extra allowance.

- Talk to them about costs. The other time that actual (rather than virtual) funds may be needed is to **'unlock'** items in order to either advance in the game or level up with higher-quality **additions** (such as weapons). Have some pre-established boundaries about whether you are happy for them to spend money this way and how much.

- For younger teens there are **settings** that can be used on different games/consoles to keep them age appropriate and safe.
- Understand the games they play: read about them online, show an interest and ask your teen for their views. You could even check with other parents you know whose teens may have a particular game. A quick Internet search for **ratings and reviews** may be helpful. If your teen will let you, play alongside them occasionally so that you can understand what it is that they enjoy about gaming (for example, the media art, the humour or the action).
- Games can be designed to be really complex, with storylines your teen may find captivating. Some are based around quite complicated philosophical concepts. Recognise that this can make things intense, so allow your teen **time to decompress** and relax after they've finished gaming.
- Similarly, have your teen recognise how **emotional** they may become during and after gaming — this may apply to particular games more than others. Once they see this, they may moderate their own choice of what they play, when, for how long and who with.
- Ensure they are clued up on **media manners** and **digital citizenship**.
- Have your teen be mindful that with extended use of VR headsets there's a possibility of them being so 'in the moment' that they fall over the family pet. Get them to **suss out the space they are gaming in,** as they may need a fair bit of room. Also, bear in mind that extended use of VR headsets can result in motion sickness for some, so it can help to set time limits here.
- Another consideration is their **comfort**: there is a real market for gaming chairs. And remind them to eat and drink!

Kōrero with Molly

I've grown to enjoy gaming as an adult, but I never really cared for it as a teenager. As for my brother, though, he loved it from the get-go. I can remember the rules around how much time he was allowed and the arguments when he was asked to come for dinner and was in the middle of some event that would ruin his ratings if he left at that moment. On the other hand, I also remember being amazed at how much factual information he got from some of the games. I know he also played to relax and have fun.

For my sister, who has special needs, it was an opening to a social network that was amazing. There are some truly accepting communities of people out there. However, there are also some unsavoury people that use these channels to harass others. For this reason, it can make me a little nervous to see more vulnerable people (like my sister or my younger family members) interact with online gamers.

There is an incredible range of games out there, and honestly, there is something for everyone! I used to think it was all shooting and fighting, but more recently I've found gaming to be a creative outlet and a great way to connect with friends.

A word on gambling and gaming addiction

A growing trend in games, prevalent even in those rated PG, is to contain opportunities to spend money over and above the initial cost. Examples of this may be an in-game purchase of additional armour, or a shortcut to another level. Perhaps more concerning, though, is the inclusion of casino-style flashing lights with 'random rolls' and 'loot boxes'. These require a payment of real-world money, but there is also some risk element involved — with the equivalent of a roll of a dice, players will find out whether their loot box contains something useful and prestigious or of little value, or even whether it is empty. This is gambling by any other name. Gambling is obviously a recognised addiction, whereas gaming currently is not. With that said, the World

Health Organization (WHO) recently identified 'gaming disorder' as a condition within its International Classification of Diseases (ICD). WHO describes gaming disorder as a pattern of gaming behavior (including both digital gaming and video gaming) characterised by impaired control over gaming, increased priority given to gaming over other interests and priorities, and continued or escalated gaming despite negative consequences from the behaviour. To meet the ICD classification of gaming disorder, the behaviour must be sufficient in severity to result in significant impairment in personal, family, social, educational, or occupational areas of functioning over a twelve-month period.[32]

If you are worried about your teen, seek further assistance (see Resources/Rauemi, page 123).

Can your teen control their gaming?

WHO uses defined criteria to assess whether a young person is suffering from gaming disorder:

- *Does gaming affect my child's ability to complete homework, get to school on time, or focus on educational needs?*
- *Does gaming negatively impact my child's relationships with parents, siblings, other family members, or peers?*
- *Does my child experience uncontrollable outbursts when told to stop gaming, including physical aggression?*
- *Does gaming take precedence over other areas in my child's life?*
- *Does gaming impede healthy habits such as eating, hygiene, and exercise?*
- *Does gaming result in significant changes in mood?*[33]

The future

There's no way to predict the future — the world of today looks nothing like most of us would have anticipated in the early nineties. Life will look very different again in the 2050s. Our teens are already very open to the idea of innovation, and this is something to be celebrated. They may even teach us a thing or two — in few years' time, a lot of them will be involved in the development of new technology. Any current obsession with phones, the Internet or gaming may yet provide your teen with the skills they need for their career of tomorrow.

How can I have this conversation? / Me pēhea tēnei matakahi?

The Internet, cell phones, social media and gaming can be fun and have some amazing benefits. There are definitely concerns, but these can be managed with your input.

> **This is why we need to have the conversation, and primarily the message here is that technology is an opportunity, not a threat.**

At the same time, it is important to have strategies to make sure that your teen is safe when they are surfing. Essentially it is important to foster an environment where your teen will come to you with any of their online concerns. By letting them know they will be taken seriously and sympathetically, with no blaming or shaming, you are setting up reassurance that you are glad they trusted you and that you will work things through with them. If you are unable to successfully assist your teen in dealing with their emotions after an online fright, it is important to encourage them to reach out for additional support.

Points to keep the conversation going

- Most teens would prefer a private space with an Internet connection for homework, making it tricky to insist on a centralised space in your home for all Internet use. Try to find somewhere that works for you as a family, and that also allows them to work within your **house rules**. Explain that the more they can demonstrate they are a good digital citizen, the more you can trust them to be autonomous.

- Have your teen show you any new apps they think you might find fun. **Ask them** what they enjoy.

- Raise the idea of having **tech-free days** with your teen (alongside the usual day-to-day tech-free times, such as during a meal and at bedtime). Get them to plan some alternative activities.

- Chat with them about any **tech-related concerns** you may have. Ask them what they think about the research that exists — get them to do an Internet search to find out more. Work out with them whether or not any findings are 'fake news' and discuss the agenda of anyone who may have funded the studies.

- Ask your **teen to assist you** in setting up your own profile on a platform (for example, Spotify or Instagram), including organising privacy settings (hopefully this will also prompt them to think of their own).

- Google yourself and get your teen to Google themselves: discuss what, if anything, you find and whether you are okay with **what can be publicly seen**. This may lead to reviewing privacy settings or prompting a conversation about how to remove information online. Ask them what they think about prospective employers looking them up.

- They will undoubtedly be covering **Internet safety at school**, so ask them what they have learned and how you can apply it at home. This is a great discussion if you also have younger children: ask your teen to help you set up a safe Internet policy for them.

- Ask your teen to construct a **plan around their gaming** if you think it's required. (They will be more invested in it if you allow them this input.) Chat about how long they can play in any day or week. Is it different on the weekend? Agree on giving them some time to finish off a game before you need them to switch it off. Is gaming going to be a privilege only to be accessed once homework is complete?
- Get your teen to show you how games are rated, and **make a decision together** about what you will allow and why. Perhaps get them to show you the game in action; you may even want to join in.
- In an opportune moment, ask them:
  - if they think gaming content could affect their **emotional health**;
  - if they think there are specific issues or problems that relate to multiplayer gaming and what they think the solutions could be;
  - how they manage negative emotional experiences online; and
  - how they'd potentially support someone who was having a hard time online.
- For teens who are starting to develop their social media profile, consider whether or not their account should be dependent on letting you be a friend/follower. It's worth having a discussion at this point about where the line should be drawn between **their privacy and their safety**. When it comes to passwords, there's a balance to be had: your teen's security is paramount, so they need to learn not to disclose their personal details. Where they are struggling, however, an alternative approach might be required.
- Does your teen think you are online or gaming 'too much', and do they feel you get distracted by your phone or social media? This can be a brave and eye-opening question to ask, but may seem only fair if you are asking them to account for their own behaviour.

Talking box questions

What is meant by your digital footprint?

Can you imagine life without the Internet?

Think up some new technology that
would help developing countries.

Resources / Rauemi

ONLINE	Seven steps for whānau wanting to stay safe online: netsafe.org.nz/online-safety-for-parents A parent toolkit for online safety: netsafe.org.nz/advice/online-safety-parent-toolkit Resource hub for staying safe online: keepitrealonline.govt.nz/parents Guides to a variety of social media for parents: commonsensemedia.org/parents-ultimate-guides Guides to teen slang and the language of social media: smartsocial.com/teen-slang-emojis-hashtags-list verywellfamily.com/the-secret-language-of-teens-100-social-media-acronyms-2609651 Information about keeping yourself safe online and protecting your data: internetmatters.org/issues/privacy-identity/learn-about-privacy-and-identity-theft pmgt.org.nz/online-safety Safety guides for key social media platforms: tiktok.com/safety/en/guardians-guide snapchat.com/l/en-gb/safety youtube.com/yt/policyandsafety/safety.html about.instagram.com/safety about.twitter.com/safety/families facebook.com/safety/tools/safety

6. DRINKING, PUFFING AND PARTYING

#drugfree #smokefree #dontdrinkanddrive

'A child's job is to test her boundaries, a parent's to see she survives the test.'
— ROGER MACDONALD

Kōrero with Molly

I used to think that my parents were pretty strict about enforcing things like curfews and other house rules when it came to partying. In retrospect, it was those rules that kept me safe. No matter what time, or where I was, I could always ring or text them and ask them to pick me up. Either Mum or Dad would show up, no questions asked (at least not until the morning . . .). I remember when I got permission to throw a party at home. Mum and Dad stayed in the house, which I thought might be a bit embarrassing, but I was so pleased to find they kept to their room, except for one occasion when Dad came out to put on a big pot of chilli, which made everyone really happy! My friends were actually pretty respectful. They made sure that the furniture was protected, the music didn't get too obnoxious and they even helped to clean up in the morning. In high school, I did hear about some parties that got a little out of control. Most of the time, those events don't live up to your expectations. People do some pretty silly things to impress their friends and, thanks to social media, it can be harder to live down. To be honest, my favourite parties were the ones when everyone brought their favourite snack, we played board games and sang karaoke, and no one finished the night with their head in a toilet.

What do you mean by that? /
He aha te tikanga o tāu kōrero?

First things first: this book is not designed to condone any illegal behaviours, and there is legislation in Aotearoa covering some of the topics in this chapter.

The law on drugs and sexual activity

Below is a brief summary of where the law currently stands on the sale and use of drugs, and on the age of consent.

- In New Zealand the sale or supply of tobacco and vaping products is restricted to those over 18 years of age. The law is not about making the young person wrong for vaping, but the legal responsibility lies in those who sell vapes and deliver vapes to our young people.[1]
- As noted by social change initiative Cheers: 'Under the Sale and Supply of Alcohol Act [2012] the minimum legal age for the purchase of alcohol in New Zealand is 18 years but there is no minimum legal drinking age. In other words, although those under 18 are unable to legally purchase alcohol themselves, they are legally permitted to consume alcohol. The law is based on the premise that parents should determine how and when their children are introduced to alcohol, so it makes it illegal for anyone to supply alcohol to someone under the age of 18 years without the consent of their parent or guardian.'[2]
- The use of cannabis in New Zealand is regulated by the Misuse of Drugs Act 1975, which makes unauthorised possession of any amount of cannabis a crime. This legislation also applies to all other Class A to C drugs.[3]
- In Aotearoa, you must be over 16 years of age to consent to sexual activity.[4]

Your teen needs to understand the framework set out in legislation — it's the law of the country, after all, whatever their personal preferences might be. Some teens will be avid party-goers, others would be if they could just get an invite, and others could think of nothing worse. Your parenting approach will obviously be determined by where your teen stands on this spectrum. It's sensible to have conversations with them well before they reach the age when they might be showing an interest in partying and all that can go with it. Recent research indicates, for example, that 'there may be benefits of alcohol education resources for children as young as 12 years'.[5]

There will also be the dreaded hormones playing their role in all socialising, platonic or otherwise. Parties can be the catalyst for the start of longer-term connections. They can also be seen as opportunities for sexual encounters (see page 224). But whether your teen engages in a one-off hook-up or a more committed personal relationship, the framework around consent (see Chapter 11) and the issues around how individuals should treat one another remain the same. These topics are covered in more detail in separate chapters.

The need for boundaries is also generally applicable: any ground rules in relation to smoking, drinking, drugs and sex are there for your teen's protection, especially if they are underage. Develop parameters with your teen that work for you all as a family, giving them room to spread their wings socially while still keeping them safe. Make sure they understand the reason behind these boundaries: as ever, they will be more likely to follow rules they are invested in. The goal here is that they are sufficiently informed and sufficiently confident to recognise and manage potentially risky situations. Not all parties are dens of iniquity; not all parties mean binge drinking or drugs or hook-ups. Partying can have some real pros, including increasing independence and social networking.

Teens need to let off steam sometimes, and partying can be a good way to do this. To some extent they are geared to think that it is almost expected of them — a rite of passage. If you consider the media they consume, in almost every 'coming of age' movie there's a story arc about characters nagging to go to parties, nagging to have a party, or telling their parents just how strict and uncool they are for not allowing a party. As a parent, you may feel it's a no-win situation. It's certainly difficult to strike a balance between being underprotective, being overprotective, and being protective enough while allowing them the space to healthily expand their horizons. Teens need the opportunity to gain your trust while also gaining their own confidence, but they need a context in which to do this. They may be worrying just as much as you, so sometimes having some boundaries imposed is just what they are wanting, not least because it shows you care about them. Cast your mind back to when you were a similar age: being worried about peer pressure, how to handle yourself socially, whether or not you were viewed as popular, whether or not that mattered. Perhaps remembering your own teenage years makes you worry all the more, knowing how much luck was involved at times. It's worth addressing any baggage of your own; just because you enjoyed going to parties doesn't mean your teen will, and vice versa.

Keeping communication lines open is key here (as ever) because peer pressure will mount: teens will want to experiment. You may feel that you are experiencing a constant stream of dissatisfaction from them, but in reality they may just be using you as a sounding board. By openly discussing boundaries, and knowing which are flexible and which are set, your teen will understand that socialising is a balance between self-expression and good decision-making. Ultimately, their ongoing behaviour will influence where you, the adult, draw the lines. Pushing boundaries is normal, but teenagers need to realise that they are not invulnerable, and that their behaviour and that of their friends can put themselves and others at risk (for instance, spiking drinks).[6] This is why continuing conversations with them on this topic is critical.

While your teen is still underage, you are ultimately in charge. This means knowing where your teen is and what they are doing, and that's not unreasonable. Agree on a time that you can expect them, as negotiating a curfew ensures you are on the same page. If you're not collecting them, it's a good idea to be up and ready to welcome them home. They may not go into great detail about their night, but it does let them know you are monitoring the situation alongside the fact that you care. It also gives you the opportunity to assess their wellbeing and whether they are sober — although as long as they aren't dangerously drunk or needing your assistance, it's better to let them get some sleep before tackling any conversations and consequences.

Sometimes you and the parents of your teen's peers are also connected socially. Most of us have heard the expression 'it takes a village', and if you are part of such a group, it can be really useful to get together to chat about some ground rules that you can stick to collectively. At the same time, be mindful of the concept of 'group think': any such agreement needs to be realistic, centred around keeping everyone's teens safe and within the law. At the end of the day, though, the rules that you have decided on as a family are the ones your teen needs to follow. The key information for any party, home or away, is:

- Where is the party?
- How many are attending and how will any uninvited guests be managed?
- Will there be alcohol and, if so, how much and of what kind, and how will it be provided/monitored?
- Will food be provided?
- When will the party finish?
- Is there adult supervision, and by whom?
- Is there anyone you can contact by phone?

Although you will hear your teen's groans and see their eye-rolls from kilometres away, it's worth giving the host's parents a quick call to get answers to the above questions, particularly with younger teens. Hopefully the host family will understand why you are getting in touch and will be happy to share information with you and, for example, exchange contact details. If you are the one hosting the party for your teen, you will need to address these points so you can field enquiries from other parents.

Tell me more . . . / Kōrero mai anō . . .

As your child grows into an independent teen they will likely take more of an interest in socialising with their mates. For younger teens in particular there may be limited options. And you may not be keen for them to hang out on street corners. You may be the kind of parent who prefers having their home as 'friend central', or you may prefer to keep it as a space for family most of the time; either way, you want to know your teen is safe. As they start to find their own way in the world, your teen will experience an uptick in exposure to smoking, vaping, drinking and drug use. They will need strategies to navigate all of these tricky topics, whether or not they also become '24-hour party people'.[7]

Let's start with some generalised statistics (all of which relate to New Zealanders):

- A 2019 study found that, on average, young people who smoked began at 15, and those who smoked daily were doing it at 16–17.[8]
- A 2018 Youth Insights Survey found that 38 per cent of 14–15-year-olds had tried vaping. This was up from 20 per cent in 2016. Two per cent vaped on a daily basis (up from 1 per cent in 2014).[9]
- In a 2019 study, the average at which young people first tried alcohol was 12.6. Almost half of the 14–15-year-olds reported never having tried it.[10]
- Government figures show hazardous levels of drinking in 12 per cent of 15–17-year-olds and 32 per cent of 18–24-year-olds.[11]
- In a 2020 survey, nearly a quarter (23 per cent) of teens had tried cannabis, and 4 per cent were using it at least weekly. Just 4 per cent had tried other drugs.[12]

Patterns over time may be changing — for example, there is a decrease in the numbers of teens who are smoking, but an increase in the numbers who are vaping. Alcohol and drug usage statistics may also vary, in part along socio-economic lines.[13]

Harms

Our job is to keep our teens informed and to steer them away from obvious harms. These harms can be physiological, psychological and social; they can impact on the individual user, but also spread through to other individuals and through to society at large.[14] The following information can be useful, not only for you as adults setting ground rules, but also in explaining to your teen why you have them.

For instance, exposure to chemicals and substances as a teen can lead to long-term consequences:

- Owing to differences in metabolism, teens absorb drugs and alcohol into their bloodstream more quickly than adults do, and their bodies are less efficient at breaking down toxic by-products.[15]
- Nicotine use can lead to long-term changes in brain function. For instance, it's known to cause alterations in the cell activity responsible for attention, learning and memory.[16]
- Alcohol abuse has also been associated with structural brain abnormalities. For example, it affects the hippocampus (the part of the brain that is important for memory and learning)[17] and can reduce brain volume.[18]
- The use of marijuana is associated with reduced cognitive function in teens.[19] One study found that teens who regularly use marijuana lose an average of 5.8 IQ points by the time they reach adulthood.[20]
- Another recent study found that marijuana has a more negative impact on a teenager's cognitive development than alcohol.[21]

More immediately, alcohol and drugs — especially if combined — can dangerously affect behaviour, leading to loss of inhibition, poor decision-making and increased risk-taking. So with this information in mind, you may want to know what to look out for. Some signs are more obvious — such as slurred speech and/or lost coordination when drunk, along with the tell-tale smell of alcohol or cannabis — while others are less so. Cannabis can cause the eyes to become reddened and puffy.[22] (For information on other drugs, see Resources/Rauemi, page 149.)

How can you tell that this may be becoming a problematic behaviour? Change, after all, is part of being a teenager. There may be signs (also covered in Chapter 8) that suggest your teen is struggling with alcohol or substance misuse, such as:

- using incense or air fresheners in the bedroom,[23]
- a chronic cough, a lack of energy and general lethargy,[24]
- memory problems,[25]
- physical problems such as hangovers or, more seriously, alcohol poisoning,[26]
- responding with hostility when the negative effects of drug use are discussed,[27]
- persistent lying, evasion or secretive behaviour, along with frequent unexplained phone calls,[28]
- personality changes, along with mood swings, bursts of anger or withdrawal,[29]
- the appearance of new friends on the scene, combined with a reluctance to introduce these friends,[30] and/or
- unusual or suspicious requests for money, and even cash or valuables going missing.[31]

More extreme consequences can include car accidents and other unintentional injuries, such as burns or falls. And, of course, driving or physically hurting someone while drunk can lead to brushes with the law.[32]

If your teen does arrive home drunk or high, try to hold off on any lectures or repercussions until they are safe and sober. Know how to assess their wellbeing: if they are really intoxicated and/or vomiting, stay with them and make sure they are in the recovery position. If necessary, take them to hospital or call emergency services.

In addition to the harms that apply more generally, there are issues that attach more specifically to smoking, vaping, drinking and using cannabis. Let's look at each of these in turn.

Smoking

Most people understand the risk of smoking cigarettes. It harms not only the smoker, but also those within their environment. Other people may find it antisocial and smelly, and in recent years there have been huge restrictions on smoking in public places. There have also been large increases in the price of tobacco products in a deliberate attempt at deterrence, and World Smokefree Day is held on 31 May each year. In 2011, Aotearoa announced a goal to be smokefree by 2025, with several initiatives, including: protecting children from exposure to tobacco marketing and promotion; reducing the supply of, and demand for, tobacco; and providing the best possible support for quitting.[33] In December 2021, the Ardern government doubled down on this, announcing plans to outlaw smoking effectively from the next generation on.[34] Overall, the anti-smoking message seems to have permeated through, with the statistics showing us that smoking is now much less popular than it might have been when you were a teen. There is still work to be done, though. A 2018 study of 14–15-year-olds found that Māori were 2.5 times more likely to smoke than non-Māori, that Pasifika were twice as likely to smoke as non-Pasifika, and that students at low-decile schools were twice as likely to smoke as those at high-decile schools.[35]

What's the harm in a cigarette?

According to SmokeFreeNZ:

Cigarettes typically consist of tobacco, chemical additives, a filter, and paper wrapping. The smoke inhaled from a burning cigarette contains a mix of over 7000 harmful chemicals. More than 70 of these chemicals are linked to cancer. There is no evidence that cigarettes advertised as 'organic', 'all-natural', or 'additive-free' are any safer or less harmful. Cigarette smoking harms nearly every organ of the body, and causes many diseases, including heart disease, strokes, and lung cancer.[36]

The school curriculum will teach your teens about why smoking should be avoided, and as a parent you need to reinforce the message. Your teen is more likely to pick up a cigarette if they are being influenced by peers, wanting to fit in or feeling the need to rebel in some way. A 2018 Youth Insights Survey found that 40 per cent of smokers 'were given cigarettes by a friend or person their own age',[37] although other powerful influences include seeing celebrities smoking; a young person is also seven times more likely to take up the habit if both their parents smoke. On the plus side, they are also more likely to quit if their parents quit;[38] and if they can make it to their mid-twenties without smoking, there's a strong chance they'll never begin. Unfortunately, the nicotine contained in cigarettes is addictive, so once someone starts it may be more difficult to stop than they'd thought.

If you start smelling the whiff of ashtrays (or mints) on your teen's breath and their money seems to be disappearing at a rate of knots, it might be time for another chat about smoking and, if necessary, to work with them to quit. If you yourself smoke, you can at least be honest about how hard it is to give up, and this, plus the side effects you struggle with, may help put them off. Teens tend to think they're bulletproof, so just talking about the longer-term health issues may not be enough. But most of them will at least want to avoid yellow fingers, teeth and nails, and stinky breath. Over time, smoking can also make it harder to participate in sports. It's also become phenomenally expensive — even teens with Saturday jobs tend to get paid only minimum wage, with the average price of a pack of cigarettes easily costing nearly twice this hourly rate.

Vaping

Vaping was initially promoted as a safer alternative to smoking and a possible step towards breaking a tobacco addiction. It relies on an electronic device (known as a vape, electronic cigarette or e-cigarette) that heats a liquid (also known as e-liquid or juice) to deliver the active vapour into the lungs. In Aotearoa you must be over the age of 18 to purchase a vape. Although nicotine-free liquids are available, the majority have varying strengths of nicotine in them. They are available in flavours that are appealing to teens, such as bubble gum, cotton candy, gummy bear, frozen lime-drop and raspberry ice cream. Some can almost sound healthy: apple, grape, strawberry and watermelon.

Although vaping has been around for a decade or so, the design and marketing have stepped up a gear in the last few years. Adolescent psychiatrist Sarper Taskiran suggests that this may account for a recent rise in its popularity: 'teens are after innovation and they're attracted by sleek design and ease of use. [Vapes] look like an Apple product.'[39] This marketing focus means that teens may not be aware of the connection between vaping and nicotine content. And while it's relatively easy for a smoker to calculate their daily nicotine intake, it's very much harder where vaping is involved, as it depends on the concentration of nicotine within the juice, the number of puffs taken and how often, and the kind of vaping device used. Vaping has also become popular at parties and get-togethers: some teens buy a non-refillable vape for an event and will often pass them around to be shared. According to studies:

- Vaping is common in schools of all deciles, and the majority of students vaping had never smoked.[40]
- The recent increase in vaping occurred across most demographics.
- Most subjects said they vaped because they liked the flavours/ taste and enjoyed vaping with their friends (both 59 per cent).[41]
- The use of vaping increased with age, with 24 per cent of

13–14-year-olds, 41 per cent of 15–16-year-olds and 47 per cent of 17–18-year-olds having tried it at some point.[42]

There are, as mentioned, nicotine-free vape juices, but while these are arguably not addictive physiologically, they may nonetheless be habit-forming. And given the high proportion of e-liquids that do contain nicotine, some research indicates vaping may be a gateway to cigarette use.[43] This would be ironic in a tool initially designed to help smokers quit.

To date, not much is known about the short- and long-term health implications of vaping. There have certainly been a few health scares recently. One relates to the additive diacetyl — a butter-flavoured chemical in foods such as ready-made popcorn — which some studies suggest can lead to a bronchial condition nicknamed 'popcorn lung'.[44] Another study, from the US, concerns an illegal unregulated e-liquid containing vitamin E acetate.[45]

So while vaping is currently generally considered much less problematic than smoking cigarettes, it may not be entirely harm-free. The words of Michael Blaha, a director of clinical research in the US, are of interest here: 'What I find most concerning about the rise of vaping is that people who would've never smoked otherwise, especially youth, are taking up the habit. It's one thing if you convert from cigarette smoking to vaping. It's quite another thing to start up nicotine use with vaping.'[46] Today, legislation is being introduced to regulate vaping products in New Zealand. The law aims to 'strike a balance between ensuring vaping products are available for smokers who want to use them to reduce the harm to their health, and making sure these products aren't marketed or sold to non-smokers, especially young people'.[47] Finally, there are additional concerns that vaping can be used as a way to consume cannabis or other illegal drugs.

Hookah/shisha
A hookah is a traditional smoking device for burning tobacco or herbal products (known as 'shisha') and filtering the smoke through

water before it is inhaled via a pipe. Prior to the pandemic, shisha lounges were becoming more popular in Aotearoa. These are places where groups can gather to eat, and to share a shisha, passing around the mouthpiece. The practice has long been a fixture in Southeast Asian, Middle Eastern and North African communities and is now becoming more widespread globally. Legally, no one under 18 years can visit a shisha lounge, but it is simple and inexpensive to buy (or make) one to use at home, and oftentimes these make appearances at parties.

Unfortunately, shisha, even if flavoured, usually contains the same nicotine and other harmful agents as are found in cigarettes. The British Heart Foundation estimates that 'in a typical shisha session (which usually lasts 20–80 minutes), a shisha smoker can inhale the same amount of toxins as a cigarette smoker consuming over 100 cigarettes'.[48] Some education here is a good idea, as it may be that your teen falsely believes smoking shisha isn't harmful; common misconceptions are that the smoke is healthier because it is first drawn through water, or that the tobacco-free versions are somehow safer than a cigarette.

Alcohol and binge drinking

It is quite possible that if alcohol were introduced now it would be highly legislated or banned. As WHO puts it, 'Alcohol remains the only psychoactive and dependence-producing substance that exerts a significant impact on global population health that is not controlled at the international level by legally binding regulatory instruments.'[49]

Looking back on your own teenage years, at the very least you may remember tales of raids on parents' drinks cabinets to 'pre-load', or people using fake IDs to purchase the cheapest and most potent beverage, very much with the intention of getting drunk. Many of us will have memories of our parents' drinking habits during our teenage years, and this may well have influenced our own behaviour. (After all, 93 per cent of adults will try alcohol at some point in their lives.)[50]

The same will be true for your teens: if you binge, they are more likely to do so too.[51]

Parents are often the conduit through which their teens gain access to alcohol: historically, it seems that allowing teens to drink alcohol in a controlled way was believed to ease them into a healthy drinking culture. But this is not necessarily the case. According to neuroscience educator Nathan Wallis, 'the earlier you have alcohol with your child, the more likely they are to have a drug and alcohol issue'.[52]

And that's not the only problem with consuming alcohol as a teen, as research indicates:

- A US study found that teens who began drinking before age 15 were 12 times more likely to be injured, seven times more likely to be in a motor vehicle crash, and 10 times more likely to get into a fight than peers who waited till the legal drinking age.[53]
- Another US study found that teens who began drinking before age 15 were five times more likely to develop alcohol issues later in life than those who waited till the legal drinking age.[54]
- Binge drinking, as opposed to moderate drinking, has also been connected with poor educational performance, higher risk-taking, being a victim of dating violence, attempting suicide and using illegal drugs.[55]

Aotearoa lowered its drinking age from 20 to 18 years in 1999. Prime Minister Jenny Shipley said, 'New Zealand's 18- and 19-year-olds are responsible enough to drink alcohol in pubs and cafes, and I welcome our society's recognition of that.' But, she added, 'Families must also take more responsibility in controlling their children's access to alcohol. Parents must also share the responsibility of knowing where their young people are in the early hours of the morning.'[56] Not everyone was on board with this decision, and many continue to petition to retract the change. There are some indications that lowering the legal drinking age led to higher levels of drinking and alcohol-related harm.[57] However, over time it seems that there is a decreasing trend in the number of teens drinking, down from 74.5 per cent of 15–17-year-olds in 2007 to 57.5 per cent in 2020.[58] Nonetheless, when teens do drink, many consume to a level that is harmful. This is especially true as they reach the end of their teens and head into their twenties. Definitions of binge drinking vary, but that used by the Youth2000 Survey Series is five or more drinks in a session (within four hours).[59]

Patterns around drinking alcohol may be about a multitude of things, including generally enjoying the convivial atmosphere it often creates, and its ability to lower inhibitions. It becomes more concerning when drinking is connected to peer pressure and wanting to fit in, or unsafe behaviours result from the false confidence it can generate. Parties in particular can be occasions where teens might be pressured into drinking games like beer pong, or challenges such as downing a yard glass of beer (2.7 litres) on a 21st birthday. Other events, such as 'crate day' (a radio station initiative to buy a crate of beer and drink from midday onwards), can feed into an unhealthy drinking culture. Such activities may make those who might naturally prefer to stay more teetotal feel excluded if they don't participate.

A 2015 New Zealand study of university students aged 18–25 years found 'excessive consumption [of alcohol] was expected, held in high regard, shaped students' positive social identity and their inclusion in the student drinking culture, and was enforced through peer pressure'. It found that 'intoxication is the goal and alcohol is used as a tool to achieve the desired state. There is an "all or nothing" culture in which students are expected to "go hard or go home". Thus, students perceive drinking in moderation to be illogical because it will not achieve drunkenness and, as such, is a waste of calories and money.'[60]

Popular drinks for teens sometimes centre on what is cheap and accessible, such as the budget high-strength lagers. RTDs or 'alcopops' containing spirits are also a go-to, with the flavours and packaging being attractive to younger drinkers. Of course, it is actually the percentage of alcohol that's important, rather than the volume consumed. What's more, the 'safe units' for adults will not be appropriate for those whose bodies are still developing, for reasons explained earlier.

There is a very difficult balance to strike here: your teen may be facing issues around alcohol on a fairly regular basis; but in terms of permission, the law leaves these decisions in your hands. The bottom line is that you will be wanting to help them develop a healthy relationship with alcohol, and making sure that they are informed about the potential harm is a key part of this. You can also help your teen find strategies to negotiate social settings when they want to avoid alcohol.

The advice, then, is clear: model safe and sensible behaviour around alcohol consumption, and delay introducing alcohol to your teen for as long as is feasibly possible. Discuss with them why you are making these decisions. Explain that there are potential health issues for under-25s who use alcohol, so this is not just a case of 'do as I say, not as I do'.[61] Try to come to an agreed solution for social events, and explore alcohol-free alternatives.

Drinking and driving

As a parent, you'll be wanting to know that your teen doesn't drive a car after drinking alcohol, or get into a car driven by someone who's been drinking. Research shows clearly that as a person's blood alcohol level rises, so does their risk of accident, injury and death from driving. With teens and those in their twenties still new to handling a car, and with their bodies still processing alcohol less efficiently, these statistics are at their worst. And, as stated by the New Zealand Ministry of Transport: '[F]or every one hundred drivers who die in road crashes where alcohol/drugs were a contributing factor, 27 of their passengers and 32 other road users died with them.'[62]

In addition, it seems that our boys are at highest risk: in 2017–19, 82 per cent of drivers in New Zealand who died in crashes linked to alcohol or drugs were male (within the 20–24 age range this figure was 44 per cent male, versus 19 per cent female).[63] New Zealand's grim teen road toll has provoked a number of advertising campaigns. Some have avoided the usual shock tactics, instead encouraging friends to look out for one another, as in the memorable 2011 'ghost chips' ad, or 2018's 'stop a mate driving drunk — legend'.

We need to let our teens know that, according to the law, 'there is a zero alcohol limit for anyone aged under 20. Anyone under 20 could be charged with drink driving if they consume any alcohol and then drive.'[64] And we need to let them know why. It's also imperative they know there is always a plan B: that no matter where they are, what they're doing with whom, and when, they can call on your help rather than get in a vehicle drunk, or with a drunk driver, without fear of reprimand (even if you need to talk through their actions at another time).

Cannabis

There is all sorts of slang and jargon relating to the use of cannabis, with different words used by different groups, and different terms used for the various methods of consuming the drug. So it may be helpful to explore some of the key words and terms:

- **Cannabis** derives from the leaves and flowers ('buds') of the hemp plant *Cannabis sativa*. (In its more innocuous industrial form, the hemp plant has many by-products, such as seed oils and natural fibres.)
- **Marijuana** is a Mexican slang word for cannabis leaves and flowers.
- **Hash,** short for hashish, is made of pressed resin from cannabis buds, and is therefore stronger in effect.[65]

Whatever you want to call it, cannabis/marijuana/hash is usually rolled and smoked like a cigarette (joints or doobies), or put in hollowed-out cigars (blunts), pipes or water pipes (bongs, cones or bowls). Recently, it has become increasingly popular for people to vape marijuana or stronger marijuana extracts (also called 'dabbing').

Some people mix it into food or brew it as a tea.[66]

There are also many kinds of **synthetic marijuana**. These artificial compounds are chemically similar to tetrahydrocannabinol (THC, the main active psychotropic ingredient in cannabis), and they can be lethally powerful.[67]

With the 2020 referendum on the legalisation of cannabis in New Zealand, there's been a lot of debate as to the potential harms of the drug. It's certainly readily available and almost definitely a substance your teen will come across and probably be offered. Whatever you may feel about its legal status and its use, the evidence shows that, as with alcohol, teenage exposure to cannabis can have negative outcomes, as noted earlier in this chapter.

One of the problems with cannabis is that its effects on users can vary widely depending on the individual, and on factors such as how it is ingested, how the user is feeling at the time and the nature of the user's immediate environment.[68]

Internationally, cannabis is the most widely used psychoactive drug among young people, with about 5 per cent of 15–16-year-olds using it at least once.[69] Just over 4 per cent of New Zealand teenagers use cannabis on at least a weekly basis, which makes it more prevalent than cigarette smoking (3 per cent).[70] US research indicates that about one in 10 cannabis users will become addicted; for people who begin using before age 18, that proportion rises to one in six.[71]

Although there is growing support for the use of cannabis to help treat some medical conditions, recreational use of the drug remains illegal in Aotearoa. This puts it into a different category to smoking/vaping and alcohol, since its usage can lead directly to involvement with the criminal justice system. Your teen may not be thinking in terms of long-term employment prospects at the moment, but they need to be aware that some employers regularly conduct drug tests, and marijuana stays in the system for some time after use.

Is cannabis a gateway drug?

There is some concern that the use of cannabis will lead to usage of other drugs. A recent review of research by the US National Institute on Drug Abuse (NIDA) suggested that 'the majority of people who use marijuana do not go on to use other, "harder" substances'.[72] Interestingly, research has shown 'that in Japan, where cannabis isn't as accessible . . . 83.2 per cent of users of recreational substances did not use cannabis first'.[73] One explanation explored in the NIDA review was that 'people who are more vulnerable to drug-taking are simply more likely to start with readily available substances such as marijuana, tobacco, or alcohol, and their subsequent social interactions with others who use drugs increase their chances of trying other drugs'.[74]

A word on addiction

Whatever first spurs a teen to try alcohol or drugs — it might be peer pressure, boredom, a shot at rebellion, or a lack of confidence and wanting to 'fit in', for instance — they may continue using for a whole new set of reasons.

They may, for instance, like the way the substance makes them feel. Both alcohol and drugs have the effect of increasing the feeling of pleasure through the release of endorphins and neurotransmitters such as dopamine; they can also impact on the body's ability to produce these chemicals naturally. Usage won't necessarily lead to dependence, but, as one publication puts it, 'teens have a higher risk of addiction because their limbic systems are very sensitive to dopamine. As a result, they may crave drugs more strongly than adults. The earlier someone starts drug use, the higher his or her addiction risk.'[75]

It's about teens taking responsibility for their behaviour, and this becomes less easy for them to do if they start to consume any substance irresponsibly — when experimentation becomes something more serious. It's vital, however, not to be judgemental;

addiction can happen to anyone, regardless of character.[76] Ultimately, as noted previously, the teenage years coincide with the brain's greatest susceptibility to damage.

If you find that your teen is experimenting with any type of illegal substance, try to find out what's driving their behaviour. You will need to discuss their alcohol and/or drug use with them and help them access support to get things under control. Useful helplines and websites are included in the Resources/Rauemi section (see page 149), including support for you and other family or friends who are impacted.

How can I have this conversation? / Me pēhea tēnei matakahi?

We have learned over the years that the philosophy of 'just say no' doesn't work for teens.[77] They want to have an explanation as to why they should and shouldn't be allowed to do something. There's a lot of peer pressure involved and they may feel that you are not up to speed with the current trends when setting your expectations and house rules. Messages around harm prevention (e.g., 'don't drink') need to be combined with messages around harm reduction (e.g., 'if you do end up drinking, make sure you drink a lot of water at the same time').

Set rules with your teen about their behaviour: they can be involved in developing these, but you are the parent, so you get to decide where there is flexibility (e.g., they can stay over at a particular friend's house for a party as you know the family well) and where there is not (e.g., they are not allowed to stay up until the small hours on a school night). Conversely, spell out in advance the consequences for any breaches of agreed rules. Again, your teen can be involved in developing these, but it's your job to see that they are fairly but consistently enforced.

**This is why we need to have the conversation,
and primarily the message here is to
set age-appropriate boundaries.**

Your teen will almost certainly have a lot to say about this topic. You may find it helpful to have a plan so that you don't get bulldozed into agreeing to something that makes you feel uncomfortable.

Points to keep the conversation going

- **This is not a one-off conversation,** so use relevant opportunities to revisit the topic often — when something crops up in a movie, or when you pass a liquor store, or if you smell someone's vape, for example. This can provide a chance to chat together about your ground rules and expectations. Try to speak in a way that will not put your teen off coming to you to talk things through when they have problems.
- Another way to open the topic is to expand on others' risky behaviours: there might be a celebrity talked about on the car radio, or your teen might relay to you an incident they heard about at school. Again, watch your tone — you could say, for example, 'It must be really hard for them to be going through this.' A **non-critical approach** can help to open up conversations rather than close them down.
- **It's useful to role-play** and have your teen practise a few 'get out of jail free' phrases, enabling them to say no — to cigarettes or vapes, or other substances — without feeling they have lost kudos. Also explore how they might leave a scene if they feel uncomfortable. You may want to organise a code word (see page 103) with them: they can text you this word to alert you they are struggling. You can then ring them immediately, and tell them something's come up and you have to pick them up straight away. They then have the opportunity to duck out, blaming you for such an over-the-top and unreasonable request . . .
- Give them the **facts and the evidence** when **setting your limitations. Be open to compromise** if it falls within your safety zones. Consider sharing with them harm-reduction strategies should they decide to do something you consider off

limits — for example, making sure they eat before drinking alcohol. Be clear that actions will have reactions: follow through with any consequences you set.

- **Discuss ideas, dilemmas and strategies** with your teen (age appropriately): ask them what they would do in various situations and chip in with ideas. Examples might be:
  - How can they keep themselves and their friends safe at a party?
  - How do they know when someone has had too much to drink and may be at risk?
  - Why do they think people smoke, vape, drink alcohol or take drugs?
  - If they felt at risk, or thought someone else was at risk, what would their action be?
  - What would they do if someone who was supposed to give them a ride home had been drinking?
  - Would they think it okay to hook up with someone who's been drinking? Or if they had?
- **Having a cell phone** (with enough credit) is a necessity these days, and it's not a bad idea to also get them a mini battery charger for their bag.
- If you are in the position to, give them access to a taxi or ride-share account for **emergencies**.
- Chat with your teen about looking out for their friends and their friends looking out for them. Encourage your teen to have this conversation with their tribe and be prepared to share phone numbers. This means that you are **always contactable** — if, for instance, your teen has broken a curfew and you are wondering where on earth they are, or they need to be collected early from a friend's house because things have come unstuck.
- Make a pact with your teen that, no matter what, they have an exit plan. Let them know time and time again that whether or not they might be in the wrong or have made a bad call,

you will be there for them. Let them know that whatever the time of day or night, whether they are drunk, high or sober, or wherever they are, you will bring them back to safety. Then stick to this, no matter what.

- Remember your own youth: **draw on the wisdom of your experiences** and try to be open-minded if your teen comes to you to talk about what is happening to them. Firstly, thank them for being prepared to share their concerns. Listen non-judgementally, ask them questions and be curious about what they think. Find out how much they know. Avoid the 'just say no' trap. Remind them of short- and longer-term harms. Find ways to make sure they have support.

Being a teenager is tricky, but don't panic. Again, try not to focus on the pitfalls, but find ways to make sure that your teen has some structure to keep them happy, healthy and safe.

Some tips if you are hosting a party at home

- Encourage your teen to pass on your **contact details** to those invited so you can be available for other parents who may have questions.
- Make sure your teen has kept the **invitations in a closed forum** and been precise with their friends about whether they can bring a plus-one or extend the invite to others.
- Ensure there is **food available** — if you pass this out yourself from time to time, you can keep a check on how everyone is going.
- Make sure there are **non-alcoholic drinks readily available.** Ideally, the best outcome is if the party can be **alcohol-free.** If, however, there is to be alcohol, think about a **limit and type/strength** you are comfortable with. You may decide to have the alcohol in one place, so perhaps have some stickers at the ready so each person's alcohol can be labelled.
- Decide if your property is **smoke-/vape-free**; if not, dedicate

an area outside for smoking and provide ashtrays. Consider having a back-up plan in case it rains.

- As you are responsible for any youth on your property, perhaps **invite other adults** to help you keep an eye on things and sort out issues if they arise. Consider having an **adult on the door** — this ensures that only those invited come in and also gives you an oversight of how many teens are there, along with how much alcohol.

- Close off and clearly label areas that are **out of bounds** (your bedroom, for example).

- If issues arise, make sure you have a **plan for dealing with problems**. If someone needs to be sent home, you may want to call their parents and will certainly want to ensure they are safe. If someone is not safe or is threatening your safety, call 111.

- Give some thought about the end of the party before it begins. When does the party end? Will friends stay over? If so, where will they sleep? For those that are leaving, how are they getting home (especially if alcohol is involved)?

Talking box questions

✂ Can you demonstrate the recovery position?

✂ What emergency contact numbers
might you need if you go to a party?

✂ How would you help a friend who
has had too much to drink?

Resources / Rauemi

ONLINE	Information packs about substances and young people:
	tepou.co.nz/uploads/files/resources/MR-Youth-AOD-resource-WEB.pdf
	drugfoundation.org.nz/assets/uploads/drugs-education-discussion.pdf
	Conversation planner with tips, tricks and comics to help facilitate a chat with your teen about substances:
	drugfoundation.org.nz/info/did-you-know/conversation-planner
	Educational online games that explore what happens to the brain and body when drugs are used:
	teens.drugabuse.gov/teens/games
	A website offering support to empower young people whose lives are influenced by alcohol and other drugs:
	amplify.org.nz
	Alcohol
	Resource hub for having conversations with your teen about alcohol:
	cheers.org.nz/parents-and-teens
	Resource hub including information about New Zealand law around alcohol, pouring standard drinks, alcohol's impacts on the body and more:
	alcohol.org.nz/parents
	Vaping
	The facts about vaping:
	vapingfacts.health.nz
	Marijuana
	Information pack about marijuana for teens:
	teens.drugabuse.gov/sites/default/files/2020-08/FINAL_NIDA_MindMatters_Marijuana_2020_508.pdf

7. BODY TALK: SELF-ESTEEM AND BODY IMAGE

#healthateverysize #loveyourbody #bodyneutrality

'And I said to my body. Softly.
"I want to be your friend."
It took a long breath. And replied,
"I have been waiting my whole life for this."'
— RUPI KAUR

Kōrero with Molly

I've not always had the easiest road to developing body satisfaction. Before puberty it just didn't seem to be an issue for me, but from then on the struggle got real. I remember when I was a teenager, going shopping at the mall with friends. One of us would point out some sparkly outfit in a shop window and we'd go in to try it on. It almost never looked like it did on the mannequin . . . although now, we realise that most mannequins are not representative of the myriad body shapes that exist. At the time, it was easy to blame ourselves for not looking the way we thought we should. Clothes shopping was not such a fun experience for me until I had the tools to critically analyse what I was seeing on the posters, on television and on social media. I'm still a work in progress! It takes time to really value yourself and accept every aspect of your identity. These days, I'll buy that sparkly outfit because it makes me feel happy and confident, and I'll do my best to avoid comparisons to unreal expectations. Looking back to my teenage years, however, it felt much harder to do that.

What do you mean by that? / He aha te tikanga o tāu kōrero?

You may well be asking how on earth you can raise a self-confident, body-confident teen today, given the unrealistic representations shown in the media, particularly in advertising, along with the pressures of the culture of social media and the moving target of the latest 'perfect body'. Well, it isn't easy — but it is possible to open your teen's eyes so they can consciously analyse the constant barrage they're receiving rather than just be unconsciously affected by the subliminal messages. Being able to analyse the information they receive may, in turn, encourage them to be critical of the cause and effects of certain narratives around body image. It will also allow them to see the positives alongside any negatives — to be able to brush off unrealistic aspects and enjoy the rest. This will then give them some context to review their behaviour and that of their peers.

Although sometimes you will hear the terms used interchangeably, self-esteem and body image are two different things. They are nonetheless interconnected, and they influence each other.

Self-esteem accounts for the way we see ourselves as a whole person, including our values (see table below).

HIGH VERSUS LOW SELF-ESTEEM	
A person with high self-esteem:	A person with low self-esteem:
• is confident • sets clear boundaries and can say 'no' to others • has a good sense of self and rates themselves as equal to others • looks forward with positivity and doesn't dwell on the past • is non-judgemental of themselves • is accepting of failure and gives things another go.	• lacks confidence • struggles with boundaries and saying 'no' to others • feels they are not as good as others, and rarely puts their own needs first • has trouble letting go of issues and moving forward positively • is judgemental of themselves • worries, stresses and can feel out of control.

Research across various age groups consistently demonstrates that higher self-esteem is linked to a more positive body image.[1] It's likely that if you can help your teen build their self-esteem, any body image issues will also be positively impacted.

Body image is specifically centred on how a person feels and reacts to their physical body, and it involves emotions, attitudes and beliefs (see table opposite).[2] The teenage years are a time when many have a growing, natural and healthy curiosity about their own and other people's bodies. Unfortunately, this could also mean that they start to compare themselves with those around them, both in real life and in the media. Many are also preoccupied with wanting to 'fit in' and so are highly sensitive to real or perceived judgements from peers. Some may develop a highly critical inner voice, and, boy, does that inner voice get loud at times. It can be a confusing and stressful time and, consequently, teens can be hard hit by a dip in their self-esteem, and that in turn can potentially lead to them having a more negative body image.

Research in New Zealand and overseas bears out how strongly young people feel about body image. In one study, nearly half (46 per cent) of 12–24-year-olds named 'body image' as a major concern, topped only by 'succeeding in studies and getting good grades' (49 per cent).[3] Another found that three-quarters of New Zealand female teens wanted to be thinner.[4] In other research, more than two-thirds of boys reported changing their diet, and two-fifths reported exercising more, to boost the appearance of their muscles.[5] And UK research found that 36 per cent of young women and 24 per cent of young men sometimes avoided taking part in certain activities (such as sport) because they worried about the way they looked.[6]

POSITIVE VERSUS NEGATIVE BODY IMAGE	
A person with positive body image may:	A person with negative body image may:
• be confident in their own appearance and not compare themselves to others • embrace their whole self rather than looking at individual body parts • understand that looks have nothing to do with someone's worth • celebrate body difference and diversity • appreciate what their body can *do*, rather than focus on how it looks, or on diet/weight issues.	• judge and compare their body to others and feel that their body is lesser • see certain features as problematic and obsess about them • struggle to disentangle their appearance from their self-worth • have a narrow view of acceptable body type for self • feel uncomfortable about their body and have concerns about food or weight.

Body image is very much in the mind. If your teen has issues around body image, then no matter how many times they look at their body in the mirror, their mental picture of that body will not match its true shape and size. Those with a negative body image can struggle to accept their body, find clothes to fit, or feel attractive.[7] Moreover, body image issues are far from static: different people experience them in different ways, and a person may feel different from one day to the next depending on their current mood and environment.

Feelings matter

Here's an exercise you can do with your teen to help explain body image.

Imagine you had a fantastic day at school. There was no drama with your friends and you got an excellent grade on a paper. When you look in the mirror, your reaction is, 'I look great!'

You take a picture of the reflection.

Now imagine you had a horrible day at school. You had a big fight with your friend and failed an assignment. When you look in the mirror, your response is, 'I look awful!'

Again, you take a picture of the reflection.

Here's the thing — for anyone else looking at these two pictures, you look practically the same! You just *felt* different. Body image is influenced by feelings. It's all about self-perception; you don't have to believe everything you feel![8]

As set out in the table on page 153, a positive body image has broader additional benefits. The ultimate aim is that your teen accepts themselves and is comfortable in their own skin. This in turn means they are able to 'be themselves' in every way.

Tell me more . . . / Kōrero mai anō . . .

It is useful to encourage your teen to think of their body image as part of their relationship with themselves. As with any relationship, to stay healthy it needs to be looked after, cherished and nourished. And there will be ups and downs. If your teen were to stop paying attention to their body and neglect to put any energy into this relationship, they might notice their mood start to decline. Another way to harm this relationship is if they constantly try to reshape their body or to push it beyond its comfortable limits. Fads including 'thinspiration' and 'fitspiration' are affecting teens' ideas of what constitutes the 'perfect body'.

This is particularly problematic at a time when teenage bodies have not yet finished forming. It's about helping your teen to understand that everybody's body is a little different and that what they see in a person doesn't necessarily depict health, ability or beauty. And it isn't even necessarily what other people see: while *they* may despise their natural hair colour, most other people might covet it. In addition, everyone has their own psychological make-up: body image issues can be tied to mental health pressures, such as anxiety, feelings of a lack of control and depression (see pages 193–197). At the same time, since a person's perception of their body image is ever-changing and adaptable, any unhelpful patterns can be addressed.

Topics to discuss with your teen could include:

- the 'perfect body',
- understanding body diversity,
- the influence of traditional media, including advertising, image manipulation and representation,
- the impact of social media, including the use of filters, peer attitudes and judgements, and
- the role of whānau/family.

This can help them develop a sense of body wonderment, which embraces the idea that their body is an 'instrument, not an ornament'.[9] They can then begin to challenge unhelpful language and practise body neutrality. So let's take a closer look at all these factors and drivers.

The 'perfect body'

Western ideals of the perceived perfect body have altered through the centuries and also the decades (remember eighties hair? — dig out that family photo album!). This 'perfect body' is therefore constantly changing. It might also be interesting to look at beauty ideals across different cultures and across the world, all of which can help your teen see how different body types, shapes and looks have dipped in and out of fashion over time. For example:

- Nineteenth-century men wanted to be as large as possible — this body shape was a status symbol because if you could afford to purchase excess food, you were obviously wealthier. There were even several exclusive clubs that men could join if they were over a certain weight, the implication being that they were therefore prestigious.[10]

- During the 1920s, when there was a degree of female emancipation following the First World War, the sought-after look for women was slender and boyish because, as actor and writer Amber Petty puts it, 'they were gaining a taste of men's power'.[11]
- Suntans first became popular in the twentieth century. Popularised by Chanel, they were considered ultra-chic in the 1930s,[12] when only the wealthy could afford to travel to sunny foreign locations. In previous centuries, pale skin was sought after; if you had a tan, it implied you were a manual labourer.[13]
- A curvy figure was popular and sought after when Marilyn Monroe was trending in the 1950–60s.[14]
- Muscles were 'in' during the eighties with the rise in popularity of actors such as Arnold Schwarzenegger.[15] Supermodels such as Cindy Crawford also popularised athletic forms.[16]
- In a reaction against this, in the nineties the waif figure was all over every catwalk.[17]
- Currently the 'fitspiration' is deemed the latest body to have, along with the Kardashian 'full booty' figure.[18]

It's worth pointing out that it isn't physically possible to be all these things. A body shape that is currently in vogue may well be out of favour in a few years' time. It's therefore better for your teen to learn to feel comfortable in their own body shape and find a look that suits them.

> *'Don't be into trends. Don't make fashion own you, but you decide what you are, what you want to express by the way you dress and the way you live.'*
> — GIANNI VERSACE

There are also geographical variations in the cultural ideals of mana, prestige or attractiveness. For example:

- Using henna to temporarily mark the skin in patterns symbolises various celebrations. This originated in Pakistan, India, Africa and the Middle East, but is increasingly practised worldwide.[19]
- While tattoos are globally popular, they also serve in traditional rites of passage, as in the Samoan peʻa (for men) and malu (for women). To wear tā moko (a tattoo) on your face is a great honour in Māori culture.
- Stretched earlobes and a shaved head are considered a sign of important transitional moments and also a mark of bravery for men and women in Kenya and other parts of Africa.
- An elongated neck is a mark of beauty and cultural identity among the women of the Kayan people of Myanmar and Thailand. From a young age, they wear rings around the neck to extend it, adding ever more rings over the years.

Something to broach with your teen is how our subconscious can be impacted in relation to our sense of self. Even as a child, we are receiving subliminal messages about what bodies 'should' and 'could' look like. Superhero toys are a fascinating example: take a look (via Google) at how the evolution of the Batman toy from the 1970s to the present day illustrates the changing shape of the 'idealised' male body. Another example is the Barbie doll: researchers who generated a computer model of a woman with Barbie-doll proportions found that her body would be too narrow to contain more than half a liver and a few centimetres of bowel, and her back would be too weak to support the weight of her upper body, forcing her to walk on all fours. A real woman built that way would suffer from chronic diarrhoea and eventually die from malnutrition.[20]

Understanding body diversity

We are intersectional human beings (see page 360). All aspects of our identity — including skin colour, height, weight, sexuality and any physical disabilities — feed into our body image. They all impact on our sense of self and, consequently, our body image in different ways.

To date, for instance, most research and discussion focuses on women and girls. But boys suffer from body image issues, too — and yet, as educator Collett Smart explains, 'boys are far less likely to address their own body image concerns and are more likely to struggle alone'.[21] Research also shows that people who identify as LGBTQIA+ can find body image issues particularly challenging.[22] It's rare, too, to see images of people with disabilities in body-positive campaigns.[23]

Ethnicity and race are additional factors. One US study reported higher rates of body dissatisfaction among Asian adolescents;[24] another found that body self-appreciation was highest among African American women and lowest among white women, while skin tone satisfaction ranged from highest among Latina women to lowest among multiracial women.[25]

Regardless of ethnicity or race, some studies have found that the more a person adopts westernised views, the more they find themselves measuring up to thin ideals, which in turn negatively impacts on their body image and self-esteem.[26] The converse also appears to be true, in that people who identify strongly with their cultural background will more readily relate to a larger figure. This is borne out in recent New Zealand research.[27] Much of the understanding around a healthy weight currently centres on a person's body mass index (BMI), and this is being challenged by other approaches such as Health at Every Size®. The key message, as eating disorder specialists Amanda Sainsbury and Phillipa Hay spell out, is that '[s]haming people into trying to lose weight, when the most likely outcome in the longer term may well be gaining weight, will only create or add to people's poor self-esteem and despair and worsen physical health'.[28]

Ultimately, as your teen builds on their relationship with themselves, you can help them embrace all of the things that make them who they are *and* appreciate the diversity of others. This may not always be reflected in the world they see around them. Mass media sometimes portrays stereotypes that are unrealistic: these can be potentially harmful to our teens, or even promote prejudice and further stigma.[29]

The influence of traditional media

The images we see in the media affect all of us, not just teens. A recent US study found that 87 per cent of women and 65 per cent of men compare their bodies to images they consume on traditional and social media, and the majority of both of these groups do so unfavourably.[30] Adults clearly struggle with interpreting images critically, and it is even more difficult for our teens, who don't yet have as wide a perspective. It is therefore vital to check in with them regularly to ensure they can critique what they see, stream, hear and read. That way, they can enjoy their media and challenge content where required.

Advertising

Advertisers have a specific agenda: they are trying to sell you stuff, of course. Advertising does not aim to enhance your sense of self or body acceptance. And because advertising is everywhere, it would be near impossible to bring up our teens in some sort of ad-free bubble. All around them there are billboards, magazines, movies, shop fronts, videos and clickbait, cleverly timed and specifically targeted for this audience. Often these images promote unhealthy or unachievable body ideals.

In addition, the use of algorithms now means that teens can be inundated with specifically directed advertisements through their social media. This programming is so effective that it is sometimes hard for your teen to work out the extent to which their interests are being directed.

Advertisers play a huge part in influencing the way teens think and behave, but currently regulation in this area is limited. The New Zealand Children and Young People's Advertising Code is trying to address this, and states specifically that '[a]dvertising must not provide an unrealistic sense of body image or promote an unhealthy lifestyle'. It defines advertising as any content that is 'controlled directly or indirectly by the advertiser, expressed in any language and communicated in any medium with the intent to influence the choice, opinion or behaviour of those to whom it is addressed'.[31]

Image manipulation

Ever since photography was invented, images have been tinkered with. Today, processes that used to be magical secrets of the darkroom can be replicated in the blink of an eye on a smartphone.

Our job as parents is not to discourage our teens from learning amazing digital programs that enable them to enhance images. After all, they may grow up to be an extremely happy and well-balanced graphic designer, and these programs take creativity, intelligence and skill to master. There is, of course, a difference between manipulating images and manipulating the people for whom those images are intended. In a 2015 interview the inventor of Photoshop, Thomas Knoll, likened the program to a tool and explained that 'like any tool it can be used to do good things or bad things'.[32] Dove's *Evolution* video, for instance, shows how easily our perception of beauty can be manipulated. It's worth encouraging your teen to watch this, too, as it lays the beauty myth bare (and has also been proven to boost young people's body image).[33] Jesse Rosten's video *Fotoshop by Adobé* also highlights these issues in a lighthearted way.[34]

The vast majority of media content is 'tweaked' before it's published for the viewer. On some occasions, fashion photography is so heavily manipulated that the model would in reality need to have several ribs removed in order to replicate the waistline shown in the picture, or would need a brace around their impossibly slender neck in order to support their head. There's not much point in your teen aspiring to look like that! Younger children may not yet be aware of how extensively these processes are used in media and advertising, or how detrimental they can be — so education is really important. It's important, too, to continue this conversation as they reach their teenage years. As *Guardian* columnist Rhiannon Lucy Cosslett has pointed out, 'we're beyond needing to teach girls about the artifice behind image manipulation. They know very well. But that doesn't mean that they are immune to its effects, that they don't desperately feel the need to change themselves as they compare their young bodies to those of supermodels.'[35]

In other words, our teens are negatively influenced by images despite knowing they are not real. Although we need to draw their attention to what's going on and encourage them to call it out, this in itself is not enough. We also need to think more laterally in order to create a positive environment. This will make our teens more resilient to subconscious messages about the 'perfect body' that are continually coming their way.

There has been some kickback over the last decade, with several well-known personalities — among them Kiwi Instagram star Jess Quinn[36] and actors Kate Winslet and Tracee Ellis Ross[37] — publicly criticising the press for reshaping or changing photographs of them. Interestingly, some publications are now using a different approach. For instance, while *Girlfriend* magazine does include some manipulated images of young women, it flags them with a labelling system called 'Reality Checks'. *Girlfriend* editor Sarah Tarca calls this system 'a media literacy tool' that 'makes our readers smart and aware as to what goes into a shoot'.[38]

Representation

Having talked about body diversity, it's also crucial to examine why it's important that images of people in the media should reflect the diverse communities around us.

Audiences will feel alienated by a lack of representation. If your teen can't see themselves in the media they access, they may not feel 'seen'— which in turn can dent their self-esteem. And that's true for all ages. For instance, in a vox pop conducted in 2020 by the UK government, 57 per cent of adults reported 'rarely' or 'never' seeing themselves or people who look like them regularly reflected in images in media and advertising.[39] A related issue is stereotyping, which, according to a US study, is a particular problem among LGBTQIA+ individuals and people (especially women) of colour. As researcher Ilyssa Salomon says, 'For teens that belong to or identify with these groups, cultural body standards can be even more limited and unrealistic, potentially eliciting greater feelings of shame toward their own bodies.'[40]

It seems bizarre, really. Even if media and advertisers are just out to make money, wouldn't it make sense for them to represent the customer? All is for All is an up-and-coming New Zealand creative agency that, among other things, represents people with disabilities in the world of media and fashion. As its website explains, 'disabled people represent 15% of the world's population and US$8 trillion in annual disposable income, but they are frequently misunderstood . . . All is for All was launched to bring about understanding. [We] started as champions of accessible fashion, believing that the power of fashion would help shift minds and hearts.'[41] In 2019, a model with a physical disability opened New Zealand Fashion Week for the first time. Wheelchair user Grace Stratton, the CEO of All is for All, commented: 'People talk about diversity and inclusion a lot, and the discussion is great, but that discussion has to follow through and turn into action.'[42]

The impact of social media

As the first fully digital generation hits its teens, we are only just beginning to understand the impact of social media and the Internet. In a 2020 Nielsen survey of New Zealanders aged 13–24, more than one-quarter (28 per cent) overall regularly viewed online posts that made them feel negatively about their body image, social situation or background. That figure rose for those who were bisexual (45 per cent), had a disability (45 per cent), were aged 19–24 years (38 per cent) or were female (35 per cent).[43]

And nor are adults immune. As highlighted by a US study, around half of us will spend four minutes or more modifying a selfie before posting it — only to feel disappointed if it receives fewer than 20 'likes'.[44]

It's not as if our teens don't know that social media images are manipulated — they are well used to tweaking their own selfies and painstakingly constructing the best of their day to circulate on whichever platform they're using. Only 'the good stuff' will make the cut, similar to a 'highlights reel'. At some level, most teens understand that even though the feeds they follow look effortless, these are in fact carefully crafted and curated, representing a very limited view of reality. This doesn't stop some teens from feeling that their life is pretty mundane and imperfect when everyone else is apparently living their best life.

The use of filters

Digital filters are effects that can be placed on photos, videos, selfies and TikToks. They are widely used on social media posts. They can change the colour of a picture — to sepia, for example — or can hide blemishes on your face, recolour your hair, and change the shape of any part of your body, from your nose to your toes. They allow the user to change, tweak or 'beautify' their selfies. These filters can also be interactive when used live. You can add bunny ears while you are FaceTiming or become a cat while Zooming.

Filters aren't intrinsically harmful, and they can be fun (who doesn't want to turn themselves into a unicorn with rainbows pouring out of their mouth every time they speak?), and yet in some situations they can prove problematic. Constant exposure to other people's 'best selves' can have a negative effect on your teen's body image and self-esteem — even if they know that their friends' photos are filtered and therefore unrealistic. Moreover, if your teen's filtered selfies garner lots of praise, then they may increasingly feel that unfiltered shots are inadequate. In a recent UK survey of girls aged between 11 and 21, more than one-third (34 per cent) said they wouldn't post a photo without a filter.[45]

One way to counter this is to watch a 'woke up like this' YouTube vlog (video blog) together with your teen. This can open a discussion about selfies and media tweaking, and underscore the difference between the expectations created by what is posted online and the realities. Since the pandemic, with so much remote working involving online meetings, we parents may now have a greater insight into why our teens are so concerned about their social media presence.

Interestingly, research conducted in New Zealand shows that teenagers themselves have identified ways in which they could be made to feel more secure online:

- *Social media channels should highlight when a photo has been digitally enhanced or altered*
- *Social media platforms should do more to make it clear when influencers are being paid to say or do something*
- *And young people themselves have identified peer-mentoring support as an effective way to help guide and support younger students with their management of social media.*[46]

Peer attitudes and judgements

The perceived attitudes and judgements of peers can have a huge influence on a teen's self-esteem and body image. It isn't uncommon for them to base their self-worth on how many 'likes' they get on a social media post, or what rating they get on the emoji slider.[47]

Media-savvy teens might post their selfies only at a certain time of day, using multiple hashtags to get the most 'likes' possible, and will even take down a post if they don't get enough responses. As a parent, you need to be alert to such practices to try to help your teen control their social media, rather than let social media control them. Privacy settings on all platforms dictate the size of any possible audience and so will affect how many people will be able to see and 'like' your teen's posts. On the flip side, imposing boundaries can offer an out clause to help ease the pressure on them ('It's the parents' fault I can't get the likes 'cause they make me close down my privacy settings' — eye-roll).

And let's not forget that social media is useful and oftentimes fun. Nobody would use it otherwise. What's more, there is growing evidence that it can provide a landscape for inclusive and accepting spaces, which could in turn increase understanding of all body types.[48] One New Zealand study of 13–24-year-olds found that 'two in five have regularly connected with a group that makes them feel positive about themselves and 31 per cent have regularly got involved with online groups that have helped share their ideas or creativity in a positive way'.[49]

The role of whānau/family

While there's a growing research base around the impact of social media on self-esteem and body image, there are fewer studies that examine the role of whānau. In other words, there's less data about interactions with real people. Unsurprisingly, too, if someone spends more time on digital platforms it can leave less time for whānau/family to exert their influence. Where your teen is a heavy user of social media it's important to maintain your credibility with them when presenting them with information that may contradict any teenage echo chamber.

At the same time, what research there is has shown that you have a job to do in supporting your teen. They are going to follow your lead when it comes to forming a relationship with their bodies and building their self-esteem. (Friends, and church, will also influence young people, and this can depend to some degree on ethnic background.)[50] You may feel you've been sold a myth around beauty and bodies. You may have your own lived experience of body shame or diet lifestyle or unhealthy exercise practices. Having teens and watching them develop their own sense of self can often bring this into sharp focus. To encourage empathy in your teen you are going to need to be alert to your own innate judgements and, if necessary, challenge them. There is, for instance, a body of research suggesting that children and adolescents learn from their family and friends that they should be thin and that being overweight is unappealing.[51] It's impossible to overestimate the positive or negative impact you can have. When healthy body image is reinforced in childhood, it can lay firm foundations for good physical and mental health later in life.

A word on body positivity and body neutrality

Body positivity introduces an inclusive way of thinking designed to bring attention to, and celebrate, all body shapes, weights, sizes and colours while calling out unrealistic body standards. It challenges the stereotyping of beauty and sends a strong message about the importance of acceptance of bodies, particularly those belonging to people in any type of marginalised group. It reiterates that everyone should be treated with respect regardless of their physical appearance.

There are many upsides to this — including, for some, improving individual body image. However, one of the downsides is that body positivity still centres on a person's external appearance, with all the deep-seated and sometimes very personal thoughts and feelings associated with that.

Another way that people are starting to think about bodies is by *not* thinking about them (in regard to appearance, anyway). This is known as **body neutrality**. Instead of focusing on how your body appears, body neutrality puts a spotlight on all the things your body can do or allows you to be able to do. For example, 'Your body gives you the ability to hold hands or hug someone you love. Your body gets you from point A to point B.'[52] Thanks to your body, you can touch, move, experience, push limits, express yourself and so much more.

'The more we focus on how our bodies feel,
how they get us around and manage
us then it's harder to criticise how they look.
It's like once you get to know someone well,
and understand how they tick, once they
become a true friend, you can't judge them.
You stick up for them.'
— ANGELA BARNETT

How can I have this conversation? / Me pēhea tēnei matakahi?

It's essential that you create space for your teen to share thoughts and emotions about their body. With the best will in the world, there will be times when your teen is unhappy with their looks or when another has poked fun at them. Appearances at times can feel all-important, so it's good to let them know you appreciate the pressure they are under. The framework and the language you give your teen to find perspective will be invaluable. There are lots of opportunities to engage with them so that they understand each person is unique, growing in their own individual way physically, mentally, emotionally, spiritually and socially (see also the section on the Māori philosophy of hauora, page 178). This knowledge can be used to reiterate for them that there's little point in making comparisons. The focus here is on body neutrality: if you can get the concept across to them that 'their body houses who they are', you're doing a great job.

This is why we need to have the conversation, and primarily the message here is that both self-esteem and body image are always a work in progress.

They need to know they have a safe space with you. They also need to know that you are interested and curious about how they are feeling about themselves as they explore their world more fully — a world in which, it is hoped, diversity will be more and more widely celebrated.

Points to keep the conversation going

- Talk with your teen about how they can grow their self-esteem and enhance their body image:
  - It may sound a bit silly, but it can really help if your teen says **affirmations** out loud to themselves in the mirror. There is science behind this: it can serve to solidify the healthy relationship they need to have with themselves.[53] It can also help to shape the way their inner voice speaks, especially about their body. It's okay to start small, maybe even a simple 'you're doing all right' each morning.
  - Encourage them to **check in with their feelings** about their body, how they think about themselves and the way they speak about themselves to others. We've all done it — those times when you're not confident about a fashion choice so you take the mickey out of yourself first to 'protect' yourself in case of criticism. This can backfire, as

others could take it as permission to wade in with their views. Negative comments may feel like banter to some people, but they can be soul-destroying if you're on the receiving end. And when that is not just a fashion choice, but something about your appearance that you can't change, it ends up being very undermining.

- Explain to your teen the importance of engaging in **self-care** and let them see you doing the same.[54] Moving the body, eating well, sleeping well and looking after the soul (MESS, see page 202) are all parts of this. Self-care is intrinsically interwoven with positive self-esteem and good body image. Ultimately self-care is about spending time 'with' yourself, doing what you love and getting to know yourself. To take this one step further, investigate with your teen pursuits that cultivate a mind–body connection; this can help them focus on how they feel inside, rather than on their appearance. You could suggest they try a simple massage, yoga or martial arts. These can go a long way towards helping your teen embody their inner self within their outer one, so that they feel more grounded and able to value all of themselves. The less time they spend focusing on the outside, the more room it gives them to understand what's going on inside.

• Share accurate and evidence-based information, and try not to follow food and exercise trends. Get your teen into the habit of **moving their body regularly**, remembering that this is not about whether or not they are going to be the next All Black or Silver Fern. 'Remember, your body belongs to you,' as Healthline puts it. 'It doesn't exist to be admired or objectified. When you respect it and care for it by giving it the fuel, rest, and movement it needs, you'll probably notice improvements in how you feel and function.'[55] Focus on the following:

- Exercise is important for managing mental health and feeling strong. It's equally important that it should be fun and/or useful — dancing, riding a bike or walking to school. Your teen should be exercising because of how it makes them feel, not how it makes them look.

- Find out what works for them. Exercise should always be properly structured and age appropriate. All too often teens, their bodies not yet fully grown, are working out in the gym without specific instruction and with problematic intentions. A study has shown that nearly three-quarters (72 per cent) of fitspiration posts emphasise appearance, while fewer than one-quarter (22 per cent) put the accent on health.[56]

• Food is food. For some teens it can also be a bit of a minefield. Recent research showed that New Zealand children were exposed to an average of 27 junk-food ads every day.[57] You can help steer their food choices by being careful about how you label different foods, and by setting up mealtimes to be all about enjoying the meal. Keep the following in mind:

- There is **no 'good' food or 'bad' food**. Everything should be enjoyed in moderation — right? Sometimes we enjoy foods and drinks that we know aren't adding to our health, and that's okay. What's not so okay is when we think of foods as bad and then punish ourselves or feel bad for eating them. So to foster a healthy relationship with food in your family, be sure to **avoid diet vocabulary**. As long as the majority of the time your teen is eating nutritious and colourful meals, has a general understanding of nutrition and knows the importance of hydration, they're ticking most of the boxes.
- **Mindful eating** is about encouraging your teen to give their full attention to their food and to take time to enjoy each mouthful. It's also about understanding their feelings around it — for example, the difference between hunger, thirst and boredom. It can be easy to eat meals at random times in front of a screen, but mindful eating

is about setting a time, creating an enjoyable space with others to eat and eliminating distractions. In order to cultivate a positive relationship with food, it can help your teen to practise mindful eating with friends and family, considering where the food came from, how it was prepared and all the flavour notes in each mouthful.[58]

- Language is important. When having conversations with your teen, be careful which words you use. Try to:
  - Give them the skills and words to respond in their own peer environment if they hear language they feel is demeaning or body-shaming. Some tips:
    - Don't engage; instead, try changing the subject:
      Comment: 'Wow, you look so toned!'
      Respond with: 'How is your day going?'
    - Don't empathise with the comments; instead of saying 'me too', try something positive:
      Comment: 'Ugh, I feel so flabby.'
      Respond with: 'Let's do something that will make us feel happy!'
    - Use every opportunity as an educational moment:
      Comment: 'That guy is so spotty!'
      Respond with: 'I don't think it's very nice to talk about people in that way.'
  - **Choose not to size-shame.** Remind your teen that words can hurt. For example, there's a lot of stigma attached to the word 'fat'. It's worth working with your teen to critically analyse language and reframe the way we talk about bodies. Remind them, too, that there are many reasons for people living in larger bodies, and that the size of a body isn't necessarily indicative of health. Focus on staying healthy in body and mind, and emphasise that **we come in different shapes and sizes,** all of which can be healthy (also known as '**health at every size**').

- **Avoid passing judgement on anyone's appearance** (whether they be in a larger or smaller body, live with a physical disability, choose to dress differently, etc.), and encourage your teen to do the same. Curiosity is one thing, but **kindness is *the* thing.** You could even help your teen model this by giving them regular compliments about something other than their appearance. This may help them to do the same to others, and you may even get a few compliments yourself. It can be a fun and challenging activity to think of an **alternative praise** every time one is delivered that focuses on looks.
  - **Create a culture of diversity and acceptance** in and out of your home — understanding that health and wellbeing are all-important. Intentionally adopt body acceptance and celebrate the differences that are around us every day.
- If you haven't already, get your head around **social media.** Ask your teen to help you do this. Apologise in advance for how much you will annoy them when you still don't understand the difference between a gif and a meme after the twelfth time they have run through this. (Perhaps compare this to how complicated they seem to find the washing machine . . .). Here are some suggestions:
  - Know which applications your teen is using. There are some awesome online tools (see Resources/Rauemi, pages 123 and 175) that will give you the lowdown on how they work and any factors you may need to be aware of. Learn the terminology of these apps (such as 'influencer'). Talk through the default settings on the apps and programs your teen often uses. For example, are search engines using voice recognition to tailor the ads that they see? What are their cookie settings? What are their privacy settings?
  - If you don't have an Instagram or TikTok account, ask your teen to help you set one up, and together

choose who you might like to follow — give them the opportunity to be the teacher (and don't be surprised if they don't allow you to follow them). Or, if they feel that those kinds of accounts are more their turf, then perhaps stick to Facebook, which tends now to be seen as more the domain of older generations.

- Discuss with your teen who they are choosing as their **online role models.** Who are they 'following'? Talk about finding accounts that boost their confidence rather than tear it down. These can help when their self-esteem takes a bit of a knock from a rough day at school. Ask your teen to take note of **how their social media makes them feel.** Do the people they currently follow make them feel good about themselves? If not, remind them they can unfollow them.
- Everybody has their challenges, and we can all grow from others' experiences. Ask your teen if they have thought of 'following' someone different from them — perhaps someone who's a similar age but from a different culture or country, or is dealing with adversities. Social media can provide a wonderful opportunity for them to **learn about diversity.**
- On the flip side, suggest that they may need **time off social media daily** (and not just when they are asleep . . .). This might feel like lighting a fuse, but some teens just need the permission to do so. You could offer it as a challenge and then see the results.
- Use your voice and encourage your teen to find theirs:
  - **Be an activist for positive change.** Together you can **verbalise, challenge and call out issues** you see around advertising and bodies. Let your teen hear your voice on this topic and encourage them to use theirs.
  - Share examples: once sold as a feminine stereotype, Barbie now comes with much more choice — diversity in skin colour, size, ability and career choices — and is a great

example of how consumer pressure can have an impact.
Part of that pressure came from agitators such as Lammily,
a community-funded start-up founded by Nickolay
Lamm, who created a doll carrying the tagline: 'average
is beautiful'. It is designed with positive body image in
mind. The doll is based on the United States Centers for
Disease Control and Prevention's measurements for an
average 19-year-old. It is also made with clothing for a
photographer, astronaut and president; there's a wheelchair
option, as well as stick-on scars and stretch marks.

- Take a further look with your teen at how social media was
created and who regulates it. Recent reports can add to your
discussions:
    - An ex-employee of Facebook has recently reached out
    to the US Congress claiming that the negative impacts
    of social media, particularly towards teens, tweens and
    children, were already recognised by the company,
    citing an alleged unactioned internal report concluding
    that '13.5 per cent of teen girls said Instagram makes
    thoughts of suicide worse and 17 per cent of teen girls
    said it makes eating disorders worse'.[59]
    - Social media platforms are evolving, which raises more
    questions about who is making the rules and how they
    are being policed. When changing the name of his
    platform to Meta, Mark Zuckerberg announced the
    development of '3D spaces in the "metaverse" [that] will
    let you socialize, learn, collaborate and play in ways that
    go beyond what we can imagine'.[60]

Talking box questions

Name three things your body
did for you today.

Name a vlogger/influencer who
inspired you, and why.

Think of a compliment that
doesn't involve looks.

Resources / Rauemi

ONLINE	See how the 'perfect body' ideal has changed over the decades: greatist.com/grow/100-years-womens-body-image
	Beauty across the world (paywalled): nationalgeographic.com/magazine/article/beauty-today-celebrates-all-social-media-plays-a-role-feature
	Teens explain why on-screen representation matters: pbs.org/newshour/arts/why-on-screen-representation-matters-according-to-these-teens
	Discussions on disability and body image: disabilityhorizons.com/2015/12/disability-and-body-image-fitting-in-when-your-body-does-not sunrisemedical.com/livequickie/blog/december-2020/women-with-physical-disabilities-body-image
	A guide for parents on social media and self-esteem: parents.au.reachout.com/skills-to-build/wellbeing/things-to-try-social-media/self-esteem-and-social-media
	An introduction to body positivity: bodyimagemovement.com goodmagazine.co.nz/body-positivity-what-does-it-mean-and-how-did-this-movement-begin

8. WELLBEING AND MENTAL HEALTH

#checkonyourmates #thelowdown #itsoktonotbeok

'What mental health needs is more sunlight, more candor, more unashamed conversation.'
— GLENN CLOSE

Kōrero with Molly

I know now that for more than one of my friends, there were days when they had to drag themselves out of bed to get to school, and basic things like eating breakfast or jumping in the shower felt almost unachievable. At the time, no one knew the effort they had made just to show up to class. This reminds me of how important it is to acknowledge that you never really know all of what's going on for people. I remember when I wasn't feeling my best, just a casual expression of kindness or a smile lifted my mood or even helped to change my perspective. I guess my motto has developed into a simple 'be kind to others' but also 'be kind to yourself' (which might mean taking a restorative PJ day once in a while, as long as it's not all the time). I also love positive affirmations, which I drive my flatmates a little mad with by sticking them everywhere. Looking back to high school, I saw some mental health issues get pretty serious, fairly quickly. This taught me a lot, including the importance of knowing where my boundaries were when it came to offering help. I don't think I or any one of my friends escaped some sort of struggle at some point, which is nothing to be ashamed of or embarrassed about. It's only getting easier to reach out and ask for help as we continue to deconstruct stigma and learn new strategies for self-care and caring for others.

What do you mean by that? /
He aha te tikanga o tāu kōrero?

With so many changes happening all at once, teens can face major mental health challenges. Some are able and willing to discuss their feelings fluently, whereas others struggle. With this in mind, it's not always easy to keep track of your teen's wellbeing. Knowing the difference between the normal mood swings that come with being a teenager and a more serious mental health issue allows you to support your teen in the right way. They've got a lot going on for them, what with their hormones surging, the rewiring going on in their brain, the move to high school and wanting to fit in with peers. It doesn't hurt to know a little more about what 'good' mental health looks like. That way you can lay positive foundations with them that will serve through to adulthood. In addition, you are informing yourself so that you can be on the lookout for anything that might be more than transient stress.

It can be especially difficult to speak of mental health when historically there has been such stigma surrounding it. In recent times this stigma has been more readily refuted. There are public campaigns to inform and educate, schools/kura are gradually introducing mental health and wellbeing programmes into the curriculum, and there is widening provision of counsellors, helplines and even a variety of useful apps designed specifically for teens, including ones on mindfulness (see Resources/Rauemi, page 206). This last concept centres mainly on two principles: awareness and acceptance. It includes being aware, for instance, of what is happening to you — both internally and externally — in the present moment, and accepting your thoughts for what they are. The ultimate goal of mindfulness is release from stress and anxiety.

There is beginning to be a real recognition that mental health is pivotal to wellbeing as a whole and that everyone struggles from time to time. The Māori philosophy of hauora, which is recognised by the World Health Organization (WHO), is a useful tool for all of us. Many schools teach this way of thinking. It is well worth discussing it with your teen: a visual representation is included overleaf.

Hauora takes the holistic vew of health: it views a person as being made up of four different yet connected parts, and aims to achieve a balance between these. The whare tapa whā, a model conceived by Dr Mason Durie in the early 1980s, compares hauora to the four walls of a whare/house, with each part supporting the others. We need balance because if we do not look after one part of ourselves then this will impact on all the other parts. In Durie's model, the four parts are:

1. **Taha tinana/physical wellbeing**: the physical body, its growth, development, and ability to move, and ways of caring for it.
2. **Taha hinengaro/mental and emotional wellbeing**: coherent thinking processes, acknowledging and expressing thoughts and feelings, and responding constructively.
3. **Taha wairua/spiritual wellbeing**: the values and beliefs that determine the way people live, the search for meaning and purpose in life, and personal identity and self-awareness. (For some individuals and communities, spiritual wellbeing is linked to a particular religion; for others, it is not.)
4. **Taha whānau/social wellbeing**: all-inclusive of our environment, this encompasses family relationships, friendships and other interpersonal relationships; feelings of belonging, compassion and caring; and social support.[1]

An additional element to consider is **whenua**, which can be thought of as your place of belonging, or connection to the land or environment. As such, it serves as a foundation for the other aspects of hauora. A connection to the land is a key element in wellbeing.[2]

Reaching this balance may allow us to achieve a better under-standing of looking after not only ourselves but also others. This is so important, especially with the reality that, even before the pandemic, a New Zealand survey reported that 'four in five adults (aged 15 years or more) have experienced mental distress personally or among people they know' during their lifetime.[3] This statistic means it may well be that we have our own very specific understanding of some of these

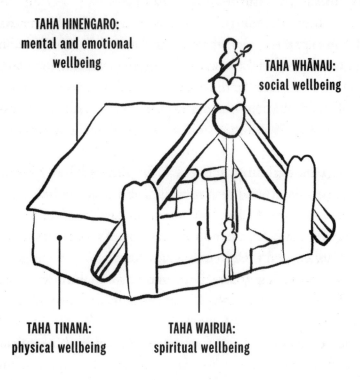

TAHA HINENGARO:
mental and emotional
wellbeing

TAHA WHĀNAU:
social wellbeing

TAHA TINANA:
physical wellbeing

TAHA WAIRUA:
spiritual wellbeing

The whare tapa whā: Mason Durie's model for hauora.
Illustration redrawn with permission.[4]

issues. Be aware of this, as it may have an impact on how you respond to your teen.

We need to demonstrate that mental health is just as much a priority as all other parts of health. This will give your teen an environment where it is natural for them to do the same. That way, they will hopefully feel able to speak openly, and we will be able to listen (and not project). Also, while your teen might be coping, those around them may be struggling, and this will have repercussions, particularly if your teen is empathetic. We all want our teens to live in a supportive and inspiring environment within a community where they can grow and thrive.

Tell me more . . . / Kōrero mai anō . . .

Aotearoa is known as being a safe, happy and healthy place to live. The 2020 *World happiness report* ranked information from 156 countries, and listed cities around the world by how happy their citizens perceived themselves to be.[5] This landmark survey looked into how the social, urban and natural environments combined to affect happiness. On the list of cities, Wellington ranked third globally, with Auckland sixteenth and Christchurch seventeenth.

Against this backdrop, though, New Zealand has some pretty shocking statistics around teen mental health concerns:

- In 2019, Youth19, a longitudinal study of young New Zealanders and their health issues, found that the proportion of teens with 'significant' depression had doubled in 20 years, and that more than half (57 per cent) of rainbow youth reported symptoms of depression.[6]
- The Youth19 study also found New Zealand's youth suicide rates to be the highest in a list of 41 OECD and EU countries, twice that of the US and almost five times that of the UK.[7]
- Another survey, Counting Ourselves, surveyed trans and non-binary people in 2018; it found that those who reported discrimination (on the basis of their sexual identity) were twice as likely to attempt suicide as those who did not report it.[8]

Despite New Zealand's many positive attributes, then, our mental health outcomes are among the worst in the developed world. How can we understand this disparity? If we discover what is burdening our teens, we will be able to better support them? While research into this is ongoing, it is clear the issues are multifaceted. Youth19 lists the following as probable contributing factors:

- *the impact of smartphones and social media*
- *the impact of early childhood experiences, including stressed parents, linked to poverty, inequity, housing costs or financial crisis issues*

- *increased exposure to violence*
- *the ongoing or increasing impact of intergenerational trauma and the impact of colonisation and racism*
- *the impact of increased parental and social monitoring, and lack of unstructured or unsupervised time*
- *increases in perfectionism and expectations in schooling and other areas*
- *the impact of future worries as teens look to adulthood and consider climate crisis, employment and housing challenges.*[9]

It's totally normal for your teen to have mood swings, get angry, shed tears and be down from time to time. Everyone has moments like this. Your teen's wellbeing is an ongoing process: as they grow, their strategies will be greatly enhanced by building **resilience**, increasing their **emotional intelligence** and practising **gratitude**. All of these skills can be learned and developed. Where possible, it's a good idea to work on these three areas with your teen (and we look into each of them below). It's never too late to start on this type of self-care, either for your teen or for yourself. And it is worth remembering that a mental health diagnosis is no one's fault and that help is available.

So what are the signs your teen is displaying good mental health? Most will be fairly obvious. They seem happy and positive about themselves, take part in extracurricular activities, and feel a sense of achievement in what they do. They get on well with family and friends, and feel settled within their community. And they're likely to be taking regular exercise, eating a healthy diet and sleeping well.[10] But even if they seem to tick all these points, don't stop here because there will certainly be times when life is a bit more tricky.

Let's look in more detail at those three areas relating to wellbeing.

Resilience

This is a concept explored by pediatrician Ken Ginsburg, who says, '**Resilient people** do experience stress, setbacks, and difficult emotions, but they tap into their strengths and seek help from support systems to overcome challenges and **work through problems**.' To illustrate this he outlines seven 'building blocks':

- *Competence: When we notice what young people are doing right and give them opportunities to develop important skills, they feel competent. We undermine competence when we don't allow young people to recover themselves after a fall.*
- *Confidence: Young people need confidence to be able to navigate the world, think outside the box, and recover from challenges.*
- *Connection: Connections with other people, schools, and communities offer young people the security that allows them to stand on their own and develop creative solutions.*
- *Character: Young people need a clear sense of right and wrong and a commitment to integrity.*
- *Contribution: Young people who contribute to the well-being of others will receive gratitude rather than condemnation. They will learn that contributing feels good and may therefore more easily turn to others, and do so without shame.*
- *Coping: Young people who possess a variety of healthy coping strategies will be less likely to turn to dangerous quick fixes when stressed.*
- *Control: Young people who understand privileges and respect are earned through demonstrated responsibility will learn to make wise choices and feel a sense of control.*[11]

This '7 Cs' model lays out a framework that is accessible for both parents and teens, and it provides a toolbox to gradually increase resilience over time through small steps that are measurable and achievable. This sends a really positive message without being overwhelming. Here are some examples that might help you think about ways of putting the model into practice:

- To increase **competence**: give your teen the space to figure out what they need to do if, say, they have dropped a friend's phone and damaged it, instead of leaping in to solve the problem. There are many components here, including taking responsibility for what's happened, communicating that they are sorry and dealing with the financial consequences.

- To build **confidence**: encourage them to participate in a school activity, outing or event that is outside their comfort zone. Trying things out like this will not always work out, but tell them how proud you are of them for giving it a go.

- To grow **connection**: help them to grow by making sure that safe people are available to them to talk things through — maybe they want to go for a coffee with an aunt who shares a particular interest of theirs, or maybe they want to join a drama group to be with like-minded people their own age outside of the school environment. The more safe spaces where they can be themselves, the more security they have behind them. This also underscores that they are someone others want to spend time with. Obviously, also make sure that they are aware you are always there for them.

- To build **character**: ask them to unpack their thinking if they, or a friend of theirs, has been given a detention and they feel it's unjust. Seeing others' points of view of a particular circumstance will also allow them to understand the roles played by each of the parties. We want our teens to learn how to accept personal responsibility for their actions. They will need to rely on their own moral compass in the future. Integrity and honesty are key characteristics of this.

- To recognise **contribution**: encourage them to participate in schemes such as the Duke of Edinburgh's Hillary Award that require participants to undertake some sort of voluntary work. These provide opportunities not only to give to others, but also to realise it's okay to ask for assistance. In fact, asking for help can be seen as a strength, not a weakness, as it means they are learning to acknowledge any current limitations. This in turn makes it easier not to be judgemental when others need support. Going further, it introduces the concept of altruism, as it encourages teens to give a helping hand, whether or not they themselves benefit.

- To improve **coping**: have a discussion with your teen to enable them to identify strategies that really help when their feelings are mounting up and they are getting stressed — though maybe don't try this on a day when you know they are already stressed! They could think through some ideas in advance: perhaps they could go for a run, play some music, do some baking, or just down tools and take time out for a while. This may not always work, so find ways to celebrate the fact that they are trying. The more they practise coping strategies, the more this will become a natural reflex; they will come to realise they will feel better if they take some positive action.

- To improve **control**: talk through any house rules that they are finding slightly more limiting as they mature. Perhaps if they are able to demonstrate that they can keep their room tidy (without being nagged) and maybe start to do the washing, then you might be happier to trust them with some additional independence. Consistency is important here, as respect runs both ways. You are trying to let them know that they are being seen and heard, but that doesn't mean they are entitled to a later curfew just because they want it, or that they can go to the mall after school just because their friend does. Having boundaries does not make you mean, or the strictest parent in the world, so ignore the pleas of 'but everybody else does . . .'.

All of the above 7 Cs allow your teen to enhance their wellbeing. Although it would be nice to imagine the state of being well is permanent, this isn't realistic. Learning **resilience** will help them get back to that position as quickly as possible and deal with what life throws them a little more easily.

Emotional intelligence

The term 'emotional intelligence', or EI, was initially used in 1990 by American psychologists Peter Salovey and John Mayer, but has now found its way into our general vocabulary. The *Oxford Dictionary* calls it 'the ability to understand your emotions and those of other people and to behave appropriately in different situations'. A recent literature review found 'evidence of the connection between emotional intelligence and resilience, both concepts being adversely related to perceived stress'.[12] In other words, the more emotionally intelligent someone is, the greater their resilience is also.

The American author and science journalist Daniel Goleman has written extensively about EI and argues that it can matter more than a person's IQ. He has recently expanded this concept in a way that works well for a business setting, but initially divided it into five categories, which you may find works better for your teen. These are:

- self-awareness,
- self-regulation,
- motivation,
- empathy, and
- social skills.[13]

Let's look at examples of how you could help your teen develop these:

- You could help them develop **self-awareness** by teaching them how to reflect. Saying something like 'think that one through' or 'what's your part in this?' will prompt them (to paraphrase Robert Burns) to see themselves as others see them. That is not to say that they should change the way that they are; they just need to be sensitive to how they might be coming across. Reflection allows for your teen to stop and think about how they reacted to something or someone. To show them how to do this, find a regular time for a debrief to enable them to think back over what has happened to them recently. Once

they are more familiar with this process, they may wish to do it
through journalling or keeping a diary.

- To help your teen develop **self-regulation,** teach them to pause.
It's important they can stop, pause and feel without reacting
immediately in a way that may have untoward consequences.
They will want to be their authentic self, but this doesn't mean
that they won't sometimes need to use a filter: they need to
realise that they may speak in one way with their peers, but
in quite another with their grandparents. At first, they may
need help to recognise their feelings and remember to take a
moment and breathe. If you are noticing that this is an issue
for them, ask them if there is some sort of subtle signal you
can give them that might alert them to the fact they need to
manage themselves at that moment. Take the lead from them
on this: it's designed to be grounding, not infuriating. It's a
learning curve for both of you.

- A way of improving **motivation** might be through using
phrases such as 'why do you *really* want that?' and then getting
them to strategise to achieve a particular goal. Initially they
may think of what's in it for them. If they are going to a party
and want to wear a certain item of clothing, they may be more
motivated to put it through the wash rather than leave it lying
under their bed. They may even be motivated to iron it. Simple
building blocks like this will teach them self-motivation —
so this will work only if, for example, you haven't already
scooped the treasured hoodie up and left it clean on a hanger
back in their wardrobe! Be aware of your and others' impact
on your teen: is it really their motivation that is driving their
behaviour? Are they getting good grades only in order not to
disappoint you? Are they people-pleasing rather than trying to
work out what they want? If this is the case, they may find that
they lose their way when left to their own devices. Learning
motivation can help them balance longer-term goals against
the desire for instant gratification. They may need your help to

get started, but as they find things that they are really excited about, they will set their own goals. Once they have their own reason behind doing things, motivation will come from within.

- To cultivate **empathy** in your teen, when something tricky happens you could ask them, 'What *don't* you know?' Imagine that they have tested out their new-found self-awareness, but even after having checked 'their part' in a situation, one of their friends still seems in a bad mood with them. This question may nudge them to consider what else is going on for that person. To paraphrase poet Mary Torrans Lathrap, you can't understand someone until you've walked a mile in their shoes. So ask them to consider how their friend might be feeling. Brainstorm in a way that tries to avoid negativity. This insight may give them cause to stand up for others or find ways to help mediate, or even want to apologise. All teens are different, but in terms of averages, girls tend to start to develop more empathy about the age of 13 and boys a little later, at 15 or so.[14] Bear in mind that it may take a while for them to be able to put this improved understanding into practice, and that they may not always get things right. But that is true of adults, too.

- Building **social skills** may feel especially challenging in this digital age, when most teens seem to spend their lives with their phone in their hands. One way they can show that they are being 'in the moment' and are appreciating the person they are with is by putting the phone down (a very scary concept, agreed). Without a phone in front of them, they will start to realise the importance of establishing eye contact, actively listening (see page 26) and trying to read body language. All of this is important to communicating in person. Not only this, but it's useful if your teen can try to be inquisitive about the subject matter being discussed. It's about being interested. This will make others realise they are seen and heard by them. A more structured way of growing your teen's **confidence** and their world view could be exploring the talking box questions included at the end of each chapter. This may even inspire them to get involved in any school or local debating society. Active listening is contagious: finding out about others' perspectives can be enlightening, and they may even discover something new about a person. Giving this space allows conversations to grow organically, and they will then find that they are talking as well as listening. They may even start to enjoy it.

Learning these five sets of EI skills is a fairly full-on task when your teen has so much else going on in their lives, so be kind to them and yourself while on this journey. Resilience and emotional intelligence are going to be vital to ongoing good mental health.

One way to model EI is to ensure that your teen sees you trying to work through your own responses to tricky situations. If they see you doing this wisely and thoughtfully in the here and now, this will encourage them to recognise their own emotions, develop their own responses and in turn perhaps better empathise with others. They can then build out from this in ways that feed into a resilient approach to life. They will also learn to draw on their thinking to guide their emotional response, rather than let emotion rule their behaviour.[15] If they can then draw on practical strategies — for example, stopping and taking a moment — they may be able to turn a situation around before it escalates. In addition, the more they practise, the more they will be able to do this whether or not you are there.

Gratitude

Since the start of the 2020s there has been much discussion as to whether we should reassess our value system and start to embrace (in a socially distanced way!) the concept of **gratitude**. This idea feeds into a sense of wellbeing — it forces you to look outside of yourself and maybe helps to challenge any spiralling negative thinking. It's a relatively recent focus for psychology, dating back only 20 years or so — possibly, say researchers, 'because psychology traditionally focused more on understanding distress than on understanding positive emotions'.[16]

Although seemingly simplistic, there is more to gratitude once you further explore it than just the occasional please and thank you — although these are obviously appreciated. There's a difference between voicing thanks and being thankful. The latter means being appreciative of what people do for you — and sometimes you will also be able to show them some kindness back. Other times you can be kind in a way that isn't reciprocated. This is the objective behind the 'pay it forward' and 'random acts of kindness' movements (see Resources/Rauemi, page 206). It's about thinking differently.

> '*Happiness is the new rich.*
> *Inner peace is the new success.*
> *Health is the new wealth.*
> *Kindness is the new cool.*'
> — SYED BALKHI

There are any number of ways your teen could engage with this way of thinking. Some suggestions are given below:

- Choose a journal for your teen from one of the many now available for purchase; alternatively, any scraps of paper can be used to write down the smaller and bigger warm fuzzies from a day.
- Get your teen one of the many books from the library that tell the stories of people who have contributed to society, or perhaps ask them who they follow on Instagram for inspiration.
- Regularly compliment your teen on the skills and gifts they offer, whether it be their awesome singing voice or their patience with a sibling.
- When in the car or around the table ask everyone to name one negative and two positives from their day. Then ask what they learned from each or how they would have been

THE KIDS WILL BE ALL RIGHT

impacted if one of the positives hadn't happened.
- Plan and do something fun together. Laughter, as they say, is the best medicine, so make the objective fun.

Suggesting to your teen that they write down some things they are thankful for may help them focus. They could write a list of people that they are happy to have in their lives, or positive things that have happened. They may even decide to write a letter addressed to someone to say why they are grateful. Some people refer to these as 'letters of gratitude'. They don't even need to send what they write. This needs to be private; they only need to share it with you if they want to (this is another way to enhance trust that their space is respected). If your teen is struggling to think of things to be grateful for, check out some of the websites in the Resources/Rauemi section (page 206) for ideas. The point is for your teen to create a 'thankfulness habit', rather than focus only on what they *don't* have.

One thing to flag is that although gratitude is proven to be useful for a teen's wellbeing, they also need to know it's okay on occasion to feel miserable. They already know there are people with worse problems than theirs — but everything is relative, and they might not ever have felt this way before. A part of good mental health is working through emotions and validating them: issues that aren't dealt with may end up being revisited over and over again. So they are allowed to — and should give themselves permission to — feel their feelings, be sad or be frustrated. Sometimes they are right: things *are* unfair, and at such times it is a little harder to find ways to be grateful. **It's okay not to feel okay.**

Everyone gets stressed

Stress is normal . . . in moderation. Although it can put a fire in your teen's belly and get them going, in situations where stress is extreme or prolonged you may start to notice it negatively impacting on their lives in a number of ways, including socially, mentally and physically. As much as you can, look out for signs of stress overload and gently remind them of the basics: eating, showering, sleeping and focusing on the positives.[17]

Stress (see page 42) can show itself in many different ways. Tell-tale changes in behaviour include:

- having trouble sleeping or sleeping too much,
- anxiety around food, or eating a lot less or a lot more,
- concerns about body image (see Chapter 7),
- physical manifestations such as a headache or stomach ache,
- being worried, nervous or anxious,
- being tearful, moody, grumpy, irritable or short-tempered,
- being aggressive either at home or at school,
- getting into trouble at school or with authorities,
- grades dropping or homework being forgotten,
- having trouble with their usual day-to-day activities or lacking motivation,
- not wanting to go to school or avoiding their friends, and
- becoming socially withdrawn.

If possible, find the right time and space and ask your teen if they want to talk — let them know what you're seeing in their behaviour. Try to do this non-judgementally and try to find a way to spend some one-on-one time with them. This will show them the importance you place on their mental health and on ongoing communication. Ask open questions (see page 26). Provide lots of silence for them to fill. Let them know it's *their* time. Let them know they can take their time. Some teens prefer to step away, process and come back to you later. Either way, let them know the door is open. You will be available whenever they are ready. And **listen, listen, listen**. Reassure them that no matter what, you've got their back, will support them and will try to understand things from their perspective. Don't second-guess them, because that doesn't leave them room to say what's going on in their head. Sometimes they may be able to express *how* they feel, yet not *why*; but talking things through is a start.

Make sure your teen knows they don't have to deal with everything on their own. A strong, loving relationship with your teen definitely has a positive impact on their mental health. Remind them frequently that there's a bunch of people around them who want the best for them and are on their side. Get them to think about who — aside from you, of course — these people might be. With a little prompting they may think about another family member, a friend or, for example, their youth group mentor or the school counsellor.

Steps towards mental wellbeing

The Youth19 survey completed in New Zealand in 2019 not only reported its findings, but also proposed practical steps 'in our homes, schools and communities to help prevent problems and to support young people when times are tough'. The report states:

Things that help promote good emotional and mental wellbeing and reduce distress include:
- *caring and supportive families, including a strong relationship with a caring adult*
- *fostering a strong sense of cultural identity and belonging*
- *acceptance of identity (ethnicity, abilities, sexual and gender identity, etc.)*
- *having fun and being around people who care*
- *a sense of purpose or achievement in daily life and hopes for the future*
- *supportive schools, where there are adults who care, teachers have high expectations and students are treated fairly*
- *activities, sports, arts and groups that offer a sense of belonging*
- *having good friends to talk to and who look out for each other*
- *other adult supports and mentors (coaches, youth workers, church leaders, etc.)*

- *freedom from violence, bullying and discrimination*
- *safe communities where there are things to do*
- *opportunities to achieve, lead and learn*
- *volunteering and employment opportunities*
- *help when things go wrong, such as from school-based health teams, youth one-stop shops, or Whānau Ora, or via online, phone and texting services.*[18]

One thing that has developed in the course of the Covid-19 pandemic and lockdowns is a multitude of mental health supports, including helplines, online provision, apps and text services (see Resources/ Rauemi, page 204). Your teen may not want to talk things through with anyone they know, and these resources may offer them a safe, neutral space to articulate what they are feeling or find tools to help.

Kōrero with Molly

The pandemic has affected everyone's mental health and wellbeing. I remember how much I depended on my peers during high school, and not having the ability to see them every day must have been extremely difficult (talk about FOMO!). Not only that, but teens also missed out on their school balls, school productions, sports fixtures and a variety of social engagements. Even for the introverted among us who probably appreciated a little more time to themselves, the pandemic has put a lot of stress on everyone. It has shown me how crucial it is to take it easy on ourselves and our peers in times like this. Life throws us a curveball sometimes and we all adapt in different ways.

What if it's more than just a bad day?

What's been discussed to this point has focused on wellbeing and understanding how this feeds into good mental health, along with how most teens will encounter stress as part of the normal ups and downs of everyday existence. Everybody has good days and bad days. However, if you are witnessing your teen's stress getting out of control or becoming chronic, or they are becoming socially anxious, it might be time to think about a more structured approach.

If they won't or can't talk about it and you see the situation deteriorating, **don't wait too long**. Suggest they visit their school nurse or counsellor, or offer to book them a GP appointment. You don't want to go behind your teen's back and cause distrust, so if you can discuss this with them in advance and express how concerned you are, you can keep any actions transparent. You can always let their form teacher or counsellor at school know you're worried and check if they are also noticing changes. Generally, information discussed between your teen and a health professional is confidential unless they are at risk to themselves or others. However, you can speak to your teen's GP in advance of any appointment to voice your concerns without breaking doctor–patient confidentialities. At the same time, it's worth being aware of your teen's rights. The Office of the Children's Commissioner clearly states: 'Parents don't have an automatic right to know health-related information about their child . . . When they're making a decision about consent, medical professionals will look at lots of factors, including the circumstances and the child's level of understanding and maturity.'[19] For more detail on this, visit the Privacy Commissioner's website (see Resources/Rauemi, page 206).

This book doesn't set out to provide medical advice in any way. A doctor or therapist would be the one to diagnose a mental health condition, and there are particular criteria they look for to figure out what's going on and how to address it. Treatment options are varied and personalised. They may include checking your teen's sleeping and eating patterns, flagging lifestyle stressors and addressing them, considering therapies, and in some cases using medication. **Early intervention is key**, as if left untreated, teens' mental health conditions can continue into adulthood, with major consequences. If you are concerned about any of the mental health conditions covered in this chapter, **consult a health professional** so that your teen can be assessed and, if appropriate, diagnosed and treated by a therapist or doctor.

WHO states that '[m]ental health conditions account for 16 per cent of the global burden of disease and injury in people aged 10–19 years'. The organisation lists emotional disorders, self-harm and suicidal thoughts, and eating disorders as the most common diagnoses seen in teens with mental health conditions. And it adds, 'Globally, depression is the fourth leading cause of illness and disability among adolescents aged 15–19 years and fifteenth for those aged 10–14 years. Anxiety is the ninth leading cause for adolescents aged 15–19 years and sixth for those aged 10–14 years.'[20] It's worth taking a closer look at depression and anxiety: how they manifest themselves, their effects, and how we might deal with them.

Depression can be caused by a variety of factors. It affects all parts of a person and can manifest itself in a number of different ways. There are many very successful treatment methods out there, and learning how to manage the condition early can help your teen later on in life. For more information about the signs and symptoms of depression, see Resources/Rauemi, page 205.

A lot of people misname **anxiety** as stress, and vice versa. In fact, anxiety can trigger stress, and stress can trigger anxiety. Both can be a fairly normal occurrence for teenagers. You yourself may recall — or still experience — those occasional feelings of agitation, worry and obsessing, along with physical manifestations such as sweaty palms, rapid heartbeat, nausea, shaky hands and more. They are not pleasant.

Like stress, however, anxiety is not all bad. In fact, it's the body's way of alerting you to a potential threat ahead. In that sense, it's a natural protection system, and with practice we can learn to 'switch it off' when it's not needed. However, it can get out of hand at times, and this is when it causes problems.

Sometimes your teen may need some extra help in recognising anxiety and switching it off, or at least managing it. If what your teen is experiencing is ongoing, affecting their day-to-day life, particularly intense or restricting their activities, they might be showing signs of an anxiety disorder. These include, for example, panic disorders, phobias and obsessive-compulsive disorder. New Zealand figures for the year ending June 2021 revealed that 8.3 per cent of young men and 24.8 per cent of young women between the ages of 15 and 24 were diagnosed with an anxiety disorder.[21] For more information about the signs and symptoms of anxiety, see Resources/Rauemi, page 205.

Other mental health issues that can surface among teens include self-harm and eating disorders.

Self-harm is when a person deliberately hurts themselves in an attempt to deal with overwhelming feelings. This can happen in different ways and often your teen may try to hide it. Up to 25 per cent of youths and young adults have self-injured at least once. One-quarter of these have done it many times.[22] For more information about self-harm, see Resources/Rauemi, page 205.

Eating disorders (ED) can affect anyone — large or small, young or old — to various degrees and in different ways (see box). The website of support organisation EDANZ defines them as 'serious, biologically influenced illnesses' that, 'if left untreated, [will] have a devastating impact on affected individuals and their loved ones'.[23]

What are eating disorders?

The Mental Health Foundation of New Zealand provides a succinct summary of the main eating disorders and how they manifest themselves:

Eating disorders are mental health problems that involve:
- *always thinking about eating, or not eating*
- *feeling out of control around food*
- *using food to meet needs other than hunger*
- *having an obsession about food, weight and body shape.*

*There are **four types** of eating disorders we most often hear about:*

- *Anorexia: Where a person believes they are fat, even when they are not and may have lost a lot of weight.*
- *Bulimia: Where a person eats very large amounts of food . . . Then they worry about gaining weight so they make themselves vomit, take laxatives or exercise to extremes.*
- *Binge eating disorder: Where a person eats an excessive amount of food within a short period of time (two hours) and feels a loss of control while eating.*
- *Other eating disorders: Where a person has signs of either bulimia or anorexia but not enough signs to definitely state they have these conditions. This category is often called Eating Disorder Not Otherwise Specified (EDNOS) by doctors, and usually occurs at an early age. It is very common and doctors treat it as seriously as the other categories of eating disorders.*[24]

During the past few years New Zealand has seen a huge increase in the numbers of those presenting with EDs and trying to access ED supports.[25] This has further spiked since the 2020 pandemic lockdown.[26] This pattern is echoed in many other countries. In addition, in the past there's been some unhelpful and incorrect commentary about what causes EDs, and misdirected blame, both of which can stop teens and their parents from seeking assistance. Although presently it's difficult to find meaningful, accessible, accurate and recent data on the prevalence of EDs in teens, there are research projects under way that will hopefully dispel any lingering stigmas, enhance treatment options and address any lack of funding.[27] For more information about the signs and symptoms of an eating disorder, see Resources/Rauemi, page 205.

For information on other mental health diagnoses such as risk-taking behaviours (see page 130), psychosis and childhood behaviour disorders, go to **mentalhealth.org.nz**.

If your teen ever mentions suicide, even indirectly, is self-harming or talking about doing so, or starts to give away personal items while displaying other signs of depression and avoidance, stay with them and seek help immediately.

A word on how this affects you

As a parent, it is important to recognise your own fragilities. It is devastating to feel powerless when you can see your teen is having a hard time. Use the strategies that you are hoping to pass on to them. Try to practise what you preach — model and talk about how you deal with your own stress, and openly use coping mechanisms. When you are tuned in to addressing your own wellbeing and mental health, you will be more tuned in to your teen's. This might mean you spot something sooner.

If your teen is really struggling, it can help to acknowledge the following points:

- You will both be on a journey and it can be challenging. You may be fearful and deeply upset that your child is having to go through something like this. Things might feel really unpredictable right now.
- If your teen is struggling in a way that is uncharted territory for you, it may take a while to learn how to handle things and to start to plan the next steps together.
- Recognise that we *all* make mistakes, and don't beat yourself up if you feel there was something you missed (such as bullying at school). Even with the best of intentions you can deal with a situation only as you understand it at the time. How can you help from this point forward?
- It's vital to respect confidentiality and your teen's privacy. At the same time, you may find you need a space where you can talk things through, be this with a trusted family member or friend, or perhaps a health professional, or by using online provision or

helplines. There is strength in asking for help when you need it.

- Remind your teen that they have coped with difficult times before; remind yourself that you have done likewise. You will see your teen grow through this.
- Progress may be slow. Celebrate every achievement and milestone, and admire your teen's tenacity. They may well show you just how courageous they are.

How can I have this conversation? / Me pēhea tēnei matakahi?

There will probably be occasions when you need to have dedicated discussions on specific mental health topics, whether related to your teen directly or to someone in their sphere. Timing is key, so let your knowledge of your teen guide you in how, when and where these should take place.

> **This is why we need to have the conversation, and primarily the message here is to keep the channels open.**

Considerations around wellbeing and general mental health need to be integrated into every part of life. There are plenty of teachable moments in which to emphasise strategies and remind your teen to keep at it. It takes practice to develop resilience and learn how to handle stress. They need a workout for their mind as much as for their body.

Points to keep the conversation going

- Chat about the amazing hormones released when you **move your body**. Research has shown that exercise enhances mood. Sometimes when we feel low and don't have the energy, exercising will actually revive us, even if this may seem counterintuitive. It's also important to include messages about **nourishing your body** (see page 169).

- Be interested in how well they slept. If you notice any evidence of them struggling to sleep, appearing overly tired or constantly oversleeping, revisit this with them at an appropriate time (perhaps not as soon as they get up!). Come up with a plan together. **Sleep** is crucial in maintaining mental health.
- Get them to discover **what makes them happy** — art? music? theatre? something else? (And remember that being artistic can be so much more than whether or not you can just draw stick figures. Check out blackout poetry by Austin Kleon for an example of some unconventional art.)
- **Laugh**! Ideally create an atmosphere of fun and laughter — for example, have a blind taste test at the dinner table. There's a place for silliness.
- Have some fun figuring out how to **breathe.** This may sound ridiculous, but there are even breathing therapists you can consult. Breathing mindfully can be therapeutic. Try relaxing the shoulders and breathing deeply in and out of the nose while counting. This can then be a 'go to' if stressed.
- Sunscreen is so important, but so is getting out into the **sun** for 20 minutes or so every day. It will give your teen vitamin D and enhance their mood. Go for a walk with them, and talk about the importance of being out in **fresh air** and **nature**. Play Pooh sticks! Go outside at night and point out the stars.
- Have them think about their **music choices**. It's a useful exercise to have them figure out a playlist that will lighten their mood, give them energy or help them relax. **Analyse** how other playlists can exaggerate a darker mood. They can then determine what's constructive for them in that moment.
- Talk about the benefits of hanging out with people who make them feel good and have a **positive vibe.** This applies to who they are 'following' on social media too.
- Practise **gratitude** and do good things for others. Check out the many 'random acts of kindness' websites for suggestions.
- What are your teen's **coping skills** when they are upset or

stressed? Do they have a 'go to' to make themselves feel better — playing with the family pet, going on a walk, bashing a pillow or playing the drums? It's definitely worth talking in advance about **strategies**.

- Emphasise the importance of **relaxation**. Whether it's spent having a bubble bath or watching some mindless Netflix, time out is crucial, and so is learning how to turn off. Give them time and space to do what brings them joy, and let them see you doing the same.

- When you're chatting, encourage your teen to **unpick what they're saying,** because if they're verbalising it you can bet they're also internalising it. Remember it goes both ways: you need to **respond positively** if they ask you to explain where you're coming from.

- Gift them a journal or notebook. **Writing** can be therapeutic. They can write their gratitudes, list their achievements and record their goals. This has to be a safe space that they can keep private or share as they choose.

- There are a number of **calming techniques** that could help your teen. Here are a few you may like to learn more about together:
  - affirmations,
  - meditation,
  - mindfulness,
  - prayer,
  - tapping (a technique designed to send calming signals to the brain — see Resources/Rauemi, page 205), and
  - yoga.

- Remind your teen of their **positive attributes** and what they're good at. **Challenge negative self-talk,** and help them to remember times when things have improved. Building wellbeing is a gradual process and not necessarily achieved in a straight line. Life's about relationships, and these connections are all-important to physical and mental health. Take every opportunity to let them know how proud you are of them and their accomplishments.

*'The most beautiful people we have known
are those who have known defeat, known
suffering, known struggle, known loss, and
have found their way out of the depths. These
persons have an appreciation, a sensitivity,
and an understanding of life that fills them with
compassion, gentleness, and a deep loving
concern. Beautiful people do not just happen.'*
— ELISABETH KÜBLER-ROSS

Kōrero with Molly

One of the ways I connect with my mental health is by asking myself about MESS (movement, eating, sleep and soul). Occasionally, I'll do this with my partner or I'll give Mum a call on my way home from work. It's a lovely way to share and notice but with no judgement — that's the rule. Sometimes, it can be a way to ask for suggestions to make things better, and sometimes it's simply helpful to vent. Ultimately, it opens a dialogue with myself which, on occasion, I choose to share with others. I find it grounding and it reminds me to check in with my mental health in a fun and useful way.

M: movement — How did I move my body today? It might be a jog, some stretching, a walk on the beach or even a dance party in my kitchen while I make dinner.

E: eating — How did I nourish myself today? Did I have energy for my day? Did I have enough water?

S: sleep — Did I sleep well? Did I remember to turn my phone off before winding down? Am I getting the hours that I need?

S: soul — What happened that made me feel happy or thankful? Was it something that happened to me or something I did for someone else? Did I spend some time in nature or making some art? (This can encapsulate so many things surrounding my emotional health.)

Talking box questions

Write a compliment about everybody at the table — pass a piece of paper around with each person's name at the top so they can take it away with them (it's easier to remember the bad things, so this can serve as a reminder of the good).

Name three things you are grateful for and why.

Resources / Rauemi

If you need more information, you may find the following websites and resources helpful (among other things, they include signs and symptoms to look out for). If you are concerned, consult a health professional so that your teen can be assessed and, if appropriate, diagnosed and treated by a doctor or specialist.

ONLINE	A hub for New Zealand mental health resources: mentalhealth.org.nz
	A website that assists parents, whānau and friends to recognise and understand the difficult situations that young people experience in their lives: mentalhealth.org.nz/common-ground
	Parenting guides around mental health: allright.org.nz/tools/parenting-guides
	Anxiety and depression self-tests to assess wellness (this website is part of a national public health programme, the National Depression Initiative. It includes The Journal, an online self-help programme aimed at people over 16 years of age): depression.org.nz
	Information on teen safety and other topics: pmgt.org.nz/teen-safety
	Mental health services for young people: healthnavigator.org.nz/healthy-living/m/mental-health-services-for-young-people
	Like Minds, Like Mine is an organisation working to increase social inclusion of, and end discrimination towards, people with experience of mental illness: likeminds.org.nz
	Just a Thought: Staying on track — a web-based e-therapy tool with structured, step-by-step online courses for people who feel pressure or distress (e.g., from the impacts of Covid-19). Developed by clinicians and researchers, it offers free cognitive behavioural therapy (CBT) courses online. CBT teaches people how to improve their mental health through learning how to interact differently with thoughts and identify behaviours that enhance wellbeing. justathought.co.nz
	All Right? Getting through together — resources to enhance mental health and wellbeing. Includes some youth-specific resources. allright.org.nz/articles/not-all-right

ONLINE	Le Va — supporting Pasifika families and communities to unleash their full potential and have the best possible health and wellbeing outcomes. Includes some youth-specific resources. One of their online tools, 'Aunty Dee', helps people cope at stressful times. leva.co.nz auntydee.co.nz An explanation and illustration of **hauora**: healthnavigator.org.nz/healthy-living/t/te-whare-tapa-whā-and-wellbeing A guide to how **tapping, or EFT** (emotional freedom technique), can help alleviate stress: thetappingsolution.com/tapping-101 AnxietyNZ Trust is a non-profit organisation that supports people suffering from **anxiety**: anxiety.org.nz A guide to symptoms and common causes of **depression**: mentalhealth.org.nz/conditions/condition/depression Resources relating to **self-harm**: youthwellbeingstudy.wordpress.com/resources helpguide.org/articles/anxiety/cutting-and-self-harm.htm Resources relating to **eating disorders**: ed.org.nz/eating-disorders-explained Love Your Kite — (Eating disorder Recovery app: associated cost) loveyourkite.com Guidance on helping people with mental health issues around **Covid-19**: education.govt.nz/covid-19/covid-19-and-wellbeing/talking-to-children-about-covid-19-coronavirus/tips-for-teachers-parents-and-caregivers-supporting-young-people An online '**resilience** check': bwcharity.org.uk/resilience-check

| ONLINE | An introduction to **emotional intelligence:**
allright.org.nz/articles/emotional-intelligence

Resources on **gratitude:**
payitforward.kiwi
begreat.co.nz/the-thankfulness-project
randomactsofkindness.org
antimaximalist.com/gratitude-list

Resources on **mindfulness:**
healthnavigator.org.nz/healthy-living/m/mindfulness
mindfulnesseducation.nz
mentalhealth.org.nz/our-work/mindfulness

A brief guide to **youth law on medical decisions:**
youthlaw.co.nz/rights/health-wellbeing/medical-decisions/#if-im-under-16-do-medical-professionals-need-to-at-least-consider-what-i-want

Resources on **privacy:**
privacy.org.nz/blog/parents-right-to-know-childrens-right-to-privacy |
| ONLINE FOR TEENS | **Aroha** — the Mental Health Foundation of New Zealand provides a range of free services, including this chatbot, which offers young people somebody to talk to.
tiny.cc/aroha

SPARX — a computer game that helps young people with mild to moderate depression. It can also help young people who are feeling anxious or stressed.
sparx.org.nz

The Lowdown — a website to help young New Zealanders recognise and understand depression or anxiety. Free-text 24/7 service: text number 5626.
Email: team@thelowdown.co.nz
thelowdown.co.nz |

ONLINE FOR TEENS	**Livewire NZ** — an online community for young people who are dealing with some tricky stuff, such as illness or disability, with crews who understand and offer a little extra support. livewire.org.nz **Youthline** — this e-therapy package is a free, texting-based programme for young people with mild to moderate anxiety and/or depression. youthline.co.nz
APPS	**HeadSpace** — provides resources for meditation and mindfulness (associated cost). headspace.com **Melon** — gives access to an online community of Kiwis who may be experiencing the same thoughts and feelings. Includes a health journal, self-awareness tools and other useful resources (free, but requires a referral from GP). melonhealth.com/mental-wellbeing **Mentemia** — an app that coaches mental wellbeing. mentemia.com **Piki** — through specifically selected peers, professionals and technology, Piki aims to equip youth with tools to help overcome adversity and strengthen their wellbeing (free, with the option to self-refer or be referred by a GP). piki.org.nz

COMMUNITY	There are a number of free or low-cost in-person counselling options for your teen. Talking to a trained professional can be a really helpful way to work through anything that you are finding challenging. There are lots of different talk therapies available.
	Ask your GP about free counselling sessions that may be available through your local primary health organisation (PHO).
	You may be eligible for 10 free counselling sessions (or more if clinically indicated) and other assistance through a WINZ Disability Allowance.
	If you are in paid employment you may be able to access free confidential counselling through your company's employee assistance programme — talk to your employer.
	Youthline has free counselling for young people aged 12–25 years and their families in various locations across Auckland and also Dunedin.
	You can ask your doctor for a referral or you can find a counsellor, psychotherapist or psychologist yourself. To find low-cost or free counselling in your area, search the Family Services Directory, contact your local Citizens Advice Bureau (CAB) or seek out your local Youth Hub — or, if you identify as a woman, you can reach out to a local women's centre.

9. MORE BODY TALK: PERSONAL AND SEXUAL HEALTH

#grabyourgonads #periodapp #nofeargosmear #safesex

*'Take care of your body. It's the
only place you have to live.'*
— JIM ROHN

Kōrero with Molly

My experience of health class at school was that it was awkward and didn't really meet anyone's needs. Some of the things that stick out in my mind are when all the girls were given the 'talk' about periods. I think half the class had already started their periods, so it was actually a bit of a missed opportunity. We were shown a tampon in a glass of water, which was kind of freaky at the time for those who didn't know it doesn't expand quite like that inside a human! Another occasion was when we were shown how to put a male condom on a banana. I recall that even the teacher didn't seem very comfortable. And I certainly won't forget the class where some horrifying pictures of various infected genitals were passed around, I think to ward us off having sex at all, ever! Overall, it felt like we barely even touched the surface of everything a teen needs to know about how to look after themselves and others.

As someone who menstruates, I know there is always a time when you are going to be caught short and need a pad or tampon when you aren't prepared, especially when your cycle is still sorting itself out. Many of us were familiar with the confusing 'walk of shame' to the nurse's office in high school, only to be supplied with just one pad that resembled a diaper. Not comfortable at all or particularly conducive for a PE class! I was really excited when the period-tracking apps started coming out for smartphones. I don't know many menstruators now who don't use one to prompt them that their period is due and teach them a bit about their cycle. Nowadays I wouldn't be worried at all about asking a colleague for a tampon or chatting about periods, but I do still find some male attitudes disappointing when you see them sneering at you and disregarding your opinion as 'PMS'. There's definitely a long way to go: can you believe a friend of mine started a job recently, only to discover there was not one period product disposal bin in the building — even though it was also open to clients?

Ultimately, conversations about looking after our personal and sexual health should not feel so scary or so awkward, especially as a teen when everything is new. We all deserve up-to-date information, free from shame or stigma, about the things that everyone is going through.

What do you mean by that? / He aha te tikanga o tāu kōrero?

Puberty involves some complex body changes. Your teen might not feel comfortable with the idea of their body changing, but you can make sure information is communicated in a way that they can understand it. This may mean some gentle nudges about showering more regularly, popping clothes in the wash more often, and perhaps considering some type of deodorant (of which there are many choices, including eco-friendly varieties). Not only will teenagers' bodies be maturing physically, but also the way they think and feel may increasingly include aspects of their sexual self. Most of us remember the so-called sex ed classes at school, and most of us would agree they were found wanting. In some schools they weren't delivered at all. It seems there has always been an element of debate as to what this type of learning should cover and who should deliver it: for example, does it belong squarely at home or should it also be an integral part of schooling?

In New Zealand, relationship and sexuality education (RSE) is a compulsory part of the curriculum. The exact nature of what will be taught is decided through community consultation, which should be held every two years. This means each school/kura may end up teaching slightly different parts of the available content. Once this is decided, some parents may then also choose to remove their teen from these lessons. The concern here is that across the country there are huge variances in the quality and quantity of information our teens receive. Every young person needs education in these matters that is evidence-based and up to date, so the school/kura does seem to be a natural place for this to happen. This is particularly true for those who aren't having such conversations at home. Where there's a vacuum of information, teens may be getting their 'knowledge' from one another and online, which could be problematic and misleading. Some parents worry that introducing topics such as sex might inadvertently 'put ideas in their teen's head'. In reality, generally speaking, those ideas are already there in one form or another. Furthermore, the research strongly indicates that talking about RSE-related topics actually does the opposite of speeding things up; here are just three examples from peer-reviewed journals:

> Developmentally appropriate and evidence–based education about human sexuality and sexual reproduction over time provided by pediatricians, schools, other professionals, and parents is important to help children and adolescents make informed, positive, and safe choices about healthy relationships, responsible sexual activity, and their reproductive health. Sexuality education has been shown to help to prevent and reduce the risks of adolescent pregnancy, HIV, and sexually transmitted infections for children and adolescents.[1]

> Parents are a trusted source of health information and can help prepare adolescents for developing healthy relationships and navigating challenges.[2]

> *Parent–teen discussions about sexual and reproductive health are associated with delayed sex and higher contraceptive use among teens.*[3]

In years gone by, the main, if not only, focus of sexuality education seemed to be on stopping teenagers from having sex, contracting sexually transmitted infections (STIs) or getting pregnant. Scare tactics tended to be a major teaching tool — for example, by showing shocking photographs or highlighting worst-case scenarios. This does not necessarily help in terms of dissuading those who are sexually interested and may actually distress those who are not yet at that stage.

More recently, it has been realised that creating fear, alienating or stigmatising is an unhealthy and unproductive approach to these topics, not least because it can set people up for relationship and sexual problems in adulthood. In addition, it creates an environment within which teens feel unable to reach out for resources and support, both at home and within the community.

It no longer has to be this way. Indeed, it really shouldn't be this way. 'Adolescence', as recent US research underlines, 'is a critical development period when youth begin to develop their romantic and sexual identities and is an important time to learn about how to engage in healthy romantic and sexual behavior, which then sets the stage for healthy adult relationships.'[4] As with other sensitive issues, then, it is vital that your teen knows they won't be judged or shamed if they have questions or want to access services. Use of healthcare provision needs to be normalised, so that environments are created where teenagers are welcomed and treated fairly, discreetly and promptly, and where they can feel comfortable and accepted.

Talking to your teen about these topics before they leave home (and preferably much younger) will hopefully encourage them to take a holistic look at their wellbeing and influence their health-related decision-making. As teenagers get slightly older, they may start to access medical professionals independently (from age 16, teens in New

Zealand have the right to access — or refuse — their own medical treatment). Alternatively, when you also attend an appointment, some medical professionals may ask whether your teen would prefer for you to step out of the room. If your teen is comfortable with this, respect their decision: as ever, let them know that you are there to support them when they need you. They are more likely to share with you if you give them the space to do so.

Tell me more . . . / Kōrero mai anō . . .

As a grounding for speaking with your teen effectively about RSE, having a basic understanding yourself about puberty, periods, fertility, sexual health (including contraception and STIs*), and intimate personal care is obviously invaluable. What's more, RSE isn't just about the birds and the bees — it also covers consent and healthy relationships (so much so, we have entire chapters on both; see Chapters 11 and 12).

Puberty

Puberty usually begins somewhere between nine and 15 years in a boy and eight and 14 years in a girl (although it could be slightly younger or older than this). It usually lasts between two and five years — although, again, this is different for everybody. Driven by hormones, it causes physical changes to the genitals (primary sex characteristics) and to the body more generally (secondary sex characteristics).

During puberty, your teen will grow in **height** and become **stronger**, their **body shape** will change, they will **sweat** more and their skin may become more **oily**. Puberty also means more **hair growth**, including pubic, underarm and (for boys) facial hair. The **voice deepens** (most noticeably in boys, of course). Some of these changes will result in

---

* You may have heard of the term 'sexually transmitted disease' (STD), but as not all infections result in disease, and as a way to address stigma, the term 'sexually transmitted infection' (STI) is now commonly used.

increased **body odour** and, potentially, **pimples**. The order for all of these changes is individual to each person.

In and among all these physical changes you will also notice your teen's social and psychological state in flux. At the very least, their mood may be more changeable. Around this time, try to work in a general conversation about hygiene — this can range from familiarising them with the concept of soap and water, to reminding them that others also require access to the bathroom, especially if you're on tank water. This conversation should include a chat about the importance of a skincare regimen (although this doesn't mean they have to buy every product on the market).

It may also be useful to have a discussion about body hair, recognising that perceived or actual pressure from peers or partners can play a huge role, as can what is stereotypically considered feminine or masculine. There's a spectrum for girls in particular, from shaving body hair (to a smaller or larger degree) through to leaving it as a feminist statement. Getting your teen to understand where any pressures come from can help to empower your teen to make their own choices. Make sure that they feel comfortable talking through with you whether or not they should, for example, shave their lower legs or bleach their top lip. If they really want to remove or disguise hair, ensure they have age-appropriate and hygienic options to do so. In addition, some boys may have mixed feelings about their body hair and struggle to raise the issue. As ever, it's about supporting them to make healthy decisions.

Most of us will remember how embarrassed we were when a massive boil appeared on the end of our nose just before the school social, so tread carefully around the subject of your teen's complexion. It's worth talking through with them that having pimples does not mean someone isn't keeping themselves clean. Pimples are perfectly normal during puberty and beyond. If your teen is having this type of issue, you could suggest they change their pillowcase a bit more frequently and drink lots of water throughout the day. There are also various products available from your local pharmacy or supermarket to help with the treatment of pimples. If pimples turn into acne, then the condition has moved on from what's considered the norm for puberty and really requires input from a health professional, who may advise medication. Acne can be devastating to a teen's self-confidence and should be taken seriously.

It's important that all teenagers have an understanding of what they and their peers are potentially going through, with differences being celebrated. For some teens, puberty presents particular challenges as they try to understand their own identities. Let's look in a bit more detail at what happens to the adolescent body during puberty.

In those born with a penis and testicles

Puberty means enlargement of the **testicles and scrotum** (usually one testicle will hang slightly lower than the other) and later the **penis**. There are changes to the body shape, such as **broadening shoulders and chest**. For about a quarter of boys there is some swelling around the upper chest area; if they are alarmed about this, reassure them that it is just a reaction to the balance of hormones and usually settles within a couple of years. Moving to the pubic area, the penis seems to take on a life of its own and often has spontaneous **erections**, sometimes at inconvenient moments. This often warrants the need to 'tie a shoe' or stay in the swimming pool a little longer. When the hormone **testosterone** gets to a high enough level, the sperm (male reproductive cell) is manufactured in the testicles for the first time (spermarche); this generally happens around 10–12 years of age, but can be sooner or later, and it leads to the first ejaculation. This commonly occurs as a nocturnal emission, or **'wet dream'** — ejaculations during sleep — which tend to happen more during puberty than at any other time and will typically tail off or stop altogether in later years. About a third of adolescent boys (or adult men) will experience penile pearly papules: pinkish-white pimple-like growths around the head of the penis. They are harmless, but if your teen is distressed by them, you or they could consult a healthcare professional.

As the vocal cords thicken and the larynx (voice box) grows, some might struggle with the way they experience their **voice changing**. Others may take this in their stride. Not only can their voice unpredictably 'crack' or 'break' mid-sentence for a while, but the larynx also becomes more prominent (known as the 'Adam's apple') and can be really noticeable in some. **Facial hair** growth may be one of the final changes and at this stage teens generally require some instruction on shaving.

It's important that your teen appreciates changes happen at different times and in slightly different ways for everyone. For instance, some will get broader than others, some will get more body hair than others, and penis size will vary. Comparisons are rarely helpful. There really is a lot going on for them and although you may feel they are withdrawing from you at this time, they still need your subtle reassurance.

Not many teens will be super comfortable about discussing such intimate events as erections, wet dreams and ejaculation. Even so, it is definitely worth having a chat to try to prepare them in advance so that they understand what's going on when it happens for the first time — not least so that they know it's perfectly natural and nothing to be worried about. If this feels too difficult, the library is full of really awesome books that you can leave on your teen's bedside table to browse. Another way to avoid possible embarrassment would be to make sure your teen is used to using the washing machine. That way, they can deal with their own sheets no matter the reason (and they may even start to take responsibility for some of their clothes-washing once they get the knack!). For a more pointed encouragement to clean up, you can always leave a small towel or kitchen roll in their room.

In those born with a uterus (womb) and ovaries

The formation of **breast** buds is the first visual sign of puberty for the majority: a firm, round, tender lump under the nipple. It's normal for one side to produce a breast bud first, with the other following soon after. These buds go on to form breasts. The **nipples** themselves increase in size slightly and may darken in colour. Breasts may grow a little unevenly and may be sore, and the nipples itchy, at this time.

Your teen may want a singlet or bra, not only to support their growing breasts but also to maintain their privacy — for example, in situations at school when they need to change in an open dressing room. Many also find that a singlet or bra protects them from clothing that, due to increased sensitivity, they are more likely to find scratchy or otherwise uncomfortable.

Alongside this there are changes in body shape, such as **broader hips and thighs** and a more defined **waist**. In addition, the **vulva and vagina** get a little bigger. **Vaginal mucus** produced at the cervix increases and can be seen on underwear (commonly known as vaginal discharge).

The **start of menstruation** (menarche) generally occurs a couple of years following the start of breast growth (although, as with everything, it differs for everyone). The average age for menarche in New Zealand is just over 13 years, although around half of all girls begin having periods when at intermediate school and some start even earlier (6.3 per cent) during primary school;[5] if your teen's period hasn't begun by age 16, you might consider consulting a healthcare professional. Without prior knowledge these changes can be alarming, so it's crucial either to have a conversation or provide some information to ensure they know it's perfectly natural and nothing to be worried about. Driven by hormones, including oestrogen and progesterone (produced in the ovaries), these changes are simply preparing the body for reproduction, with the ova (eggs) that have been inside the ovaries since before birth now able to mature and be released in a cyclic rhythm.

All these changes can be a lot for teenagers to get their heads around, particularly when it comes to periods: these may begin earlier or later than in anyone else they know; they may have a lighter or heavier flow, which they find easier or harder to deal with; their cycles may be very regular or completely unpredictable; they may or may not have mood swings in the lead-up to them; they may or may not have period aches and pains; and they may or may not be in an environment at school that they consider understanding and supportive. In addition, some teenagers may be concerned about the vaginal discharge they experience between periods. Daily changing of their underwear (preferably an absorbent fabric such as cotton) should be sufficient to cope with this, but some also choose to wear panty liners (washable or otherwise). With all these uncertainties, your job is to make sure that they learn how to listen to their own body so they are able to navigate their way through. Meanwhile, be sure your teens born without a uterus are also informed about periods and related products. Menstruation is completely natural and should be spoken about without stigma or shame.

Periods

While still within what is considered 'normal', there can be quite a variance between people's experiences of their menstrual cycle, and this continues into adulthood. It is usual for each cycle (counted from the first day of the period until the day before the next period) to be about a month in length; however, anywhere from 21 to 40 days is completely normal. Interestingly, only one in 10 women actually fits the commonly quoted cycle of 28 days.[6]

Occasionally periods are totally predictable from the outset, but for many it can take a while — up to three years, even — for them to settle into a regular pattern. Periods themselves usually last about five days, but may range from three to seven days. The amount of blood lost in a period is typically 30–40 millilitres (2–3 tablespoons),[7] but again this can vary.

Often, people experience discomfort such as mild stomach cramps, lower back ache and tiredness. Your teen might find a number of strategies to help them cope with this: for example, using a wheat heat pack, going for a brisk walk (which can alleviate cramping) or getting an early night. This may also help with premenstrual syndrome (PMS), which can affect up to three-quarters of people who menstruate. This includes physical symptoms (such as aches, muscle pains, tiredness, breast tenderness, constipation/diarrhoea, pimples, bloating and clumsiness) and emotional or behavioural ones (such as low mood, mood swings, anger, tears, food cravings, insomnia and poor concentration).[8] Fortunately, most people experience only a few of these at most.

In addition to not feeling completely themselves, your teen also has to deal with the practical implications of having periods. Teens describe worrying about being allowed to leave the classroom urgently, participating in sports (particularly swimming), and dealing with the inevitable leak or the unexpected arrival of a period. Some of this could be put down to reactions resulting from a lack of education, or immaturity of other peers, specifically boys. Unfortunately, there may still also be a lack of understanding and empathy from some adults. These are genuine concerns and well worth unpacking with your teen. Although you cannot cover all possibilities or make everything all right for them, you can ensure they have your ear — and, more pragmatically, a kit in their bag containing a spare pair of underwear, some wipes and some products they feel comfortable using.

Suggest, if they haven't already done so, downloading an age-appropriate period app: it may be worth checking these out together and deciding which one suits. These apps tend to cover a range of fertility tracking, and they often have the option to switch off content that may cover more than your teen needs. Apps can be a fantastic aid, allowing teens to work out if their cycle is becoming more regular, to keep a track of their period length, and to get a notification through their phone that their period is expected (the app creates an algorithm over time). While your teen may choose to keep this information private, having some data can also give them an opportunity to open up a conversation if they are experiencing anything they are concerned might be outside of the norm.

Although some will find their periods annoying and inconvenient, there is a difference between this and symptoms indicating health conditions that shouldn't be ignored and may require treatment. Menstruation can act as an overall health indicator. (For example, pregnancy is the most common reason for periods stopping, and breastfeeding can cause changes to the cycle. However, issues relating to the pituitary, thyroid or adrenal glands can also stop periods, as can reproductive problems, and eating disorders, overexercising and extreme weight loss can interrupt the normal cycle.)[9] So having a basic knowledge of the menstrual cyle and paying attention to it can be useful in being able to flag changes or concerns. Indicators to look out for include: heavy or long periods (menorrhagia), very light or sporadic periods (oligomenorrhoea), painful periods (dysmenorrhoea) or no periods at all (amenorrhoea). In addition, any bleeding between periods or after sexual intercourse warrants a check-up. In saying that, it is still not unusual for period problems to be brushed off or dismissed without proper investigation. This means that too many people are putting up with problematic periods and unnecessary discomfort. It's like building a jigsaw puzzle: one thing on its own may not be relevant or concerning but, put together, things can start to form a picture. For example, if your teen is in such pain when they have their period that it prevents them from being able to function as they normally would, or they are struggling with excessively heavy or long periods, it would be a good idea to contact a healthcare professional for advice. This would also be the case where a hormonal issue may be indicated — for example, if your teen didn't get their period until a bit later than most, their period hasn't settled down into a pattern after a year or so (especially if there are long gaps in between), they have started to put on a large amount of weight, their skin is particularly prone to pimples, and/or there is hair growth in places outside of the pubic area and underarms. In general, the sooner a health condition is investigated and recognised, the sooner any required treatment (holistic and/or medical) can begin. Conditions such as **endometriosis** and **polycystic ovarian syndrome (PCOS)** need to become more easily and more promptly diagnosed. For instance, Endometriosis New Zealand advises that, 'Internationally, there is a diagnostic delay of eight or more years from first presentation of symptoms to a doctor with diagnosis, which means unnecessary suffering for those it affects.'[10]

Perhaps some of the stigmas and barriers to conversations about periods are beginning to break down due to a recent increase in media attention. The topic of period poverty is now a talking point, regularly featuring in the news and highlighting the inaccessibility of period products for some. There are many associated negative outcomes —

including missed days at school. New Zealand schools are now able to opt into a programme providing free products for all menstruating students in addition to health promotion initiatives.

Period products

In previous decades, any adverts featuring menstrual products seemed to feature women wearing white swimsuits. Eye-roll! The absorbency of a pad or tampon was frequently demonstrated by the use of a blue, rather than red, liquid. We're finally getting a bit more real and, with that, there are now more comfortable and convenient ways to manage period flow, including environmentally friendly options. Our parents or grandparents may have relayed stories about their having to use big, bulky pads secured by loops onto a belt around the waist (they may even have found the subject of periods too taboo to mention at all). If you (and we're talking to dads as well as mums) are a parent of a menstruator, it's useful to know that there are now various options:

- Both **disposable pads and tampons** are now available in a range of synthetic materials or environmentally friendly cotton (or a mixture of both), which will impact on how quickly they break down after use. Tampons might be used alongside panty liners, pads (washable or otherwise) or menstrual underwear.
- You can now get modern-day **washable pads**. These are not the wads of material used in olden days and have been reinvented. They come in different sizes and various colour schemes. There is generally a popper underneath to keep them in place, with most designed to wick the blood away from the surface so they are cool and comfy. These are primarily available online.
- And then there's the new kid on the block — **period underwear**, which is just like normal underwear but with various levels of absorbency sewn into the gusset. These are not necessarily the cheapest option, although they are becoming more affordable. The fit is important: they actually need to be snug so they don't leak. They are now being released in togs,

too — this is a bit of a game-changer for many.

- Instead of a tampon you can use a **menstrual cup or disc**, which is reusable and can last up to 5–10 years depending on what it's made from (generally either TPE — a high-quality polymer — or medical-grade silicone). Beware: all cups/discs are not made equal, and some of the cheaper online brands may not be ideal. While using a menstrual cup/disc definitely involves a learning curve, it is an increasingly popular option. If your teen is interested, they could investigate a couple of different brands to get the best fit.

Try to remove any embarrassment around this topic so that your teen can always come to you to talk things through if they have questions. Encourage your teen to try out a few combinations. They should not feel guilty if a particular option doesn't work for them; it's all about choice. A level of hygiene is important whatever they choose to use, so make sure that they know to wash their hands frequently. They should also familiarise themselves with the instructions for each of the products they use — for example, how long each should be used for, how to clean reusable products, and how to dispose of disposables. There can be health implications if products are not used as recommended.

Fertility

Once a body goes through puberty it is capable of reproduction. Understanding the effects of hormones and the consequences on fertility can be empowering for all teens, and for this they first should understand the mechanics of both reproductive systems. If they choose to delve further, those with ovaries can even learn simple charting (monitoring temperature and cervical mucus). Known as fertility awareness, this allows them to recognise some of the female body's signals, which can be both useful and fascinating. These signs can confirm ovulation, help them to predict when their next period will be, explain moods at certain times in the menstrual cycle, and alert them to issues such as infection. There are books on the topic written specifically for teenage readers, with the focus on health, such as *Cycle Savvy* by Toni Weschler.[11]

A FEW FACTS ABOUT SPERM AND EGGS	
• Sperm production begins at puberty and is then **continual and ongoing**. • Sperm is produced at a rate of about **90,000 per minute** (most are reabsorbed into the body).[12] • It takes about **three months** for sperm to mature. • One ejaculation contains **300 million to 500 million sperm** but it takes only one to fertilise an egg. • The chromosome from the sperm determines the sex of a baby (XX = female, XY = male, and combinations such as XXY = intersex).	• All ova (eggs) are already in the ovaries at birth. • No matter how long or short the menstrual cycle is, the ovum (egg) survives a maximum of 24 hours once released from the ovary. The average is 18 hours. • Sperm can survive at least five days, and up to seven in favourable conditions, so fertilisation of the egg can occur days after intercourse. • Ovulation usually occurs 10–16 days before the next period begins.

Often the focus of RSE for teens is on contraception and avoiding STIs; information about achieving a pregnancy is rarely mentioned as part of any school programme. As such, it can come as a shock later down the track if they are among the one in four Kiwis who encounter fertility issues.[13] It might be helpful to chat with your teen about preserving their fertility (by not smoking, and by eating a healthy diet, for example).[14] Introducing the idea of family planning can also be constructive. Obviously there's no great rush or imminent crisis, but it will help them to know that, if they are planning a naturally conceived family — especially if they want several children — it might pay to factor that into their fertile years.

And in terms of the chances of becoming pregnant, age has a lot to do with it. Women under 30 have a roughly 20 per cent chance (per monthly cycle) of getting pregnant naturally. By the time they reach 40, this figure is down to 5 per cent. For men, the chance of fathering a child reduces after the age of 40.[15]

Infertility, as one New Zealand report explains, 'is equally attributable to male and female issues — in about 40 per cent of infertile couples the problem is a female factor, in about 40 per cent it is a male one, and for the remaining 20 per cent there is a joint problem or the cause is unknown'.[16] Assisted reproductive technology (ART) will normally double your chances of conceiving; however, doubling, for example, a 5 per cent chance means the likelihood of getting pregnant is still only 10 per cent. It is possible now to freeze either eggs, ovarian tissue or embryos to use later in life, but currently none of these techniques gives any guarantees, and all involve cost and medical procedures.

Masturbation

Talking about such a private topic can be tricky. At the same time, it's worth it so that your teen knows masturbation is totally normal. By becoming familiar with their own body, they get to know what feels safe and good for them. Their privacy is crucial (for them and for you!). Be alert to the difference between healthy sexual exploration and behaviours that might become concerning or are not age appropriate. Some of these are covered in Chapter 13, which discusses porn.

Sex

Remember back to your youth and how sex was edging its way into conversations, including who'd had it and who hadn't — and some of what was said was even true! People become interested in the idea of sex at different stages and to different degrees, or perhaps not at all. Teens will be hearing information from their schools — and, of course, their peer group — as well as at home. They may be sexually active or that may be years away, and they may or may not choose to share this information with you. It may be that your teen is not heterosexual. All teens need to be properly informed about sex to allow them to make safe, age-appropriate choices. Not everyone will make the same decisions: for example, preserving virginity and waiting for sex until after marriage is of great importance to some people, but less so for others. This can be for a multitude of reasons, including religious and cultural beliefs. Others see sex solely in terms of physical enjoyment. The basic parameters for sex are that it is within the law, safe, consensual and also enjoyable for all involved.

Teens may have different views as to when it is appropriate to become sexually active — and these views may or may not overlap with yours. Even if your teen is not yet at that stage, they will be receiving a barrage of very mixed messages from the world around them. While it is natural and normal for them to be curious about sex, sometimes the media they access seem to be encouraging them to hurry up and grow up. Virginity is often presented in the context of 'getting it over with', or as a rite of passage, but in reality this is a highly significant step for most people; research has found that only around 3 per cent of us cannot remember our 'first time'.[17]

Sex is an act that requires trust and respect. When it forms an integral part of a relationship, it also involves a degree of intimacy that requires some emotional involvement. We will have people within our own social groups that have a range of opinions on what is and isn't acceptable and appropriate behaviour. We may have felt pressures as teenagers — and indeed as adults — around what was 'expected' in certain situations, whether or not we then acted on those expectations. We need to recognise that the same will be true for our teens and give them strategies to deal with these situations. As parents, we should be alert to the fact that there may be a generation gap between our own perspectives on hook-ups, 'friends with benefits' and the 'rules' of dating, and those of our teens. It can be a very confusing time for us and for them. This is why it is important to have ongoing discussions — to make sure that your teen values themselves and gains the confidence to formulate their own opinions. They will be developing an idea about what their boundaries are and getting comfortable about communicating these.

The reality is that some teens will be having sex, and they need to be able to take care of themselves and others. Alongside understanding respect and consent (see Chapters 11 and 12), that care includes knowing about hygiene, contraception and STIs. Their communication skills should be at a level where they can hear what their partners are saying and verbalise their own wants and needs.

Ideally, all this is something they should be informed about in advance of their first sexual experience. Your teen will be making their own personal decisions, which are all influenced by your input and their own values and beliefs (framed within, for instance, their family, social groups, culture and faith). In addition, there may be reasons why they choose not to have a sexual relationship until they are older.

AGE AND SEXUAL ACTIVITY Figures from longitudinal studies in New Zealand show that today's teens are waiting till they are older to have sex, compared to those in previous years.		
AGE OF RESPONDENTS	PERCENTAGE WHO HAVE EVER HAD SEX	
	2012[18] (CUMULATIVE PERCENTAGES)	2019[19] (CUMULATIVE PERCENTAGES)
13 yrs & under	8%	6%
14 yrs	14%	8%
15 yrs	24%	19%
16 yrs	37%	25%
17–19 yrs	46%	41%

If you can, find a way to check in with your teen regularly (but not intrusively) so that conversations relating to sex are normalised. Clarify that you don't want details; you just want to know that they are feeling safe and in control of this aspect of their life, and that they are aware they can come to you if they have any concerns. Research shows that a positive home environment is conducive to your teen's sexual health and use of contraception.[20]

A word on abstinence education

Abstinence, if taken to mean absolutely no sexual contact at all, including outercourse, is the only 100 per cent effective family planning method of avoiding pregnancy. That being said, people interpret the term in different ways — if someone's criteria for abstinence includes being able to touch intimately, for example, there is still opportunity for pregnancy to occur, however unlikely, where there is potential for sperm to come into contact with the vulva. In addition, it is still possible to transmit STIs via skin-to-skin contact or through bodily fluids whether or not penetrative sex has taken place.

If abstinence is the approach you would prefer your teen to take, let them know your definition and that this is your preference, and explain your reasoning behind this. At the same time, respect that their views may not completely overlap with yours. Whatever your perspectives, it is still important to ensure that your teen understands the mechanics of any sexual activity and has sufficient knowledge of STIs and pregnancy prevention: abstinence is not something that can be taught in a vacuum. US research offers clear evidence that 'programs promoting abstinence-only until heterosexual marriage occurs are ineffective'.[21]

Contraception

A broad knowledge of contraceptive options is key, for both teens having sex and those not having sex. Information will assist them in making decisions as to what is right for them, such as avoiding pregnancy at an age when they're not necessarily mature enough to cope with the consequences. Some types of contraception can also help to limit the spread of STIs.

While there seems to be a trend towards teens starting to become sexually active at a later age, recent research has highlighted some concerning statistics around the low rate of contraceptive use. (It is as yet unclear whether or not this is because of difficulties accessing healthcare.) The Youth19 survey in New Zealand found that, in 2019, 41 per cent of sexually active students always used condoms, compared with 49 per cent back in 2001. Among those who were sexually active, just over half (52 per cent) reported that they or their partner always used contraception.[22]

There are several different contraceptive options, most of which are available in New Zealand and are Pharmac-funded. Each type has a varying level of effectiveness, ease of use and affordability. For informed decision-making, it is useful to understand any potential side effects, and how each method works to prevent STIs or stop a pregnancy. Prior to initial use, some methods of contraception require a medical consultation and prescription. Not all types are suitable for all people (for example, weight or family/personal health history may be a factor). In New Zealand, youth under the age of 16 can be given contraceptive information, services and prescriptions without parental permission if the health professional has assessed the young person as being able to make an informed decision. Contraceptives can be divided into the following five categories, with some overlap.

Barrier contraceptive

Barriers include the external condom, used on the penis; the internal condom, used in the vagina; and the diaphragm or cap. In all cases they put a physical barrier between the sperm and the ovum (egg). They also provide some protection against STIs (the internal condom can be used in the anus), and they are often used in addition to other contraceptive methods.

Your teen will need to learn the key rules around using these. When using the external condom, check the expiry date on the individual packet and open it carefully (not with scissors!), and if the outside of the packet is sticky, discard it. When fitting the condom, pinch air out of the top bulb before rolling it down over the penis, taking care no sperm gets on the outside of the condom. After ejaculating, remove the condom before the penis becomes flaccid so that it does not slip off, and keep it away from any partner at this stage. Do not reuse condoms, and discard them appropriately.

Note that using two condoms at once is not safer and moreover can cause the condoms to break. (This would be true of two condoms on a penis, or a condom on a penis used in conjunction with an internal condom.) Friction during intercourse can also cause a condom to break, and lubrication ('lube') can help to prevent this. Use only a proprietary lube (widely available from chemists and superstores or online); avoid things like vegetable oil or petroleum jelly, which degrade condoms.

The diaphragm or cap is getting hard to purchase. It's not available from New Zealand clinics, and, if ordered online, it still needs to be checked by a nurse via a pelvic examination to ensure it's the appropriate size for any individual or it will be ineffective. The diaphragm or cap should first be checked for holes or tears before applying spermicide, which also has availability issues in New Zealand. It is then inserted into the top of the vagina prior to intercourse and must remain in place for at least six hours afterwards. If sex occurs again in those six hours, more spermicide must be applied. Once removed, it should be gently washed and dried flat, then returned to its protective case.

Hormonal contraceptive

These include the oral contraceptive pill (OCP, 'the pill'). This may take the form of a combined oral contraceptive pill (COC) containing progestogen and oestrogen, or a progestogen-only pill (POP). A progestogen injection (Depo-Provera, or DP) is also available. Other products include a hormone patch or hormone ring, but these are not available in New Zealand.

COCs (and some newer progestogen-only pills — desogestrel progestogen) are designed to prevent ovulation.[23] In addition, they target changes in the cervical mucus, making the path of the sperm difficult, and they reduce the motility of the egg through the fallopian tubes and alter the lining of the uterus to prevent implantation. Some POPs will not stop ovulation, but are effective in terms of the other roles. Some hormonal contraceptives are prescribed in such a way that the period (known, during pill use, as the withdrawal bleed) is less frequent: this can be achieved, for example, by not leaving gaps between active pills.

Healthcare professionals should discuss any health risks and potential side effects prior to prescribing any hormonal contraception. Many side effects do dissipate after the first few weeks, but different medications suit different people and occasionally a change needs to be made.

The Depo-Provera injection is given at a clinic by a healthcare professional about every 11–13 weeks.

Long-acting reversible contraceptive (LARC)

LARCs include the arm implant and intrauterine devices (IUDs). These options are known as 'fit and forget' and can last between three and 10 years, depending on the device.

The funded implant available in New Zealand, under the brand name Jadelle®, can last up to five years. The implant (also known as 'the rods') is inserted under the skin on the upper arm. In some users it causes irregular periods, which can be problematic. To remove it is a relatively simple procedure, usually carried out by a nurse or GP, requiring some numbing of the site and a small incision. Once the implant has been taken out, fertility usually returns promptly.

Some IUDs (including the Mirena® and Jaydess® brands) release the hormone progestogen, while another version is non-hormonal and made of copper, which acts as a spermicide. IUDs require fitting by a medical professional, which involves a pelvic examination and the use of a speculum for insertion. The modern designs mean that having previously given birth is now no longer a prerequisite. They are some of the most effective contraceptives available.

Knowledge

This contraception category includes either understanding and utilising natural fertility information or practising the withdrawal method.

If your teen chooses to use fertility awareness to avoid conception, they will be charting fertility signs in their body to accurately determine when they are fertile in each menstrual cycle. At that time, they would either avoid having intercourse or use a barrier form of contraception. This method requires dedication and discipline to engage in the learning process, which is best achieved through a qualified fertility educator (rather than via a book or the Internet). Fertility awareness can also help with managing PMS.

The withdrawal method relies on the penis being withdrawn from the vagina before ejaculation. This can be problematic, as feelings may be running high in that moment . . . In addition, a small amount of pre-ejaculate exits the penis (to clear the urethra of urine) immediately prior to ejaculation. It's possible that this may contain some sperm, and, if there is cervical mucus present, this can help the sperm move up the female reproductive tract and could result in pregnancy. As such, withdrawal is not recommended as a reliable method of contraception.

Permanent contraceptive

The options for permanent contraception include laparoscopic clip sterilisation (for females) or vasectomy (for males). They involve, respectively, the clipping, blocking or tying of the fallopian tubes or the vas deferens. These procedures are generally reserved for those who have completed their families and are not usually an option for teens. Although reversal (through surgery) may be possible, results are not guaranteed.

When stating the efficacy of a product, most contraceptive literature will draw a distinction between 'perfect use' and 'actual use', taking into account that many people don't use contraception exactly as prescribed. For example, daily pills can get forgotten. Doubling up on contraception types is often recommended (except for doubling up on condoms) — for example, using condoms while on the OCP. Here are a few other contraception considerations:

- Some methods require pre-planning to use (e.g., the diaphragm or condom), whereas others don't interrupt activity (e.g., the implant).
- Similarly, some methods rely on the user remembering to take/ use them (e.g., the pill), whereas others are 'fit and forget' (e.g., an IUD).
- Some methods are prescribed for a dual purpose or specifically as a medication — for example, to treat acne, or painful or irregular periods, or to assist in the management of those with endometriosis or PCOS.
- Contraception should not be assumed to be the sole responsibility of one partner or the other. At the same time, it is perfectly reasonable for a female to carry a condom.

If this is not a conversation that either you or your teen feel comfortable having, there are some excellent resources for more detailed information. In addition, in New Zealand there are local Family Planning clinics and Youth Hubs that are confidential and free for those under 22 years (see Resources/Rauemi, page 244).

Emergency contraception

Accidents happen, and so it makes sense to ensure your teen is aware of emergency contraception. There are two types of back-up methods available when there are concerns because unprotected sex has occurred or contraception has failed:

- **Emergency contraceptive pill (ECP):** This is a single tablet that can be accessed from the GP, either free or at the cost of a prescription, or directly from a chemist without a consultation with a doctor or nurse. The latter is more expensive. You may know it as the 'morning-after pill'; however, as it is suitable for use up to three days (in some cases four) after the event, it has been renamed. It has slightly lower rates of effectiveness in those who weigh over 70 kilograms. Note that the ECP is not designed for multiple uses (although it can be taken more than once). If your teen is repeatedly using it, it is highly recommended they switch to an effective contraceptive method. This pill should not be confused with a medical termination, which uses a completely different medication and terminates a pregnancy at an early stage.
- **Insertion of an IUD:** Obviously this option is more invasive than the ECP, but can be useful for those who weigh over 70 kilograms and is also effective up to seven days after unprotected intercourse. It requires a GP or a clinic appointment. Generally, once in, the IUD remains inserted for ongoing pregnancy prevention; or it can be removed when the next period starts.

Teen pregnancy

In 2019, the rate of live births for the 15–19-year-old female popula-tion in New Zealand was 12.76 per 1000 population. Although this is well down from 33.11 in 2008,[24] our teen pregnancy rate is still higher than in many other OECD countries.[25]

If your teen has found the courage to let you know they are (or their partner is) pregnant, they will be needing your support more than ever. You may initially feel overwhelmed. You can bet they do. Emotions are likely to be running high, but your teen now has a plethora of decisions to make, particularly if they are the one who is pregnant. They may be fearing unpleasant opinions from others, including their peers, teachers and some of their wider whānau, so your non-judgemental communication is going to be key.

There are options that your teen will need to consider seriously, including whether they wish to continue the pregnancy and then parent (either with their partner or alone), choose adoption, or terminate the pregnancy (which is free in New Zealand for anyone eligible for funded healthcare). Many factors will play a part in their decision and your guidance.

Seeking medical advice promptly (initially through their GP or a local Family Planning clinic; see Resources/Rauemi, page 244) allows them to access all their options in good time. Teen pregnancy comes with higher health risks, including the chance of miscarriage, so healthcare supports and knowledge of supplements and lifestyle changes are important. And if they decide on a termination, they have more options earlier in the pregnancy: at less than seven weeks (from conception) they may be able to take the medical route (tablets) rather than surgery. Whatever they choose, they will need wraparound understanding, support (including counselling) and care, potentially also including schooling options. In some locations there are specific teen pregnancy units attached to schools, or there are online education routes.

Avoiding sexually transmitted infections

There is a health education issue here, which ideally your teen needs to understand prior to becoming sexually intimate with another: once sexually active, regularly checking their sexual health is all part of caring for themselves and others. This is true whether they are currently abstinent, having sexual relations with one partner in a committed long-term relationship, or exploring other options. The future is not predictable, and due to the serious implications of STIs, testing should be viewed as just another health check.

The reality is that although nobody sets out to contract an infection, STIs are common among those who are sexually active. And though it may not be the most pleasant subject to talk about, it's an important one. After all, more than half of us will contract an STI at some point in our lives.[26]

Caused by microbes (such as bacteria and viruses) or external parasites, STIs can be passed on during penetrative sex, or simply through intimate bodily contact, particularly where bodily fluids are shared. They can infect the genital and anal area, the mouth and the throat. In New Zealand, they are most common among young people up to the age of 25,[27] and teens aged 15–19 are also particularly at risk,[28] but STIs can happen to anyone. Symptoms may be obvious or entirely absent, which means that you can pass STIs on without ever having realised it.

There are three types of STI:

- **Parasitic:** These involve external parasites such as pubic lice and scabies. They are treatable and curable, usually by means of creams and lotions.
- **Bacterial:** These include chlamydia, gonorrhoea and syphilis. They are treatable and curable, although there are some concerns that certain bacterial strains are becoming resistant to the antibiotics currently available.
- **Viral:** These include herpes, human papillomavirus (HPV) and human immunodeficiency virus (HIV). They are currently

incurable but have many treatment options. There are ongoing research programmes into preventative and curative measures. For example, there is now a vaccine for HPV, which is highly effective for those not already infected. It is offered to young people from intermediate-school age with the intent to vaccinate before exposure (it is funded in New Zealand for anyone aged nine to 26 years old). It targets the HPV types that are most widely known to cause cancers of the cervix, mouth and throat, as well as genital warts.[29] Also, in regard to HIV, prevention and treatment have vastly improved in recent years, with medications such as PrEP (taken to protect someone from contracting the infection) and antiretrovirals (drugs designed to treat someone with HIV and, in many cases, bring their viral load to undetectable levels, which means they will not transmit the infection via sex). Herpes can cause uncomfortable blisters around the genitals and surrounding areas, but again there are medications available that can moderate symptoms and greatly reduce the incidence of flare-ups.

Try not to present any information in a way that might put your teen off even thinking about ever having sex. But do make sure that your teen is informed about how STIs can occur and strategies to prevent infection (e.g., use of a condom or a dam*). Talking about this subject in a non-judgemental and factual context will mean that they know they can come to you to talk about any concerns. It can also help to break down stigma and means that they can be an accurate source of information for others. It should not be a taboo subject, even though it is a private one. It's about their safety: STIs can impact on health and fertility, and can even be life-threatening. A really important point to

---

* A dental dam is a thin sheet of latex that was initially produced for dentists to isolate a tooth, hence the name. Designed for protection against STIs (as opposed to pregnancy), it is placed as a barrier between the mouth or fingers and the vulva. If a dam is not available, it is possible to cut a condom in half longways and use this instead. This is obviously the only time to go near a condom with scissors!

stress is that many of those infected have no symptoms, but can still suffer the impact of infections and also pass them on. Ensure that your teen is aware that free STI testing in New Zealand is available for those under 22 years old. There are some clinics set up specifically for teens and young adults that are designed to be welcoming, confidential and non-judgemental. Testing is generally a fairly straightforward process, involving, for example, a swab, a urine test or a blood test.

Again, if this conversation is not one you or your teen feel comfortable with, there are many resources available (see Resources/ Rauemi, page 244).

Intimate body care

There is probably going to be a time when your teen will want to have autonomy over their healthcare, including attending medical appointments by themselves. This is entirely normal, and it's never too soon to start conversations around personal and sexual health. They are moving into adulthood and teens benefit from knowing about things in advance, including aspects of adult body care they won't access until a bit later (such as cervical screening programmes). You can talk to them about the various practices you do to monitor your health. Inform them about any pertinent family health history and susceptibilities without scaring them. Most are already aware about diseases such as cancer, and most are aware of various health promotion initiatives in the community, even if these are not specifically targeted at them.

Not only is this good for their general knowledge, but being properly informed can also allay fears: for example, some girls can be worried about a perfectly natural lump behind their nipple at puberty (breast buds) and may confuse this with breast cancer information they have come across. If they are confident that they can raise these concerns with you, you can make sure that they are not worried unnecessarily. As they mature, inform them how important it is to spend time getting to know their body and thereby establish what is normal for them (for example, young men should regularly check their testicles for lumps). For both testicular and breast care, there's plenty of information online as to how and when to do this. If they are familiar with their body, they are more likely to be able to recognise any untoward changes. Prompt action generally means an easier journey in dealing with health issues.

As with all information in this chapter, the following is useful for all genders to know; after all, your teen may find themselves supporting a partner or friend in the future. Again, if this feels like an awkward conversation for either of you, check out the Resources/ Rauemi section (page 244) for alternative approaches.

Some sex-specific guidance includes:

- **Penis health**: In an uncircumcised penis, the foreskin should be pulled back gently and washed underneath to remove any smegma. This cheesy-looking substance is a natural lubricant that keeps the penis moist, but if it builds up under the foreskin, it can start to smell and become a breeding ground for bacteria. Your teen may be wanting to take a bit more control of the types of underwear they wear, and there may be some specific types needed for protection during particular sports. Whatever they choose to wear, it's important that they are addressing their hygiene by changing their underwear and showering or bathing daily.

- **Testicular health**: In New Zealand, testicular cancer is the most commonly diagnosed cancer in men between the ages of 15 and 44. While rare, if detected and treated early it is one of the most survivable and curable forms of cancer. The symptoms vary — there may or may not be localised pain, for instance — but anything that feels unusual, such as an enlarged or lumpy testicle, or a dull lower back pain, warrants a visit to a healthcare professional. This means that your teen needs to get to know their testes and scrotum, preferably by checking them (e.g., in the shower) every month or so.

- **Vulva and vaginal health**: A daily bath or shower, washing around the vulva, and wearing cotton or breathable underwear takes care of genital hygiene. Make sure your teen knows that the vagina cleans itself and does not require douching. When the vagina is healthy, it keeps the perfect balance of bacteria and pH levels and this can be disturbed if additional elements are introduced. If your teen does notice a discharge that is out of the ordinary, it's always best to see the GP: it may just be thrush (*Candida*), a yeast infection usually accompanied by itching, which is quite common and easily treated with an antifungal cream (some people are more prone to it than others). It's also worth a word with them about not removing pubic hair: it's there for good reason, reducing friction during sex and helping to keep bacteria and other pathogens at bay.[30] If they really want to, encourage them just to give it a trim rather than eliminate it altogether.

- **Breast health**: Usually breast self-examination should start in the twenties, but if your teen is keen they can begin earlier. Although it is extremely rare to get breast cancer this young, establishing a monthly breast self-examination is a good routine to get into. It is important for them to understand that, since they're still maturing, their breasts may still be growing. Also, as breasts are affected by hormones, timing is important: day eight of the menstrual cycle is ideal, which is when they are least likely to be overly tender and lumpy: turn a figure 8 on its side and they even have a visual reminder!

- **Pelvic examination**: Your teen may require a pelvic examination for health or contraceptive reasons. Some contraceptive options (such as the IUD) are inserted using a speculum, for example. Give your teen information beforehand to ensure they can be an active partner in their own healthcare. Encourage them to find out in advance what might happen, if there's likely to be any discomfort and what they can do to prepare. The following online tips from the Ministry of Health may be useful:

- *Wear a skirt you can leave on.*
- *Use the sheet or blanket provided to keep you covered and comfortable.*
- *Ask for a female [doctor or nurse].*
- *Request someone from your culture.*
- *Try to breathe deeply and relax your legs.*
- *Try lying on your side [if this is an option].*
- *Take a friend or whānau for support.*[31]

- **Cervical screening**: Research has shown that treating cervical issues before the age of 25 is mostly counterproductive.[32] For this reason, in New Zealand cervical screening now doesn't start until someone is over the age of 25 and has become sexually active. Times are changing when it comes to the cervical smear. Almost all cervical cancer is caused by HPV, so in New Zealand from 2023, testing will concentrate on the presence of this virus. This will not necessitate the same type of examination and procedure: instead, swabs will be sufficient, with the option to self-test. The frequency of screening will also move from three-yearly to five-yearly, including for those who have been vaccinated against HPV (as this doesn't cover every single possible cancer-causing strand). This screening is for women and trans or non-binary people with a cervix, and also applies to those who have had sex only with other women.

Kōrero with Molly

I strongly recall getting my first smear was nerve-racking, and I was lucky to have had a fairly in-depth understanding of how it all worked and what to expect. A lot of my friends went in for their first pelvic exam or smear knowing next to nothing. I was also lucky to have a lovely doctor looking after me and she explained the process further as we went along. I walked out of the clinic feeling like a pretty powerful woman. It's easy to ignore how serious this self-care is, especially when the procedure can feel a little uncomfortable, which is why I am that friend that reminds my group to book the appointment. It's also a good idea if you stick a little card with some breast examination info on the shower so you remember to do it once your period has finished.

Thinking back, and even now, while my female peers knew the bare minimum, it often felt like my male peers knew even less! It's difficult for me to speak to the body education that male teens receive, but I do know that the culture impacts everyone. Perhaps deeper conversations about sex and intimate body care require a sense of maturity and vulnerability that can be harder to access as a teen. At the end of the day, we are all growing and going through similar changes, which is nothing to be ashamed of. In my opinion, the earlier we learn about how to look after ourselves and others, the better.

How can I have this conversation? / Me pēhea tēnei matakahi?

If teenagers have the tools and knowledge, they can make good decisions about health. As previously mentioned, teens themselves are asking for more non-judgemental, open communication from adults about their personal and sexual health.

> **This is why we need to have the conversation,
> and primarily the message here is one of
> normalising and destigmatising messages.**

Points to keep the conversation going

- Start conversations young. This can **take embarrassment out of the topic** and allow for freer discussions.
- Use **teachable opportunities**: for instance, you may know someone who's about to have a baby or has recently announced

a pregnancy. Share with your teen when you have an appointment for a smear, mammogram or prostate check, so that they think of these things as part of a normal routine.

- Always make sure they know the **correct terminology** for body parts, including the more intimate ones, when talking about their anatomy. A teen should feel comfortable calling their 'willy' a 'penis', or referring to their 'boobs' as 'breasts'. In addition, make sure that they are naming these body parts accurately. For example, the anatomy between a female's legs is collectively called the vulva, not the vagina. The vagina is the internal canal that has its opening as part of the vulva and leads to the base of the uterus (the cervix).

- When it comes to talking about **periods**, look to reduce stigma and shame: discuss periods openly. For example, keep up to speed on media coverage of period poverty. Include those without a uterus in these discussions, as this will encourage respect and empathy. Find out if your teen's school is taking the same approach. If you are a menstruator, consider sharing with your teen that you have your period and, for example, are feeling like an early night. Have products in the bathroom and don't hide them away; have a bin with a lid in there, too, for easy disposal. When shopping for products, don't be embarrassed or shy about collecting them from the shelf.

- If your teen has a **disability**, access additional information and support as necessary. Ensure they have a full and thorough understanding of how their individual body works so they can meet their personal, sexual and health needs. For example, it may be that certain period products work better for them.

- It is also important to **avoid talking to your teen in a stereotypical gendered way**. Try not to make comments or assumptions based on outdated and incorrect views (for example, that it is somehow 'unladylike' for girls to carry condoms, but it is 'macho' for boys to do so — their health and safety are what is important here).

- If your family has specific circumstances such as same-sex parents, or your teen is LGBTQIA+, there are lots of resources, supports and services available.
- Try not to associate personal and sexual health only with anatomy and physiology. It's also about your teen's values and feelings, and their getting comfortable with themselves. Talk about your family's attitudes, values, beliefs and circumstances. Think together about other families' situations — and if they differ from yours, how. **Celebrate differences**.
- Express to your teen that an intimate moment like having **sex is supposed to be fun** and feel good (or even great) for both them and their partner/s. Yes, there may be some embarrassment, funny noises and odd smells, but the experience should be more positive than negative.
- Sexual contact needs to take place **within the context of consent and within the law**. This is discussed in more detail in the chapter on consent (see page 268).
- Have a **conversation about boundaries** when it comes to overnight stays at your home or if your teen asks to stay over at their partner's. There's a lot to consider before this chat happens, and your teen needs to feel heard too, even if you don't agree with each other. If they feel heard, they will be more likely to listen to you, and understand and respect your decisions (whether this be a hard no or a conditional yes, for instance with specific sleeping arrangements). It's about recognising that teens become sexually active at different stages; but, ultimately, when it's your house, it's your rules.
- **Share resources with your teen**, allowing them their privacy but at the same time trying to be open and approachable yourself. They may prefer a new GP from the one you all use as a family. There are also specialised clinics that welcome youth, such as Youth One Stop Shops and Family Planning clinics (see Resources/Rauemi, page 244).

Talking box questions

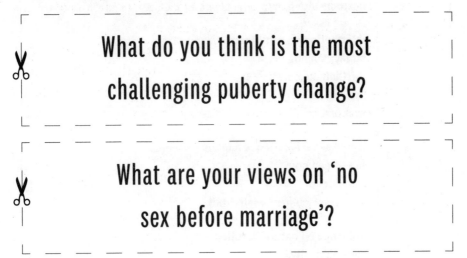

What do you think is the most
challenging puberty change?

What are your views on 'no
sex before marriage'?

Resources / Rauemi

There's loads of information (and misinformation) on the Internet about personal and sexual health, with some sites aimed at helping parents talk to teens and others for teens themselves. You may want to direct your teen towards the more reputable sites (some of which are listed overleaf). The library is another good option. A positive development around menarche is the introduction of period preparation pamper kits (such as the Nest.Box), which contain a variety of menstrual products alongside other goodies and information.[33]

ONLINE	The Nest.Box is a period preparation pamper kit: nestconsulting.nz/product/nest-box Information on contraception and STIs: familyplanning.org.nz justthefacts.co.nz hpv.org.nz nzaf.org.nz Useful sex education resources for teens: scarleteen.com bishuk.com villainesse.com/therealsextalk Guidance on natural fertility: naturalfertility.co.nz Breast examination explained: breastcancerfoundation.org.nz/breast-awareness/taking-care-of-your-breasts/under-20 Testicular examination explained: kidshealth.org/en/teens/tse.html A support hub for endometriosis sufferers: nzendo.org.nz Guidance on PCOS: womens-health.org.nz/health-topics/polycystic-ovarian-syndrome
CLINICS	Family Planning: familyplanning.org.nz New Zealand Sexual Health Services: nzshs.org/clinics Youth One Stop Shops: healthnavigator.org.nz/healthy-living/y/youth-one-stop-shops Termination of pregnancy services: abortion.org.nz

10. RAINBOW TEENS

#LGBTQIA+ #queerculture #pride

*'We have to be visible. We should
not be ashamed of who we are.'*
— SYLVIA RIVERA

Kōrero with Molly

A lot of movies and TV show episodes I watched as a kid, in retrospect, were really perpetuating harmful stereotypes about the rainbow community and normalising discriminatory behaviour. Looking back now, I'm horrified to think what influence this must have had on impressionable audiences. I hope that nowadays we are more able to have critical conversations about how important it is to recognise all types of diversity.

Having attended a couple of schools as a teenager, I got to see how different school cultures around sexuality and gender can impact on students. There were places where 'gay' or 'lesbian' were treated like dirty words, and we weren't even given the space to be curious about what they meant. There were also places that celebrated everything that made us different.

For the most part, getting to know yourself and what works for you can be a long journey. A lot of my queer friends and whānau feel comfortable and confident in labelling themselves LGBTQIA+. I can respect that by addressing them how they like to be addressed and using their pronouns. Everyone is different and we all deserve respect and equal opportunity at happiness. Our understandings of gender and sexuality are constantly growing and changing, which can feel intimidating. For me, it's about keeping an open mind and an open heart.

What do you mean by that? /
He aha te tikanga o tāu kōrero?

Diversity (see page 360) is all the ways we're different from one another, including race, ethnicity, religion, culture, physical ability, mental ability, family make-up, socio-economic status, sex, gender and sexuality. We know it's important to avoid stereotyping, to embrace and accept differences in people, and to celebrate individuals for who they are. Generally, stereotypes are a problematic attempt to 'box' people, and these boxes can be limiting and unhelpful. They may also be totally inaccurate, which in turn can be detrimental to those who find themselves expected to fit in with others' preconceived ideas. It is healthy to challenge stereotypes.

A simplistic example of this is the use of the colours pink and blue, from gender-reveal parties through to clothing and toys, to reinforce stereotypical expectations in the behaviour of girls and boys.[1] It is a heteronormative assumption that pink girls and blue boys will grow up to be cisgender* and have heterosexual relationships. However, this is to ignore the fact that gender and sexual identity are multifaceted, and involve a number of dimensions that may overlap. It's all a mixture of how we see ourselves and how we wish others to see us, along with who we might be attracted to sexually, physically, emotionally, romantically or intellectually. And some of us may not feel attracted to others in this way at all. As concepts associated with being female and male are more readily challenged, space is created for teens to discover and explore much more freely their own sexual and gender identity and the way they choose to express it. Whatever their, or your, individual views, our teens are part of a changing world, one that takes a much more fluid approach to the concepts around defining identity.

Families can all look a little different: some have one parent, some have two or more, and in some cases the parents are the same gender

---

* **Cisgender** — a person whose gender aligns with their biological sex; for example, someone born with a vulva identifying as female, or someone born with a penis identifying as male.

as each other. Some teens are being parented by grandparents, grow up in foster care, or live in a group home or at boarding school. Teens are entitled to feel good about themselves, and as parents, our desired outcomes for them will undoubtedly be similar: that they are safe, healthy, resilient, open-minded and kind. Ultimately, we want our teens to be non-judgemental and respectful to others.

Tell me more . . . / Kōrero mai anō . . .

In New Zealand, as affirmed by the Human Rights Commission, all people 'have the same rights and freedoms, regardless of their sexual orientation, gender identity and expression, and sex characteristics'. These rights are protected by the New Zealand Human Rights Act 1993, which states: 'It is unlawful to discriminate on the ground of sexual orientation.'[2] The age of consent (16 years) applies to everyone, again regardless of their sexual orientation, gender identity and expression, and sex characteristics. It is legal for both same-sex couples and heterosexual couples to marry, and to adopt children. Aotearoa is considered by many to be a socially progressive country. Examples of this include the passing of recent legislation relating to the processes of self-identification on formal documents and the banning of conversion therapy. New Zealand was the first place in the world to fly the intersex flag in Parliament. It was the first country to have an openly transgender member of Parliament, and currently also has several other MPs and local politicians who proudly represent the rainbow community. This openness, and that of some LGBTQIA+ celebrities and sports stars, has provided role models for rainbow teens; it has also helped on the journey to destigmatising non-heteronormative views on sexuality and gender. In June 2021 Lonely Planet rated New Zealand second on the list of the most gay-friendly places in the world.[3] This is a really positive non-discriminatory message. With all that said, transphobia and homophobia are still prevalent, and we all must be aware of this. There is much work to be done to continue to dismantle harmful discrimination. As reported in a 2019 survey conducted at the University of Waikato, many of our rainbow youth across Aotearoa experience a variety of barriers to gender-affirming care — for example, prohibitive cost, lack of support from whānau and lack of information.[4]

DEFINITIONS		
Anatomical/biological sex		This is different from gender. The Safe Zone Project describes it as 'a medical term used to refer to the chromosomal, hormonal and anatomical characteristics that are used to classify an individual as female or male or intersex. Often referred to as simply "sex", "physical sex", "anatomical sex", or specifically as "sex assigned at birth".'[5]
Gender can be understood by looking at identity and expression:	Gender identity	A person's sense of self: being feminine, masculine or non-binary. Gender identity doesn't necessarily match with that person's chromosomes or genitalia, or how they present themselves.
	Gender expression & gender presentation	The way someone expresses their gender, for example, through clothing, hairstyle, make-up, behaviour, body language or voice. Typically a person will express their gender in a feminine, androgynous or masculine way, or they may choose to switch between these.
Attraction/sexual orientation		A person's sexual and romantic sense of self and who they choose to share it with.

Research has found that some students are aware of the nature of their sexual attractions before they leave primary school, while others will be at high school and some will be older still before they feel they understand their sexual identity, and whether it is fluid. The Kinsey scale, developed by Alfred Kinsey and others, explains more about the fluidity of sexuality.[6] A recent New Zealand survey found that '16 per cent of 13–18-year-olds identified as same- or multiple-sex attracted, not sure, or not attracted to any sex'.[7] Another found that 'young people aged 18–24 were more likely to identify as bisexual or gay/lesbian than any other age group'.[8]

Your teen may identify with the rainbow community, or have friends and peers that do. With this in mind, it's really useful for them and you to be informed. The table opposite provides some definitions.

The rainbow community is an umbrella and inclusive term for those who are LGBTQIA+. The term 'queer' was once used by homophobic people as a derogatory and hateful slur. It has been reclaimed by the rainbow community and is often used as another umbrella and inclusive term (although, given its history, it's best to check before using this term). Language can provide validation for an individual's identity: some people find empowerment referring to themselves in a particular way, while others use words more fluidly and feel labels do not define a person. Some of the terms used within the LGBTQIA+ spectrum are listed and loosely defined in the box below.

A rainbow glossary

LGBTQIA+ stands for: L = lesbian, G = gay, B = bisexual, T = transgender, Q = queer or questioning, I = intersex and A = asexual, with the + acknowledging that there will never be a definitive list of the ways people choose to describe themselves in the rainbow community.

The terms denoted by LGBTQIA+ 'may mean different things to different people', according to the New Zealand rainbow support organisation OutLine, which offers the following glossary of 'generalised descriptions':

AFAB — *a person who was assigned female at birth but whose gender identity is that of a man. Terms sometimes used: trans man. [Appears in original source as FtM, but AFAB is generally preferred.]*

THE KIDS WILL BE ALL RIGHT

AMAB — *a person who was assigned male at birth but whose gender identity is that of a female. Terms sometimes used: trans woman. [Appears in original source as MtF, but AMAB is generally preferred.]*

Asexual — *a person who experiences no sexual attraction to other people, and/or no desire for sexual activity. However, the term asexual to some is an umbrella term and includes demisexual, graysexual (see definitions below). (Also known as 'ace'.)*

Bisexual — *a person who experiences romantic attraction and/or sexual attraction towards people of more than one gender.*

Cross-dresser — *a person who wears clothing (accessories/make-up) that is typical of the opposite gender. May do this full-time or only sometimes.*

Demisexual — *a person who only experiences sexual attraction to people with whom they form an emotional connection.*

Gay — *a person who experiences sexual and/or romantic attraction to those of the same sex. Predominantly this term is used for those who identify as male.*

Gender fluid — *a person who does not identify as having a fixed gender.*

Gender nonconforming, gender variant — *a person whose gender expression is not limited by the stereotypical masculine and feminine gender 'norms'.*

Genderqueer — *an umbrella term for people whose gender identity and/or expression is different to the binary male or female.*

Graysexual — *sometimes referred to as the grey space between sexuality and asexuality. People who identify as graysexual (or 'grey-A' or 'gray ace') sometimes experience sexual attraction towards others (some say infrequently or mildly), and may or may not have any desire to have sexual contact.*

Intersex — *a person who is born with sex chromosomes, external genitalia and/or internal reproductive parts of both genders.*

Lesbian — *a person who identifies as female who is sexually and/or romantically attracted to others who identify as female.*

Non-binary — *a description of a gender identity that [exists outside of the gender binary].*

Pansexual — *a person whose sexual and/or romantic attraction is based on personalised traits/connection/physical characteristics, regardless of the other person's assigned gender or gender identity.*

Polysexual — *a term that means a lot of different things to different people. Some say it is the attraction to more than one gender, therefore bisexuality and pansexuality are under this umbrella term. Some believe it is the attraction to some but not all gender expressions.*

Queer — *an umbrella term encompassing all identities and expressions outside of the heterosexual, monogamous and gender-normative majority.*

Questioning — *a person who is in the process of questioning their gender identity, sexuality and/or gender expression.*

Straight — *a person who experiences sexual and/or romantic attraction to those of the opposite sex.*

Transgender — *a person whose gender identity differs from that which was assigned at birth.*
- *Transfeminine* — *a term for a range of identities where the female identity or femininity is prominent.*
- *Transmasculine* — *a term for a range of identities where the male identity or masculinity is prominent.*

Transsexual — *a person whose gender identity differs from that which was assigned at birth and who has taken steps to physically transition their body to that which more closely aligns with their gender identity.*[9]

In addition, OutLine explains some Māori and Pasifika gender diversity terms as follows:

Ira tāngata: Gender diverse. (Note the macron over the 'a' in 'tāngata' defines the broadness/diverseness of gender.) How people live their life.

Takatāpui: The traditional meaning of takatāpui is 'intimate companion of the same sex'. Many Māori people have adopted this term to describe themselves, instead of or in addition to terms such as lesbian, gay, bisexual, queer, or transgender. It refers to cultural and sexual/gender identity. Also spelt takataapui.

Tangata ira tāne: Someone born biologically female who has a male gender identity.

Whakawahine, hinehī, hinehua: Terms describing someone born biologically male who has a female gender identity.

The following terms have wider meaning and are best understood within their cultural context.

- *Fa'afafine (Samoa, American Samoa, and Tokelau);*
- *Fakaleiti or leiti (Tonga);*
- *Fakafifine (Niue);*
- *Akava'ine (Cook Islands);*
- *Mahu (Tahiti and Hawai'i);*
- *Vakasalewalewa (Fiji);*
- *Palopa (Papua New Guinea).*[10]

A word on pronouns

Try not to make assumptions about how to address someone, as getting it right is integral to your recognition of their identity and gender expression. It's important to use the pronouns that the person is comfortable with (see table below).[11] To misgender someone is to use their incorrect pronoun. Deadnaming is when someone's 'old name' is used after they have informed you of their new name. Oftentimes this applies to someone who is transgender or non-binary and has changed their birth name to a name they are now using. Both misgendering and deadnaming can be undermining and hurtful.

PRONOUNS				
Subject	She	He	They	Zhe (pronounced 'zee')
Object	Her	Him	Them	Hir (pronounced 'here')
Possessive	Hers	His	Theirs	Hirs (pronounced 'here's')

Health Navigator provides some helpful advice around the importance of pronouns and what to do if you make a mistake:

> *Try not to make any assumptions about a person and what*
> *pronouns they might use. Stop and think before 'assigning' someone*
> *to a gender. If you make a mistake, apologise, correct yourself and*

move on. Don't dwell on it as this may embarrass the person. If you
witness someone using incorrect pronouns in relation to someone
else, let them know what the correct pronouns are. This is especially
important if it's being done repeatedly or maliciously.[12]

Wellbeing and mental health

Wellbeing and mental health (see Chapter 8) are important for all teens, but there are additional pressures for those who are part of the rainbow community. A Ministry of Health report found that LGBTQIA+ people 'have higher lifetime risk for mental health problems, including depression, anxiety, suicide and self-harm, substance misuse and eating disorders than their peers'.[13] As noted in Chapter 4, rainbow teens are more likely to be bullied. In New Zealand, according to the Youth19 survey, 'almost half of queer youth had seriously thought about taking their own life in the previous year'.[14] Another recent report found that '71 per cent of trans and non-binary people reported high or very high psychological distress, compared with only 8 per cent of the general population in Aotearoa. Fifty-six per cent had seriously thought about attempting suicide in the last 12 months; 37 per cent had attempted suicide at some point.'[15]

Although rainbow teens are disproportionately represented in these upsetting statistics, these issues are starting to be recognised, and measures are being put in place to improve support networks, to increase public awareness and to tackle discrimination. There are new initiatives in schools in Aotearoa, such as the Ministry of Education's Inclusive Education programme.[16] In addition, your teen's school may take part in Pink Shirt Day (see page 91) or be considering initiatives such as gender-neutral uniform choices. All these are reflective of how we are becoming more inclusive of our diverse community.

Coming out

Coming out refers to someone choosing to be more open about their sexual orientation and/or gender identity. If someone feels confident enough to communicate this to you, you should take it as a huge compliment, since it indicates that they feel secure in their relationship with you. This is especially true if they are your teen: it's a huge decision on their part to share this with you.

If your teen has come out or is exploring their identity, or wants to support friends who are on this journey, there are many resources available, including helplines (see page 393). You can also help simply by listening and providing a judgement-free space.

The UK support organisation Stonewall offers some advice to parents who may be struggling with their teen's disclosure:

> *The truth is, if you've got a problem with the idea of your child being LGBTQIA+, you're going to have to live with it and accept it. The best thing you can do is put your feelings to one side and remember that, regardless of your child's sexual orientation and gender identity, you love them and want them to be happy. As for other family members: if they don't react well initially, put some rules in place and establish what can and can't be said in front of your child.*[17]

Every family has its own values and its own way of dealing with personal and relationship issues, and if your teen has come out to you, you will probably have the best idea of how to respond. But if you find it difficult, here are a few dos and don'ts that may be useful:

- **Don't ignore it.** It's particularly important to acknowledge your teen when they come out to you. Saying nothing (whether or not you are happy with the news) could leave them agonising over whether you are okay with it, or not, or even whether you were listening in the first place. At the same time, they may be expecting you to be a little lost for words, and sometimes the best thing is just to acknowledge as best you can and suggest a time that suits you both to catch up and talk further. After all, there will be lots more conversations on this topic.[18]
- **Don't assume it's just a phase.** For most teens, this will be

one of the hardest secrets they've had to disclose, so they're not taking it lightly. At the same time, they may be still be on a gender-questioning journey, and are some way short of knowing themselves fully. That makes it all the more important to assure them you're walking beside them on their journey, and you're not going to try to 'talk them out of it'.[19]

- **Do respect their terminology.** If they want to change their pronouns, then you owe it to them to practise getting them right. If they choose to use a label to define their gender or sexuality, then that's the label you need to be using, too. Make sure other family members do likewise.[20]

- **Don't say, 'We already knew.'** (Even if you did.) If you downplay the news, they may feel deflated and just a little smaller. The act of coming out belongs to them — this really is their big day out — so let them own it.[21]

- **Do tell them you love them.** You don't need to know all the correct LGBTQIA+ terms off by heart; you simply need to reassure your teen that you love and accept them, no matter what, and that you are always there for them if they need you. It is hugely important that they hear this.

- **Do ask them how you can support them.** You may be the first person they've come to and they may need your help in making the next move. Or they may already have told others, having been nervous about how you'd react. Either way, it's your job now to be their rock, and if there are practical steps you can take — talking to a teacher about bullying or a school support network, perhaps, or paving the way with more strait-laced members of the whānau — then take them.[22]

- **Do honour their discretion.** If they don't want to come out more openly (again, extended family members can be the hardest sometimes), then you need to keep their confidence until they're ready. **Outing** them — making their gender/sexual identity public against their wishes, or before they are ready to out themselves — is effectively taking away their choice about something that should very much be on their own terms. To do this, even accidentally, can be devastating, and you may have to work hard to regain their confidence and trust. By the same token, respect their wishes if they do ask you to tell others; it may hurt them considerably if they feel you're ashamed to go public with the news. You can also help them if they're struggling to find ways of telling others; perhaps the two of you could try some role-playing.[23]

Ultimately, be proud that you have such an awesome relationship with your teen that they felt comfortable enough to have this conversation with you. Remember that you will need support too, so that you can help them (and be a role model to other parents of rainbow teens). Should your teen choose to share more widely, encourage them to give people a little space and time to absorb their news. For some people, it can take a while to process news about another's diverse identity — this does not mean, however, that once they have had a chance to do so, they will not become a supportive advocate. Help your teen to feel safe should they receive a less-than-positive initial response: remind them that this may not be a person's final response.

Kōrero with Molly

I always felt that, in my house, there were no conversations that were off-limits or out of bounds. There was an ongoing dialogue that I could rely on and ask questions about as I grew into the queer woman I am today. However, I found picking a label to be pretty stressful — in fact, it made me quite miserable. I don't remember seeing much media representation of lesbian and bisexual women. I just couldn't squeeze myself into any of the categories that had been laid out for the rainbow community. It took a lot of time to make my peace with that, and I think that the same is often true for many teens and young adults.

Safety

Worldwide, the culture of acceptance for the rainbow community is still relatively new, and not all countries take the same progressive stance as Aotearoa. Historically, LGBTQIA+ individuals and groups have faced ostracism and discrimination. While there is more social and legal support for our rainbow communities, so many are still struggling with homophobia and transphobia today — particularly those who are from transgender or gender non-conforming communities and, even more so, transgender people of colour.[24] Community inclusion is an important part of identity and health. The way forward should be one that ensures our teens are respectful and mindful of their peers with the knowledge that we are all different. Whatever a person's personal belief system, there is never a reason to treat another badly. It's important to celebrate all individuals.

Being an ally

In this context, an ally is someone who does not identify as LGBTQIA+, but stands up for the rights of the rainbow community. When well-known figures use their platform to speak out, it sends a clear message of support and encourages acceptance:

> **'It's so important to be proud of the person you are.'**
> — THE DUKE OF CAMBRIDGE (STRAIGHT ALLY OF THE YEAR AT THE 2017 BRITISH LGBT AWARDS)

Another way to show solidarity is through brand choice: UK research showed that two-thirds of LGBTQIA+ respondents 'said they would not use products or services from brands that have been reported as discriminatory or homophobic'.[25] There are also fun ways to show support: for example, by attending one of the many LGBTQIA+ events held throughout the year, including Pride festivals around the country. On an individual level, teens can also stick up for one another to create an inclusive environment that celebrates people's differences.

How can I have this conversation? / Me pēhea tēnei matakahi?

This chapter may be informative for some and challenging for others. It's not unusual for parents to state that they feel uncomfortable or out of their depth when considering this topic, firstly because of its sensitive and private nature, and secondly because the terminology and understanding continue to evolve. It's all about recognising individuality.

> **This is why we need to have the conversation,**
> **and primarily the message here is one of**
> **respecting others' wishes to be themselves.**

Opening up these avenues of conversation also gives your teen a chance to share with you what they already know about the issues of gender stereotyping, diversity and acceptance — you may even find you can learn lots from them.

Points to keep the conversation going

- As always, there are plenty of **teachable moments**: it might be that your teen shares about someone they know at school who has come out, a storyline in a film may prompt discussion, or perhaps you have seen an advert for a Pride festival. You could have a discussion about some of the rainbow flags that are now more frequently seen in the community, particularly those representing intersectionality.
- Be **mindful about male/female stereotyping**:
  - Try not to use expressions such as 'be a man' or 'be more ladylike'; you could also discuss with your teen the '#likeagirl' campaign.
  - While shopping with your teen, it can be fun to challenge them to point out what products are marketed stereotypically towards male or female demographics, and get them to discuss the impacts this might have.

- Chat with your teen about what toys you played with when you were young, and get them to discuss whether they were gendered.
- Give your teen room to make their own choices about clothes, hairstyles and make-up.

- If your teen does remark on someone's sexuality or gender expression, take the time to continue the conversation. **Don't allow for any discrimination or slurs**. It's worth discussing with our teens that **language is powerful** and, as such, negative expressions can be extremely derogatory and harmful. If your teen uses the expression 'that's so gay', for example, ask them what they mean by that and then unpick it with them.
- Ask what your teen knows about some of the newer **LGBTQIA+ vocabulary**: practise using **non-gendered pronouns** with them — perhaps there are some celebrities who are openly part of the rainbow community you could relate this to.
- Discuss how your teen can **be an ally** and ask them why they think allies might be important — there are plenty of resources out there to help with this. Ask whether they know about any organisations they could contact for support, either for themselves or for one of their friends.
- Despite New Zealand's steps towards an inclusive society that is supportive of everyone, it still has a long way to go. Consider with your teen what we could be doing better in the LGBTQIA+ space through legislation, services, resources and recognition of intersectionality. How can we ensure access and choice for all, particularly our friends and whānau of colour? How can we further reduce stigma and discrimination?
- When you watch or listen to the **news**, keep up with new **legislation** — bring policy and events related to LGBTQIA+ into the conversation and ask your teens for their opinion.

If your teen asks you a question that you aren't sure how to answer, don't be afraid to take a beat. Reassure them that their questions are valid and that you want to have a conversation about it when you are both prepared. Take an evening to do some research and sleep on it before circling back and answering the questions your teen has.

Talking box questions

What do the initials LGBTQIA+ stand for? What does diversity mean?

Why is it wrong to stereotype people?

Why is positive media representation of diverse groups important?

Resources / Rauemi

ONLINE	Nest Resource Hub, with links to clips, diagrams and more information: nestconsulting.nz/parents-teachers-resources/sexuality-education
	A resource hub for takatāpui and their whānau: takatapui.nz
	An animated resource hub with information about sexual orientation: amaze.org/?topic=sexual-orientation
	InsideOUT provides workshops, resources and support to help make schools, community organisations and workplaces inclusive for rainbow people: insideout.org.nz
	Rainbow Youth provides support, information, resources and advocacy for queer, gender diverse, takatāpui and intersex youth in Aotearoa: ry.org.nz
	Find out your legal rights related to being queer or gender diverse: rainbowrights.nz
	The genderbread person diagram (constantly reviewed and updated), while not without its issues, is a useful tool: genderbread.org
	Thinking outside of the gender binary: thebodyisnotanapology.com/magazine/5-ways-to-help-kids-think-outside-the-gender-binary teenvogue.com/story/9-things-people-get-wrong-about-being-non-binary

11. CONSENT

#consentismandatory #nomeansno #consentculture

*'You need a yes, without duress,
and nothing less will do.'*
— MS MOEM

Kōrero with Molly

It's upsetting to think about the times my friends or I had our consent disrespected. Whether that was an unwanted sexual image sent via Snapchat or someone's partner pressuring them into doing something they felt uncomfortable with. This sort of behaviour made us feel a variety of negative things. It made us feel small. I'm grateful that it's getting easier to have conversations about it. We all deserve to feel safe and respected.

What do you mean by that? / He aha te tikanga o tāu kōrero?

In some ways this should be a short chapter, because the message is very basic: **NO MEANS NO. It's never okay to be in someone's space if they don't want you to be there.**

Does your teen still let you hug them? Do you ask your teen's permission before you dive in? Although it might seem the only way to get a hug, it's a good idea to foster a culture of consent by first checking they're okay with it. In fact, there are many opportunities to role-model negotiating consent in age-appropriate ways from the time a child is born. In any case, some teens avoid this type of contact for a while — as a parent you may find this upsetting, but it's completely natural and healthy as they become more independent and try to understand their own boundaries. They usually welcome contact again as they get slightly older, and that is also completely natural and healthy. Remember, the way they're interacting with their peer group is changing, too. They're all trying to figure out their comfort zones and these might not be the same as those of other people they know, or what they see in the media. At some point, your teen is going to need the skills to be able to *tell* any partner that they're giving consent for intimacy. In addition, they need to be able to *hear* this type of consent *from* their partner. Asking whether it's okay for a hug is one way you can help them model this behaviour. You are helping your teen to have clarity about their boundaries, and about how their body is touched and by whom. Emphasising this, along with the fact that these decisions are *theirs*, is the starting point to understanding this topic.

You may think consent is simply saying yes, or agreeing to something. However, when it comes to consent and sexual encounters, it soon becomes clear that there are additional intricacies that we must explain to our teens. There are several parts to achieving consent and keeping safe, which is spoken to in detail below. Some of these also have a legal dimension (for example, a person's age). This conversation could potentially be a minefield: you don't want to overwhelm your teen so that you put them off having sex at any point in the future, but instead give them skills so that they don't feel pressured into any intimacy before they feel themselves to be ready. And fully understanding and practising consent makes for a fun and respectful relationship: it's an essential ingredient for a mutually pleasurable sexual experience. Communicating these positives, rather than solely focusing on the more negative aspects that can come out of conversations about consent and sexual assault, is a useful way to frame the discussion.

Consent is in fact an empowering topic, rather than a scary one. When it comes to sexual activity, everyone has the right to decide when they do it, where they do it and how they do it — as long as it's **consensual** and otherwise **legal**. They also have the right to decide *not* to do it. It's never too soon to begin actively talking about this topic: by discussing sex with your teen, you are not telling them you think it's a good idea for them to become sexually active. There is also room for you to explain why, at this stage in their life, you think maybe it *isn't* such a good idea. They themselves might realise they're not ready. At the same time, for older teens, you need to recognise that it might be you that is not ready for them to have sex, whereas they are starting to think about it — or may even have started to do more than just think about it.

In some ways, the dictionary definition of consent — 'voluntary agreement to or acquiescence in what another proposes or desires'[1] — is unhelpful. We need to be teaching our teens about affirmative consent. A concise definition comes from California legislation:

> 'Affirmative consent' means affirmative, conscious, and voluntary agreement to engage in sexual activity. It is the responsibility of each person involved in the sexual activity to ensure that he or she has the affirmative consent of the other or others to engage in the sexual activity. Lack of protest or resistance does not mean consent, nor does silence mean consent. Affirmative consent must be ongoing throughout a sexual activity and can be revoked at any time. The existence of a dating relationship between the persons involved, or the fact of past sexual relations between them, should never by itself be assumed to be an indicator of consent.'[2]

Why is this important?

In the light of **#metoo**, we can look back at and review with new clarity occasions that may have made us feel uncomfortable as teens. If we were lucky enough not to have experienced unwanted attention ourselves, we will almost certainly remember times when our friends were distressed by something that happened to them. That these memories are so clear even now indicates the long-term impact of the times when we felt ourselves to be out of our depth. Talking about such topics with teens can be tricky and awkward — you may remember having embarrassing conversations with your own parents or teachers when you were a similar age. With these experiences in mind, we can hopefully be sensitive when we deliver this information because we must help our teens recognise the key role played by communication and the fundamental need for respect; that means respect for others as well as for themselves. An open dialogue on a number of levels about consent is aimed at giving teens a much clearer framework. Most schools/kura are also beginning to include this topic in the curriculum, which is very different to what the majority of parents encountered when they were teenagers. This is often included within their relationship and sexuality education programme, which also covers other components of sexual healthcare (see Chapter 9).

The following statistics (all bar the last two are from New Zealand research) emphasise why this is important:

- Thirteen per cent of students stated that they had received unwanted sexual messages, most commonly by mobile phone (52 per cent), the Internet (44 per cent), or letters or notes.[3]
- Twenty-six per cent of female students, and 14 per cent of male students, reported unwanted sexual contact, which was defined as being touched sexually or being made to do sexual things that they did not want to.[4]
- Eighteen per cent of male students and nearly twice as many female students (38 per cent) reported that the last time they had experienced unwanted sexual contact it was bad (pretty bad, really bad or very bad).[5]
- Only two-fifths of young people who had experienced sexual abuse had disclosed the experience to someone else.[6]
- Māori students (18 per cent) and Pacific students (22 per cent) were more likely to report having experienced sexual abuse or coercion than their New Zealand European counterparts (who reported 12 per cent).[7]
- Young people were most likely to experience unwanted sexual contact from a boyfriend/girlfriend or friend. This highlights the importance of supporting young people in understanding concepts such as consent and developing respectful friendships and relationships.[8]

- Children with disabilities are 2.9 times more likely to be victims of sexual violence. Children with mental or intellectual impairments appear to be among the most vulnerable, with 4.6 times the risk of sexual violence than their non-disabled peers.[9]
- Twenty-three per cent of LGBTQIA+ students who had dated or went out with someone during the 12 months before the survey had experienced sexual dating violence in the prior year; 18 per cent of LGBTQIA+ students had experienced physical dating violence.[10]

These are shocking figures, and they may make us want to wrap our teens up in cotton wool. They show not only that our teens are experiencing unwanted sexual contact, but also that, in a significant proportion of cases, this can affect them in very negative ways. In addition, the figures draw attention to the higher risk of marginalised groups.

These statistics can provide a springboard for conversations to help our teens navigate safer interactions with others. If we can unpack the data, we find that the majority of unwanted contact is from people within the same social group. This underlines how giving teens practical approaches can have a real impact, both now and in the longer term. As parents we can try to help them find strategies that work for them as individuals: if they are feeling uncomfortable by any dynamic — from friendships to hook-ups, and through to longer-term relationships — they need to know that we are there for them.

A global problem

This isn't something that just affects New Zealand. Teens in all countries are reporting struggling with the same issues, as the following statistics outline:

- A survey of 1559 UK teens found that in the course of a year almost a third of girls aged 13–17 years (31 per cent) received unwanted sexual messages online from their peers (compared to 11 per cent of boys).[11]

- An Australian study found that the statement 'Someone made sexual gestures, rude remarks, used body language, touched, or looked at me in a way that embarrassed or upset me' was true for both girls (30 per cent) and boys (15 per cent).[12]

- A UK survey found that only 39 per cent of young people aged 14–17 thought it was okay for someone to withdraw consent if they were already naked.[13]

- A US survey stated about one in eight female and one in 26 male high school students reported having experienced sexual dating violence in the last year.[14]

- US data stated 26 per cent of women and 15 per cent of men who were victims of contact sexual violence, physical violence, and/or stalking by an intimate partner in their lifetime first experienced these or other forms of violence by that partner before age 18.[15]

- Around 53 per cent of Indian children reported experiencing different kinds of abuse, which included inappropriate touching, being forced into nude photography, assault and sexual abuse.[16]

Tell me more . . . / Kōrero mai anō . . .

So, as clear-cut as the issue of consent may initially seem — 'no means no' — this topic does in fact require further discussion to give it context.

The law

As we know, laws are there to regulate behaviours, to discourage or prevent those that a society agrees are not appropriate or criminal. In New Zealand there are a range of laws that regulate sexual acts. The key common denominator of these laws is: if someone imposes any sexual act on a person who doesn't want to participate (this could be through comments, sharing of intimate pictures, showing someone pornographic material, kissing and touching, or any kind of penetration), that act is **non-consensual**.

Sexual consent law in New Zealand states that a person (of any gender) must be over 16 years of age to give consent to sexual activity.[17] Consent laws in some other countries include a clause stating that the law is applied slightly differently when all those involved are below the age of consent (it's also important here to remember that the age of consent varies between countries). This is sometimes called the 'Romeo and Juliet' clause. There is no such provision in New Zealand legislation. This means that, in Aotearoa, if anybody underage is involved in any sexual activity it is **against the law**. Although it lacks a 'Romeo and Juliet' clause, the law in New Zealand is intended to protect young people from harm, abuse or violence instigated by older people, not to criminalise underage sexual activity.

Sexual consent law also identifies other instances and circumstances in which people are not able to consent to sex — for example, if they are incapacitated in any way (including under the influence of drugs or alcohol), or if they are asleep or unconscious. In these circumstances the law states that the person does not consent to sexual activity. Consent can also be brought into question in other situations, which are covered more fully later in this chapter.

This is why conversations about consent are so important: we are supporting our teens to understand that age is not the only factor in consent. Being over 16 years of age does not in and of itself indicate that a person is ready for, or wanting to have, sexual contact.

The language of consent

We need to normalise this language for our teens, which may feel more than a little awkward — so have a practice talking it through with a partner or a friend first if you think that will help. See the Resources/Rauemi section (page 284) for other ways of going about this if you need an alternative option.

It's useful to check with your teen that they have some examples on how to use the language of affirmative consent: it needs to be, as one support website puts it, an 'explicit and enthusiastic agreement to participate in a sexual activity'.[18]

With that in mind, below are five ground rules for consent that everyone needs to know.

1. Respect boundaries. The first thing that your teen needs to do is check in with themselves as to what they want. Once they have established their own boundaries and what they are feeling comfortable with, they can then check in with the other person. They need to remember to respect the other person's boundaries in the way that they are expecting theirs to be respected. Examples might be:

- 'What would you like to do?'
- 'Is there anything you wouldn't feel comfortable doing?'
- 'Are you up for . . . [be specific]?'
- 'I'm okay with touching from here up but not anything below here.'

And there should be no judgement if the other person says no.

2. Everyone has the right to change their mind. No sexual contact can begin without consent, and if consent is revoked, any activity must stop immediately. Everyone involved must feel able to say 'no' at any time. Examples of checking in might be:

- 'Let me know if you want to stop or if anything isn't feeling good, okay?'
- 'Are you okay to keep going?'
- 'Do you want to stop?'

And there should be no judgement if the other person says no, **even if consent was previously established.** The relationship advice blog *Never Settle* cites a neat example of this from the movie *Scott Pilgrim vs. the World*:

Scott Pilgrim and his crush Ramona are kissing in bed and appear to be leading up to sex. Halfway through, Ramona stops and says, 'I changed my mind . . . I don't want to have sex with you, not right now.' She's clear that she reserves the right to change her mind about it and have sex at another time. He responds, 'Okay, well this is nice. Just this,' and immediately accepts how she feels without pressuring or questioning her, or making her feel guilty. This is a perfectly kind and sweet way to respond when someone withdraws consent.[19]

3. Consent is specific to a particular action and does not cover more than that. In other words, if consent is given for kissing, then any progression — for instance, to touching — needs to be agreed.

- 'May I now touch your . . .?'
- 'Would it be okay if I moved my mouth to . . .?'

And there should be no judgement if the other person says no.

4. There are cues other than a verbal 'yes' or 'no', and it is vital that teens be attuned to these. Some can seem very subtle: even if the non-verbal cues that someone is giving seem to be positive, it is always a good idea to check in with them and ask if they are enjoying the experience and are happy to continue. Everyone needs to know how to **listen and observe** for consent: through, for example, body language or changes in eye contact. This can be tricky to interpret whatever age you are and whatever stage your relationship is at. So if there's ever any uncertainty as to what a person is trying to say, it's important your teen knows they should **stop** and ask for **clarification**. Examples of when someone is not certain about the situation could be:

- if the other person says something that sounds like 'I'm not sure' or is silent,

- if the other person responds with an 'umm' or a 'maybe',
- if the other person appears unenthusiastic or becomes passive, and/or,
- obviously, if the other person looks sad, looks away, cries, backs away, isn't responding positively, or for example starts putting their clothes back on.

In any such instance, your teen needs to **stop and check**. And there should be no judgement if the other person is letting them know it's a no.

5. Consent is mandatory and cannot be assumed. It needs to be reassessed not only continually during any sexual encounter, but also **before any new encounter,** even if that is with the same person. Just because something happened consensually the last time, that **isn't a guarantee** it's okay next time. Hooking up at one party doesn't mean that they have to hook up at the next one. Kissing at the movies doesn't mean that they feel comfortable making out in the park. Examples of how to talk about this might be:

- 'Did you enjoy it when we [intimate action]? Can we do it again?'
- 'Can we do what we were doing at [location], here?'

And there should be no judgement if the other person says no.

Withdrawing consent

Just as important is preparing your teen with **the skills to withdraw consent.** Remind them that they are entitled to do this at any time — even after they had previously given enthusiastic consent. They may feel that, in fact, they aren't ready, that things are going too fast, or that they don't feel comfortable or safe. As discussed above, **everyone can change their mind,** and after communicating this, their decision should be respected. They can:

- let their partner know verbally that they'd like to slow down or stop, or
- redirect touch to something they prefer by moving a hand or asking their partner to do so.

If they are feeling unsafe, they can:

- say 'no' or 'stop',
- use their hand as a stop signal, and/or
- pull away.

If things are becoming extremely unsafe, they can:

- shout for help,
- use self-defence or any other means to get away, and/or
- tell someone what has happened so that they can get support.

It is important to note, especially if your teen comes to you for help, that a 'freeze' response in this situation is a normal reaction to trauma. They may need reassurance if they feel they could not use, or were not safe to use, any of the above strategies.

A framework like this, if respected by all involved, will help to ensure that any encounter is safe for your teen. Affirmative consent requires ongoing communication so that the encounter always remains consensual. Let them know consent is no less important in a long-term relationship or marriage — **all the same rules apply**.

Are there situations where a 'yes' is not consent?
In addition, it's good to discuss with your teen that sometimes a 'yes' is **not actually a 'yes'**, including the following situations:

- Someone may initially say 'no' to a sexual activity, but another person doesn't accept this and tries to change their mind by tactics such as **persuasion, guilt burdening, bribing or wearing**

them down. If this is the case, even if someone ultimately says 'yes', that yes is actually a 'no'.

- There may be circumstances where a person is being **threatened, pressured or blackmailed** (for example, through threats to expose private images) to engage in a sexual activity, or a person is trying to **force** a 'yes' by use of violence. If this is the case, even if someone says 'yes', that yes is actually a 'no'.

- There are times when a person **deliberately gets another person drunk or drugged** (or takes advantage of someone who is drunk or under the influence of drugs) in order to get them to say yes to a sexual activity. If this is the case, even if someone says 'yes', that yes is actually a 'no'.

- If a person is **asleep or for any other reason not aware of their environment,** they are not able to consent to any sexual activity. If this is the case, even if someone has previously said 'yes', that yes is now a 'no'.

It's essential to talk with your teen about consent in situations where people have been drinking or using drugs. **Intoxication can impact on the capacity to give clear consent.** Not only is assuming consent (obviously) not the right thing to do, but also a person's non-sober 'consent' may not be considered informed and therefore might not be legal. Your teen may find this idea complicated, but there are ways in which you can help them understand it. Here is another example from *Never Settle* — in this case, the movie *10 Things I Hate About You*:

> *A core element of this movie revolves around attitudes towards sex and dating. When Kat gets too drunk at a party and Patrick drives her home, she leans in for a kiss at the end of the night. He rebuffs her, knowing it wouldn't be right to take advantage of this moment because she's too intoxicated to freely give her consent.*[20]

There are other times when a 'yes' is not considered consent, even if both parties are over 16 years old. The law is designed to protect vulnerable people from those who would exploit their position of power — for instance, in cases where one person has charge of the other, or is in a position of trust or authority (such as a teacher, boss or doctor), which could lead them to take advantages. Let's look at this in more detail:

- If there is a guardian–dependant relationship, the age of consent is 18 years old.
- If a person has a significant physical, intellectual or mental health condition that means they are unable to give or convey consent, sexual contact would be illegal.
- If a person allowed sexual activity, mistakenly thinking the other person was someone else, it does not amount to consent and is therefore illegal.
- If consent is given for a physical examination, but during that examination the physician performs a sexual act, it is against the law. The initial consent did not cover this unwanted act.

Your teen needs to know that there are huge **consequences** when consent is not mutual. This is because **consent must be given freely and willingly**, otherwise it can be considered **sexual coercion, assault or rape**. This is more than unacceptable behaviour. These are criminal offences.

What's more, the physical and psychological impacts of sexual assaults on survivors are significant and ongoing.

Without wanting to scare your teen, they need to be aware that sexual assaults do happen. You also need to make sure that they have strategies to cope. This is one of the worst things imaginable, but your teen needs to know they can come to you and that you will not be judgemental in any scenario (for example, if it happened at a party they weren't supposed to be at). You will need to be there for them and potentially also find them support, such as a counsellor. In addition, they may decide that they want to speak to the police. What is vital is that you listen to them and let them tell you exactly what happened in their own words. Let them know you recognise how difficult it is for them to have disclosed this to you. Let them know that they are believed.

In all of this, you will need coping strategies and supports, too.

'Rape culture'

The phrase 'rape culture' date backs to the early 1970s.[21] It's a term that we are now much more familiar with due to campaigns such as **#metoo** (which began with Tarana Burke's online initiative encouraging women to speak out about sexual harassment, abuse and rape culture). It describes a form of societal conditioning that is expressed well by the United Nations group UN Women: 'While no one may disagree that rape is wrong, through words, actions and inaction, sexual violence and sexual harassment is normalized and trivialized, leading us down a slippery slope of rape culture.'[22]

What does this mean for our teens? It's complicated and we need to unpack it first.

The impact of rape culture is such that sexual harassment seems to be tolerated, along with sexually explicit jokes. The incidence and degree of sexual assaults, and the distress that they cause, are downplayed. Survivors are blamed, with a commentary on the way that they dress, whether they had been drinking and whether they were known to have been sexually active in the past. Stereotypes of a dominant male and submissive female are reinforced. Statistics that challenge these unhealthy perspectives on sexual assault and rape are themselves challenged and trivialised.[23]

The proportion of sexual assaults that find their way into the criminal justice process is alarmingly small: for every 100 cases of sexual violence reported to police, only 31 result in court action, 11 in convictions and six in a jail sentence.[24] Bear in mind that only 6 per cent of incidents are reported to the police in the first place, and that younger people are more at risk of sexual assault.[25] Distressingly, victim-blaming continues even within the court setting — with casual misogyny appearing even at these levels.[26] (This affects male survivors, too.) Currently, fear of shame and ridicule is one of the reasons both men and women often do not report sexual violence. This will be even more true of teens.

Some would argue that rape culture is, in fact, an example of toxic masculinity rooted in patriarchal beliefs, power and control. This extends all too often to our teens, as the statistics earlier in this chapter show. But we have begun to realise that the way things are is not necessarily the way things should be. Recent sexual violence legislation in New Zealand has made changes aimed at lessening the traumatic side effects of criminal trials on the survivor and their family. In addition, the government has appointed the first minister for family and sexual violence, and in December 2021 launched the first national strategy to eliminate family violence and sexual violence in Aotearoa.[27] This comes amid New Zealanders of all ages protesting in the media, at schools and on marches, demanding changes, including:

- adequate and sustainable funding for sexual violence support services,
- educational programmes to be set up focusing on rape prevention and awareness, and
- new police measures providing better support for survivors.[28]

Until these and other changes come to fruition, we will still want to protect our teens in a society that seems to condone many problematic behaviours. Fundamentally, we need to remember that unwanted sexual contact is extremely distressing and it is imperative that people with harmful sexual behaviours are held to account.[29]

A word on consent in the media

We are trying to tell our teens about affirmative consent. We hope that they learn about this topic from home and from school, but we also know they learn a lot from the media they interact with (one study found, for instance, that almost 40 per cent of 14–17-year-olds learned about consent from TV and film).[30] It would be great

Deconstructing rape culture is imperative.

then, if these media more commonly portrayed situations with good modelling of how to ask for consent, even demonstrating that consent can be a positive part of a sexual encounter. Unfortunately, we seem to consistently see consent shown at best in an ambiguous way. This can be confusing for those learning about relationships.

Teens may identify with characters and situations in the things they watch or stream and, because of this, they may be soaking up any messages both consciously and subconsciously. We need to grow their media literacy — to encourage them to think critically about what they are watching so that they understand any subtle messaging that may be involved.

Our teens live in a world where sex seems to be ever-present: on television, social media, radio and billboards, and in the movies. Music is also an important dimension of most teens' lives, often being one of the ways in which they identify their tribe. Much as we want to respect our teens' choices, it can be hard not to sometimes feel judgemental about what can be fairly explicit content. The concern is that this degree of saturation may lead to desensitisation. And this in turn can appear to contradict the positive messages that we are trying to communicate in relation to affirmative consent.

A US article succinctly reiterates how good it would be if consent (as presented in this chapter) were normalised in the media our teens consume:

> As our culture advances, the hope is that consent will become more normalized within media and pop culture. We, as a culture, have already made leaps and bounds, but we do have much further to go. Music is typically a part of most people's lives and is a great avenue for awareness, education, and normalization. The more consent is talked about honestly, the more our culture will shift. So, support music that is honest and consent-positive! Support artists who make music about vital cultural issues! It may not happen overnight, but I believe we can create a culture where our children respect the bodies of others. A culture where women do not have to fear walking home alone or wearing a low-cut top. A culture where young girls are taught that they are independent beings and have control over their bodies and their sexuality. However, as we wait for this ideal culture to develop, let's applaud the artists who are already fighting for consent, and be wary of those who ignore it.[31]

How can I have this conversation? / Me pēhea tēnei matakahi?

Parents are not expected to be experts, and it's okay not to know everything. What is useful is learning to hear your teen, supporting them towards pro-social behaviours, and reaching out for help when you need it.

Consent is clearly at the foundation of any teen's learning about interpersonal relationships. The information given needs to be age appropriate and must be added to as they mature and their sexuality education broadens.

This is why we need to have the conversation, and primarily the message here is one of respect and communication.

Different teens will be at different levels of understanding and in need of different sorts of strategies, so we need to make sure that we pitch things accordingly. For the young and young at heart, Disney's *Frozen* shows a positive example of affirmative consent between the two characters Anna and Kristoff. When Kristoff hugs Anna, he says, 'I could kiss you!' but then pauses and presents his wish as a question: 'I mean I'd like to. May I, may we?' She responds by kissing him on the cheek and verbally confirming, 'We may.' They then kiss.

There are opportunities everywhere to talk about consent in context. There may be a story in the news, or a programme that is going viral. If you notice a good example of consent (or the opposite) on the radio or television, ask for your teen's viewpoint. Perhaps don't ask during every single film you watch, or maybe wait to the end — otherwise just listen to those groans as they see you reach for the remote. The important thing is that you are talking — and that you are listening.

'There is much discussion about consent within the context of sex. But consent is about so much more than that. Consent is about time and it's about energy. It's also spatial in scope. Physical space and mental space. People will act entitled to your time, energy, and space. They need to understand that they're not entitled to these things; these things require your consent.'
— C. JOYBELL C.

The lessons learned about consent around sexual encounters can be extrapolated more generally so that our teens can develop respectful interpersonal relationships. This applies in all settings where they have dealings with others: lending or borrowing a book, making plans to meet up or communicating over social media, for example. It becomes a language of good interaction in which we would like our teens to become fluent. Over time, through this type of interaction, they will gain confidence from doing the right thing, particularly in relation to sexual encounters. Then if they find themselves in a situation that makes them feel uncomfortable, or the person they are with feels uncomfortable, they are more likely to be able to trust their own instincts.

Points to keep the conversation going

- Acknowledge your teen's growing **maturity** and their expanding **boundaries**, and check in with them frequently.
- As with other topics, use the **media** you watch together to **kick-start conversations** on whether the behaviours you've witnessed are respectful and consensual or not — there are some examples earlier in this chapter.
- There are many topical and celebrity news items you and your teen will hear about that can lead into further discussions about **consent** (or generally, the lack of it) and **consequences** — use these to get your teen's views and also to build their **understanding of the law**.
- Find films and series for them to watch with **positive examples of consent**, or even dig out specific age-appropriate educational resources, such as the YouTube clip in the Resources/Rauemi section (page 284).
- Encourage your teen to **critically analyse their music** and call out artists who perpetuate concerning culture.
- Ask them straight out what the word 'consent' means to them.
- Be interested in (or ask the school directly) what they are **learning at school about consent** — most schools/kura have

programmes running that you can build on at home.

- Discuss what they know of the **#metoo initiative**, how it came about and what it means, and be open to hearing their thoughts. Talk with them about the **statistics**. This may be upsetting, but it's real and will ground them in the knowledge that you are informed and open to this conversation.

- **Make awkward normal** and, perhaps with a dose of humour, practise how respecting others can come across in conversation, including those all-important ways to check in about intimate consent. Importantly, make sure they know that it's totally okay for them to say 'no' to anything they are uncomfortable with at any time.

> **We need to send a clear message: it's not just a case of listening for a 'no', but also hearing and seeing a clear and positive 'yes'.**

Talking box questions

How can we mobilise our society
to challenge rape culture?

What do you think victim-blaming means?

Can you think of a film or TV
programme where consent either
was or was not displayed?

Resources / Rauemi

ONLINE	This media cartoon made for the UK Thames Valley Police by Rachel Brian and Emmeline May explains consent in the most simplistic way using a 'cup of tea': youtube.com/watch?v=oQbei5JGiT8 Advice and services regarding consent and sexual assault from New Zealand Police: police.govt.nz/advice-services/sexual-assault-and-consent Resource hubs for learning about consent: bodysafe.nz/consent teentalk.ca/learn-about/consent A resource hub for learning about sexual harm: safetotalk.nz/what-is-sexual-harm Test your knowledge of consent with this quiz: archive.youthline.co.nz/info-zone/sex/getting-and-giving-consent Tips for standing up against rape culture: un-women.medium.com/16-ways-you-can-stand-against-rape-culture-88bf12638f12 More information about how alcohol impacts consent: everydayfeminism.com/2016/05/alcohol-and-consent-questions

12. SAFE RELATIONSHIPS

#saferelationships #boundaries #healthyrelationships

*'A healthy relationship will never
require you to sacrifice your friends,
your dreams, or your dignity.'*
— DINKAR KALOTRA

Kōrero with Molly

For just about all of us, romantic relationships played a part in the social dynamics of high school. Looking back, it all felt like a pretty big deal at the time. There were always people getting together or splitting up or gossiping about who had hooked up at a party. Going out with someone so that you could say that you were with someone was never a good idea. At the same time, there seemed to be pressures about being with someone, and then when you were, there were pressures about how a relationship should look or make you feel. Something a lot of us were guilty of was semi-abandoning friends when in a relationship: a boyfriend or a girlfriend could soon become all you'd think about, and sometimes this had a bad impact on grades, friendships, relationships with family and even mental health.

Most teenage relationships came to an end — sometimes that was a good thing. But it was always tricky, especially when both of you were attending the same school . . . It was like awkwardly bumping into your ex at the supermarket every single day, except it was at a place where you were trying to concentrate and learn! Peers would pick sides, and social media exacerbated everything. Usually these things blew over fairly quickly — but again, that didn't mean it wasn't hard at the time, and more so if you'd really liked someone. Other people trying to be kind by saying it would all be all right in the long run wasn't really all that helpful. It just made it feel like something that was important to you was insignificant to everyone else. When a relationship didn't look right, I remember people used to talk about it, but no one really seemed to know what friends were supposed to do to be supportive. When I was at school, there wasn't much information or any school programmes that talked through what you were entitled to expect within a healthy relationship. I think that the work that is happening nowadays is a really great development.

What do you mean by that? / He aha te tikanga o tāu kōrero?

People who are in your life should make you feel safe, especially if you are not yet an adult. This is true of family, whānau, friends and acquaintances, or, for example, people who are in a position of authority (such as teachers, youth leaders or bosses). There are certain standards of behaviour that would be deemed to be appropriate in any context: these centre on mutual acceptance and respect. A teen's initial experiences of relationships will generally be close to home. How they themselves are treated, and what they witness, provides them with their base of understanding for what to expect from others and what others can expect from them. Teens are also constantly picking up information about how people can connect with one another from their friends, from school, from their social networks or from other media such as television, movies or celebrity news. Not all these model healthy relationships, so it is critical that you, as their parent, have some input: if you can develop a good relationship with your teen, they are more likely to relate well to their peers.[1]

A huge part of any type of relationship (whether it be platonic, romantic, intimate or sexual) relies on effective communication (see Chapter 1) and conflict resolution skills. At the very least, your teen needs to be able to relay their needs, to be able to hear and understand others' needs, and to learn the importance of emotional intelligence. It's your job to nurture their self-worth and self-esteem (see page 151), which will in turn enable them to 'own' their own feelings. Negative emotions and behaviours erode even the healthiest relationships; and if your teen doesn't feel good about themselves, they may inadvertently externalise responsibility for their own happiness (or internalise the other person's happiness as their responsibility). This could leave them vulnerable to reliance on others for validation, whether or not those others have their best interests at heart. Relationships need to be balanced in all meanings of the word. Ideally, you will want your teen to have the space to really think about the kind of person or people they want to be around, and for them to know that they do not have to settle for anything less.

We have already discussed friendships in Chapter 3, so here we will concentrate on more intimate relationships. This conversation is an opportunity to establish some dating ground rules with your teen. Hearing your thoughts and messages allows them to internalise your protective boundaries. We will want our teens to know that any form of violence within a relationship is absolutely unacceptable.

> ### 'Young love is common, but that doesn't mean it's not precious.'
> — EOIN COLFER

Dating: that word alone is enough to give some parents butterflies. Your teen's early relationships are pivotal because they can set patterns moving forward, influencing how they may behave towards others and what behaviour they are likely to accept. Should these patterns look concerning — such as withdrawal from a usual social circle, or inequalities within the relationship — try to find an opportunity to tactfully discuss what the boundaries in their connections with others should look like.

You may have your own memories and experiences — some good and some not so much — that are informing what you want for your teen. So, whether you dated widely (or not so much), whether you met the love of your life at a young age (or rather older), and whether you are currently dating — whatever baggage you bring along — try to make space to listen to your teen's perspective. And don't hesitate to get support for yourself if need be.

What you will also know is that the landscape has changed a fair bit since your own teenage years. Dating may not even be a word in your teen's vocabulary: current terminology may include some slang you are not familiar with. Chatting, talking, seeing, hanging out, chilling, getting with someone, hooking up, Netflix and chill, no strings attached (NSA), friends with benefits (FWB), exclusive, going out — all these have nuances that feel a little like a foreign country to anyone who was around when *The Simpsons* first aired. Sometimes, due to the generation gap, we may understand very different things from the same words. Don't worry: find out (sensitively) the meaning of the phrases that your teen uses and keep your conversations within that framework (yikes!).

These conversations might even allow you to give a little guidance, but remember the course of true love doesn't always run smoothly. It's about them, not you, so try to avoid creating a Romeo and Juliet dynamic. There's a lot your teen will be learning: who they want to be with and why; who they *don't* want to be with and why; what they are seeking from a more personal relationship and why; and the extent to which they are prepared to negotiate these expectations. Some teens feel more keenly than others about 'needing' a boyfriend or girlfriend. Discuss these pressures and what they think they will get out of such a relationship. After all, young love is as much about them establishing who they want to be as it is about establishing who they want to be *with*. As with friendships, you may witness your teen going through some ups and downs, and the downs can feel like heartbreak. Most of us remember that feeling, so make sure that you are there for them if and when this happens. Take the opportunity to talk about the support they already have from family, friends and others, as these connections provide a great safety net. It's important your teen knows not to abandon their wider group because they are so smitten: engaging with only one person can potentially lead to them becoming isolated.

Tell me more . . . / Kōrero mai anō . . .

Types of relationship

Some relationships involve teens living in each other's pockets and seeing a lot of each other, whereas others seem to take place only online and are just 'Facebook official'. Some teens are not sexually driven or may choose not to make a relationship physical, some are monogamous, and others have wider boundaries. It may be that intimacy and romance are not commonly seen as a precursor to sex. In fact, for some, sex may be the precursor to a more long-term partnership. It may also be that modern-day teens are less judgemental about their own and others' choices — highlighting an often much more casual approach to relationships by teens of all genders. It should however, be remembered that there's a degree of emotional maturity required where connections start to include a physical dimension.

A word on online dating

Online dating is hugely popular with adults and most teens are well aware of its existence. Teens generally have many opportunities to meet people, so this may not be their first port of call. There are many different sites catering to a variety of demographics — to many teens the idea of setting up a profile online and then swiping left or right may sound fun. As an adult you can probably already see the problems and pitfalls of this type of app for those under 18. The potential Internet dangers range from catfishing (where someone sets up a false online profile; see Chapter 5) through to grooming.[2] You may think your teen is protected from using these sites by age restrictions, so it's worth knowing that there are some that allow younger users. Up until 2016, Tinder registered users from 13 years of age (7 per cent of users were registered in the 13–17-year-old age range, with Tinder allowing them only to 'match' with other users in the same range). It's unsurprisingly not unheard of for teens to enter an incorrect date of birth in order to join an over-18 dating app. As we are all aware, older users may also lie about their age.[3]

Communication

There's a wonderful intensity to finding your person, and technology makes it incredibly easy to be in constant touch. Your teen may see their person 'in real life' (IRL) or they may choose to supplement this contact with a seemingly endless stream of direct messages (DMs), FaceTime, texts and Snapchats. They may even go old school and send the occasional letter. Whichever way they connect, communicating assertively (see page 24) yet respectfully is integral to any ongoing close relationship,[4] and this calls for some universal ground rules:

- Find a way to be open and honest, as this builds trust.
- Have mutual respect and support each other.
- Find ways to express and receive affection.
- Understand the practice of consent (see Chapter 11).
- Be able to speak up and be heard — but equally, remember to listen.
- Establish a balance that allows for give and take.

There are several dimensions here: your teen needs to be able to communicate with their boyfriend or girlfriend (or whatever terminology they may be using to describe their connection), but they will also want to be able to talk about their relationship with other people. This will help them to reinforce what's good and positive, but also to talk about anything that might be bothering them. And while your teen will appreciate your respecting their privacy, they need to know that you are keeping a weather eye on things. There may have been a time at that age when you were convinced that no one else could understand how important a particular person was to you. In many ways this is true: you can't understand the dynamics of other people's relationships from the outside. Your teen's choices are their choices — and anyway, even if those choices might not be yours, it can sometimes be counterproductive to criticise. This is why it's important for you to know what an unhealthy relationship looks like — so you can ensure your teen knows, too.

It's also helpful for them to understand some of the pressures and contributing factors to behaviours that can lead to unhealthy relationships, and societal gender roles do have a part to play here.

A word on redefining masculinity

The impact of gender stereotyping is now recognised as problematic, and as such is more likely to be challenged. According to UN Women, a United Nations entity for the empowerment of women, research indicates that 'children start absorbing stereotypes by age three, causing the world to expand for boys and shrink for girls by age 10. That's why we have to start conversations about gender roles early on, and challenge the features and characteristics assigned to men and women at home, in our daily routines, in school and in places of work.'[5]

For a teen who is struggling to find themselves, exposure to this sort of negative messaging can be harmful, and those who identify as male may feel under particular pressure to conform to the models of masculinity (toxic or otherwise) that they see in the media around them. And those who identify as female may feel pressured into accepting these norms. This situation will be amplified if patterns of behaviour in the adults within their circle imply that in order to 'be a real man' you must 'Be strong / Don't cry / Don't show emotions except anger (even when you're sad) / Want sex all the time / Be aggressive / Do a physical job, be the boss / Be rich/successful / Be a baller/gangsta'.[6]

Recent research shows that this perspective is not only unhelpful, but can in fact be damaging to individuals and to society in general. As a 2021 Australian study finds, 'There is a consistent gap between men and women when it comes to views of gender roles. Young Australian men are less aware than young women of sexism and more supportive of male dominance and violent attitudes toward women.' And, it adds, 'Conformity to traditional masculinity is a well-documented risk factor in domestic violence.'[7]

One of the best ways to break down stereotypes is to talk things through, to name and call out behaviours that are toxic, and to champion healthier alternatives. That Australian study again: 'We need to promote ideals for boys' and men's lives that are positive, diverse and gender-equitable.'[8]

See also the section on feminism (pages 364–370).

Healthy and unhealthy relationships

This topic's relevance to teens has now been recognised as so fundamental that it has been included as part of the national curriculum for all school-age groups in Aotearoa.[9] Your teen needs to be fully aware that any healthy relationship is based on respect and should be an equal partnership. If they are not currently with someone themselves, they need to understand this not only for their own future, but also in order to be supportive to their friends. In this way, they will be better able to distinguish healthy relationships from unhealthy ones, and be conscious of how one can shift into the other (perhaps they start to feel that they have grown apart, or are constantly bickering). As a general rule, it's a good time to review a relationship if it's starting to make you more unhappy than happy.

Arguments and disagreements happen. Relationships will fluctuate: not many can say that things are 100 per cent all of the time. Sometimes there are opportunities for escalating problems to be addressed in order to get things back on course. There is, however, a difference between having an off-day, or being in a relationship that needs work — or perhaps is not fixable — and being in one that is abusive.

A RELATIONSHIP HEALTH CHECK

This table, adapted from an article published on the website Verywell Mind,[10] summarises some of the most noticeable differences between a healthy relationship and one showing signs of problems.

CHARACTERISTICS OF A HEALTHY RELATIONSHIP	SIGNS OF PROBLEMS IN A RELATIONSHIP
Trust/openness and honesty: • Trust in your partner is a key component of any healthy relationship. • Trust is also established by how partners treat each other. When you see that your partner treats you well, is dependable and will be there when you need them, you are more likely to develop this trust. • Being open and honest, firstly with yourself and then with each other, not only helps you feel more connected as a couple, but also helps foster trust. • Healthy boundaries in a relationship allow you to still do the things that are important to you, such as going out with friends and maintaining privacy, while still sharing important things with your partner.	• Lack of privacy or pressure to share every detail of your life with your partner. • Being afraid to share your opinions or thoughts.
Mutual respect: • In close, healthy relationships, people have a shared respect for one another. They don't demean or belittle each other, but offer support and security.	• Feeling pressured to change who you are. • Unequal control over shared resources, including social status, money and transportation.

Affection: • Healthy relationships are characterised by fondness and affection . . . However, it is important to remember that physical needs are different for each individual. • There is no 'right' amount of affection or intimacy, but it should always be consensual. • A nurturing partnership is characterised by genuine affection for each other, expressed in a variety of ways.	• Feeling that spending time together is an obligation. • Avoiding one another.
Good communication: • Healthy, long-lasting relationships, whether they are friendships or romantic partnerships, require the ability to communicate well.	• Poor and inconsistent communication — for example, gaslighting.
Give and take: • You do things for each other because you genuinely want to. This doesn't mean that the give and take in a relationship is always 100 per cent equal. At times, one partner may need more help and support.	• Neglecting your own needs in order to put your partner first. • Being pressured to quit the things you enjoy. • Attempts to control your behaviours. • Facing criticism for what you do, who you spend time with, how you dress, etc. • Lack of fairness when settling conflicts. • Yelling. • Physical violence.

If you have concerns about your teen's current partner, try to get them to focus on what they think a healthy relationship looks like. This will give them space to review their choices.

Ending relationships

Teen romances can be on again, off again, which is a good reason to avoid bad-mouthing your teen's current partner or recent ex. Some relationships do come to a more permanent end — and it can definitely feel like some should . . . Your teen needs to know that it's okay to break off a relationship, or to be broken up with. That's not to trivialise what has happened. Whichever way things end, there's likely to be some intense feelings on both sides, and they may need some TLC. If you have previously had the chance to highlight examples where relationships have been broken off respectfully, any advice you might offer in these painful circumstances is much less likely to be taken by your teen as a personal criticism of them when they are already feeling fragile. Again, this comes back to those communication and emotional skills.

Here are some tips you can forward to your teen for healthy break-ups (although, if there is abuse happening in a relationship, this list might look different):

- Empathy is the key here, and treating people how you'd like to be treated is the way to go.
- Be the one to talk to your soon-to-be-ex-partner. Be assertive and respectful, and honest about why you have decided things need to end. Avoid breaking up through another person, or via a text or social media.
- Talking of social media, construct a plan as to when you will both be changing your relationship status, and avoid bad-mouthing or spilling secrets online (or anywhere else).
- If one of you doesn't want to break up, remember it's not healthy to try to get the other to stay by emotionally manipulating them (and it wouldn't last even if they felt guilted to stay).
- No matter how your ex responds, maintain your own integrity and manners. If it gets too difficult, seek support.

Red flags

As a relationship progresses, there can be subtle changes indicating that the nature of the connection also becomes different. Some behaviours present more obvious challenges, such as lying or cheating. However, teens may find it harder to recognise other signals that things have hit rocky ground: encourage them to tell you how they are feeling and to reflect on how they are feeling about their partner.

It may be time to review things if someone in a relationship feels:

- things just aren't fun any more and it's influencing their mood and attitude,
- they are no longer able to discuss with their partner how they feel or what they need,
- the connection has worn off and they have little to share or talk about,
- the partnership is unbalanced, with one person always getting their way,
- they are being undermined and trust is becoming an issue, and/or
- they are becoming isolated from others, including their family and friends.

Watch out for more intense issues that may indicate the relationship is sliding into an abusive one. These can range from feeling dominated or intimidated, to experiencing threats of suicide or violence.

Unfortunately, some risky behaviours may be confused by our teens as just being a part of their youth culture. They may interpret a partner's behaviour as being romantically intense, when it's actually possessive, controlling and problematic. It's not okay if your teen's partner is constantly belittling them — for instance, by telling them their opinion is worthless — nor is it acceptable for them to dictate your teen's choices, whether that's around clothing, or music, or birth control.[11] There is a spectrum of behaviours within relationships that can move from healthy to unhealthy to abusive.

New Zealand teens are not immune to abusive relationships, as a recent study bears out:

Violence and abuse in adolescent relationships are serious problems in New Zealand and internationally. These issues do not receive the same level of attention as violence in adult relationships. Adolescence is a key time to intervene and to support young people to build healthy relationship skills . . .

Compared with other New Zealanders, adolescents between the ages of 15 and 19 have the highest rates of intimate-partner violence . . .

Intimate-partner violence is perpetrated by and against people from all communities, ethnic groups and socio-economic backgrounds, but marginalised groups are at higher risk.[12]

Abuse can happen within a variety of types of relationship and is known as intimate partner violence. It is characterised by one person exerting power and control over the other, denying the other's freedom and/or forcing them into behaviours they wouldn't otherwise choose. The result can be physical and/or emotional damage. Physical violence is rarely used alone; it is most often used together with a mixture of verbal abuse, emotional and psychological abuse, coercive control, dating violence, cultural abuse, financial abuse, cyber abuse and sexual violence.[13] Non-physical violence should not be dismissed as any less serious than physical violence, and many survivors state that it's even harder to recover from. While men are usually the abusers, some men do experience intimate partner violence themselves.

Research suggests that in New Zealand, 23 per cent of females and 14 per cent of males who have been abused by an intimate partner first experienced it between the ages of 11 and 17.[14]

Sadly, this means that it's highly likely your teen might need some strategies should a friend disclose to them that they are having problems of this sort. If so, they may find the following template helpful. You may also find it useful if you suspect that your teen is the one experiencing abuse.

How you can help

This template is adapted from a resource used by New Zealand Police, and was designed originally with Year 12 students in mind for the Loves-Me-Not programme aimed at preventing abusive behaviour in relationships.[15]

Listen
Hear what they say and try not to interrupt. Let them talk at their own pace. Show them you are listening by making eye contact and nodding. Don't worry if they stop talking for a while — silences are okay.

Believe
Try not to overdo the questions, as this can make it seem like you doubt their story. They need to see you're on their side.

Validate
Tell them that what they're feeling is right. Let them know you think their feelings are real and normal, by repeating the feeling word they've used (e.g., 'it's okay that you feel scared'). Acknowledge that you have feelings about it too, but try to keep the focus on them.

Shh
It's important that they trust you and feel like they're in control of the story. If you think someone else needs to know, check with them first. You can think together about who can be trusted, but don't tell anyone else until they are okay with it.

No blame
In our society, it's common for victims to be blamed for their experience of violence. Try to avoid questions such as, 'Why did you go there?' and 'Why did you go out with them?' because that might make them think they're responsible for what happened.

> ### Ask
> If you feel a bit helpless, ask them what sort of help they'd like from you. They're not expecting you to solve the problem, and you've already done heaps just by listening. Asking will also help them think about what to do next.
>
> ### Get help
> Talk with them about what would help stop the violence (if it's still happening), or what they feel they want. Encourage them to tell a trusted adult who can do something about it, such as a relative, a teacher or a school counsellor.

How can I have this conversation? / Me pēhea tēnei matakahi?

The strength of teens' emotions can often result in their heart seemingly ruling their head, and they may take what you intend as a helpful suggestion to be a deeply personal criticism of their love life. Ultimately, all you are trying to do is encourage them to treat others in the way they deserve to be treated. And they themselves deserve to be treated like the wonderful human being that they are:

This is why we need to have the conversation, and primarily the message here is one of respect and equality.

Make sure they know, as ever, that no matter what happens you are there for them. And try not to say, 'There are plenty more fish in the sea.'

Points to keep the conversation going
- Draw attention to any movies or series, or celebrities, that seem to **model healthy relationships**. Weave in questions on:
    - what they think are the pros or cons of being in a relationship,

- what their ideal relationship would be like,
- what people look for in a boyfriend/girlfriend/partner,
- what comes to their mind when they think of 'real love',
- whether there is peer pressure to be in a romantic relationship,
- how they balance their relationship with their other commitments,
- whether friends and support networks still matter when someone is in a relationship, and
- whether they think boys and girls expect the same from relationships.

- Once you have more of an idea about your teen's thoughts, you will be better placed to understand the type of support they might need in this context. Try not to be judgemental if their ideas differ from yours — after all, you want the conversation to continue — but do share your perspective and the reasoning behind your views (be they due to experience, religion or culture).
- If your teen has let you know they have broken up with someone, it might be useful to get them to **reflect** on anything that went well or not so well — **timing is key** here, as there may well be a grieving process to go through first.
- If you find yourself chatting with your teen about a relative's or friend's relationship (e.g., someone who is getting married, or has just announced they are having a baby), pick out some of the things that you observe in their and their partner's behaviour that make you happy for them. This can open the door to checking out the way your teen defines **what makes a healthy relationship**.
- Sometimes your teen might share with you that they are worried about a friend who has recently started going out with someone — for example, a previously happy-go-lucky friend has become very withdrawn. **Thank them for sharing this information** with you, and sensitively ask them if they

have ever seen behaviour that concerns them or makes them consider that this friend is in an unhealthy relationship or even an abusive one. Acknowledge how tricky it might feel to intervene with offers of help. You could go through the 'How you can help' box (see page 298) together, so they become more comfortable with hearing a disclosure. By being open and honest about these matters, you will hopefully encourage them to do the same.

- Check out your teen's views on why it's hard to leave an abusive relationship, and ask what they know about **support networks**; share **resources** with them (see the Resources/ Rauemi section, page 303).

Talking box questions

What do these words mean to
you in terms of relationships?
Authenticity, equality, fairness, freedom,
kindness, respect, security, trust

How would you help a friend who was
unhappy in their relationship?
What signs might tell you
that this was the case?

Resources / Rauemi

ONLINE	A resource hub for learning more about respectful relationships: loveisrespect.org
	A podcast about masculinity and what it means to be a modern man: interactives.stuff.co.nz/2021/01/hell-be-right-masculinity-podcast/
	Information about the Duluth Power and Control Wheel: theduluthmodel.org/wheels
	An adapted Power and Control Wheel and an Equality Wheel for teens: safe-sound.org/wp-content/uploads/2020/06/SPEAK-Teen-PC-and-Equality-Wheels-MERGED.pdf
	See also the list of support services for victims of sexual violence in the Helplines section (page 394).

13. THE PROBLEM WITH PORN

#pornisnotlove #theproblemwithporn

*'Porn is everywhere — it's harder
to avoid it than it is to see it.'*
— ITSTIMEWETALKED.COM

Kōrero with Molly

From my experience and that of my friends, porn was really impactful when it came to relationships, body image and early expectations of sex. I distinctly recall my first exposure to it. I was 14 years old and a boy in my class was passing around a clip on his phone. He thought the whole thing was really funny and it seemed like no one wanted to call him out on it . . . Actually, what he was showing was pretty full-on and certainly nothing I had ever even thought of before, let alone witnessed. It wasn't really funny at all. I have to be honest: it didn't make me want to emulate what I'd seen. Nonetheless, I've definitely (and I know my peers have too) felt the pressure to act and look like what we see in much of porn. It's stressful! Through work on our own body image and education about what porn is, we learned that sex is on our terms, too. Usually this education is something women have to do on their own, as parents are less likely to address their daughters about this subject. Sadly, it often isn't addressed until it's too late. While the rudimentary sex education we were taught in school when I was there is slowly becoming more progressive, it has only just begun to tackle topics like pleasure and intimacy. Awkward and uncomfortable, yes, but also imperative, I feel, especially for women and those in the LGBTQIA+ community. It ties into issues around consent and the understanding that sex does not revolve around what a man wants (or has been conditioned to want after watching hours of porn).

What do you mean by that? /
He aha te tikanga o tāu kōrero?

There's little to no chance of your teen spontaneously letting you know they have seen porn or want to have a conversation about it, so it's probably you, as their parent, who needs to broach the subject. Oh yay! Granted, this isn't the easiest topic. Porn and sexualised images are everywhere online, and by the time children have reached their teens most have had access to laptops, tablets or smartphones for some time. Over the pandemic it became even more essential that they had access to Wi-Fi to continue learning. Given the abundance of sexualised images within mainstream media, the odds are your teen has already seen some sort of pornography, whether purposefully or accidentally.

It's obviously not ideal for a young person's first exposure to information about sex to be via porn. Porn can depict sexual behaviours that don't highlight consent (see Chapter 11), mutual pleasure or equal partnerships. Also concerning is when children see sexualised images well before they are ready: they may find it traumatising. And for those teens with a history of sexual abuse, porn can be very triggering. Many teens are likely to have been exposed to sexual imagery well before they are having sex, or even before they are at the point of understanding their body and other people's bodies in that way. Bearing in mind the teenage brain is still developing (see page 21) and hasn't fully formed its pathways, all this can be confusing and confronting. They may not know how to process the mixture of feelings elicited by watching porn: they may feel guilt and shame, yet at the same time experience feelings of excitement and being sexually engaged. In some cases a negative cycle can begin: engaging in porn, feeling ashamed, and then re-engaging to feel better. This may be particularly true where teens come from a faith or cultural background where there are additional taboos around porn.

Overexposure to pornography and a potential lack of counter-messaging may mean that teens forge unrealistic expectations of any partners and their own future sexual behaviours. Research by the Office of Film and Literature Classification (OFLC), the government body responsible for classifying publications that may need to be restricted or banned in New Zealand, has also found that some groups can be particularly vulnerable to the impacts of porn, such as rainbow teens, teens who are neurodiverse and teens who have disabilities.[1]

Pornography is defined by the *Oxford Dictionary* as '[p]rinted or visual material containing the explicit description or display of sexual organs or activity, intended to stimulate sexual excitement'.[2] When we're talking about consenting adults, pornography is a personal choice. And adult consumption is different to that of younger people for several reasons, including being able to self-manage their porn usage better, usually having real-life sex scenarios to compare porn to, and being able to think more critically about the content (for example, when it contains problematic themes).

Some adults might enjoy porn (whether it be looking at it, reading it, listening to it or watching it), and there's nothing inherently wrong with that. It may be that they choose to enjoy it solo or within a relationship. Some would argue that, if mutually pleasurable, it can encourage communication, exploration and sexual pleasure. Other adults might find porn to be an absolute no-no and have strong feelings about anyone's exposure to it, and there's nothing inherently wrong with that either. It's important to recognise that we all bring our own viewpoint, understanding and (potential) baggage to this conversation, and these will be influenced by our age, gender, orientation and experience.

It's equally important to accept that our teen is becoming sexually aware (see Chapter 9). We need to take care not to demonise, on account of our own issues, topics such as masturbation and other age-appropriate sexual discovery. It can be difficult to discuss such subjects at the best of times, but any kind of perceived negative response could put our teens off raising issues with us in the future. The last thing that we want to do is alienate them at a time when they need us to be non-judgemental. Our primary concern, as ever, is their safety. It might be horrifying to find out your teen has been 'sexting' — sending nude images — that have then been shared online, but it's important that they feel able to let you know so you can figure out together the next steps to take.

It seems that what our teens are dealing with is different to the pornography of the past. Although porn genres have always drawn on stereotypical examples of sexuality, what is becoming more common is the amount of misogynistic content and normalisations of violence, which very often intersect: much recent research shows that a 'significant portion of pornography contains depictions of aggression against women with no negative responses'.[3] This is a disconcerting message on many levels for all teens, who should be trying to develop a grounded understanding of appropriate behaviour. Not only are they witnessing aggression towards women, but this aggression is also presented as acceptable and, in the majority of cases, met with pleasure, wanted or enjoyed. As outlined in a large-scale 2020 content analysis study led by sexual health communicator Niki Fritz:

> *If the only responses seen when women are the target of aggression are pleasure or non-response, male viewers may assume women either enjoy aggression or that their feelings or feedback regarding aggression is simply not important. This may normalize a script of a woman's body as an object or recipient of aggression. Women may also learn that they are supposed to experience pleasure with aggression or that they should ignore any discomfort they do experience and give a neutral response.[4]*

Added to this, pornographic content is now freely available and accessible via the Internet, and moreover is no longer restricted to porn sites. Teens can access it via a multitude of mainstream sites, apps and social media platforms. And sometimes it finds them: they see it without even looking for it in unexpected and unwanted pop-up ads, for example. There are even animated genres, such as 'anime porn', which are harder to filter as they target younger demographics. As Lacy Bentley of Women United Recovery Coalition states, 'Just because it's a cartoon, does not mean it is not pornographic.'[5]

This barrage makes it difficult for teens not only to avoid sexual content, but also to be able to think critically about what they see, particularly if there is an absence of counter-messaging. They need your help to develop a robust and resilient approach so they can process what they will inevitably be faced with.

In the words of Netsafe, a New Zealand Internet safety guideline provider, 'Pornography can negatively impact a young person's mental health and wellbeing and their knowledge, attitudes, beliefs and expectations about sex and gender. Exposure to pornography has also been found to shape sexual practices and strengthen positive attitudes toward sexual violence and aggression.'[6]

Tell me more . . . / Kōrero mai anō . . .

It can be tricky to navigate your way through the current research in this area and be sure you are adequately informed. Evidence reliant on self-reporting studies can be fraught with ambiguity since people (both teens and adults) may well want to keep their personal porn-related preferences and behaviours private. The ethics of deliberately exposing teenagers to pornography in order to study its effects would be questionable, to say the least.

This topic is now on the agenda — as evidenced by government-level policy groups around the world. The New Zealand government was concerned enough to set up a Porn Working Party, including the OFLC, Netsafe, and the Health, Social Development and Education ministries. Their work is ongoing, with some research already reported.

To date, the OFLC has produced information in a number of stages. The *NZ youth and porn* report (2018) surveyed the views of more than 2000 nationally representative 14–17-year-olds to examine their use of pornography.[7] This was followed by the *Breaking down porn* report (2019), which analysed the most-watched pornography films in New Zealand in order to 'understand what New Zealanders are watching in general, and what that might say about the kind of content that younger viewers are also accessing'.[8] Next came *Growing up with porn: Insights from young New Zealanders* (2020). This report is based on in-depth interviews with diverse young people from across the country, focusing on 'why young people view porn, why it matters, and why we need to rethink our approach to it'.[9]

Here are some key findings from the 2020 OFLC report:

- Porn is normalised for young people, whether they watch it or not.
- Young people are curious about sex, and porn is a default learning tool.
- Girls watch porn, too, for similar reasons as boys, but see a double standard.
- Porn can have a negative impact on body image/confidence.
- Young people think porn can negatively influence sex.
- Young people and adults are not talking about porn.
- Young people want comprehensive sexuality education that includes information about porn.
- Young people had varying views about filters or age verification but agreed that children shouldn't have access to porn.[10]

Although the OFLC research didn't overly focus on the impacts or harms of viewing porn, more and more studies *are* presenting research that points clearly to potential harms associated with consumption by teens and their (in)ability to constructively analyse content.

Porn is normalised for young people, whether they watch it or not

The 2018 OFLC report suggested that the average age at which respondents had first seen porn was 13 (see table overleaf).[11] These figures are echoed in research in other countries. A 2014 UK study found that seven out of 10 youth thought 'accessing pornography was seen as typical'.[12] Interestingly, the same research reported that eight out of 10 thought it was too easy to accidentally see pornography. Other UK research released in 2020 by the British Board of Film Classification stated that 'viewing pornography has been normalised among children from their mid-teens onwards, with more encountering it on networks such as Snapchat and WhatsApp than on dedicated pornography sites'.[13] So if porn is normalised, is it shaping what is considered normal?

PORN VIEWING HABITS OF NEW ZEALAND TEENS The following statistics are from the 2018 OFLC report.[14]			
	Girls	Boys	All
First seen by 14 or younger*	51%	68%	60%
First seen by 17 or younger*	68%	81%	75%
Watch monthly**	9%	21%	15%
Watch weekly**	3%	13%	8%
Watch daily or almost daily**	0%	5%	2%

*excludes 7 per cent who preferred not to answer the question
**based on all respondents

The largest study of online pornographic content to date, published in 2021 by the *British Journal of Criminology*, asserted that 'sexual violence in pornography is mainstream', and that 'coercion, deception, non-consent and criminal activity are described in mainstream online pornography in ways that position them as permissible'.[15]

Young people are curious about sex, and porn is a default learning tool

When teens are curious about all things to do with sex and relationships, porn can become one of the easiest and most readily accessible resources to look for answers to the many questions they naturally have. A concern here is that those who are accessing porn regularly for sexuality education may not then utilise other more rounded sources, and so potentially end up with a viewpoint that's informed by the porn industry. And for groups who might struggle to find much of any sexuality education specific to their needs, this is an even greater possibility: the OFLC research found that rainbow teens were twice as likely to be regular viewers and learn about sex from porn, and that teens who have long-term health issues or to disabilities were twice as likely to watch porn for stress relief or to help with sleep, and to try something out that they had seen in porn. This latter group were also four times more likely to watch porn to help with sadness and depression.[16]

Additional statistics from the OFLC findings show that, of those who view porn regularly, nearly three-quarters (73 per cent) report using it as a learning tool, and one in five recent viewers have tried out something they've seen in porn. More than one-quarter (26 per cent) state that porn is one way in which they've learned about sex; this is twice as likely with boys (34 per cent) as girls (17 per cent).

Another OFLC statistic states that friends (at 69 per cent) are the most common source of sex information, followed by teachers (62), parents or adult caregives (57), and television and the media (44). That being said, it isn't difficult to conceive that many of these friends have found what they're sharing from pornography.

Considering pornography often doesn't prioritise safe relationships and safe sex, it would be concerning if it was the only source of sex and relationship education. For example, most porn does not actively demonstrate consensual behaviour. The OFLC found that 35 per cent of porn showed explicitly non-consensual or coercive behaviour; and in a much larger British review of 150,000 videos, one in eight videos were described as containing sexual violence, almost all against women (with scenes such as spanking, gagging, slapping, hair-pulling and choking).[17]

Neither does porn encourage condom or dam use[18] (see page 235). Porn actors may rely on regular STI checks instead, but this would obviously be off-camera. Teens may therefore not realise they are only receiving partial (and potentially problematic) information, which could impact on their understanding of their health choices. To at least balance out what they may be seeing, it seems imperative for home and school to be stepping in and creating alternate learning tools to fill the gaps.

Girls watch porn, too, for similar reasons as boys, but see a double standard
Surveys of young people have shown both boys and girls are watching pornography, although, across each age group, boys are watching more and doing so more often. It seems that girls' experience of porn may be unequal in other ways, such as how they perceive they are expected to behave. This is possibly unsurprising considering that much porn is generally made by men, for men.

Statistics bear this out:

- In a 2014 British survey of 500 18-year-olds, 75 per cent of women said that 'pornography has led to pressure on girls and young women to act a certain way'.[19]
- According to a British Girlguiding survey of 2015, seven in 10 girls and young women aged 11–21 think that pornography gives out confusing messages about sexual consent, or that it makes aggressive or violent behaviour towards women seem normal (both at 71 per cent).[20]
- In the OFLC's 2020 report, girls described a greater sense of taboo or stigma around sex and sexuality, and this 'double standard extended to watching porn'.[21]

It's not uncommon for girls to report that they have been asked to do something their partner saw in porn. We can see that girls who view porn are not always finding it a positive activity, and they are also experiencing some of the negative fallout of boys watching porn. So it's worrying to note from the 2018 OFLC survey that 'parents and caregivers were almost twice as likely to raise the topic of porn with boys than with girls'.[22]

Porn can have a negative impact on body image/confidence
Given all of the above, it's perhaps not surprising that teens are comparing porn to what they see in real life. Porn is one of the few ways that teens can view other people's naked bodies, after all. Part of growing up and developing healthy self-esteem and good body

image (see pages 151–153) is understanding and celebrating the vast array of differences between people (see page 360). This includes their body type, gender, race, disability and sexuality. There is a lack of this representation within most media as a whole, and porn is no exception.

In the British Girlguiding survey, nearly nine in 10 young women aged 17–21 agreed that pornography 'creates unrealistic expectations of what women's bodies are like' (87 per cent), while around three in four (73 per cent) thought that 'it creates unrealistic expectations about men's bodies'.[23] And according to the OFLC's 2020 report *Growing up with porn*, both boys and girls 'were concerned that watching porn could make young people feel more self-conscious about their bodies. The young people thought it would be common for girls to feel bad about their bodies after watching porn because their bodies did not match up to the "ideal" portrayed in porn.' For boys, the biggest source of worry was penis size.[24]

Teens may worry, if comparing themselves to porn actors, that their body doesn't measure up, concerned that body parts are too small, too large, the wrong shape or too hairy. Male porn actors tend to be muscular and well-endowed, with an unrealistic amount of stamina. Most female porn actors tend to be slim yet curvaceous, with hairless body parts. In addition, mainstream pornography will use adult actors and models, so teenagers whose bodies are still in the process of maturing may look completely different. These comparisons can be detrimental at a time when body image and confidence can already be fragile. (These particular points don't necessarily apply to the ever-increasing amount of amateur porn, which may have less stereotypical body shapes and sizes, but given the lack of regulation this content is concerning for many other reasons.)

Young people think porn can negatively influence sex

Much of the time in porn it appears as if the man is in charge and his needs are the only important ones. The woman is seemingly willing to have sex at any time, anywhere and in virtually any way to please the man. Even lesbian porn is generally scripted by and for men, which can be especially damaging to our queer youth. It's hard to make sense of storylines that show characters who are seemingly always 'up for it' and taking pleasure in all encounters, even when others are doing painful or aggressive things to them. This confusion can be exacerbated for those teens who lack other information or experiences to counter what they are seeing.

Repeated viewing can seem to normalise these situations. Research now suggests repeated porn usage can shape sexist attitudes and that unrealistic expectations of sex can develop as a result if unchallenged.[25] According to a recent Australian study, 'Gaps between expectations and reality can produce "sexual uncertainty" about sexual beliefs and values and may also be related to sexual dissatisfaction, anxiety and fear.'[26] More concerning still is the question of whether this young exposure to porn, particularly violent, rough and aggressive porn, normalises sexual violence, and, if so, whether it can lead to the everyday acceptance of sexual aggression in youth sexual culture or even a rape culture (see page 276).

In addition, there has been an increase in the overlap between porn and virtual reality: as this becomes more popular and the equipment for it more affordable, porn now has a growing market for another level of participation. It's difficult to imagine, when so immersed in something not relevant to a healthy relationship, that it won't have some damaging effects, especially if consumed by teens whose brains are still developing (see page 21). Some teens will tell you that they understand porn is not real and will report laughing between themselves about the situations they are viewing. In the words of Gail Dines, an American scholar of pornography and professor of sociology and women's studies:

> *They may be laughing about it but they are also masturbating to it. They say they know it's fake, but what does that mean? You haven't got one brain that processes fake stuff and one that processes real stuff. You have one brain and one body that's aroused. If you begin*

by masturbating to cruel, hardcore, violent porn, studies show that you are not going to grow up wired for intimacy and connection.[27]

There is increasing attention on what is referred to as 'porn addiction', perhaps better conveyed as 'problematic or compulsive usage', when people (teens included) are unable to stop or cut down their porn use and become 'hooked' for psychological or other reasons. Over time, we will likely become aware of the true impact of the way teens are currently accessing and using pornography. In the meantime, there are a number of concerns as to how porn could negatively influence sexual behaviour, including:

- erectile dysfunction (the notion that the overstimulation of watching porn renders teens unable to reach an erection or ejaculation in a real-life sexual situation),
- aggression in intimate scenarios,
- the depersonification of women, and crimes that come from this,
- other general difficulties in understanding and participating in relationships,
- a perceived pressure on a teen to sext or even to make amateur porn movies themselves, something they may later regret, and
- anxiety, guilt and shame around porn usage, especially when teens use porn to manage stress and negative emotions.

Netsafe reports that, 'Although over-consuming porn is not technically classed as an official addiction, there is evidence to suggest that some people can become overly reliant on watching online porn and develop compulsive porn usage. It's a good idea to talk about the fact that some young people may use porn to avoid things in their everyday life and or in a way that makes them feel unhappy or out of control.'[28]

If you are concerned about your teen's relationship with porn, it's good to seek some help, but in the meantime you can set some ground rules. Keeping screen time restricted to a public place can be useful, but cell phones go everywhere and you cannot supervise teens 100 per cent of the time. Perhaps a rule about no tech in the bedroom after bedtime is a useful boundary. Ultimately, as parents we need to have some input — we need to check in with our teen and check out what influence porn is having on them. Again, it's all about safety.

Young people and adults are not talking about porn

Interesting to note is that our teens want help in managing porn. A number of research projects report that they're actually asking for assistance — and are letting us know that they don't think the adults around them are adequately informed. This makes it tricky for them to have the conversations they want and need. There seems to be a mismatch of opinions between adults and teens as to how large a problem this is.

In one British survey, 75 per cent of parents thought their child hadn't seen pornography online, but in reality 53 per cent of their children reported that they had in fact seen it.[29] And according to the 2020 OFLC report, teens talked about persistently hearing only negative and sometimes simplistic messages about pornography from adults, which often don't fit with their own feelings and experiences. They noted that overly negative and unrealistic talk about porn gets in the way of their seeking help and guidance and created a climate of fear and anxiety around porn and sexuality more generally.[30]

If all that teens are hearing from adults is that porn is a negative thing and shouldn't be viewed under any circumstances, it can remove the opportunity for discussion when they already feel themselves to be in an information void. Shame, guilt and secretive behaviours can creep in, rather than an open environment that allows for conversation and understanding. In Utah, USA, porn has been officially labelled by politicians as a 'public health hazard'.[31] This 'just say no' idea could be counterintuitive and serve only to pique teens' curiosity.

Note that for our neurodiverse teens, porn can be especially difficult to process and deal with, and they may require greater support in this area from parents and caregivers.[32]

Young people want comprehensive sexuality education that includes information about porn

It's awesome that our teens are actually asking for more input on sexuality. If they are curious and seeking answers, this can only be a good thing. It may indicate that they are asking for help so that they can make healthy and safe choices. The OFLC report from 2019 revealed that, out of all the porn films they examined, only 29 per cent showed some form of affection, whereas 35 per cent showed some non-consensual behaviour and only 3 per cent showed condom use.[33]

If we aren't including information and discussion about porn in sexuality education, who is outlining the dangers of what teens viewing porn are being exposed to? And without giving them this context, does it undermine the other messages that we are trying to give them? With regard to sexuality education, the OFLC states that, 'along with sexual violence, porn was the least covered topic in New Zealand schools', and as a consequence, 'some young people are missing out on in-school learning about porn, and in-depth coverage of aspects like consent, relationships, sexual violence and digital technologies'.[34]

What is becoming very clear is the need for broader sexuality education to keep up with the times and cover so much more than the birds and the bees. Ideally this occurs at home as well as at school, but wherever it happens it's important that it is open and non-judgemental. It may also mean that parents are requiring additional information and skills as to how to talk with their teens (such as this book!).

Young people had varying views about filters or age verification but agreed that children shouldn't have access to porn

The OFLC report of 2018 found that 89 per cent of New Zealand teens 'agreed that it isn't okay for children to look at pornography'. And 71 per cent 'believed children and teens' access to online porn should be restricted in some way, including half (51 per cent) of regular viewers of pornography.[35] British research, likewise, found that 'two-thirds of young women and half of young men think growing up would be easier if porn was more difficult to access'.[36]

There are various parental controls you can install on your teen's computer and the home router, but, although these are useful with younger children, teens are harder to police. You can block certain sites (the notorious *Pornhub* would be a good place to start). There are also programs that notify you if any such sites are accessed. And if they are, it might be time to have a conversation, if you haven't already. However, even with safeguards in place, it's important not to be complacent given the ubiquity of online porn. That's not to say it's not worth doing, and if you do decide to explore these options it's a fairly straightforward process. At the same time, it's highly likely your teen is more tech-savvy than you are and could easily get around any restrictions. This is why it's important to talk things through with your teen.

Ethical porn?

Along with the issues raised above, many also believe those involved in the porn industry are exploiting, abusing and generally disempowering people, some of whom may even be underage. Porn is a billion-dollar industry, so those making it will be concerned with profit and not necessarily the health and safety of those involved and those accessing the end product. There has been particular worry that some of the most popular porn platforms are hosting non-consensual (such as underage pornography), stolen (such as sexual images and videos which were never intended for public viewing, uploaded from hacked private accounts) and abusive content including harmful digital imagery. Activists have been campaigning for changes to these platforms in the way they verify their content. *The Guardian* newspaper has also reported up to 350,000 people signing various petitions and joining campaigns such as #NotYourPorn.[37]

Ethical porn, 'fair trade' porn and feminist porn are various types of pornography that some consider to be made in a positive, fair and safe way. This means the performers and crew are not exploited financially, the actors' ages are verified, the actors consent to the content being online, and the content usually (but not always) shows mutual respect, care and pleasure. Importantly, consent is demonstrated. It is thought generally to be more realistic, inclusive and representative. The type of sex it shows is not invariably centred around male pleasure, and the actors featured are drawn from a much more diverse group of people who are therefore more representative of the 'normal' population.

Ethical porn isn't for the most part free, it isn't spotted in pop-ups, and most can be found only by specifically searching for it. It's also not made for teenagers, and the content is therefore age restricted. Some ethical porn can still contain aggressive content, so it can still have some or a major negative impact on any teens viewing it.

A word on nudes and sexts

According to Netsafe, one in five 14–17-year-olds in New Zealand have been asked to share a nude photo, and although girls tend to be asked more frequently there is an equal amount of boys and girls who do. According to the Youth2000 survey, '13 per cent of students stated they had received unwanted sexual messages, most commonly by mobile phone (52 per cent), the Internet (44 per cent) or letters or notes (4 per cent)'.[38] Sexting and sending nudes is making sexual images and sharing them using a phone or by posting them online. They can be of the person themselves or of another person, and are either partially or completely nude. Most teens have, at the very least, heard of the practice and some would state they have 'consented to' sending nudes or sexts and consider them fun.

One of the issues here is your teen's understanding of their 'digital footprint' (see page 107). This means the trail of data they intentionally and unintentionally leave online. Whether they create a social media post, send an email or comment on a web page, the content can potentially be seen, examined, used and collected by others. To be a good digital citizen your teen needs to know how to take part in online community life in a safe, ethical and respectful way.

Images, once shared, can end up out of your teen's control and dispersed widely. They may also crop up at an embarrassing point in the future, such as when making applications for jobs or colleges. It can be extremely difficult to get back what's been posted online. That even goes for Snapchat, where images that are designed to disappear after a few seconds can be screen-shot and saved by others.

There are legal avenues (for example, the Harmful Digital Communication Act 2015) to pursue if nude or nearly nude images have been shared without permission, as it can be considered 'image-based abuse'. Successful prosecutions can result in large fines or prison time.

Netsafe recommends that if content has been shared online without your teen's permission, they should:

- take a screenshot of the content,
- report the content at once to the relevant platform (e.g., Facebook, Twitter, etc.),
- report to the platform also the profile of the person who shared it, and
- contact Netsafe to discuss what further steps can be taken.[39]

How can I have this conversation? / Me pēhea tēnei matakahi?

As referenced earlier, 60 per cent of young New Zealanders first saw porn by the age of 14. Mounting evidence about the effects of porn on teens, coupled with the qualitative information reported from teens themselves, strongly indicates that there are some problem areas they require assistance in addressing.

This is why we need to have the conversation, and primarily the message here is to be the counter-messenger.

Ideally these dialogues need to take place in advance of your teen being exposed to porn — before they accidentally come across it or think to go looking. You don't want porn messing up your teen's emotional health or putting their future relationships at risk. Remember, you are not authorising your teen to watch porn by talking about it — and nor are you, in all likelihood, putting the idea in their head for the first time.

As a parent, you may relate to the following analogy from author Tanith Carey: 'Leaving children to find out about porn for themselves is like putting them on a motorway without a driving test: they might find their own way through it, but before they learn to take control, they could harm themselves and others during the process. They need driving lessons from the outset.'[40]

- Let your teen know you **appreciate these conversations are personal** — they can feel embarrassed, but you're going to be having them anyway.
- Let them know it's **healthy to be curious** — you're just keen they are also critically analysing the messages they are receiving.
- Talk about **consent** (see Chapter 11).

As always, a great conversation starter is to discuss with your teen what they already know and what their thoughts are on the topic. You could ask them what they'd want a younger sibling or cousin to know about pornography and why. Put them in the role of helping out — their answers will impact them too. You may find you're really impressed by how considered their opinions are. If we can open the space, they will eventually start filling it, and that's when we get to hear their worries and questions. It's about letting them know we are not judging them.

Points to keep the conversation going

- **Initiate discussions** about porn in a similar way to those suggested in Chapters 7 and 11, on body image and consent — for example, using teachable moments when the topic is referenced or when it is downplayed or normalised in the general media you watch together.
- **Be analytical (but not judgemental) about the media** you know your teen already accesses. Again, remember that the films, television and reality shows and series now routinely available are way more graphic than in days gone by. You may remember music videos being banned for showing too much skin or being considered provocative back in the day, whereas now we have reality shows and game shows that are built on nudity and sex. Some of the behaviours and messages in porn are also seen in mainstream TV shows and series. Dialogue may well contain 'normalising' references to individuals' or characters' use of pornography. This makes it harder for teens to disentangle messages around what is appropriate.
- **Sharing your own thoughts** in these conversations, throwing in some **statistics** and being inquisitive with your wonderings might just ensure that your teen, at the very least, realises porn is not a real-life example of sex.
- Let them know that if they are concerned that porn may be impacting on their everyday life, **they can talk to you** about it. If they don't feel comfortable talking to you, let them know there are **other services** who can support them.
- Teens can be really interested in the topic of porn and ethics. Here are some key points to prompt further discussion:
  - Porn is theatre, fantasy — the scenarios set up for porn are **not designed to be realistic**. Most porn stars are actors and are paid to do this job.
  - Most of what porn portrays is not what should be expected in real life.
  - Porn is not something anyone should be **worried** about

having to replicate or live up to.

- Porn may contain content that is not only misogynist, but also racist, homophobic or disablist.
- A lot of the sexually and gender diverse (SGD) porn is very aggressive and fetishes or stereotypes SGD actors.
- Porn can show **cruelty, violence and humiliation** — what is seen in porn could be physically painful or harmful in real life.
- Porn can be masochistic and **stereotypically gendered**: seemingly women are seen as willing sex objects ready any time and any place to please men.
- There is often **no consent** in porn.
- In porn, actors look like they enjoy rough or aggressive sex, but in **real-life** sex most people don't like this.
- Porn **doesn't always show safe sex** (and some porn contains illegal acts).
- Porn stars' bodies may well **not reflect the body of your teen** — or indeed that of anyone else they know.
- Porn is a billion-dollar industry and therefore has its **own agenda,** which tends to put profit first.
- Porn is not designed to provide young people with sexuality education.
- Porn is normally about the sexual act rather than intimacy, trust and healthy relationships. Watching porn can therefore **confuse feelings** around sex and intimacy.
- Watching porn can **shape sexual ideas, expectations and experiences**.
- Constantly dealing with **mixed-up feelings** related to sex can have long-lasting effects.

Talking box questions

> # Why are there age restrictions on some Internet content?

> # How might watching porn impact someone's intimate relationships?

Resources / Rauemi

ONLINE	Resource hubs including tips and information for chatting to your teens about dealing with challenging content and staying safe online:
	thelightproject.co.nz/whanau/talking-with-teens
	netsafe.org.nz
	Resource hub for teens struggling with porn-related issues:
	intheknow.co.nz
	Media designed for teens
	Real sex talks:
	tinyurl.com/yc89p2yw
	The Eggplant is a New Zealand comedy drama series that sets out to help young Kiwis navigate Internet-related issues on sexuality:
	tvnz.co.nz/shows/the-eggplant
	Keep It Real Online is a government initiative (with Netsafe) to help young people stay safe online:
	tinyurl.com/2p98jpaf

GROWING IN INDEPENDENCE

14. PREPARING YOUR TEEN FOR ADULTING

#adulting #lifeskills #flyingthenest

'... kids don't stay with you if you do it right. It's the one job where the better you are, the more surely you won't be needed in the long run.'
— BARBARA KINGSOLVER

Kōrero with Molly

I remember the Christmas before I moved out (the first time!). My brother had already started flatting and learning the realities of adulting. Santa brought me some awesome gifts that year, but I was horrified to see some of the presents my brother got . . . nail clippers, cans of baked beans, undies, socks, bed linen . . . how boring! Little did I know I would be just as excited as he was when I received similar things the following year. It meant that I could make what little money I did have as a student go just a bit further.

What do you mean by that? / He aha te tikanga o tāu kōrero?

At some point your teen will move on from the family home and begin their journey into 'adulting' and independence. This is an exciting time when you both can look forward to their future and all the opportunities that exist for them. Well before they actually leave home, you can facilitate their learning in terms of the everyday skills they will need to look after themselves: they may consider the tasks you lay out for them as just chores, but by getting them involved you are in fact giving them an advantage for when they fly the nest.

Sure, they are going to find their own way, and learn from their own mistakes, but you can give them a bit of structure so that they have had some practice for when they find themselves out in the big wide world.

The following list is a good starting point:

- **healthy habits** (food and nutrition, grocery shopping, cooking, exercise, healthcare),
- **domestic stuff** (laundry, cleaning),
- **transportation** (transport, navigation and road safety),
- **finances** (money management), and
- **career planning** (job applications and interviews).

Although your teen has Google and YouTube to answer any and every question, trying to get their head round *all* of the practicalities of day-to-day living at the same time can feel a little like their first driving lesson: there are just too many things to concentrate on all at once. It can be invaluable to have a lived experience so that everything doesn't feel overwhelming when your teen has to fend for themselves (for example, putting together a quick meal, working out which clothes need to be washed on which cycle, or remembering not to stick a knife into the toaster to unwedge the bread — least of all when it's plugged in).

It may feel like you don't want to overload your teen when they already have so much on their plate, but this is a time of transition, and if you step back while they are still under your roof, that then allows them the space to step forward. Any muck-ups can then be used as lessons in a safe environment while they continue to move towards independence. Their self-reliance and autonomy is what will see them through, even if they have some errors in judgement along the way (something that has happened to most of us at some point or another).

Statistics show that about a third of Kiwi teens go to university the year after they leave high school.[1] Others enrol in alternative further education, including modern apprenticeships, some go straight into work, and there are also those who choose the well-trodden path of the

OE (which might now look very different as a result of the pandemic). Whatever their choice, and whether they are in accommodation, flatting, travelling or still with you, you will want to know that they are confident and capable of looking after themselves. This is especially true if they end up staying with you — or you will still be washing their socks when they are 30. Many schools don't have a programme within the curriculum that is dedicated to actual living skills, in which case it will fall to you to start preparing them for adulting, and it could be argued that you can't start too soon.

You may remember the highs and lows of first living away from home. Perhaps things seemed exhilarating and scary in equal measure. Your young adult may feel the same: one Australian study of 18–34-year-olds, for instance, found that the '[h]appiness and satisfaction of those who lived away from home was much higher than those who still lived with their parents'.[2] That said, even if they do leave, for a variety of reasons you may find your teen back on your doorstep in their early twenties for another protracted stay — perhaps while they save up for a deposit on their first home. And with house prices (and rents) currently spiralling upwards, there is no guarantee how long they might be around. New Zealand statistics tell us, for instance, that the average age at which adult children leave home is 27,[3] and that, before the pandemic, about one-third of young adults were still living at home. That figure has since risen, with some 40 per cent of surveyed 18–24-year-olds living with one or both parents,[4] and around one-quarter of young people expecting some financial help from their parents.[5]

Tell me more . . . / Kōrero mai anō . . .

This book has already covered a lot of ground looking at the importance of your teen's health and wellbeing, and how they can build their social and emotional skills. This chapter focuses instead on some of the practical skills they will need. There's a lot to be said for daily routines they may then take with them into adulthood (five fruit and veg a day, for example). In addition, you can use particular events as learning opportunities. When they have invited friends over, get your teen involved in the planning, the catering, the shopping and the clean-up. If they have a sleepover, get them to help with organising sleeping arrangements. When they have a form or application to fill in, try not to take over: this will then hold them in good stead for when they need to fill in driving licence documents, enrol at uni, or apply for StudyLink or an 18+ card, for example. They will need to know their various ID numbers and store them securely (this covers everything from student ID to health ID to IRD). Decide when is a good time for them to have responsibility for their own passport and other important documents.

Most teens have access to a calendar app or Internet planner. Your family may even share a Google diary. One way to help teens start to take responsibility for not only organising their own social life, but also for letting you know their whereabouts, is to have an old-school paper calendar — it's even better if this has a column for each member of the family. This can help them to be more mindful of other people's time so that they don't commit to a film night at their mate's on the night of Gran's birthday party.

Healthy habits

Food and nutrition

We all want our teens to understand how to look after themselves, and part of this is keeping their body functional and healthy. Generally your teen will have learned at school about the food pyramid and what a balanced diet looks like. It never hurts for you to re-emphasise this, while being mindful that food doesn't become a point of stress for them (see page 169). Having your teen be hands-on is an excellent way for them to learn, and there are some great student cookbooks available that can make the perfect Christmas or birthday present. Health and environmental considerations increasingly influence our eating habits; for instance, Kiwis now rank fifth in the world for veganism.[6] Your teen is growing up with these issues being discussed, so try to respect their choices (so long as they are healthy) rather than dismiss them as fads. (You may be aware of this already when you go into a coffee shop and can choose from five different types of milk.)

Kōrero with Molly

Have you heard of the 'fresher 5'? It's a slang term for the extra weight in kilos that students tend to put on after moving out of home. It's far too easy to fall into the routine of ordering takeouts or relying solely on two-minute noodles and energy drinks for sustenance when Mum and Dad are no longer serving those home-cooked meals. Convenience is really important to young people, and I don't remember spending too much time thinking about what I was having for lunch or dinner, let alone how many fruits and vegetables I was eating. My older brother was the same until my mum convinced him he would get scurvy, like a pirate, if he didn't eat any fruit — which scared the hell out of him!

Grocery shopping

For most of us, grocery shopping isn't much fun at the best of times — and dragging along a sullen teenager won't make matters better. However, this is an important habit to instil. Perhaps send them off by themselves every now and then to get some specific ingredients. Even when life is busy and stressful, we still have to make time to get to the supermarket, or for online grocery shopping. It's a big part of anyone's routine. Of course, there's an app for that! Some apps will even generate a cost-effective shopping list from a weekly menu plan, which can be helpful in terms of budgeting.

Kōrero with Molly

I used to pop my headphones in and try to groove down the aisles and make it fun (much to my mother's embarrassment). Within my banking app I have now created an account with my food allowance for the week, and I use my phone as a calculator when I'm doing my big shop so that I stick to my budget. Some supermarkets provide you with a scanner so you can track how much you are spending as you fill your cart. Even now I find shopping a bit boring, but I like that many supermarkets have their own apps. You can log the items on your shopping list and it will organise them by aisle to make things really easy.

Cooking

Before even getting to the cooking part it's a good plan to teach and remind your teen how to handle themselves in the kitchen. They will need to:

- make sure **surfaces are clean** before they start (*and* after they finish),
- **wash their hands** regularly when handling food,
- know to prevent the spread of bacteria by thoroughly cleaning knives and chopping boards at all stages of food prep (especially if cooking with meat or fish),
- have some basic **knife skills** to preserve their fingers,
- have a **first-aid kit** in the kitchen (just in case), and
- test their **smoke alarm** regularly, and know how to use a **fire extinguisher** — which is not as straightforward as you might imagine. They should also know how to put out different types of fire in the kitchen (see Resources/Rauemi, page 349).

Once they've mastered basic safety and hygiene, teach your teen a few simple and affordable recipes that they can have under their belt. Not only is this going to be really helpful to them, but you can also use the time to catch up with them while busy chopping and stirring. You may even be able to introduce a regular time for them to cook that fits around their extracurricular activities. The more they are involved in food preparation and putting together meals, the more they will gain confidence in the kitchen. It will also highlight what they will need to make up their own 'cooking toolkit' when they do eventually move out.

Kōrero with Molly

At least once a week, my parents would have me cook a meal for the family. It really is good practice for being out in the real world. There are some basic skills that everyone should know about the kitchen — such as how to use a knife safely, the best technique for chopping an onion and garlic (the base of almost every meal I know how to make), how to check an expiry date and how to look after a non-stick pan. My dad taught me how to put every single vegetable in the fridge in a pan with some mince and canned tomato before serving it on rice or pasta. That saved me a few times. I have learned that some people just have a knack for cooking and others don't. I fall into the latter category, so instead I chop up the vegetables and do the dishes. Regardless, I would have been lost without a basic understanding of how to cook a balanced meal. Despite my aversion to cooking, I can whip up a mean stir-fry that covers the main food groups and allows me to continue to be a functioning human being. Thanks, Dad.

Exercise

The important thing here is for your teen to make keeping fit another integral part of their routine. Being active keeps us happy as well as healthy. The Ministry of Health recommends teenagers do 'at least one hour of moderate or vigorous physical activity spread over each day'.[7] As they progress through high school, your teen may decide to drop the option of PE. If this is the case, encourage them to explore other options outside of school. Is there a beach nearby where they can go for a daily walk or swim? Perhaps there are some social sports teams they could join, or even a yoga class at the community centre? There are also some incredible free resources for at-home workouts online. The possibilities are endless.

Kōrero with Molly

I tried a lot of team sports throughout my schooling. I was too afraid of the ball and found myself waving to Mum in the crowd instead of participating, so I was really happy when I found dancing. I was never really that good at it, but it was such a fun way to get my body moving. Plus, it was more time to hang out with friends outside of school. I often opted out of the more serious exams and competitions; I was there to have fun. My peers found ways to keep fit through a variety of sports, some through school and some through other clubs. Cheerleading was really popular at my school, alongside water polo, rugby, soccer and badminton. There really is something for everyone, and it set me up for finding a sustainable exercise routine to take with me after high school.

Healthcare

As your teens get older it's useful for them to start taking more responsibility for scheduling their own routine appointments. Setting a good precedent is particularly important for male teens, since in older life men tend to avoid visiting the doctor.[8] There are costs associated with healthcare — and this is known to be even more of an obstacle for the young than for the elderly[9] — but there are also ways to mitigate expenses. For instance:

- Charges for GP visits vary from practice to practice, so it's worth shopping around.
- Some teens may have access to free medical care through school.
- Some Youth Hubs and clinics waive medical fees for under-22s.

- If your teen is at uni, the affiliated health care centres are generally free.
- Teens need to visit an optometrist every couple of years (unless an issue arises in the interim); some companies do free examinations for under-16s, and others have special deals for tertiary students.
- Dental care is free for under-18s (although this doesn't include orthodontic care).
- If your teen or your household qualifies for a Community Services Card, medical fees will be significantly reduced.

Kōrero with Molly

Finding a good doctor is hard! I was very picky because I needed to find someone that made me feel heard and respected. Someone once told me to never trust a doctor with dead plants in their office. I found myself doing lots of research and discovering that there were loads of GP clinics in my area. Their prices vary and visiting the doctor can be pretty expensive. Luckily, my university offered free healthcare, so I used that while I could. My friends that chose not to go to university looked into getting Community Services Cards, which subsidised their GP visits, or they drove a little bit further to a clinic that had lower prices.

The reality is, every doctor deals with their patients in a different way, and I learned that it's okay to take my time to shop around.

Domestic stuff

Household chores can feel endless. Many of us find them repetitive and boring, as your teen will almost certainly echo. However, getting them ready for flatting or living in uni residences also means training them up to be able to at least do the basics. It's also important to understand that one chore might form only part of the process. Let's take laundry as an example:

- Ensure they put their laundry in the laundry basket and not in a heap on the floor of their room.
- Teach them to read clothing labels so that they know how to separate their laundry into the various different types of washes.
- Don't forget to show them how to turn the washing machine on (and how to check the filter) . . . and encourage them to use it!
- Explain the best ways to hang clothes on a line to get away with as little ironing as possible.[10]
- If using a dryer, make sure they are aware of the expense, the ecological impact and that there are safety implications (i.e., remind them that they need to remove the fluff that gathers each time).
- Teach them how to iron. And remind them to turn the iron off after use and not to put it away until after it has cooled down.
- Get them to put their clean clothes away and not back on the floor . . .

You may have some tips and tricks you can pass on, like their aunt's way to fold a T-shirt or Grandad's way of cleaning the oven. Or you may have some family anecdotes (or horror stories) about how not to do things. Whichever way you choose to impart your domestic wisdom, at the very least your teen should be in charge of keeping their own room clean and tidy (bear in mind that your definition of 'clean and tidy' may be at variance to theirs, but over time they will get there!). They should also take some responsibility for the bathroom they use. All this is not nagging (well, not just nagging): when they leave home they will almost certainly be sharing with others, and they don't want to be the worst flatmate ever.

'Teenagers who are never required
to vacuum are living in one.'
— FRED G. GOSMAN

Kōrero with Molly

I'll never forget moving into my first apartment. It was just above the train station. It had been a week or two and my washing pile had grown so high, I couldn't see out of my own window. I stuffed everything I had into the washing machine and then ... wait ... This isn't the same as the one I had at home ... How does this work? I'm not ashamed to say that I rang my mother and asked her how to turn it on. Something I had taken for granted was now another big part of my routine.

Transportation

Although it might feel like you are forever your teen's personal taxi service, thinking of them in charge of their own transportation can be nerve-racking. Nonetheless, many teens will be wanting to learn to drive before they leave home, particularly if they live in more rural areas where public transport options are usually limited. To drive a car independently involves a few years and a three-step process. The first stage is understanding the road rules in order to gain a **learner** licence, which your teen can do when they turn 16. Once they have achieved this they will then need driving lessons. After they've held their learner licence for a minimum of six months they can then sit a driving test. If they pass, they gain their **restricted** licence, which allows them to drive alone but only within certain hours of the day (there are some exceptions to this). At age 18 years (or 17.5 if they have taken an advanced driver course) they can sit another, slightly shorter, driving test. Passing this gives them their **full** licence, which allows them to drive unrestricted any Class 1 vehicle (see Resources/ Rauemi, page 349).

So, your teen has passed their test and is desperate to have their own car and all the independence that it brings. But before they rush out to buy the nearest rust-bucket, it's important to have a conversation (if not several conversations) about:

- what they need to use it for (the school commute, or for strapping on a surfboard and driving off into the wide blue yonder),
- who is going to fund the purchase (you, them or a combination),
- whether it will be new or second-hand, and
- who is going to fund its running costs and maintenance (you, them or a combination).

Your teen should be aware that owning a car is a substantial ongoing expense. They need to be able to factor in registration, upkeep and repairs (new tyres, for example), WOF and insurance. Although car insurance is not mandatory in New Zealand it's well worth their having it, even if only third party. If possible, get it under their own name so they can start building up their credit rating for better deals later, because, as we all know, buying, registering, insuring and running a car isn't cheap: even a modest model will set them back around $3000–5000 annually.[11]

Your teen may also be considering the environmental impact of driving. Buying an electric car is probably not yet affordable for most teens, even though they might ideally prefer to go down this route in order to reduce their carbon footprint (see page 372) — not to mention their fuel bills. Ultimately, safety should be the overriding consideration. The AA recommends that, if buying new or near-new, you look for an ANCAP five-star safety rating (a four-star rating will do if you are buying an older car). This dramatically reduces the risk of serious injury on the road.[12]

It's a good idea, too, to help your teen learn some car maintenance and safety before they are allowed their own keys. Basics should include knowing how to fill the tank, change a tyre (and check tyre pressure), jump-start a car when the battery is flat, check oil and water (and screen-cleaner), pay for parking, and cope in a breakdown or emergency.[13]

Road safety

When your teen does get out on the road, either as a driver or as a passenger, as ever, their safety is paramount. And with the legal driving age coinciding with the stage of brain development where they can potentially be at their least risk-averse (see page 21), it is perhaps unsurprising that 15–24-year-olds are, according to government figures, 'at a far higher risk of death from motor vehicle traffic crashes than any other age group except 75 years and over'.[14] It is therefore imperative that your teen knows the fundamental rules of the road before they sit behind the wheel:

- Don't use your phone while driving. Pull over if you need to make a call or send a text message.[15]
- Don't drink and drive. There is a zero alcohol limit for anyone under 20, and you may be charged if caught flouting this rule.[16] The same is obviously also true of drug-taking.
- If you are going out to a bar or to a party, make sure your group includes a designated sober driver.[17]
- If a designated driver is drunk or otherwise under the influence, don't accept a lift. (It's a very good idea to agree with your teen that they can phone you at any time, day or night, and you will come and find them, or have a family ride-share account that they can access in case of such emergencies.)

With all this talk about cars, it can be easy to forget that there are other ways to get from A to B. Public transport is slowly becoming more of an option for many. Also, if possible, ensure your teen knows how to ride a bike (it's never too late to start), understands the cycling road rules and has some general bike maintenance skills, along with a robust lock. Perhaps your family enjoy riding together: this can instil a habit that lasts a lifetime, especially when your teen starts to factor in the finances of other methods of transportation. Undoubtedly, they will also be aware of the many hire options for scooters and bikes, particularly in cities.

Finances

Wonderful as teens are, they are also expensive to run. And as they get older and more interested in money and what it can buy, the more expensive they seem to be. As with everything else touched on in this chapter, the key thing here is to give them a limited amount of responsibility as soon as they are able to cope with it, and to build things up gradually. Make them accountable (excuse the pun) for their financial decisions: if they have spent all their allowance on lollies, they will not be able to afford the next PS5 game any time soon . . .

> *'Annual income 20 pounds, annual expenditure 19 pounds, 19 shillings and six pence, result happiness. Annual income 20 pounds, annual expenditure 20 pounds ought and six, result misery.'*
> — MR MICAWBER, *DAVID COPPERFIELD* (CHARLES DICKENS)

Everyone, no matter what their incoming money (whether it is from wages, benefits, StudyLink, employment or investments), needs to be able to budget their spending and organise their savings. Money skills are no less vital for teens. Deciding on whether your teen has an allowance, and how much, is all a part of this. Giving them some financial independence can feel scary — but it also permits them to make a few slip-ups while they are still under your wing, and it will help them fend for themselves later on. You may find that your teen is influenced by the way you deal with your accounts; similarly, you may have been influenced by your parents.

The importance of being financially savvy cannot be overestimated, not least because there can be so many disagreements that relate back to money. This knowledge can be gained incrementally, but by the time they reach their twenties your teen should have the following in place:

- **A bank account**: At first, they would normally be issued with a cashpoint card, which usually can also be used for eftpos.

When they are ready, they can then move on to a debit card that can be used online. In addition, your teen will almost certainly be embracing other ways of paying, including using their phone, Apple or Google Pay, or PayPal.

- **An understanding of their statements**: Many teens will feel entirely at home using online banking and may even already access their accounts through an app on their phone. When they are first learning about money matters, or if they are needing a bit of support, discuss with them the extent to which they are happy to share their financial records with you.
- **An understanding of bank charges**: Start with teaching them the basics of interest and the result of being overdrawn. They may need you to point out the various fees banks can charge (e.g., for using a different bank's cash withdrawal machine).
- An ability to track their income and expenses, and **knowledge of how to balance** the two: There's the old adage — don't lend, don't borrow, don't overspend. You may remember the days when you had to rely on monthly paper statements, which made it easy to get caught out should there be a delay in incomings or outgoings appearing. **Online banking** makes current accounts much easier to manage.
- An understanding of the difference between debit cards and **credit cards**: Credit cards are very enticing, but have their downfalls if not used sensibly. Similar challenges may arise when considering the popular 'buy now, pay later' and layby options.
- **A habit of saving**: Many banks have developed facilities that can be really helpful here — for example, you can arrange for a fixed amount or proportion from any deposit made into a current account to be automatically transferred across to a savings account, and there are accounts where all purchases are rounded up to the nearest dollar, with the difference being transferred to a savings account. A purchase of $12.30 would therefore see $13.00 coming out of their current account, and

70 cents going into their savings account for a rainy day. As they say, look after the pennies . . .

- **An understanding of the difference between a 'need' and a 'want':** They should learn not only how to save responsibly, but also how to spend responsibly. Encourage savings goals and explain the benefits of having a 'slush fund' for emergencies. This may help them learn not to fritter away the money that is burning a hole in their pocket.
- **The confidence to ask for help:** If they get into debt, or feel themselves getting into financial difficulties, make sure they know to come to you as soon as possible to talk things through in a way that perhaps focuses on a plan of action rather than whether or not you are going to bail them out. They have to know that doing nothing will actually mean that they will be leaving things to keep on getting worse (interest rates mean that amounts can escalate exponentially). This could also impact on their credit ratings in the longer term.

Be aware, too, that sometimes debt is a signal that your teen may be struggling with other issues (see Chapter 8).

Sixty per cent of high school students get some allowance from their parents, with the median amount being around $20 a week. Around 30 per cent of students aged 13–18 have a part-time job.[18] In some families, when a teen has part-time work, they are expected to contribute to the household expenses or perhaps be responsible for a regular bill — their cell phone or a portion of Netflix, for example. You have to decide whether this approach works for you, but it can be beneficial in terms of their monetary education.

If your teen continues to live at home as they continue to grow up, or returns after uni or their OE, it's not unreasonable to expect them to contribute from time to time, or even pay some rent or board. This is certainly the case if they are working full-time, even if the idea is for them to save for a deposit, as it can help to set a routine for them. There's a balance to be had: it's a lot like the laundry, and those socks again.

Career planning

Some teens can't wait to get a job, whether part-time or for the summer. The idea of having an income stream is generally what motivates this desire. Others may have no interest or no time, with academia, sports or music higher on the agenda. Working while still at school can lead to problems — for example, prioritising paid work over study. Teens may also resent parents wanting to have a say in how they part with their hard-earned cash. Having money in their pocket increases the opportunity for them to get out and about with their friends — this is positive on the one hand, but not without problems.

There are lots of pluses about having a job: it will give them the chance to learn about managing money; it can help them develop a good work ethic and get used to working as part of a team; it helps with more general life skills, such as communicating, using their initiative and forward planning; it teaches them about the importance of good time-keeping, working to deadlines and presenting themselves well; and it may also provide an understanding of future career choices (see page 47).

The law on young workers

There is legislation in Aotearoa around the employment of teens:

- Work hours for students under the age of 16 must be outside of school hours and not between 10 p.m. and 6 a.m.
- There is no minimum wage for employees under 16, but all other minimum standards and employment rights and obligations apply.
- In various circumstances, when starting out, employees aged 16–19 years can be paid a different minimum wage than adult workers.[19]

If your teen has a job, make sure they understand that they have employment rights. These should be set out in their contract and relate to their hourly rate of pay, entitlement to breaks, and how their annual leave and sick pay are factored in. Help them to understand their **pay slip** (it's always useful for them to keep a copy of their IRD number and their current tax code, and you should have a copy, too, for when they lose them). Explain to them about **tax** so that they understand their hourly rate will be higher than the actual dollars and cents in their pocket at the end of a shift (i.e., the difference between gross and net pay). They will be offered the opportunity to join **KiwiSaver** and may need your guidance on this; this can help with their future financial planning.

The job market is continually changing. Here are some key trends currently affecting youth:

- Many employers expect a diploma or a degree for an entry-level position, particularly in certain sectors (such as architecture, banking, education, law, medicine and science).
- In addition to experience and qualifications, employers are looking for candidates with 'soft skills'. Qualities such as good communication, initiative, problem-solving abilities, positivity and a 'can-do' attitude are highly valued.
- The global market is now more transient, meaning there's a bigger pool of applicants for any job. And there's a growing number of roles that can now be automated. This increases competition in finding a job.
- Our teens will likely work in several jobs, or even across several careers, during their working lifetime. With the gig economy undermining the job security we knew, they may well not be employed on a standard 40-hour-a-week contract. This can be intimidating and exciting in equal measure.
- Added to the above, there remains the age-old problem whereby even starter-level jobs can require a bit of experience, which is hard to acquire before joining the workforce.

Job applications and interviews

Trying to find work can be a disheartening process. Your teen may put a tremendous amount of energy into an application, only to receive no response from the employer if they are unsuccessful (this practice is becoming increasingly common). Added to this, the automated software that is increasingly used to filter CVs (known as an applicant tracking system or ATS) will often reject perfectly valid applications. Sending CVs out into the ether with no acknowledgement can leave your teen feeling as though they are operating in some sort of vacuum, which can knock their confidence. Their school/kura may offer career guidance (see page 46), but you can also assist them in showing them how to construct a CV, find references and write cover letters. There are several free online tools for creating comprehensive and professional-looking CVs; some of them offer tips on getting past the ATS.

If your teen does progress to the next stage, they may find interviews to be a nerve-racking process. As with anything, practice makes perfect: let them role-play the scenario with you beforehand, and debrief with them afterwards (as constructively as possible). Try to anticipate ways that they might get slightly wrong-footed and let their nerves get the better of them — for example, post-Covid, potential employers may not be shaking hands at the start of an interview. For more advice on job interviews, point them to the Resources/Rauemi section (see page 349).

The government offers some assistance to those who are job-seeking via the Ministry of Social Development's Work and Income agency, whose Jobseeker Support includes a basic sum of money to cover rent, bills and food, as well as weekly seminars giving practical help with interviewing skills. For those who are pursuing further education, StudyLink may be available to assist with course costs and living/housing. Depending on the student's age and their caregivers' income, this money may need to be paid back through the government's Student Loan facility.[20]

Kōrero with Molly

I got my first job at 17 years old working in administration, and bounced around medical centre receptionist positions as I finished my degree. My brother got his first job at 13 doing a paper route and mowing lawns, before moving on to hospitality and retail as he finished his studies. We are never too young to learn about the value of a dollar and the value of a day's work — right? Plus that extra money in your pocket isn't so bad . . . It's hard to imagine venturing out into the real world without some idea of how to manage money and understand a pay slip (especially when none of this stuff was covered at school).

A word on emerging adulthood

The term 'emerging adulthood' is starting to gain currency as a means of referring to the period between the late teens and the twenties. Although it presents its own challenges,[21] it's also a time that is ripe with opportunity for you and your teen to work out how your relationship could look over the years ahead.

It's a time of handing over the ropes. Your teen is forging their own path and will gain confidence in the knowledge that sometimes you will agree on things and sometimes you won't, and that's okay. All you can hope for is that they will ask your opinion from time to time and occasionally take your advice. As they gather more life experiences, you may find yourself asking their opinion and seeking their help as they once sought yours. At some point it may be that they have a partner who becomes part of your family, and things will change again as they are gently incorporated into the mix. Ultimately, it all comes down to that open communication, their sense of security and the knowledge that, even as they become independent, the family remains.

How can I have this conversation? / Me pēhea tēnei matakahi?

While it's wonderful to be able to look back at all your teen's achievements and the happy family memories, you can't stop them from growing up, and neither would you want to. You can see how far they've come — so you can see their potential. It's now time to nudge them along a little, with the emphasis on reducing any anxieties and focusing on all the amazing things they have to look forward to . . .

This is why we need to have the conversation, and primarily the message here is that these times are full of opportunity.

However, it's not uncommon to experience a mishmash of emotions — you are going to feel apprehensive, but at the same time excited by all that lies ahead of them. They are going to feel the same way — just not necessarily at the same time as you.

Points to keep the conversation going

- When encouraging your teen to take on some cooking, rather than having a scratchy discussion about menu planning, look for ways to lighten things up. Choose three random ingredients and challenge them to incorporate them into one dish — you may even stumble across some interesting new recipes. Introduce a 'new food Tuesday' when you try out undiscovered recipes. Challenge them to **cook for themselves** on a $10 budget.
- Get them to practise their barista skills by making you a cuppa or a coffee after dinner.
- To avoid the plaintive cries of 'it's not fair, why's it only me that has to do this?', it can sometimes help if your teen sees that **everyone is working together** to get the more mundane chores out of the way. Remember the days when someone washed up, someone wiped and someone put away? Consider having family rotas, or set aside a couple of hours on the

weekend when everyone does their bit — whether it's sorting the recycling, mowing the lawn, tending to the vege patch, doing the dishes and so on.

- Try to encourage a little **lateral thinking** and ask them to generate a list of chores that could be tangentially relevant to keeping each room tidy — from emptying the vacuum cleaner once in a while to making sure that the loo roll doesn't run out.
- Teach them how to change a duvet cover the easy way (wait, there's an easy way?!).[22]
- Decide whether you attach chores to any allowance you might give your teen, or whether you see them as just a **responsibility** for living in the house and something that they should do automatically. If you are going to pay them for doing additional chores (for example, washing the car or cleaning out the fridge), **make sure that you are consistent** with the amount you give them and the standard to which they need to operate.
- Watch some of the Waka Kotahi advertisements on road safety when talking about purchasing a car. They are hard-hitting, very real and designed for just this audience.
- **Set a good example** when driving — no using a cell phone, no speeding — allow your teen to challenge you if they see you breaking the rules of the road.
- Teens may boomerang a few times before moving out for good: sometimes this is planned (between uni semesters, for example) and sometimes things don't work out. Let them know there is a **safe space** with you for them to find their feet again.
- If you don't think your teen is ready to move out, yet they are determined to do so, find a good time to share your concerns, **actively listen** to their reasons and find a way to keep communication channels open. If they move out but are close by, perhaps a regular meal together will **preserve connections**.
- When preparing for job interviews, there are a few standard questions you can put to them to them in a **role-play** practice, such as:

- What made you apply for this job?
- What makes you the ideal candidate for this role?
- What are your strengths (and weaknesses)?
- Can you give us an example of how you put those strengths into practice?[23]
- The government's careers website (careers.govt.nz) is an excellent resource, not only for tips on interview technique but also on what careers are out there: the qualifications your teen would need, the career prospects and so on. See also Resources/Rauemi, page 349.

'We may not be able to prepare the future for our children, but we can at least prepare our children for the future.'
— FRANKLIN D. ROOSEVELT

Talking box questions

Design a roster for the chores that works for everyone around the table.

How do you think credit cards and loans work?

Resources / Rauemi

Online	Checklist for keeping New Zealand homes fire safe: fireandemergency.nz/at-home
	Tips and tricks for budgeting and saving money: everydollarcounts.org.nz moneyhub.co.nz/money-in-a-nutshell.html
	Information about student loans and how to apply for one: studylink.govt.nz
	Information on getting a driver licence in New Zealand: nzta.govt.nz/driver-licences/getting-a-licence/licences-by-vehicle-type/cars
	Tips and tricks for building a CV and writing cover letters — including templates and a job application checklist: careers.govt.nz/job-hunting/cvs-and-cover-letters
	Interview tips for applicants: employment.govt.nz/starting-employment/hiring/interviews/interview-tips-for-applicants
	Rights and responsibilities of a young employee in New Zealand: employment.govt.nz/starting-employment/rights-and-responsibilities/young-employees

WORLD

15. GLOBAL TOPICS FOR TEENS

#justice #activism #blacklivesmatter #community
#heforshe #beboldforchange #savetheplanet

*'We all have different inspirations,
but one goal: A better world.'*
— ERNESTO ARGUELLO

Kōrero with Molly

One thing I have learned about tackling the topics we cover in this chapter is that there are a variety of opinions and a variety of ways to get involved. Some of my peers seem to have deep understandings and are clear about what they believe in. Others seem to find it quite hard to determine what their standpoint is, get a little freaked out by the bigger questions and prefer to stay near the surface. Most global topics are touched on throughout high school, but it wasn't until we left that my peers really started to find the causes they wanted to fight for and form stronger viewpoints. While working out my own perspective on things, I found it helpful to have chats with my parents without fear of being 'wrong'. Through education and discussions with the people around us, we can figure out and evolve our own manifestos. I think it's important to stay true to yourself and allow space for others to do the same.

What do you mean by that? / He aha te tikanga o tāu kōrero?

So far, this book has generally focused on how issues might impact directly on an individual teen, their family and their immediate circle. As they expand their horizons, it becomes ever more relevant that they explore their heritage in more detail, understand how they relate to the locality within which they live, and find their identity within a global perspective. As parents we all want our teens to be well-rounded human beings, as well as valued and productive members of their community or communities. This chapter is about helping them to be able to see further than themselves and further than their immediate environment. It's also about upskilling ourselves in some of the topics that are in the forefront of many of our teens' minds. They are far from oblivious and many are really invested in a lot of the key issues of the day.

When a particular topic strikes a chord with your teen, follow their lead: encourage them to share their views and point them towards more research — for example, by finding some age-appropriate websites, books or other resources. Otherwise, some gentle probing can help you discover what sparks your teen's interest; this might be something that feels more accessible to them, such as the referendum on the New Zealand flag (or, more recently, the referenda on cannabis and euthanasia). Look for ways to help them relate to the 'bigger questions' — such as the handling of the Covid-19 pandemic, or climate change — in ways that they find relatable so that they don't feel overwhelmed. Carve out time for discussions, as this will keep you up to date with where their head is at, and will familiarise them with the idea of using you as a sounding board. It may even help teach them how to listen. As we know, teens can be strongly opinionated. While it's commendable to be passionate about matters that are close to their heart, it's also advisable to be informed — and, of course, empathetic. As they mature, encourage them in their learning to be mindful and respectful of others' opinions.

'You never really know a man until you understand things from his point of view, until you climb into his skin and walk around in it.'
— ATTICUS FINCH, *TO KILL A MOCKINGBIRD* (HARPER LEE)

There's a lot going on: for instance, the Black Lives Matter movement; the #metoo movement; climate change; and the increasing understanding of the impact of child, domestic and sexual abuse. It's a lot for anyone to navigate their way through, and an awful lot for a teen. In addition, there is the added dynamic of the social media echo chambers, which can give unhealthy credence to toxic and polarising opinions. The Internet is a tool that gets used for both the good and the not so good: there are issues that can unite people, but there are also obviously some that are divisive, and it can be challenging to agree to disagree. People's different political viewpoints and cultural and religious heritage will inform their perspectives on how they wish to take part in society. With the pandemic, despite the previously unimaginable limitations that it has imposed, there have been amazing examples of how we have been able to keep connected in cyberspace. Everyone will remember these times — how they gave us an opportunity to hunt out the positives, understand one another better and become part of a more worldwide community.

Getting involved in issues, whether on a local or global scale, can encourage your teen to engage with the world beyond their doorstep and beyond their own immediate needs or wants. The phrase 'global citizen' is often used to denote someone who acknowledges the complexity of the world, and the way in which our decisions or choices can affect others. The International Development Education Association of Scotland (IDEAS), a Scottish network that promotes global citizenship education, offers this definition:

> *A Global Citizen is someone who:*
> - *is aware of the wider world and has a sense of their own role as a world citizen*
> - *respects and values diversity*
> - *has an understanding of how the world works*
> - *is outraged by social injustice*
> - *participates in the community at a range of levels, from the local to the global*

- *is willing to act to make the world a more equitable and sustainable place*
- *takes responsibility for their actions.*

To be effective Global Citizens, young people need to be flexible, creative and proactive. They need to be able to solve problems, make decisions, think critically, communicate ideas effectively and work well within teams and groups.[1]

Tell me more . . . / Kōrero mai anō . . .

It's impossible to cover every single 'big' question that your teen is going to raise with you. The separate sections set out later in this chapter aim to highlight some of the key areas that may be catching your teen's attention:

- diversity and intersectionality,
- modern feminism,
- climate change,
- politics,
- religions and beliefs, and
- giving back.

When it comes to having these conversations, it's a question of getting teens to recognise nuance. A good starting point is to have a discussion about bias. **Conscious bias** might include prejudices or opinions that we can own up to, and correct if we so choose. **Unconscious bias** (also called implicit bias), according to blogger Allaya Cooks-Campbell, refers to:

attitudes, prejudices, and judgments that we unconsciously hold about people or groups. By definition, we are either unaware of these feelings or we are unable to pinpoint where they come from. While everyone has implicit biases, the nature of these prejudices aren't universal. They're ingrained in our subconscious through our individual experiences, upbringings, and backgrounds. For example, we often have biases related to racial groups, including our own. While many unconscious biases are related to ethnicity, it's possible to have biases based on sexual orientation, education, or gender.[2]

One way to examine both the shorter- and longer-term implications of unconscious bias is by identifying and then challenging systemic discrimination. Instagram artist Harshveer Jain's graphic representation is an excellent visual way to do this with your teen. In summary, it asks us to imagine 2 sprint teams — red and blue. They race together, but the red track is clear while the blue track has hurdles. Naturally, the red players win more often. Which means that the red players are more successful:

- Red teams get more sponsors.
- Red players get more investment and training.
- When they retire, reds take positions of power in the sport — selection committee, referee, commentator, coach, etc.
- The rules, the audience, the money — the whole ecosystem of the sport begins supporting the red team.

Generations later, the hurdles on the blue track are removed, but . . . the red team still holds the accumulated wealth and power. Red players have better shoes, more training, more opportunities, more fans, more support. So even if things seem equal, and red and blue teams work equally hard, the red team has a generational advantage and the blue team does not.[3]

These conversations can be challenging and may bring up issues that have affected your family. Give your teen space to take things at their own speed. Perhaps start by drawing attention to the examples of inequality and discrimination they can see in front of them, and then broaden the scope to the world around them. To unpack this, it's useful for them to fully understand the terms **equality** and **equity**, concisely demonstrated by the metaphor shown in the redrawn graphic on the following page. Fairness is about liberating people from the barriers that may be in their way. Brainstorm with your teen to see if they can think of some unfair situations they may have observed or experienced.

How can I have these conversations? / Me pēhea tēnei matakahi?

Let your teen know you are prepared to at least try to talk about tricky topics. Also let them know that this will not always be easy, particularly when issues are contentious, but that you can offer them a safe and non-judgemental space in which to tackle hard questions. In this way, you can help your teen discuss the things that matter to them in a way that doesn't alienate their peers or relatives. Respect the knowledge your teen has already accrued on a particular subject and ask them open-ended questions if they are still figuring things out. You don't need to know all the answers, either.

> **This is why we need to have these conversations, and primarily the message here is to be open to other people's perspectives.**

Meaningfully engaging teens means making the discussion personally relevant. If they can relate an issue to something that they do, use or care about, it suddenly becomes much more attainable and real. It's about encouraging your teen to seek more information, to be curious as to why things are happening, and to be interested in what role they can potentially play. Teens are intrinsically idealistic, so play to this quality in them. What's more, there are a lot of teens out there who are starting to be heard — whether it's Malala Yousafzai speaking up for youth education, or Greta Thunberg challenging the developed nations to take action against climate change.[4]

REALITY

EQUALITY

EQUITY

LIBERATION

A visual representation of reality, equality, equity and liberation
(based on an illustration by Angus Maguire for the Interaction Institute
for Social Change).[5]

Points to keep the conversation going

- If your teen expresses an interest in **learning languages**, encourage them, or even do this as a family. Consider te reo Māori: learn to write and speak your pepeha, watch some Māori TV or find a local course (many are free).[6] Think about learning sign language (at least the basics — how to say hello, please and thank you, or the alphabet signs). Always say people's names as they themselves pronounce them and never ask for an 'easier version'.

- Some of those dinnertime conversations can include **quizzes**, such as locating countries on a map of the world or naming capital cities.

- **Watch the news** on television with your teen or explore some of the excellent online alternatives. If your teen finds news programmes a little dry, consider current affairs programmes that discuss the stories of the day.

- Discuss the protests or vigils that may be going on in our communities. Ask your teen, if they were going to organise a **protest**, what would it be about?

- Many causes have their own day, week or month in the year to **raise awareness**. For example: Earth Day is 22 April; Te Wiki o Te Reo Māori (Māori Language Week) is held each year in September; and June is Pride Month.[7]

- Look for other activities that will expose your teen to **different perspectives**. Try attending events at your local library or visiting museum exhibits. Exposure can help broaden the idea of **inclusiveness**.

- Provide them with **data**. Having stark figures in front of them can be a real motivator for action. Check out the 'Tell me more . . . / Kōrero mai anō . . .' sections throughout this book.

- Some teens enjoy **debating**, which can be an excellent outlet and a skill. If your teen's school/kura doesn't have a club, they could suggest it to a teacher or join a team outside of school.

Diversity and intersectionality

Diversity refers to the fact that we all have different characteristics, different experiences and different perspectives on the world. There's an added dimension here in the form of **intersectionality**, which builds on the debates around equality, equity and social justice. It's about how complicated it is to be a human, and, as the International Women's Development Agency puts it, 'the interplay between any kind of discrimination, whether it's based on gender, race, age, class, socioeconomic status, physical or mental ability, gender or sexual identity, religion, or ethnicity'.[8]

> *'Just like a puzzle, each person is made up of lots of different pieces . . . It's impossible to understand the full picture until you put all the pieces together!'*
> — MCKENNA SAADY

There are some examples online that bring the complexities of intersectionality into focus at a simpler level. Researcher Miriam Dobson has created a fun guide about intersectionality, based on Bob, who is proud to be a striped triangle. Unfortunately, however, Bob is struggling because there are groups of people that don't like the fact he is a triangle and there are other groups that don't like the fact he has stripes. Bob is facing oppression because these groups are working to make life a lot harder for him. Luckily, there are groups of people that are similar to Bob and they are working hard to liberate themselves by raising awareness and asking for change. However, these groups are *NOT* intersectional. So there is a group for triangles, but these triangles aren't stripey, and there is a group for stripey shapes, but these shapes aren't triangles. These groups don't like to interact with each other and they even compete against each other! Poor Bob can't work out where to go . . . He thinks to himself: 'Am I more stripe or am I more triangle?'[9]

A society should be inclusive, appreciating and celebrating everyone, rather than taking a stance that is negative or judgemental. Ultimately, everyone deserves to feel safe and to be treated with respect. Conveying this to your teen is a huge — but hopefully achievable — parenting goal.

> *'Our ability to reach unity in diversity will be the beauty and the test of our civilisation.'*
> — MAHATMA GANDHI

There's a lot of work to be done to address some of the disproportionate disadvantages experienced by people like Bob. One way to understand this is to find ways to **listen** to the voices of people affected. While it isn't Bob's responsibility to educate everyone about how it feels to be a triangle, or how it feels to be stripey, or how it feels to be a stripey triangle, it is nonetheless our responsibility not to **tell** Bob how he feels. As Sylvia Rani outlines in her article about anti-racism, we need to listen to those who have been and continue to be treated unfairly.[10]

We can inform ourselves by accessing the amazing array of resources available to us. And we can help our teens by encouraging them to do the same. We can also start to explain the issues around **privilege** — which, as McKenna Saady explains, 'is the advantage you get because of a part of your identity. For example, a person with no disabilities has privilege because it's easier for them to get around in public compared with many people who do have disabilities.'[11]

In this context, if we think back to the example of the red and blue sports teams given earlier, this may help our teens to understand more easily what the term 'white privilege' means. The Black Lives Matter movement began in 2013 and protests expanded internationally following the murders of George Floyd, Ahmaud Arbery and Breonna Taylor.[12]

If your teen struggles with some of the arguments around the Black Lives Matter movement, there are plenty of resources online that give clear responses they can use in their own debates with peers — such as this, for instance, from blogger Ryland Hunt:

> *Black Lives Matter does not mean that non Black lives don't matter. But put it this way: If one house in a neighborhood is on fire, you should call the fire department and help save the burning house. All the other houses in the neighbourhood matter too, but the one on fire needs help at the moment because that one is in danger. It is like that with Black Lives Matter. Black lives are in danger in our country and need our help.*[13]

This is not just an American problem. Published in 2021 by Te Atawhai o Te Ao Charitable Trust, *Whakatika: A survey of Māori experiences of racism* reported the following:

> *Colonial racism is both act and omission, through micro and macro-aggressions, media representations, ignorance and disrespect, and the invalidation of Māori and celebration of colonisation through colonial statues . . .*

> *[Ra]cism impacts Māori on a daily basis, in a number of ways. The harms of racism include grief and anger, and it impacts our connections to tūpuna and mokopuna across generations . . .*

> *[R]acism and discrimination are so widespread that they will never be conquered through isolated activities, such as unconscious bias training, alone. Addressing racism requires a constant, consistent, Māori-focused multipronged approach.*[14]

There is a whakataukī (proverb) that states, 'Me tiro whakamuri, kia anga whakamua', which loosely means, 'If we want to shape our future, start with our past'.[15] Schools/kura in Aotearoa are now reviewing the ways in which the country's histories will be taught to incorporate the role colonisation played in the bicultural foundation of New Zealand, and the complexities around the context of te Tiriti o Waitangi.[16] In addition, there will be a much wider sharing of te reo Māori and tikanga Māori.

'We all should know that diversity makes for a rich tapestry, and we must understand that all the threads of the tapestry are equal in value no matter what their color.'
— MAYA ANGELOU

Five further points to ponder . . .

- In age-appropriate ways, talk about how everyone is an individual and that differences should be celebrated. As UNICEF puts it, 'Conversations about racism and discrimination will look different for each family. While there is no one-size-fits-all approach, the science is clear: the earlier parents start the conversation with their children the better.'[17]

- Talk about representation: ask your teen about their favourite movie or TV show — is it an accurate representation of the various ethnicities, religions and sexual orientations that exist in society? Controversies such as the previous lack of representation at the Oscars have shown that it's also important to get diversity behind the camera as well as in front of it.

- Help familiarise your teen with terms such as bias, racism, privilege, microaggressions and marginalisation. Ensure they understand that jokes at the expense of others are not funny.

- Sometimes statistics make comparisons between ethnic groups but give little background to explain the patterns that they describe. When you encounter a radio or news report on how something has impacted differently on different populations (for example, rates of university admissions), ask your teen to think about how discrimination or other disadvantages may have had an influence on these figures.

- Find ways to be an ally and help your teen to do the same. Emphasise that doing nothing is not an option, as communicator Cecelia Kersten explains: 'By remaining in the status quo, you are directly benefiting from social structures that harm . . . marginalized communities.'[18]

Calling out racism

Futurist and tech educator Sinead Bovell offers the following template of responses to racist comments:

- *Could you clarify what you mean by that?*
- *That doesn't sound very funny to me. It sounds racist.*
- *As your friend, I feel obligated to let you know that that remark was racist.*
- *Is the person's race relevant to the story?*
- *Do you actually believe that? If so, how come?*
- *I didn't want to single you out before, but that comment made me feel uncomfortable. Here's why . . .*
- *I know you were just trying to make a joke, but here is why it was offensive . . .*
- *Hey! I wanted to follow up on why I responded, 'yikes' to your comment. Check out this article, it explains things better than I could . . .*
- *I really don't feel comfortable when you make comments like that.*
- *I saw what you posted today. To be honest, it made me feel angry. Here's why . . .*
- *I disagree. You are stereotyping . . .*
- *Hmm . . . do you have evidence to support that belief?*[19]

Modern feminism

Please don't skip this part if you are solely parenting boys. The information and conversation starters in this section are important for all teens. Feminism works towards equality, not female superiority, and has nothing to do with belittling men: it does not support sexism on the grounds of gender.

> *'I'm glad we've begun to raise our daughters more like our sons, but it will never work until we raise our sons more like our daughters.'*
> — GLORIA STEINEM

Raising feminist teens, no matter what their gender, is all about **cultivating empathy and fighting stereotypes.** Many ideas that are now considered mainstream, such as promoting body neutrality and understanding and practising consent, find their roots in feminism — as does the concept of intersectionality. Sharing the history of the movement with your own teen is one way for them to understand how far we have come in terms of equality. For example, Aotearoa was the first country to grant women the vote. The fact that it 'then took 26 years to let them stand for parliament', and that the first woman prime minister wasn't elected until the end of the 1990s, shows, however, that there is still a way to go.[20]

The ideas that sparked the feminist movement started to find traction in the late eighteenth century — Mary Wollstonecraft's *A Vindication of the Rights of Woman* was first published in 1792, for example. In her day, women in the western world were excluded from education and politics. They did not generally have autonomy over their finances, their families or even their own bodies. Their job opportunities were also limited. The reaction to the inequalities experienced by half the population as a result of their gender crystallised into what can be recognised as a politicised movement as early as 1840, and its development is now described as being organised into four waves:

Wave 1: 1840–1920

- Wāhine Māori organised across the country to advocate for suffrage: Meri Te Tai Mangakāhia (Te Rarawa, Ngāti Te Teinga, Ngāti Manawa, Te Kaitutae) was the first woman to address the Kotahitanga Māori Parliament in 1893 to call for women's suffrage.[21]

- In 1893, New Zealand became the first self-governing country in the world that allowed women to vote in parliamentary elections.
- Kate Sheppard was also at the forefront of these campaigns and Aotearoa memorialises her on the NZ$10 note.[22]
- The first Family Planning clinics were introduced in the UK and US just before the First World War, and in New Zealand in 1936.[23]

Wave 2: 1960–80

- Betty Friedan coined the phrase 'the problem with no name' in her 1963 book *The feminine mystique*.[24] We would now use the term 'systemic sexism'.
- The mid-1960s onwards saw women's liberation groups being set up around the globe, with the first groups being established across New Zealand in 1970. Women's lib looked to address issues such as reproductive autonomy, freedom from sexual harassment, equal pay and equal opportunities. There was still a divide in that women of colour continued to be left out of the conversation — feminism had not yet become intersectional (this theory was introduced in the 1980s by Kimberlé Williams Crenshaw).[25]
- Slogans such as 'The personal is political' were used to help challenge the status quo, and started to lead to results: New Zealand introduced the Equal Pay Act in 1972.
- There were many high-profile protests, such as the one against the objectification of women at the Miss America Pageant in 1968. A male-dominated media was, however, quick to try to undermine the motivations of those involved in such campaigns, as writer Constance Grady explains: 'the comfortable conservatism of the Reagan era managed to successfully position second-wave feminists as humorless, hairy-legged shrews who cared only about petty bullshit like bras instead of real problems, probably to distract themselves

from the loneliness of their lives, since no man would ever want a (shudder) feminist.'[26] Some of these unhelpful preconceptions remain today — feminism is much more nuanced than 'burning your bra'.

- The second wave seemed to give rise to the idea of women 'having it all',[27] and yet women still found themselves responsible for most of any household organisation, domestic chores and childcare.

Wave 3: 1990–2010

- Susan Faludi's book *Backlash* (1991) drew attention to the way that feminist messages were routinely undermined by a still patriarchal society. As Naomi Wolf noted in *The beauty myth* (1990), 'The more legal and material hindrances women have broken through, the more strictly and heavily and cruelly images of female beauty have come to weigh upon us.'[28]
- Third-wave feminism built on the progress of the second wave, but drew attention to the fact that, as Gender Equal NZ points out, 'Discrimination doesn't happen in isolation — and we need to recognise the negative effects of homophobia, transphobia, racism and other forms of oppression, along with sexism.'[29] There were concerted efforts to make future developments more inclusive.
- There was still an issue around the extent to which gender stereotypes continued to exist and impact on everyone's day-to-day lives. A 2010 New Zealand study looking into how long people spent on household chores found that '[w]omen spent an average four hours and 20 minutes a day . . . [whereas] men did two hours and 32 minutes'.[30]
- Issues were highlighted in an imaginative way through music, art and campaigns, by outfits such as the Guerrilla Girls, Riot grrrl and Pussy Riot.

'I raise up my voice — not so that I can shout, but so that those without a voice can be heard . . . We cannot all succeed when half of us are held back.'
— MALALA YOUSAFZAI

Wave 4: Present day

- This wave is still taking shape, but the importance of feminist issues is now getting international recognition at the UN level, with High Commissioner for Human Rights Michelle Bachelet saying: 'We need to keep pushing, to advance women's well-being; their dignity; their autonomy; and their rights.'[31]
- According to American policy and social justice coordinator Margie Delao, 'fourth wave feminism is seen as characterized by action-based viral campaigns, protests, and movements like #MeToo advancing from the fringes of society into the headlines of our everyday news. The fourth wave has also been characterized as "queer, sex-positive, trans-inclusive, body-positive, and digitally driven".'[32]

Kōrero with Molly

A lot of my male friends are struggling with how to change their perspectives as they become more and more aware of the negative impact of toxic masculinity. They often complain that they are finding it hard to do anything right and are offending people, particularly women, at every turn. But everyone has to get involved in order to push for this global shift in attitude, including men.

Being a good ally means listening, really listening, and educating yourself on how to do better. It also means calling out your mates who don't behave well around women, who make inappropriate jokes, who pursue girls under 16, or who can't take no for an answer when someone tries to reject them. The bottom line is that a lot of people are feeling unsafe because of a toxic masculine culture.

The response 'Not all men are like that' misses the point. I like to explain it using this analogy: When you see a swarm of bees, you don't think to yourself, 'Not all of those bees are going to sting me, I can relax . . .' No! Enough of the bees are going to sting you that you wouldn't differentiate between those that would and those that wouldn't — you would just assume that they all are going to sting you and get out of the way.

The same goes for me when I'm walking alone to my car in the dark. Not all men are going to try to assault me, but unfortunately there are some that might, and for my own safety I have to assume that one could and so take necessary precautions.

'Feminism isn't about making women stronger. Women are already strong. It's about changing the way the world perceives that strength.'
— G. D. ANDERSON

Five further points to ponder . . .
- Celebrate International Women's Day on 8 March. Brainstorm female role models with your teen, and point out literature, movies and music that promotes powerful women. Also draw attention to those that do the opposite and seem to ignore or misrepresent a woman's perspective.
- Discuss the history of gender roles. Why are old stereotypes not applicable to modern-day society? How should people living in the same household divide the chores between them? What about childcare?
- Have a chat about the wage gap and the implications of this (statistics and more information can be found in the Resources/Rauemi section, page 384). Think about how many CEOs are women, and how many MPs. How often is

the 'expert' on a news report someone other than a middle-aged middle-class white male? Acknowledge that things are changing for the better. But it's important that everyone sees themselves as represented in these situations.

- What are examples of progress that have been made thanks to the four different waves of feminism?
- Caroline Criado Perez writes in *Invisible women* (2019), 'There is plenty of data showing that women have, on average, smaller hands than men, and yet we continue to design equipment around the average male hand.'[33] See if you and your teen can think of other examples of unconscious bias.

Climate change

Heatwaves. Droughts. Fires. Rising sea levels. Floods. We have a role as caretakers for the environment we live in, but unfortunately we aren't passing on to our teens a world that is in the best of health. According to the pressure group Scientists for Extinction Rebellion:

75% of the Earth's land has now been severely altered by human actions such as industry and farming. Only 13% of the world's oceans remain as wilderness, free from human influence and exploitation. Today, approximately 60 billion tonnes of renewable and nonrenewable resources are extracted globally each year from our ecosystems, nearly twice the figure from 1980. According to some studies we are producing wastes and using the Earth's resources 70% more quickly than they can be absorbed or replenished, effectively using up our annual ecological budget by August each year.[34]

'It's surely our responsibility to do everything within our power to create a planet that provides a home not just for us, but for all life on Earth.'
— SIR DAVID ATTENBOROUGH

There are many topics of concern that could be included under the umbrella of **environmental issues** — from overpopulation, urban sprawl, pollution and overfarming to loss of biodiversity, deforestation, global warming and ocean acidification, to name but a few.[35] Most teens have grown up with environmental issues high up the agenda, and as such are actually already better informed than the majority of older generations. If your teen seems less aware or concerned, it's useful to ensure they have a basic understanding of key terms, although you do not want to make them anxious. (For instance, some people use 'global warming' and 'climate change' interchangeably, but they're not the same thing, as Climate.gov explains: 'global warming is one symptom of the much larger problem of human-caused climate change'.)[36] A 2019 New Zealand survey found that 55 per cent of year 9–13 students agreed that climate change was 'an urgent problem that needs to be managed now'.[37] With that in mind this section focuses on climate change. (For other environmental topics, see the Resources/Rauemi section, page 384.)

Only 0.17 per cent of global emissions come from New Zealand, but given the nation's size (5.1 million, which is 0.06 per cent of the world's population) this still places Aotearoa seventeenth out of 32 OECD countries using about three times more than what would be a 'fair share'. Road transport produces most of our CO_2 emissions, and agriculture most of our greenhouse gases overall; what's more, our net emissions have shot up by 60 per cent in just two decades.[38]

On a national level, New Zealand:

- signed the Paris Agreement in 2016, and joined 32 other nations in 2020 in declaring a climate change emergency,
- passed the Climate Change Response (Zero Carbon) Act in 2019, which commits New Zealand to reducing emissions,
- committed to a carbon-neutral government by 2025,
- formed a Climate Change Commission tasked with putting the country on a path to net zero emissions by 2050,
- is limiting landfill by promoting reusing, recycling and reducing,

- banned single-use plastic bags in 2019 and is looking to ban all problematic plastic packaging by 2025,
- is promoting renewable energy, including wind, solar and hydro methods, and
- is reviewing transportation, including promoting low-emission vehicles, electric cars, public transportation and active alternatives such as cycling.

On a more personal level, Gen Less, a New Zealand government agency dedicated to mobilising New Zealanders to be world leaders in clean and clever energy use, suggests several ways people can make climate positive decisions in their everyday life, including:

- What they eat — by replacing a meat-based dish with a vegetarian meal just once a week reduces the carbon load attributed to the food plan by an average 7 per cent.
- How they shop — teens are a key market for fast fashion and this is a 'teachable moment'. *Business Insider Australia* reported in 2020 that the fashion industry 'is responsible for 10% of humanity's carbon emissions', which is 'more emissions than international flights and maritime shipping combined'.[39] Choosing sustainable and quality purchases that are built to last will help to reduce this, alongside using charity shops (or op shops) and buying second-hand.
- Being online — running a computer or gaming device constantly has a negative effect on the environment, increasing carbon emissions and using power. People may choose to decrease their use with this in mind.
- Sharing their knowledge — being a force for change and using their voice can make a huge difference. Leading by example, campaigning, and supporting groups and organisations that have environmental policies (and voting with their feet when they don't) sends a clear message.[40]

'Some people say that we should study to become climate scientists so that we can solve the climate crisis. But the climate crisis has already been solved. We already have all the facts and solutions. All we have to do is to wake up and change.'
— GRETA THUNBERG

Five further points to ponder . . .
- Consider together anything around the home you can change to better serve the environment: for example, conserving more water, setting up a vege grow-bag or patch in the garden, starting a compost or worm bin, understanding how to recycle efficiently and making litter-free lunches. If applicable, help your teen research period product options that are reusable and/or organic (see page 221).
- For shorter trips, think about using public transport or other forms of active transport, rather than the car.
- Find an online carbon tax calculator and check out your carbon footprints together — think of imaginative ways that you might reduce these.
- Find the positives in any discussions that you have with your teen about environmental issues so that they are motivated to keep participating in change and don't become eco-anxious. The situation is not as we might want it to be, but collaborative approaches are starting to show benefits.
- Don't forget World Environment Day on 5 June each year: plan an eco-friendly or eco-awareness event or activity. Keep your eye on relevant policy changes and referenda, along with other safe activism.

Politics

Even if your teen is a way off turning 18 and being eligible to vote, they may already be beginning to form **political opinions**. As *Teen Vogue* points out, 'Figuring out a political belief system is something that takes time, and it's a process deeply influenced by how our families talk (or don't talk) about politics; the environments and historical moments in which we grow up; and the information we consume.'[41] It's vital for teens to realise the importance of political engagement — even if that just means keeping abreast of the news headlines.

> ### 'Change will not take place without political participation.'
> ### — BERNIE SANDERS

Try to engage your teen in conversations about the issues of the day, but bear in mind that they may not take the same spin on a topic as you do. It may be easier to start with issues that are closer to home — such as community mobilisation initiatives, local and national issues, New Zealand's domestic and foreign policies — and then widen the scope to include world affairs. Encourage them to bring a news story to the dinner table — for example, the local referenda on euthansaia and marijuana, the longer-term global impact of events such as Brexit or Trump's presidency, or the appropriateness of the international response to places torn by conflict, such as Afghanistan, Syria and Ukraine. A good time for a deep dive and getting them interested in politics is during an election year, when there are some excellent online resources available. It's a good idea to click through each party's manifesto, which sets out their political beliefs, values and action plans, to see who your teen aligns with the most. Other sites set out a series of questions that enable users to see which party overlaps with their own existing agenda. It can be helpful to watch the numerous campaign TV debates together and chat about what the polls say. Try to focus on discussing the issues, rather than the personalities.

We all come from different social backgrounds. We all have different views, values and perspectives to draw from when building our political beliefs. You may have different opinions to your teen. It's not wrong to disagree, but politics can be polarising and triggering. Remind them that others are entitled to their own opinions (so long as these opinions are not hateful or harmful). Encourage them to have empathy and understanding, as this will help them as they widen their world view. We can and should have debates, but we must also respect each other.

Reaching the **voting age** is an exciting rite of passage. Your teen will hopefully already realise that voting is a privilege and a right not afforded to everyone globally. The history of electoral representation is an interesting starting point for discussion. For example, in 1867 New Zealand legislation gave universal suffrage to Māori men 12 years before European men enjoyed the same privilege.[42] And, as noted earlier, this was still 26 years before New Zealand women got to vote.

Politicians are recognising that they need to be savvy to social media. For example, Green politician Chlöe Swarbrick aimed to show 'that politicians can look a little different, sound a little different, and do things a little differently'.[43] She channelled the youth vote through her social media fan base, including an Instagram following second only (among MPs) to Jacinda Ardern.[44] Your teen may already be mindful that political discussions are increasingly moving to social media, where MPs are reaching out to voters, and voters are sharing their opinions (sometimes forcefully).

The positives and negatives that attach to social media also hold true in political forums, and it's important to guard our teens against misinformation. Echo chambers of opinions and ideas mean that once they begin to interact with posts they agree with, they will find themselves seeing more posts that reflect and reinforce these ideas, rather than challenge them or present them with new information. This can become unsafe and even lead to radicalisation or extremism. You needn't normally be concerned over your teen's decisions to switch friendship groups, or beginning adopting a new style of dress, but do keep an eye out for possible warning signs of something more worrying — if, for instance, they:

- spend so much time with a new friend group that they barely see family or old friends,
- spend a lot of time looking up extremist groups online,
- begin using hateful or derogatory terms when referring to peers or others, or
- drop out of regular activities they formerly enjoyed.[45]

Check in with your teen if you can. While a change in behaviour may turn out to be some other issue entirely (in which case you'll be glad you enquired), you need to be aware if they are turning to extremism.

Five further points to ponder . . .
- Help your teen come to an understanding of how the parliamentary system in New Zealand works (see Resources/ Rauemi, page 385). What do MPs do, and how are they accountable to their voters? What is the difference between MMP and other voting systems? How is power distributed across Parliament (makes law), the executive (administers law) and the judiciary (interprets the law through the courts)? How should laws be made or updated, and how should they be enforced?
- Discuss the differences between a constitutional monarchy, a republic and a dictatorship. What are the differences between right-wing and left-wing politics? What does an anarchist believe in? What about a communist or a fascist? How do you challenge someone whose political perspective is bigoted or offensive?
- Watch *Parliament TV* and question time during MPs' debates. Does your teen feel that their interests are being represented?
- There are a number of initiatives encouraging teens to learn about, and even get involved in, policy-making, such as the Youth Parliament, the Youth Press Gallery members and the Model UN.
- Encourage your teen to attend rallies on particular issues, to take part in other activities such as fundraising or handing out leaflets, or even to do an internship with the local MP.

Religions and beliefs

Life should be full of celebrations, and our traditions and heritage often set out ways that we might celebrate, from Chinese New Year, to Eid al-Fitr, to Matariki, to Diwali, to Hanukkah, to Christmas. Many of us enjoy Easter eggs or Thanksgiving whether or not they're a direct part of our culture, meaning that your teen will be aware at some level of the existence of structured religions around the world.

> **'Each of the world religions has its own particular genius, its own special insight into the nature and requirements of compassion, and has something unique to teach us.'**
> **— KAREN ARMSTRONG**

You may have a belief system and these beliefs may include certain events or actions, such as attending church or avoiding some foods. Or you may be a non-believer, or you may have given religion little thought. Whether or not religion or spirituality is important to you, it's probable that you will have brought up your teen so that their perspective is similar to yours. Or they may be growing up in an interfaith family, and this will present its own positives and challenges. As they mature, they may or may not embrace your outlook.

While it's all too often the differences between structured religions that make the news stories, there's a lot of overlap between them, in that they all generally try to find positive ways for people to be kind and live together as a part of a community. There are many resources that outline the similarities and differences in the way that each might approach things (see Resources/Rauemi, page 385). As ever, it's all about tolerance and respect: respecting others' beliefs and respecting how others' beliefs may differ from our own. The Universal Declaration of Human Rights, Article 18, states:

> *Everyone has the right to freedom of thought, conscience and religion; this right includes freedom to change his religion or belief,*

and freedom, either alone or in community with others and in
public or private, to manifest his religion or belief in teaching,
practice, worship and observance.[46]

The issue is not whether or not someone believes, or believes in different things to you or your teen. The point is that any immoral or unethical actions under the guise of religion should be named and called into question.

> **'I believe that the only true religion**
> **consists of having a good heart.'**
> **— DALAI LAMA**

Five further points to ponder . . .

- Is your teen familiar with the basis of the different belief systems across the world? You might like to spend time with them looking up some of the scriptures and beliefs of the major religions, and looking for common positives rather than getting caught up in differences.
- Some diaries and calendars include the dates that are important to some of the major faith groups. This offers an opportunity to discuss what each of these refers to.
- Take up invitations to visit friends' places of worship or a marae so that your teen can see why faith, culture and heritage are so important to some people.
- Article 18 of the Universal Declaration of Human Rights, quoted above, was included in New Zealand legislation in the Bill of Rights Act 1990. Explain why tolerance and understanding are so important.
- There are many gods and creation stories in Māori mythology, and your teen will be learning about some of these at school. Do they have a favourite myth or legend?

Giving back

Many teens are interested in the world around them and are sufficiently observant to realise that some people find life harder than others, such as the victims of a natural disaster or a homeless person on the street. They're bound to express opinions and ask searching questions. It's important to talk with your teen about language here. We want to avoid the 'us' and 'them' mentality by acknowledging that we all need a little help sometimes.

It's also normal for your teen to want to do something to help, and there are any number of ways they might do this. It's okay to start small, and it's okay to start local, from buying fair trade products to taking part in a sponsored event to volunteering at an elderly care home. They may choose to contribute to charitable causes, and you as a parent may have a role to play here: research shows that 'children whose parents talk to them about giving are 20 per cent more likely to give than those whose parents don't'.[47]

> **'The developmental milestone of putting others before oneself is significant and can be a predictor of greater generosity, positivity, perseverance and altruism later in life.'**
> **— AARON HANSON**

We New Zealanders are, it seems, a nation of givers. In 2021, there were 28,014 charities in Aotearoa,[48] and collectively we give around $3 billion annually. Tony Paine, chief executive of charity umbrella organisation Philanthropy New Zealand, says 'it's about what you care about and things that have made an impression. Philanthropy has huge power. You're only limited by your willingness and your imagination.'[49]

> **'What do we live for, if it is not to make life less difficult for each other?'**
> **— DOROTHEA BROOKE, *MIDDLEMARCH* (GEORGE ELIOT)**

Five further points to ponder . . .

- Let your teen know about the charities that you have a connection with. Explain why these causes are important to you. Share updates and newsletters with them. If they would also like to contribute some money, or volunteer their time, talk through with them how to go about this.

- There are any number of charities that your teen might be interested in supporting: for example, animal protection, cancer and other health-related campaigns, children's rights, people with disabilities, hunger prevention, national and international relief and development, period poverty, under-represented and minority communities, women's rights, youth development. There are also any number of impromptu ways that they can help, including donating clothes, toys or other items; donating money to a charity organisation of their choice; raising money through a school fundraiser, such as a bake sale; and participating in fundraisers such as fun runs or sponsored silences.

- There are many innovative ways of giving back that have gained popularity recently. Some teens choose to do a Givealittle charitable campaign for their birthday rather than get presents. Other charities offer vouchers that cover the costs of, for example, a pump to give a village in a developing country clean water. There are also exciting initiatives such as global Pay It Forward Day (28 April).

- There are many organised ways of getting involved. The Student Volunteer Army describes itself as 'an education charity run for students, by students, focused on providing meaningful volunteering opportunities for primary, secondary and tertiary aged young people in Aotearoa'.[50] The Duke of Edinburgh's Hillary Award programme includes a volunteer component. Both the SVA and Duke of Edinburgh schemes are also excellent ways to gain experience and skills that may later help in the workplace (see Resources/Rauemi, page 385).

- It's always good to check the credentials of any organisation with which your teen is getting involved. The Citizens Advice Bureau website has some advice on how to do this.[51]

A word on the United Nations Sustainable Development Goals

In 2015, the UN set out an agenda of 17 goals and 169 targets to end poverty, to protect the planet, and to ensure that by 2030 all people enjoy peace and prosperity: effectively a 'World's To-Do List'.[52] There is a section on their website that is specifically targeted at teens to help them learn about the Sustainable Development Goals, in order to 'show them that a better world is possible'.[53]

New Zealand is one of the 193 countries taking part in this initiative, contributing through domestic action, international leadership on policy issues, and support via the New Zealand Aid Programme.[54]

Talking box questions

If you were going to set up a political party, what are the three most important things you would include in your manifesto?

What are the three changes we could make as a family that would have a positive environmental contribution?

If you were going to update our banknotes, which people would you want to see on them and why?

Think of a way to explain equality and equity to group of primary school children.

If you were going to invent your own cultural or religious festival, what would you celebrate and how would you celebrate it?

If you were going to set up your own charity, who would be the main beneficiaries and how would you run it?

Resources / Rauemi

DIVERSITY AND INTERSECTIONALITY	Pepeha is a way of introducing yourself in Māori. It tells others who you are by sharing your connections with the people and places that are important to you. This website helps you create yours: pepeha.nz The equality versus equity fence image explained further: socialventurepartners.org/wp-content/uploads/2018/01/Problem-with-Equity-vs-Equality-Graphic.pdf Learn about and join anti-racism protests: colorofchange.org

MODERN FEMINISM	Information and activities for International Women's Day: internationalwomensday.com A New Zealand collective promoting gender equality: theweavinghouse.nz A diverse group leading a national movement towards true gender equality for all New Zealanders: genderequal.nz Goal 5 of the Human Rights Commission Te Kāhui Tika Tangata: Gender Equality: hrc.co.nz/our-work/global-goals/gender-equality Information on New Zealand's Gender Action Plan: mfat.govt.nz/en/media-and-resources/launch-of-the-gender-action-plan-to-guide-new-zealands-development-cooperation
CLIMATE CHANGE AND OTHER ENVIRONMENTAL TOPICS	An international movement and community dedicated to saving the environment: extinctionrebellion.nz A resource hub with tips on minimising waste: katemeads.co.nz/pages/resources The World's Largest Lesson is working with the UN to promote the use of the Sustainable Development Goals in learning so that children can contribute to a better future for all: worldslargestlesson.globalgoals.org Can *you* fix climate change?: youtube.com/watch?v=yiw6_JakZFc

POLITICS	All about Youth Parliament, UN Youth and how to get involved: unyouth.org.nz parliament.nz/mi/get-involved/youth-parliament myd.govt.nz/young-people Information on the New Zealand Parliament: parliament.nz/en/visit-and-learn/educators-and-students/resources ondemand.parliament.nz Information on political systems: kids.britannica.com/kids/article/political-systems/390910 Ten inspiring young people: waterford.org/education/kids-who-changed-the-world An accessible news hub covering current affairs on Instagram: instagram.com/shityoushouldcareabout
RELIGIONS AND BELIEFS	Information about religions around the world: thebestschools.org/magazine/world-religions-study-starters Festivals and celebrations in New Zealand: anyquestions.govt.nz/many_answers/festivals-and-celebrations-new-zealand
GIVING BACK	Student Volunteer Army: sva.org.nz The Duke of Edinburgh's Hillary Award: dofehillary.org.nz Guidance from the Citizens Advice Bureau on authenticating a charity: cab.org.nz/article/KB00001917

LAST
WORD

YOU'LL BE ALL RIGHT: AN OVERVIEW

#parenting101 #teenagers

'There is no such thing as a perfect parent.
So just be a real one.'
— SUE ATKINS

Now you've reached the end of this book, it's time to check in with you — how are you feeling? It's a lot to take in, right? Parenting should always be thought of as a marathon, not a sprint. As such, it's useful to keep the future in mind: 20 years on from here you want to be able to meet your now-teen for a coffee, to babysit any grandchildren and to be able to celebrate holidays together. In the meantime, you aren't expected to get things right all of the time. Mistakes will happen, you'll drop the ball on occasion and you'll wish for a redo. But ultimately, if you keep the communication channels open, your teen will be okay. It can be scary, but they don't need us scared. They need us informed.

This is why we need to have these conversations, and primarily the message here is that you'll be all right too.

You've sought out and read a book on how to stay in touch with your teen and their world, and that says a lot for starters. Hopefully, some of Molly's kōrero have had you thinking back and remembering what it was like for you as a teen, along with providing an insight into your own teen's thoughts and feelings: the good bits, the bad bits and everything in between. There will be differences in your experiences, but there will also be some striking similarities.

You don't have to agree or feel comfortable with everything you've read in this book, but that's not really the point. Our teens will be talking about each and every topic anyway. By keeping yourself up to speed as much as possible, you'll be able to stay involved and even have some input, particularly should things go awry. All the time you've spent with them so far has started to lay a foundation for what they feel able to go on and do.

This investment will have shown them you are interested in them and their opinions, you care for what happens to them and you're on their side. They are learning lessons that will build their character, which includes helping them develop emotional intelligence and resilience. You are not solely there to entertain them: boredom is a gift as it enables them to take responsibility for their own time. Don't save them too much; let them fall sometimes, to help them learn that actions have consequences. They will also realise that they can cope in times of adversity, disappointment and stress. This in the long term is incredibly reassuring for both them and for you. Every time a hiccup happens, it gives them more confidence that they can cope, brush themselves off, take the lessons and move forward.

Writer Yvonne Walus illustrates this beautifully:

> Picture a tree growing on an exposed hilltop: when the wind blows, a resilient tree bends with the gust and straightens back up when the squall dies down. A fragile tree, on the other hand, might snap in half or be uprooted by bad weather. Similarly, resilient people don't dwell on their failures or wallow in self-pity: they acknowledge the situation, they learn from their mistakes, and then they move on.[1]

Your teen will model a lot of what they do on you — or deliberately do the opposite because what you do doesn't work for them. You may butt heads sometimes (or oftentimes for a while), and that's normal, as they test boundaries and become more their own person. They're not a mini-me and they are all the more interesting for that. Give each other room so that you can find ways to always be in each other's space. Gently remind them, though, that for a little while longer, it's your house rules. Don't be afraid to say no, but not all the time. Pick your fights; not everything is worth going after. It's about compromise, rather than control. It is not the time to be their buddy when they are a teen: that comes later, when they're all grown up. Keep your humour, and in the future you will be able to enjoy recounting anecdotes about where the wheels came off, even if things didn't feel quite so funny at the time.

For now they need your guidance, they need you to hold the line and they need you to be fair. Admit your mistakes and apologise if you want your teen to do the same. Make sure they know you are grateful to have them in your life: say thank you when they are open and share their thoughts and experiences with you. You take a lead role in their support team, and this will continue to be true as they become more independent and self-sufficient. It's not as if things are all sorted once they turn 18. You are both working towards laying the groundwork for your future relationship with each other where you both interact as adults.

If they are moving out imminently, listen to any concerns that come up for them and assist them in solving things for themselves. If you don't take over and don't judge them, it will show your teen not only that you think they are capable, but also that you trust them to do a good job. At the same time, it's important they realise that asking for help doesn't mean they aren't adulting well.

Always look for the best in them, even in those moments where it seems hard: these are the times they probably need it the most. Let them know that they are appreciated and enjoyed for who they are and that they are someone people want to spend time with.

Remember that you love them, and you're already nine-tenths of the way there.

> 'Ka whāngaia, ka tipu, ka puāwai.'
> 'Nurture it and it will grow, then blossom.'
> — MĀORI WHAKATAUKĪ (PROVERB)

ACKNOWLEDGEMENTS

From Robyn

Thank you to Gary, my partner in this parenting malarky, who has constantly reassured me that 'the kids will be all right', while making sure I am all right too.

From Molly

Thank you to Tyla, whose support has been unwavering and whose resilience has been inspiring.

From Robyn and Molly

Thank you to Debbie, who, over an extraordinary amount of early-morning and late-night calls (as we balanced UK and New Zealand time zones), allowed us our very own sounding board, challenged us on every semicolon and constantly shared her voice of wisdom.

Thank you to Billy H., Gus, Nicola, Karen and Krissy, who took the time to read through and provide such insightful feedback. We and the book have benefited greatly from it.

Thanks to the following specialists and colleagues who shared their knowledge and their time to ensure accuracy and authenticity of specific chapters: Waratah Taogaga, Cultural Director at Helensville Primary School, in regard to the use of te reo Māori and tikanga Māori in Chapter 8 (Wellbeing and Mental Health) and in headings throughout; Cassandra Woollett, National Clinical Supervisor at Natural Fertility NZ, for Chapter 9 (More Body Talk); Miriam Gioia Sessa, Sexual Violence Prevention Specialist, for Chapters 11 (Consent) and 12 (Safe Relationships); and Nikki Denholm, Director of the Light Project, for Chapter 13 (The Problem with Porn). Thanks also to everyone else who supported us through this project.

And thank you to our publisher, Michelle, for this amazing opportunity, and for her support and guidance throughout. Thanks also to our project editor Leanne and everyone else in the team at Allen & Unwin, including freelance copy editor Matt Turner.

HELPLINES IN NEW ZEALAND

Find a comprehensive and regularly updated list of helplines (downloadable as a PDF) here: mentalhealth.org.nz/resources/resource/helplines-and-local-mental-health-services

MENTAL HEALTH HELPLINES

Need to talk? — Free call or text 1737 any time for support from a trained counsellor.

Lifeline — 0800 543 354 (0800 LIFELINE) or free text 4357 (HELP)

Suicide Crisis Helpline — 0508 828 865 (0508 TAUTOKO)

Samaritans — 0800 726 666

Rural Support — 0800 787 254. Provides support (including mental health support) for those living rurally.

Victim Support — 0800 842 846

Depression Helpline — 0800 111 757 or free text 4202 to talk to a trained counsellor about how you are feeling or to ask any questions.

depression.org.nz (includes *The Journal* online help service)

Healthline — 0800 611 116

DRUG, ALCOHOL AND ADDICTION HELPLINES

Quit Line — 0800 778 778. For smoking cessation help.

Alcohol and Drug Helpline — 0800 787 797 or online chat at alcoholdrughelp.org.nz/helpline

Gambling Helpline — 0800 654 655

HELPLINES FOR CHILDREN, TEENS AND YOUNG PEOPLE

Youthline — 0800 376 633, free text 234, email talk@youthline.co.nz or chat online at youthline.co.nz/web-chat-counselling

Kidsline — 0800 543 754 or kidsline.org.nz

thelowdown.co.nz — Free text 5626 or email team@thelowdown.co.nz

sparx.org.nz — An online e-therapy tool provided by the University of Auckland that helps young people learn skills to deal with feeling down, depressed or stressed.

What's Up — 0800 942 8787 (for 5–18-year-olds). Phone counselling is available Monday to Friday from 12 noon to 11 p.m., and weekends from 3 p.m. to 11 p.m. Online chat is available from 3 p.m. to 10 p.m. seven days a week, including all public holidays.

OTHER SPECIALIST HELPLINES

Anxiety NZ — 0800 269 4389 (0800 ANXIETY)

EDANZ — 0800 233 269 (0800 2 EDANZ) or email info@ed.org.nz. A service focused on improving outcomes for people with eating disorders and their families.

Skylight — 0800 299 100. For support through trauma, loss and grief. Available weekdays from 9 a.m. to 5 p.m.

RAINBOW MENTAL HEALTH HELPLINE

OUTLine NZ — 0800 688 5463 (0800 OUTLINE). Provides confidential telephone support for the rainbow community.

HELP FOR PARENTS, FAMILY AND FRIENDS

Parent Help — 0800 568 856 for parents/whānau seeking support, advice and practical strategies on all parenting concerns. Anonymous, non-judgemental and confidential.

Family Services 211 Helpline — 0800 211 211. For help finding (and direct transfer to) community-based health and social support services in your area.

Yellow Brick Road — 0800 732 825 (northern region), 0800 555 434 (central North Island) or 0800 876 682 (South Island). A service that supports families towards mental wellbeing.

al-anon.org.nz — When you don't know where to turn because someone drinks too much, Al-Anon Family Groups can help.

SUPPORT FOR KEEPING SAFE ONLINE

Netsafe — 0508 638 7233 (0508 NETSAFE), free text 'Netsafe' to 4282 or email help@netsafe.org.nz

FAMILY VIOLENCE, INTIMATE PARTNER VIOLENCE AND SEXUAL VIOLENCE HELPLINES

Rape Crisis — 0800 883 300

HELPLine — 09 623 1700 (Auckland) or 04 801 6655 (Wellington). Available 24/7.

Safe to Talk — 0800 044 334 or free text 4334. For help for anyone who has suffered from sexual harm. Available 24/7 and staffed by trained counsellors.

MOSAIC / Tiaki Tangata — 0800 942 294. Peer support for males who have experienced trauma and sexual abuse.

Male Survivors Aotearoa New Zealand — 0800 044 344. Offers one-to-one support as well as peer and support groups for male survivors of sexual abuse and their significant others.

Tu Wahine Trust — 09 838 8700. Kaupapa Māori counselling, therapy and support for survivors of sexual harm (mahi tukino) and violence within whānau.

Are You OK — 0800 456 450. A family violence helpline.

Women's Refuge Crisis Line — 0800 733 843 (0800 REFUGE). For women living with violence, or in fear, in their relationship or family.

Shakti Crisis Line — 0800 742 584. For migrant or refugee women living with family violence.

Vagus Line — 0800 567 6666. Aims to promote family harmony among Chinese people in New Zealand, enhance parenting skills, decrease conflict among family members (couple, parent–child, in-laws) and stop family violence. Available Monday, Wednesday and Friday from 12 noon to 2 p.m.

NOTES

1. THE TEENAGE BRAIN

1 Imperial College London. (n.d.). *What is nudge theory?* imperial.ac.uk/nudgeomics/about/what-is-nudge-theory

2 Stanford Children's Health. (n.d.). *Understanding the teen brain.* stanfordchildrens.org/en/topic/default?id=understanding-the-teen-brain-1-3051

3 American Academy of Child and Adolescent Psychiatry. (n.d.). *Teen brain: Behavior, problem solving, and decision making.* aacap.org/AACAP/Families_and_Youth/Facts_for_Families/FFF-Guide/The-Teen-Brain-Behavior-Problem-Solving-and-Decision-Making-095.aspx

4 ChatBus Trust. (2018, April 3). *Helping children dealing with their anger.* chatbus.org.nz/anger

5 Skipwith, D. (2021, May 19). *Inside the teenage brain: What changes and how to cope.* Stuff. stuff.co.nz/life-style/well-good/teach-me/300291087

6 Adapted from UK Violence Intervention and Prevention Centre. (n.d.). *The four basic styles of communication.* tinyurl.com/2p8p778p

7 Topornycky, J., & Golparian, S. (n.d.). *Balancing openness and interpretation in active listening.* files.eric.ed.gov/fulltext/EJ1104498.pdf

8 Middle Earth. (2019, July 1). *Teaching conflict resolution skills to youth.* middleearthnj.org/2019/07/01/teaching-conflict-resolution-skills-to-youth

9 Morin, A. (2020, June 24). *Teen slang words every parent should know.* Verywell Family. verywellfamily.com/a-teen-slang-dictionary-2610994

2. LEARNING AND LOOKING TO THE FUTURE

1 Farrington, C. A., Roderick, M., Allensworth, E., Nagaoka, J., Keyes, T. S., Johnson, D. W., & Beechum, N. O. (2012). *Teaching adolescents to become learners. The role of noncognitive factors in shaping school performance: A critical literature review.* Chicago: University of Chicago Consortium on Chicago School Research. consortium.uchicago.edu/publications/teaching-adolescents-become-learners-role-noncognitive-factors-shaping-school

2 Kelly, A. (2018, July 26). *My child is unhappy at school. Should we change schools or will it make things worse?* Nest Psychology. nestpsychology.com.au/uncategorized/my-child-is-unhappy-at-school-should-we-change-schools-or-will-it-make-things-worse

3 Figure.nz. (n.d.). *Home-schooled students in New Zealand.* tinyurl.com/yfjxuzw2

4 Stats NZ. (n.d.). *Life expectancy.* stats.govt.nz/topics/life-expectancy; Stats NZ (n.d.). *New Zealand abridged period life table: 2017–19.* stats.govt.nz/information-releases/new-zealand-abridged-period-life-table-201719

5   ZME Science. (2019, April 19). *'Cool' light improves learning and academic performance.* zmescience.com/medicine/mind-and-brain/lighting-and-mind-study

6   Gifted & Talented Education. (n.d.). *Gifted learners: Characteristics of the gifted.* gifted.tki.org.nz/define-and-identify/characteristics-of-the-gifted-and-talented

7   Singhal, P. (2017, April 30). PWC to end university degree employment requirement. *Sydney Morning Herald.* smh.com.au/education/pwc-to-end-university-degree-employment-requirement-20170424-gvrb7c

8   Investopedia. (2021, August 26). *Gig economy.* investopedia.com/terms/g/gig-economy.asp

9   Ibid.

10 Scoop. (2021). *NZ tech sector soaring since Covid.* scoop.co.nz/stories/SC2108/S00013/nz-tech-sector-soaring-since-covid.htm

11 Heissel, J., & Norris, S. (2020, December 17). Rise and shine. *Education Next, 19*(3), 54–61. educationnext.org/rise-shine-how-school-start-times-affect-academic-performance

12 Kelley, P., Lockley, S. W., Kelley, J., & Evans, M. D. (2017). Is 8:30 a.m. still too early to start school? A 10:00 a.m. school start time improves health and performance of students aged 13–16. *Frontiers in Human Neuroscience, 11.* doi:10.3389/fnhum.2017.00588

13 Morin, A. (2017, November 1). Should kids be allowed to take mental health days? *Psychology Today.* psychologytoday.com/au/blog/what-mentally-strong-people-dont-do/201711/should-kids-be-allowed-take-mental-health-days

3. FRIENDSHIPS AND FRENEMIES

1   Anderson, M., & Jiang, J. (2019, December 31). *Teens, friendships and online groups.* Pew Research Center. pewresearch.org/internet/2018/11/28/teens-friendships-and-online-groups

2   Saeri, A. K., Cruwys, T., Barlow, F. K., Stronge, S., & Sibley, C. G. (2017). Social connectedness improves public mental health: Investigating bidirectional relationships in the New Zealand attitudes and values survey. *Australian & New Zealand Journal of Psychiatry, 52*(4), 365–374. doi:10.1177/0004867417723990

3   Gee, S. (2018, August 31). *Teen goes social media free to stay connected.* Stuff. stuff.co.nz/life-style/life/106243852

4   Kvalsvig, A. (2018). *Wellbeing and mental distress in Aotearoa New Zealand: Snapshot 2016.* Wellington: Health Promotion Agency.

5   Ministry of Social Development. (n.d.). *Social connectedness.* socialreport.msd.govt.nz/social-connectedness/loneliness.html

6   Borys, S., & Perlman, D. (1985). Gender differences in loneliness. *Personality and Social Psychology Bulletin, 11*(1), 63–74. psycnet.apa.org/record/1986-06376-001

7   Webb, S., Kingstone, S., Richardson, E., & Flett, J. (2020). *Rapid evidence brief: COVID-19 Youth Recovery Plan 2020–2022.* Te Hiringa Hauora Health Promotion Agency. tinyurl.com/44y774ub

8   Mental Health America. (n.d.). *Is your child lonely?* mhanational.org/your-child-lonely-parents

9   Ibid.

10 Ditch the Label. (2021, April 21). *Are they really your friend? 15 signs that suggest otherwise.* tinyurl.com/c8f22u23

11 Gordon, S. (2020, January 19). *Is your child's friend really a frenemy?* Verywell Family. verywellfamily.com/is-your-childs-friend-a-bully-460640

12 Geller, L., & Blumberg, P. O. (2020, January 15). 15 signs you're in a toxic relationship — and how to GTFO. *Women's Health.* womenshealthmag.com/relationships/a25939904/signs-of-toxic-friendships

13 Hoffses, K. (Ed.). (2018, July). *Helping kids cope with cliques (for parents).* Nemours KidsHealth. kidshealth.org/en/parents/cliques.html

14 Whitson, S. (2014, October 20). What parents can do when their kids' friendships end badly. *Psychology Today.* psychologytoday.com/us/blog/passive-aggressive-diaries/201410/what-parents-can-do-when-their-kids-friendships-end-badly

15 Bagwell, C. (2020, June 11). *Teens are wired to resent being stuck with parents and cut off from friends during coronavirus lockdown.* The Conversation. theconversation.com/teens-are-wired-to-resent-being-stuck-with-parents-and-cut-off-from-friends-during-coronavirus-lockdown-136435

16 Preidt, R. (2021, March 15.) *Pandemic has harmed mental health of teens.* WebMD. webmd.com/lung/news/20210315/pandemic-has-harmed-mental-health-of-teens

4. BULLIED, BULLYING AND BYSTANDERS

1   United Nations Educational, Scientific and Cultural Organization. (2019). *Behind the numbers: Ending school violence and bullying.* unicef.org/media/66496/file/Behind-the-Numbers.pdf

2   Bullying Free NZ. (n.d.). *What is bullying?* bullyingfree.nz/about-bullying/what-is-bullying

3   Raising Children Network. (2021, March 11). *Teenage bullying: What to look for and how to help.* raisingchildren.net.au/pre-teens/behaviour/bullying/teen-bullying

4   *Kandersteg declaration against bullying in children and youth.* (2007, June 8–10). Joint Efforts Against Victimization Conference, Kandersteg, Switzerland. mac-cura.ca/download%20docs/KanderstegDeclarationEN.pdf

5   Programme for International Student Assessment (PISA). (2017). *PISA 2015 results (vol. III): Students' well-being.* doi.org/10.1787/9789264273856-20-en

6   CensusAtSchool New Zealand. (2015, June 11). *Verbal abuse the biggest bullying problem at school: Students.* new.censusatschool.org.nz/2015/06/12/verbal-abuse

7   PISA, *PISA 2015 results.*

8   Ipsos. (2018, August 27). *Cyberbullying in NZ 3rd highest of 29 countries surveyed.* ipsos.com/en-nz/cyberbullying-nz-3rd-highest-29-countries-surveyed

9   Green, V. A., Harcourt, S., Mattioni, L., & Prior, T. (2013). *Bullying in New Zealand schools: A final report.* Wellington: Victoria University of Wellington. wgtn.ac.nz/education/pdf/Bullying-in-NZ-Schools.pdf

10 US Department of Education. (2019). *Student reports of bullying: Results from the 2017 school.* Web tables NCES 2019-054. nces.ed.gov/pubs2019/2019054.pdf

11 Huitsing, G., & Veenstra, R. (2012). Bullying in classrooms: Participant roles from a social network perspective. *Aggressive Behavior, 38*(6), 494–509. doi:10.1002/ab.21438

12 StopBullying.gov. (2021, June 2). *Who is at risk.* stopbullying.gov/bullying/at-risk

13 Ditch the Label. (2020, November 17). *The annual bullying survey 2020.* ditchthelabel.org/research-papers/the-annual-bullying-survey-2020

14 Rivara, F., & Le Menestrel, S. (Eds.). (2016). *Preventing bullying through science, policy, and practice* [e-book]. Washington: National Academies Press. doi. org/10.17226/23482

15 Mark. (2018, July 5). *Bullying in NZ schools: What you need to know and what you can do about it.* The Child Psychology Service. thechildpsychologyservice. co.nz/bullying-in-nz-schools-what-you-need-to-know-and-what-you-can-do-about-it

16 Enough is enough. (n.d.). *Cyberbullying statistics.* enough.org/stats_cyberbullying

17 Marbaix, E. (2019, June 21). What are the 5 types of cyber bullying? *Axcis.* testblog.axcis.co.uk.gridhosted.co.uk/2019/06/what-are-the-5-types-of-cyber-bullying

18 BroadbandSearch.net. (n.d.). *All the latest cyber bullying statistics and what they mean in 2021.* broadbandsearch.net/blog/cyber-bullying-statistics

19 PrivacySavvy. (2020, December 31). *40 cyberbullying statistics for 2021 (it is time to take action).* privacysavvy.com/security/safe-browsing/cyberbullying-statistics-facts

20 Harmful Digital Communications Act 2015, No. 63. legislation.govt.nz/act/public/2015/0063/latest/whole.html

21 Edwards, K. (2017, March 23). *What to do if your child is the bully.* Stuff. stuff.co.nz/life-style/parenting/big-kids/five-to-ten/90775899

22 Branson, C. E., & Cornell, D. G. (2009). A comparison of self and peer reports in the assessment of middle school bullying. *Journal of Applied School Psychology, 25*(1), 5–27. doi:10.1080/15377900802484133

23 Katz, B. (2020, December 23). *My child is a bully: What should I do?* Child Mind Institute. childmind.org/article/what-to-do-if-your-child-is-bullying

24 Gordon, S. (2021, February 4). *8 reasons why bullies engage in hurtful behavior.* Verywell Family. verywellfamily.com/reasons-why-teens-bully-others-460532

25 Edwards, What to do if your child is the bully.

26 Branson & Cornell, A comparison of self and peer reports.

27 Ibid.

28 Edwards, What to do if your child is the bully.

29 Ibid.

30 Branson & Cornell, A comparison of self and peer reports.
31 Ibid.
32 ReachOut Parents. (n.d.). *My teen has been called a bully, what should I do?* parents.au.reachout.com/common-concerns/everyday-issues/things-to-try-bullying-behaviour/my-teen-has-been-called-a-bully-what-should-i-do
33 StopBullying.gov. (2021, May 21). *Bystanders are essential to bullying prevention and intervention.* stopbullying.gov/resources/research-resources/bystanders-are-essential
34 National Bullying Prevention Center. (n.d.). *Bullying facts.* pacer.org/bullying/resources/facts.asp
35 Thornberg, R., Tenenbaum, L., Varjas, K., Meyers, J., Jungert, T., & Vanegas, G. (2012). Bystander motivation in bullying incidents: To intervene or not to intervene? *Western Journal of Emergency Medicine, 13*(3), 247–252. doi:10.5811/westjem.2012.3.11792
36 Hollaback! (n.d.). *Bystander resources.* ihollaback.org/bystander-resources
37 Pink Shirt Day. (n.d.). *Kōrero mai, kōrero atu, mauri tū, mauri ora.* pinkshirtday.org.nz/about/korero-mai-korero-atu-mauri-tu-mauri-ora
38 Child Mind Institute. (2019, March 21). *Harvard goes gaga against bullying.* childmind.org/blog/harvard-goes-gaga-against-bullying; Child Mind Institute. (2019, March 21). *Celebs share their bullying stories on video.* childmind.org/blog/celebs-share-their-bullying-stories-on-video/; Osborne, E. (2012, September 19). *Rihanna: 'I was bullied, but now I'm in a much bigger world'.* Capital FM. capitalfm.com/features/famous-people-celebrities-bullying/rihanna

5. TEENS AND TECH

1 Gerritsen, J. (2021, May 9). *NZ teens among world's biggest internet users.* RNZ. rnz.co.nz/news/national/442196/nz-teens-among-world-s-biggest-internet-users
2 Pacheco, E., & Melhuish, N. (n.d.). *New Zealand teens' digital profile: A factsheet.* Netsafe. netsafe.org.nz/wp-content/uploads/2018/02/NZ-teens-digital-profile_factsheet_Feb-2018.pdf
3 Ibid.
4 Ibid.
5 Ibid.
6 NZ On Air. (n.d.). *Children's media use survey 2020.* nzonair.govt.nz/research/childrens-media-use-survey-2020
7 CensusAtSchool New Zealand. (2019, April 29). *One in three high-school students spends too much time on social media* [Press release]. new.censusatschool.org.nz/category/press-releases
8 Roehampton University. (2021, February 23). *The impact of Covid-19 lockdown on internet use and escapism in adolescents* [Press release]. roehampton.ac.uk/psychology/news/the-impact-of-covid-19-lockdown-on-internet-use-and-escapism-in-adolescents
9 Ann & Robert Lurie Children's Hospital of Chicago. (2020, September 1).

Parenting teens in the age of social media. *Lurie Children's Blog*. luriechildrens. org/en/blog/social-media-parenting-statistics

10 CensusAtSchool New Zealand, *One in three high-school students*; Gerritsen, *NZ teens among world's biggest internet users.*

11 Perficient, Inc. (n.d.). *Mobile vs. desktop usage in 2020.* perficient.com/insights/ research-hub/mobile-vs-desktop-usage

12 Collins, S. (2019, August 26). School census: Most kids have their own phones by age 11. *New Zealand Herald.* tinyurl.com/2ket3yr6

13 Hinton, T. (2021, March 9). *New Zealand: Internet users.* Statista. statista.com/ statistics/680688

14 Netsafe. (2018). *New Zealand teens and digital harm: Statistical insights into experiences, impact and response.* women.govt.nz/sites/public_files/NZ-teens-and-digital-harm_statistical-insights_2018.pdf

15 Netsafe. (n.d.). 'User Agreement Template — Secondary' in *Student user agreements.* netsafe.org.nz/the-kit/wp-content/uploads/2018/06/Netsafe-Kit-Student-User-Agreement-Template-Secondary.docx

16 CensusAtSchool New Zealand, *One in three high-school students.*

17 Martin, A. (2021, July 3). Ollie Robinson clear for cricket return after ban over racist and sexist tweets. *The Guardian.* theguardian.com/sport/2021/jul/03/ollie-robinson-clear-for-cricket-return-after-ban-for-offensive-tweets

18 Coughlan, S. (2018, May 21). *'Sharenting' puts young at risk of online fraud.* BBC News. bbc.co.uk/news/education-44153754

19 Casserly, M. (2020, November 12). *Top tips for keeping your kids safe when using Facebook, YouTube and the whole internet.* Tech Advisor. techadvisor.com/feature/security/how-keep-your-kids-safe-online-3411255

20 Corcione, A., & Elizabeth, D. (2017, September 17). 9 signs you're being catfished. *Teen Vogue.* teenvogue.com/story/signs-youre-being-catfished

21 Central Bank. (n.d.). *Seven tips to avoid online fraud.* centralbank.net/personal/security/security-news/seven-tips-to-avoid-online-fraud

22 Roach, J. (2021, August 23). *What is a vpn and how does it work?* Forbes. forbes. com/advisor/business/software/what-is-a-vpn-and-how-does-it-work

23 BulliesOut. (2021, March 17). *Trolling.* bulliesout.com/need-support/young-people/trolling

24 Brand, J. E., Todhunter, S., & Jervis, J. (2017). *Digital New Zealand 2018.* Eveleigh, NSW: Interactive Games & Entertainment Association. igea.net/wp-content/uploads/2017/08/Digital-New-Zealand-2018-DNZ18-Full-1.pdf

25 TechJury. (2021, September 9). *Video game demographics: 27 powerful stats for 2021.* techjury.net/blog/video-game-demographics

26 Brand et al., *Digital New Zealand 2018.*

27 Association for Psychological Science. (2016, July 13). *Playing action video games boosts visual motor skill underlying driving.* ScienceDaily. sciencedaily.com/releases/2016/07/160713105856.htm

28 Hurley, K. (2018, August 28). *Kids, teens, and gaming disorder: The World Health Organization (WHO) defines the mental health condition.* Psycom.net. psycom.net/gaming-disorder

29 Cybersmile Foundation. (n.d.). *Types of in-game abuse*. cybersmile.org/advice-help/gaming/types-of-abuse

30 Te Mana Whakaatu Classification Office. (n.d.). *How games are classified*. classificationoffice.govt.nz/about-nz-classification/how-games-are-classified/#who-classifies-games-in-new-zealand

31 McCarthy, C. (2016, August 2). *Protecting children from the dangers of 'virtual violence'*. Harvard Health. health.harvard.edu/newsletter_article/violent-video-games-and-young-people; Roy, E. A. (2018, December 20). New Zealand survey suggests real crime figures could be seven times official tally. *The Guardian*. theguardian.com/world/2018/dec/20/new-zealand-survey-suggests-real-figures-could-be-seven-times-official-tally

32 World Health Organization. (n.d.). *Addictive behaviours: Gaming disorder*. who.int/news-room/q-a-detail/addictive-behaviours-gaming-disorder

33 Hurley, *Kids, teens, and gaming disorder*.

6. DRINKING, PUFFING AND PARTYING

1 SmokeFree NZ. (n.d.). *Legislation*. smokefree.org.nz/smokefree-environments/legislation

2 Cheers. (n.d.). *Cheers! — Parents and teens*. cheers.org.nz/parents-and-teens

3 New Zealand Police. (n.d.). *Cannabis and the law*. police.govt.nz/advice-services/drugs-and-alcohol/cannabis-and-law

4 Health Navigator New Zealand. (n.d.). *Consent*. healthnavigator.org.nz/health-a-z/c/consent

5 Campbell, S., Jasoni, C., & Longnecker, N. (2019). Drinking patterns and attitudes about alcohol among New Zealand adolescents. *Kōtuitui: New Zealand Journal of Social Sciences Online, 14*(2), 276–289. doi:10.1080/1177083x.2019.1625934

6 New, M. J. (Ed.). (2014, October). *Date rape (for teens)*. Nemours KidsHealth. kidshealth.org/en/teens/date-rape.html

7 Happy Mondays. (1991). 24 hour party people [Song recorded by Happy Mondays]. On *Squirrel and G-Man twenty four hour party people plastic face carnt smile (white out)*. London Music, William George Entertainment Ltd., Warner/Chappell Music Publishing Ltd.

8 Gurram, N., & Martin, G. (2019). *Disparities in age of smoking initiation and transition to daily smoking in New Zealand*. Wellington: Health Promotion Agency.

9 Lucas, N., Gurram, N., & Thimasarn-Anwar, T., (2020). *Smoking and vaping behaviours among 14 and 15-year-olds: Results from the 2018 Youth Insights Survey*. Wellington: Health Promotion Agency/Te Hiringa Hauora Research and Evaluation Unit.

10 Campbell et al., Drinking patterns and attitudes about alcohol.

11 Ministry of Health. (n.d.). *Key indicators*. minhealthnz.shinyapps.io/nz-health-survey-2019-20-annual-data-explorer/_w_c09d8b2a/#!/key-indicators

12 Fleming, T., Ball, J., Peiris-John, R., Crengle, S., Bavin, L., Tiatia-Seath, J.,

Archer, D., & Clark, T. (2020). *Youth19 Rangatahi Smart Survey, initial findings: Substance use*. Auckland and Wellington: Youth19 Research Group, University of Auckland and Victoria University of Wellington.

13 NZ Drug Foundation. (2019). *Drugs in NZ*. drugfoundation.org.nz/policy-and-advocacy/drugs-in-nz-an-overview

14 Mt-Isa, S., Tzoulaki, I., Callréus, T., Micaleff, A., & Ashby, D. (2011). Weighing benefit–risk of medicines: Concepts and approaches. *Drug Discovery Today: Technologies, 8*(1). doi:10.1016/j.ddtec.2011.04.002

15 Tots to Teens. (2019, March 21). *Alcohol and teenagers*. totstoteens.co.nz/child/teens/alcohol-and-teenagers

16 Tobacco Free CA. (2020, June 19). *The effects of nicotine on the adolescent brain — vaping side effects*. tobaccofreeca.com/e-cigarettes/the-effects-of-nicotine-on-the-adolescent-brain

17 White, A. M., & Swartzwelder, H. S. (2004). Hippocampal function during adolescence: A unique target of ethanol effects. *Annals of the New York Academy of Sciences, 1021*(1), 206–220. doi:10.1196/annals.1308.026

18 Jacobus, J., & Tapert, S. F. (2013). Neurotoxic effects of alcohol in adolescence. *Annual Review of Clinical Psychology, 9*(1), 703–721. doi:10.1146/annurev-clinpsy-050212-185610; Hermens, D. F., Lagopoulos, J., Tobias-Webb, J., De Regt, T., Dore, G., Juckes, L., Latt, N., & Hickie, I. B. (2013). Pathways to alcohol-induced brain impairment in young people: A review. *Cortex, 49*(1), 3–17. doi:10.1016/j.cortex.2012.05.021

19 Scott, J. C., Slomiak, S. T., Jones, J. D., Rosen, A. F., Moore, T. M., & Gur, R. C. (2018). Association of cannabis with cognitive functioning in adolescents and young adults. *JAMA Psychiatry, 75*(6), 585. doi:10.1001/jamapsychiatry.2018.0335

20 Meier, M. H., Caspi, A., Ambler, A., Harrington, H., Houts, R., Keefe, R. S., McDonald, K., Ward, A., Poulton, R., & Moffitt, T. E. (2012). Persistent cannabis users show neuropsychological decline from childhood to midlife. *Proceedings of the National Academy of Sciences, 109*(40). doi:10.1073/pnas.1206820109

21 Morin, J.-F. G., Afzali, M. H., Bourque, J., Stewart, S. H., Séguin, J. R., O'Leary-Barrett, M., & Conrod, P. J. (2019). A population-based analysis of the relationship between substance use and adolescent cognitive development. *American Journal of Psychiatry, 176*(2), 98–106. doi:10.1176/appi.ajp.2018.18020202

22 New Zealand Police Managers' Guild Trust. (2020, April 28). *Teen safety — parenting, youth suicide, alcohol, drugs*. pmgt.org.nz/teen-safety

23 Ibid.

24 Ibid.

25 Centers for Disease Control and Prevention. (2020, October 23). *Underage drinking*. cdc.gov/alcohol/fact-sheets/underage-drinking.htm

26 Ibid.

27 New Zealand Police Managers' Guild Trust, *Teen safety*.

28 Ibid.

29 Ibid.

30 Ibid.
31 Ibid.
32 Centers for Disease Control and Prevention, *Underage drinking*.
33 SmokeFree NZ. (n.d.). *Smokefree Aotearoa 2025*. NZ Ministry of Health. health.govt.nz/our-work/preventative-health-wellness/tobacco-control/smokefree-aotearoa-2025
34 Palmer, R. (2021, December 9). *Smokefree action plan: Cigarette sales to be banned for younger generations*. RNZ. rnz.co.nz/news/political/457539/smokefree-action-plan-cigarette-sales-to-be-banned-for-younger-generations
35 Lucas et al., *Smoking and vaping behaviours among 14 and 15-year-olds*.
36 SmokeFree NZ. (n.d.). *The risks of tobacco*. teen.smokefree.gov/the-risks-of-tobacco
37 Lucas et al., *Smoking and vaping behaviours among 14 and 15-year-olds*.
38 Community & Public Health. (n.d.). *Supporting young people to remain smokefree*. cph.co.nz/your-health/stopping-youth-smoking
39 Martinelli, K. (2019, October 23). *Teen vaping: What you need to know*. Child Mind Institute. childmind.org/article/teen-vaping-what-you-need-to-know
40 Ball, J., Fleming, T., Archer, D., Sutcliffe, K., & Clark, T. (n.d.). *Youth19 Vaping Fact Sheet*. Youth19: A Youth2000 Survey. tinyurl.com/5ecp97s7
41 Lucas et al., *Smoking and vaping behaviours among 14 and 15-year-olds*.
42 National Institute on Drug Abuse. (2021, May 17). *Marijuana trends and statistics*. drugabuse.gov/drug-topics/marijuana/marijuana-trends-statistics
43 Miech, R., Patrick, M. E., O'Malley, P. M., & Johnston, L. D. (2017). E-cigarette use as a predictor of cigarette smoking: Results from a 1-year follow-up of a national sample of 12th grade students. *Tobacco Control, 26*(e2). doi:10.1136/tobaccocontrol-2016-053291; Preidt, R. (2018, October 2). *More evidence that e-cig use leads to smoking*. WebMD. webmd.com/parenting/news/20181002/more-evidence-that-e-cig-use-leads-to-smoking
44 Harvard T. H. Chan School of Public Health. (2019, February 1). *Common e-cigarette flavorings may impair lung function* [Press release]. hsph.harvard.edu/news/press-releases/common-e-cigarette-chemical-flavorings-may-impair-lung-function
45 Grady, D. (2019, November 11). Vaping illnesses are linked to vitamin E acetate, CDC says. *New York Times*. nytimes.com/2019/11/08/health/vaping-illness-cdc.html
46 Blaha, M. J. (n.d.). *5 vaping facts you need to know*. Johns Hopkins Medicine. hopkinsmedicine.org/health/wellness-and-prevention/5-truths-you-need-to-know-about-vaping
47 Ministry of Health NZ. (2021, October 4). *About the Smokefree Environments and Regulated Products (Vaping) Amendment Act*. Ministry of Health NZ. health.govt.nz/our-work/regulation-health-and-disability-system/regulation-vaping-and-smokeless-tobacco-products/about-smokefree-environments-and-regulated-products-vaping-amendment-act
48 British Heart Foundation. (2021, August). *Shisha*. bhf.org.uk/informationsupport/risk-factors/smoking/shisha

49 World Health Organization. (2021). *Global alcohol action plan 2022–2030*. tinyurl.com/yc7fhhzs

50 NZ Drug Foundation. (2019). *Drugs in NZ*. drugfoundation.org.nz/policy-and-advocacy/drugs-in-nz-an-overview

51 Olson, J. S., & Crosnoe, R. (2018). The interplay of peer, parent, and adolescent drinking. *Social Science Quarterly, 99*(4), 1349–1362. doi:10.1111/ssqu.12497 ·

52 Wallis, N. (2016, May 11). *Teenage drinking*. RNZ. rnz.co.nz/national/programmes/ninetonoon/audio/201800447/nathan-mikaere-wallis-on-teenage-drinking

53 National Research Council (US) and Institute of Medicine (US). (2004). *Reducing underage drinking: a collective responsibility*. Washington: National Academies Press.

54 Centers for Disease Control and Prevention, *Underage drinking*.

55 Miller, J. W., Naimi, T. S., Brewer, R. D., & Jones, S. E. (2007). Binge drinking and associated health risk behaviors among high school students. *Pediatrics, 119*(1), 76–85. doi:10.1542/peds.2006-1517

56 Scoop. (1999). *Prime minister welcomes lower drinking age* [Press release]. scoop.co.nz/stories/PA9911/S00633/prime-minister-welcomes-lower-drinking-age.htm

57 ActionPoint. (n.d.). *Trends in adolescent drinking in New Zealand*. actionpoint.org.nz/trends_in_adolescent_drinking_in_new_zealand

58 Ministry of Health, *Key indicators*.

59 Fleming et al., *Youth19 Rangatahi Smart Survey*.

60 Robertson, K., & Tustin, K. (2018). Students who limit their drinking, as recommended by national guidelines, are stigmatized, ostracized, or the subject of peer pressure: Limiting consumption is all but prohibited in a culture of intoxication. *Substance Abuse: Research and Treatment, 12*. doi:10.1177/1178221818792414

61 American Psychological Association. (n.d.). *Brain research advances help elucidate teen behavior*. apa.org/monitor/julaug04/brain

62 Ministry of Transport Te Manatū Waka. (n.d.). *Alcohol and drugs*. transport.govt.nz/statistics-and-insights/safety-annual-statistics/sheet/alcohol-and-drugs

63 Ibid.

64 Health Promotion Agency. (2014). *What the Sale and Supply of Alcohol Act means for under-18s*. tinyurl.com/yckzm8cx

65 Here to Help. (n.d.). *Cannabis use and youth: A parent's guide*. heretohelp.bc.ca/workbook/cannabis-use-and-youth-a-parents-guide

66 Dowshen, S. (Ed.). (2018, May). *Marijuana (for teens)*. KidsHealth. kidshealth.org/en/teens/marijuana.html

67 Ibid.

68 HealthEd. (n.d.). *Cannabis and your health*. healthed.govt.nz/resource/cannabis-and-your-health

69 World Health Organization. (n.d.). *Adolescent and young adult health*. who.int/news-room/fact-sheets/detail/adolescents-health-risks-and-solutions

70 Fleming et al., *Youth19 Rangatahi Smart Survey.*

71 Centers for Disease Control and Prevention. (2017, May 12). *Fast facts and fact sheets.* cdc.gov/marijuana/fact-sheets.htm

72 US National Institute on Drug Abuse. (2021, May 24). *Is marijuana a gateway drug?* drugabuse.gov/publications/research-reports/marijuana/marijuana-gateway-drug

73 Vanyukov, M. M., Tarter, R. E., Kirillova, G. P., Kirisci, L., Reynolds, M. D., Kreek, M. J., Conway, K. P., Maher, B. S., Iacono, W. G., Bierut, L., Neale, M. C., Clark, D. B., & Ridenour, T. A. (2012). Common liability to addiction and 'gateway hypothesis': Theoretical, empirical and evolutionary perspective. *Drug and Alcohol Dependence, 123.* doi:10.1016/j.drugalcdep.2011.12.018

74 US National Institute on Drug Abuse, *Is marijuana a gateway drug?*

75 Heads Up. (n.d.). *Drugs and the teen brain.* headsup.scholastic.com/sites/default/files/NIDA17-INS1_downloadall.pdf

76 Young, K. (2020, October 27). *Teens and drugs.* Hey Sigmund. heysigmund.com/teens-drugs-parents-need-know-conversation-response

77 Lilienfeld, S. O. (2014, January 1). Why 'just say no' doesn't work. *Scientific American.* scientificamerican.com/article/why-just-say-no-doesnt-work

7. BODY TALK: SELF-ESTEEM AND BODY IMAGE

1 GoodTherapy. (n.d.). *Body image.* goodtherapy.org/learn-about-therapy/issues/body-image

2 Medical News Today. (n.d.). *Body image: What is it, and how can I improve it?* medicalnewstoday.com/articles/249190#definitio

3 O'Connell Rapira, L. (2018, September 3). *Ngā kōrero hauora o ngā taiohi; A community-powered report on conversations with 1000 young people about wellbeing.* Community Research. communityresearch.org.nz/research/nga-korero-hauora-o-nga-taiohi-a-community-powered-report-on-conversations-with-1000-young-people-about-wellbeing

4 Miller, E., & Halberstadt, J. (2005). Media consumption, body image and thin ideals in New Zealand men and women. *New Zealand Journal of Psychology, 34*(3), 189–195.

5 Eisenberg, M. E., Wall, M., & Neumark-Sztainer, D. (2012). Muscle-enhancing behaviors among adolescent girls and boys. *Pediatrics, 130*(6), 1019–1026. doi: 10.1542/peds.2012-0095

6 The Be Real Campaign. (n.d.). *Body confidence for everyone.* berealcampaign.co.uk/wp-content/uploads/2018/02/Somebody_like_me-v1.0.pdf

7 YoungMinds. (n.d.). *Body image.* youngminds.org.uk/find-help/feelings-and-symptoms/body-image

8 Nest Consulting. (n.d.). *Body talk.* nestconsulting.nz/school-programmes/body-talk

9 Kite, L., & Kite, L. (2021). *More than a body: Your body is an instrument, not an ornament.* Boston: Houghton Mifflin Harcourt.

10 Cave, J. (2016, April 1). *Fat men's clubs existed, and they were the ultimate*

celebration of body acceptance. HuffPost. huffpost.com/entry/fat-mens-clubs_n_
56fc2d77e4b0daf53aee85d2

11 Petty, A. (2021, February 11). *How women's 'perfect' body types changed throughout
history.* TheList.com. thelist.com/44261/womens-perfect-body-types-changed-
throughout-history

12 Fashion and Textile Museum. (2020, April 29). Exhibition archives:
1930s fashion and photographs. *Fashion and Textile Museum.*
fashiontextilemuseumblog.wordpress.com/2020/04/29/exhibition-archives-
1930s-fashion-and-photographs

13 Martin, J. M., Ghafer, J. M., Cummins, D. L., Mamelak, A. J., Schmults, C.
D., Parikh, M., Speyer, L.-A., Chuang, A., Richardson, H. V., Stein, D., &
Liégeois, N. J. (2009, December). Changes in skin tanning attitudes, fashion
articles and advertisements in the early 20th century. *American Journal of Public
Health, 99*(12), 2140–2146. ncbi.nlm.nih.gov/pmc/articles/PMC2775759

14 Van Edwards, V. (2020, April 21). *Beauty standards: See how body types change
through history.* Science of People. scienceofpeople.com/beauty-standards

15 Petty, A. (2020, December 15). *How men's perfect body types have changed
throughout history.* TheList.com. thelist.com/56105/mens-perfect-body-types-
changed-throughout-history

16 Thomson, L. (2020, February 21). Instagram star photoshops pics to show
how body ideals have changed over time. *Metro.* metro.co.uk/2020/02/21/
instagram-star-photoshops-pics-show-body-ideals-changed-
decades-12279753

17 Lee, T. (2020, September 17). Are the '90s responsible for our filter-obsessed
generation? *Harper's Bazaar.* harpersbazaar.com/uk/fashion/a34052490/are-
the-90s-responsible-for-our-filter-obsessed-generation

18 Jurkštaitė, D. (1966, January 1). *How the 'perfect' female body has changed in 100
years.* Bored Panda. boredpanda.com/shape-perfect-body-changed-100-years

19 St Thomas University. (n.d.). *Henna: Its history and cultural significance.* stu.ca/
lnap/henna-its-history-and-cultural-significance

20 American Addiction Centers. (2012). *Dying to be Barbie: Eating disorders in
pursuit of the impossible.* rehabs.com/explore/dying-to-be-barbie

21 Smart, C. (2020, April 1). *Boys have body image issues too.* Raising Teenagers.
raisingteenagers.com.au/boys-have-body-image-issues

22 Schuster, D. (2020, February 27). *5 people championing body positivity in the
LGBTQ community.* Goodnet. goodnet.org/articles/5-people-championing-
body-positivity-in-lgbtq-community

23 Broadwater, A. (2020, June 6). *How to be body positive without being ableist.*
Medium. medium.com/@ashleybroadwater346/how-to-be-body-positive-
without-being-ableist-cdebceb34b59

24 Bucchianeri, M. M., Fernandes, N., Loth, K., Hannan, P. J., Eisenberg, M. E.,
& Neumark-Sztainer, D. (2016). Body dissatisfaction: Do associations with
disordered eating and psychological well-being differ across race/ethnicity in
adolescent girls and boys? *Cultural Diversity and Ethnic Minority Psychology,
22*(1), 137–146. doi:10.1037/ cdp000003

25 Winter, V. R., Danforth, L. K., Landor, A., & Pevehouse-Pfeiffer, D. (2019). Toward an understanding of racial and ethnic diversity in body image among women. *Social Work Research*, *43*(2), 69–80. doi:10.1093/swr/svy033

26 Mental Health Foundation. (2020, August 6). *Body image and ethnic background*. mentalhealth.org.uk/publications/body-image-report/ethnic-background

27 YWCA. (n.d.). *Why should we still care about body image?* ywca.org.nz/media/2417/bi-report-final-compressed.pdf

28 Sainsbury, A., & Hay, P. (2014). Call for an urgent rethink of the 'health at every size' concept. *Journal of Eating Disorders*, *2*(1). doi:10.1186/2050-2974-2-8

29 Smith, S. L., Choueiti, M., Pieper, K., Gillig, T., Lee, C., & DeLuca, D. (2015). *Inequality in 700 popular films: Examining portrayals of gender, race, and LGBT status from 2007 to 2014*. Los Angeles: USC Annenberg Media, Diversity, & Social Change Initiative. researchgate.net/publication/312489186_Inequality_in_700_Popular_Films

30 Blackford, M. (2021, January 21). *Body image and social media questionnaire*. FHE Health. fherehab.com/news/bodypositive

31 Advertising Standards Authority. (n.d.). *Children and young people's advertising code*. asa.co.nz/codes/codes/children-and-young-people

32 CBS Interactive. (2015, February 19). *A look back at 25 years of Photoshop*. CBS News. cbsnews.com/news/adobe-photoshop-anniversary-russell-brown-thomas-knoll

33 Dove UK. (2021, August 10). *The* Evolution *video: The use of airbrushing and photoshop in the media*. dove.com/uk/dove-self-esteem-project/help-for-parents/media-and-celebrities/the-evolution-video.html

34 Rosten, J. (2012, January 10). *Fotoshop by Adobé* [Video]. YouTube. youtube.com/watch?v=S_vVUIYOmJM

35 Cosslett, R. L. (2016, September 8). Thinner, smoother, better. *The Guardian*. theguardian.com/commentisfree/2016/sep/08/thinner-retouching-girls-image-manipulation-women

36 TVNZ. (2018, August 30). *Kiwi Instagram star Jess Quinn speaks out against image retouching that sees bodies changed to fit 'cookie cutter mould of perfection'*. tvnz.co.nz/one-news/new-zealand/kiwi-instagram-star-jess-quinn-speaks-against-image-retouching-sees-bodies-changed-fit-cookie-cutter-mould-perfection

37 Malvindi, D. (2020, September 30). 11 celebrities who've spoken out about photo editing and unrealistic beauty standards. *Marie Claire*. marieclaire.com.au/celebrities-spoken-out-unrealistic-photo-editing

38 Delaney, C. (2012, August 29). Girlfriend m*agazine launches self-esteem campaign, editor: 'this is not a response to* Cleo *anti-airbrushing protest'*. Mumbrella. mumbrella.com.au/girlfriend-magazine-launches-self-esteem-campaign-editor-this-is-not-a-response-to-cleo-anti-airbrushing-protest-112664

39 House of Commons Committees. (n.d.). *How do you feel about your body image?* houseofcommons.shorthandstories.com/women-and-equalities-body-image-survey/index.html

40 Campbell, L. (2018, July 5). *Taking too many selfies may be bad for your teen's health*. Healthline. healthline.com/health-news/taking-too-many-selfies-may-be-bad-for-your-teens-health

41 All is for All. (2021, August 14). *Accessible communications*. allisforall.com

42 Davison, I. (2020, September 22). Entrepreneur and wheelchair user Grace Stratton opens NZ Fashion Week. *New Zealand Herald*. tinyurl.com/yck5wv8p

43 Mackay, P. (2021, May 26). *Young Kiwis ask for social media safeguards*. Graeme Dingle Foundation. dinglefoundation.org.nz/young-kiwis-ask-for-social-media-safeguards

44 Blackford, *Body image and social media questionnaire*.

45 Lee, Are the '90s responsible for our filter-obsessed generation?

46 Mackay, *Young Kiwis ask for social media safeguards*.

47 Simmons, R. (2016, August 19). How social media is a toxic mirror. *Time*. time.com/4459153/social-media-body-image

48 McGuire, J. (2019, April 16). Positive uses of social media in body image advocacy. *Eating Disorder Hope*. eatingdisorderhope.com/blog/positive-social-media-body-image

49 Mackay, *Young Kiwis ask for social media safeguards*.

50 Javier, S. J., Moore, M. P., & Belgrave, F. Z. (2015). Racial comparisons in perceptions of maternal and peer attitudes, body dissatisfaction, and eating disorders among African American and white women. *Women & Health, 56*(6), 615–633. doi:10.1080/03630242.2015.1118721; McCabe, M. P., Fotu, K., & Dewes, O. (2011). Body image, weight loss and muscle building among Tongan adolescents in Tonga and New Zealand. *Journal of Health Psychology, 16*(7), 1101–1108. doi:10.1177/1359105311400226

51 Michael, S. L., Wentzel, K., Elliott, M. N., Dittus, P. J., Kanouse, D. E., Wallander, J. L., Pasch, K. E., Franzini, L., Taylor, W. C., Qureshi, T., Franklin, F. A., & Schuster, M. A. (2013). Parental and peer factors associated with body image discrepancy among fifth-grade boys and girls. *Journal of Youth and Adolescence, 43*(1), 15–29. doi:10.1007/s10964-012-9899-8

52 Weingus, L. (2018, August 15). *Inside the body image movement that doesn't focus on your appearance*. HuffPost. huffpost.com/entry/what-is-body-neutrality_n_5b61d8f9e4b0de86f49d31b4

53 Moore, C. (2021, March 16). *Positive daily affirmations: Is there science behind it?* PositivePsychology.com. positivepsychology.com/daily-affirmations

54 Green, A. (2019, September 11). Positive body image isn't enough. *Psychology Today*. psychologytoday.com/nz/blog/psy-curious/201909/positive-body-image-isnt-enough

55 Raypole, C. (2021, January 20). *How to shift from 'body positivity' to 'body neutrality' — and why you should*. Healthline. healthline.com/health/body-neutrality

56 Simpson, C. C., & Mazzeo, S. E. (2016). Skinny is not enough: A content analysis of fitspiration on Pinterest. *Health Communication, 32*(5), 560–567. doi:10.1080/10410236.2016.1140273

57 Chambers, T. (2021, May 11). *NZ children see more than 40 ads for unhealthy products each day. It's time to change marketing rules.* The Conversation. theconversation.com/nz-children-see-more-than-40-ads-for-unhealthy-products-each-day-its-time-to-change-marketing-rules-120841

58 Healthy Food Guide. (2020, September 22). *How to embrace mindful eating.* healthyfood.com/advice/how-to-embrace-mindful-eating

59 Gordon, M. G. (2021, October 5). Ex-Facebook employee says network hurts kids, fuels division. *New Zealand Herald.* tinyurl.com/2p9fjk9k

60 Meta. (2021). *Welcome to Meta.* about.facebook.com/meta

8. WELLBEING AND MENTAL HEALTH

1 Durie, M. (1994). *Whaiora: Maori health development.* Melbourne: Oxford University Press.

2 Ibid.

3 Kvalsvig, A. (2018). *Wellbeing and mental distress in Aotearoa New Zealand: Snapshot 2016.* Wellington: Health Promotion Agency. www.hpa.org.nz/sites/default/files/Wellbeing-And-Mental-Distress-Snapshot-2016-Final-FEB2018.pdf

4 Based on an illustration in Durie, M. (1994). *Whaiora: Maori health development.* Melbourne: Oxford University Press. Reproduced by permission of Oxford University Press Australia from *Maori Health Development* © Oxford University Press, www.oup.com.au

5 Helliwell, J. F., Layard, R. Sachs, J., & De Neve, J.-E. (Eds.). (2020). *World happiness report 2020.* Sustainable Development Solutions Network. worldhappiness.report/ed/2020

6 Fleming, T., Peiris-John, R., Crengle, S., Archer, D., Sutcliffe, K., Lewycka, S., & Clark, T. (2020). *Youth19 Rangatahi Smart Survey, initial findings: Introduction and methods.* Auckland and Wellington: The Youth19 Research Group, University of Auckland and Victoria University of Wellington. Encouragingly, though, in the year to 30 June 2020 there was a decrease in the number of young New Zealanders dying by suspected suicide, particularly in the 15–19 age range (down from 73 to 59) and the 20–24 age range (down from 91 to 60). Rates for both age groups decreased, from 23 to 19 and from 27 to 18 in every 100,000, respectively. tinyurl.com/569u4dx7; Office of the Chief Coroner of New Zealand. (2020, August 21). *Chief coroner releases annual provisional suicide figures* [Press release]. coronialservices.justice.govt.nz/assets/Documents/Publications/Chief-Coroner-Suicide-Stats-2020-Media-Release.pdf

7 Ibid.

8 Counting Ourselves. (2019). *Executive summary.* countingourselves.nz/wp-content/uploads/2019/09/Executive-Summary.pdf

9 Fleming et al., *Youth19 Rangatahi Smart Survey, initial findings: Introduction and methods.*

10 Raising Children Network. (2021, May 13). *Mental health in pre-teens and*

teenagers. raisingchildren.net.au/pre-teens/mental-health-physical-health/
about-mental-health/teen-mental-health

11 Ginsburg, K. (n.d.). *The 7 Cs: The essential building blocks of resilience.* Fostering
Resilience. fosteringresilience.com/7cs.php

12 Sarrionandia, A., Ramos-Díaz, E., & Fernández-Lasarte, O. (2018). Resilience
as a mediator of emotional intelligence and perceived stress: A cross-country
study. *Frontiers in Psychology, 9.* doi:10.3389/fpsyg.2018.02653

13 Goleman, D. (2020). *Emotional intelligence.* New York: Bantam Books.

14 Melbourne Child Psychology School Psychology Services. (2013, November
4). *How to help teenagers develop empathy.* melbournechildpsychology.com.au/
blog/help-teenagers-develop-empathy

15 MentalHelp.net. (n.d.). *Resilience: Emotional intelligence.* mentalhelp.net/
emotional-resilience/emotional-intelligence

16 Wood, A. M., Maltby, J., Stewart, N., Linley, P. A., & Joseph, S. (2008). A
social-cognitive model of trait and state levels of gratitude. *Emotion, 8*(2),
281–290. doi:10.1037/1528-3542.8.2.281

17 Raising Children Network. (2021, May 14). *Stress in pre-teens and teenagers.*
raisingchildren.net.au/pre-teens/mental-health-physical-health/stress-anxiety-
depression/stress-in-teens

18 Fleming, T., Tiatia-Seath, J., Peiris-John, R., Sutcliffe, K., Archer, D., Bavin,
L., Crengle, S., & Clark, T. (2020). *Youth19 Rangatahi Smart Survey, initial
findings: Hauora hinengaro / Emotional and mental health.* Auckland and
Wellington: The Youth19 Research Group, University of Auckland and
Victoria University of Wellington, New Zealand. tinyurl.com/32aetdav

19 Office of the Children's Commissioner. (n.d.). *Health rights.* occ.org.nz/
childrens-rights-and-advice/health-rights/#disclosure

20 World Health Organization. (n.d.). *Adolescent mental health.* who.int/news-
room/fact-sheets/detail/adolescent-mental-health

21 Figure.nz. (n.d.). *New Zealand adults diagnosed with anxiety disorder.* tinyurl.
com/2p8skhy2

22 Our Health: Hawke's Bay. (n.d.). *A guide to understanding self-injury for school
professionals.* ourhealthhb.nz/assets/Uploads/Self-Injury-Schools-highres1.pdf

23 EDANZ. (n.d.). *Causes of eating disorders.* ed.org.nz/eating-disorders-
explained/causes

24 Mental Health Foundation. (n.d.). *Eating disorders.* mentalhealth.org.nz/
conditions/condition/eating-disorders

25 Big increase in eating disorder cases at New Zealand clinics. (2016, October 9).
New Zealand Herald. tinyurl.com/e9nm2v96

26 Leask, A. (2021, April 12). Eating disorders: 'endless' and 'horrendous' costs
for parents who cannot get sick teens into public health system. *New Zealand
Herald.* tinyurl.com/2tk5usbp

27 GP Pulse. (2020, March 10). *Rethinking eating disorders as both psychiatric and
metabolic.* rnzcgp.org.nz/GPPulse/Clinical_news/2020/Rethinking_Eating_
Disorders

9. MORE BODY TALK: PERSONAL AND SEXUAL HEALTH

1 Breuner, C. C., & Mattson, G. (2016). Sexuality education for children and adolescents. *Pediatrics, 138*(2). doi:10.1542/peds.2016-1348

2 Ackard, D. M., & Neumark-Sztainer, D. (2001). Health care information sources for adolescents: Age and gender differences on use, concerns, and needs. *Journal of Adolescent Health, 29*(3), 170–176. doi:10.1016/s1054-139x(01)00253-1

3 Lantos, H., Manlove, J., Wildsmith, E., Faccio, B., Guzman, L., & Moore, K. (2019). Parent–teen communication about sexual and reproductive health: Cohort differences by race/ethnicity and nativity. *International Journal of Environmental Research and Public Health, 16*(5), 833. doi:10.3390/ijerph16050833

4 Ibid.

5 Donovan, S., and Telfar-Barnard, L. (2019). Age of first menstruation in New Zealand: Findings from first ever national-level data and implications for age-appropriate education and support. *New Zealand Medical Journal, 132*(1500), 100–102. tinyurl.com/mwh4dpxp

6 Health Navigator New Zealand. (n.d.). *Menstruation.* healthnavigator.org.nz/health-a-z/m/menstruation

7 Ibid.

8 Mayo Clinic. (2020, February 7). *Premenstrual syndrome (PMS).* mayoclinic.org/diseases-conditions/premenstrual-syndrome/symptoms-causes/syc-20376780

9 Cornforth, T. (n.d.). *What teen girls should know about having periods.* Verywell Health. verywellhealth.com/answers-to-your-questions-about-first-periods-3520915

10 Endometriosis New Zealand. (2020, March 30). *Endo information: Common inflammatory disease.* nzendo.org.nz/endo-information

11 Weschler, T. (2006). *Cycle savvy: The teen girl's guide to her awesome body and all its menstrual mysteries.* Collins.

12 Dell'Amore, C. (2020, March 19). How a man produces 1,500 sperm a second. *National Geographic.* nationalgeographic.com/science/article/100318-men-sperm-1500-stem-cells-second-male-birth-control

13 Fertility Week. (n.d.). *Infertility in New Zealand.* fertilityweek.org.nz/archive/fertility-week-2019/fertility-topics/infertility-new-zealand

14 Your Fertility. (n.d.). *Understanding how to improve your chance of having a baby.* yourfertility.org.au

15 Your Fertility. (n.d.). *Why age matters for men and women who want to have a family.* yourfertility.org.au/everyone/age; Fertility Week, *Infertility in New Zealand.*

16 Fertility Week, *Infertility in New Zealand.*

17 Davis, N. (2019, January 15). Many in UK lose virginity before they are ready — study. *The Guardian.* theguardian.com/lifeandstyle/2019/jan/15/women-and-men-are-losing-virginity-before-they-are-ready-study

18 Clark, T. (n.d.). *Youth'12 sexual and reproductive health findings.* Auckland: University of Auckland. tinyurl.com/ys5xaec9

19 Clark, T. C., Lambert, M., Fenaughty, J., Tiatia-Seath, J., Bavin, L., Peiris-John, R., Sutcliffe, K., Crengle, S., & Fleming, T. (2020). *Youth19*

Rangatahi Smart Survey, initial findings: Sexual and reproductive health of New Zealand secondary school students. Auckland and Wellington: Youth19 Research Group, University of Auckland and Victoria University of Wellington.

20 Appleton-Dyer, S., Edirisuriya, N., & Bosswell, A. (2016). *Youth 2000 summary report.* Synergia. matesanddates.co.nz/assets/resources/synergia-youth2000-summary-report-2016.pdf

21 Breuner & Mattson, Sexuality education for children and adolescents.

22 Clark et al., *Youth19 Rangatahi Smart Survey, initial findings.*

23 Health Navigator New Zealand. (n.d.). *Progestogen-only oral contraceptive pill.* healthnavigator.org.nz/medicines/p/progestogen-only-oral-contraceptive-pill

24 Figure.nz. (n.d.). *Teenage fertility rate in New Zealand: 1962–2020, live births per 1000 women aged 15–19.* figure.nz/chart/wYHyiilvB9uCUP8O

25 Hughes, C. (2020, November 23). *Teenage live birth rate in New Zealand from 2010 to 2019, by age group.* Statista. statista.com/statistics/1064263

26 Young, D. H., & Coughlan, D. E. (2017, June 13). *Just the facts on STIs.* Just the Facts. justthefacts.co.nz/sexually-transmitted-infections-stis/facts-about-stis-sexually-transmitted-infections-stds

27 Ibid.

28 Ellis, S. J., & Aitken, R. (2020). Sexual health practices of 16 to 19 year olds in New Zealand: An exploratory study. *Journal of Primary Health Care, 12*(1), 64. doi:10.1071/hc19037

29 Ministry of Health NZ. (n.d.). *Questions and answers about HPV immunisation.* tinyurl.com/3kkawe35

30 Vandergriendt, C. (2021, March 12). *Why do we have pubic hair?* Healthline. healthline.com/health/purpose-of-pubic-hair

31 National Screening Unit. (n.d.). *The smear process.* timetoscreen.nz/cervical-screening/having-smear/the-smear-process

32 National Screening Unit. (n.d.). *Give your cervix some screen time.* tinyurl.com/2p9ypetf

33 Nest Consulting. (n.d.). *Nest.Box.* nestconsulting.nz/product/nest-box

10. RAINBOW TEENS

1 Springboard Trust. (2020, October 16). *Colour coded: The story of 'pink for girls, blue for boys'.* springboardtrust.org.nz/news/colour-coded-the-story-of-pink-for-girls-blue-for-boys

2 Human Rights Commission. (n.d.). *Our work.* hrc.co.nz/our-work

3 Lonely Planet. (2021, July 8). *The 15 most gay-friendly places on the planet.* lonelyplanet.com/articles/most-gay-friendly-countries

4 Veale, J., Byrne, J., Tan, K., Guy, S., Yee, A., Nopera, T., & Bentham, R. (2019) *Counting Ourselves: The health and wellbeing of trans and non-binary people in Aotearoa New Zealand.* Hamilton: Transgender Health Research Lab, University of Waikato. researchcommons.waikato.ac.nz/handle/10289/12942

5 The Safe Zone Project. (n.d.). *LGBTQ+ vocabulary glossary of terms.* thesafezoneproject.com/resources/vocabulary

6   Lucassen, M. F. G., Clark, T. C., Moselen, E., Robinson, E. M., & The Adolescent Health Research Group. (2014). *Youth'12 The Health and Wellbeing of Secondary School Students in New Zealand: Results for young people attracted to the same sex or both sexes.* Auckland: University of Auckland. See also the Kinsey scale, e.g., Ferguson, S. (2020, January 29). *What's the deal with the Kinsey scale?* Healthline. healthline.com/health/kinsey-scale

7   Fleming, T. (2021, June 25). *Same- and multiple-sex attracted students: A Youth19 brief.* Youth19. youth19.ac.nz/publications/same-and-multiple-sex-attracted-students-brief

8   Stats NZ. (n.d.). *New sexual identity wellbeing data reflects diversity of New Zealanders.* stats.govt.nz/news/new-sexual-identity-wellbeing-data-reflects-diversity-of-new-zealanders

9   OutLine. (2020, September 25). *Glossary of LGBTIQ+ language.* outline.org.nz/glossary

10 Ibid; OutLine references this material to Statistics New Zealand, and also references the 'Takatāpui' entry to 'Pega, Gray, & Veale, 2010'.

11 The Diversity Center. (2021, August 13). *Pronouns: A how-to.* diversitycenterneo.org/about-us/pronouns

12 Health Navigator NZ. (n.d.). *Pronouns — what they are and why they matter.* healthnavigator.org.nz/healthy-living/p/pronouns-what-they-are-and-why-they-matter

13 Ministry of Health NZ. (2011, December 21). *Suicide prevention action plan 2008–2012: Second progress report.* health.govt.nz/publication/suicide-prevention-action-plan-2008-2012-second-progress-report

14 Fleming, *Same- and multiple-sex attracted students.*

15 Veale et al., *Counting Ourselves.*

16 Inclusive Education. (n.d.). *Guide to LGBTIQA+ students.* inclusive.tki.org.nz/guides/supporting-lgbtiqa-students

17 Stonewall. (2020, August 13). *Advice if you think your child might be LGBTQ+.* stonewall.org.uk/help-advice/coming-out/advice-if-you-think-your-child-might-be-lgbtq

18 Family Equality. (2020, April 17). *What to do (and not do) when your child comes out to you.* familyequality.org/2018/06/01/what-to-do-and-not-do-when-your-child-comes-out-to-you

19 Planned Parenthood (n.d.). *What should I teach my high school-aged teen about identity?* plannedparenthood.org/learn/parents/high-school/what-should-i-teach-my-high-school-aged-teen-about-identity

20 Ibid.

21 Family Equality, *What to do (and not do) when your child comes out to you.*

22 Ibid.

23 Planned Parenthood, *What should I teach my high school-aged teen about identity?*

24 Ibid.

25 British LGBT Awards. (2021). *LGBT<25 survey results headlines.* britishlgbtawards.com/lgbt-25-results-headlines

11. CONSENT

1 Oxford University Press. (1989). Consent. In *Oxford English Dictionary*. tinyurl. com/4nzx2p2p

2 California Legislative Information. (n.d.). *Student safety: sexual assault* [Bill text, SB-967]. leginfo.legislature.ca.gov/faces/billNavClient.xhtml?bill_ id=201320140SB967

3 Clark, T. C., Moselen, E., Dixon, R., The Adolescent Health Research Group, & Lewycka, S. (2015). *Sexual and reproductive health and sexual violence among New Zealand secondary school students: Findings from the Youth'12 national youth health and wellbeing survey*. Auckland: University of Auckland.

4 Ibid.

5 Appleton-Dyer, S., Edirisuriya, N., & Boswell, A. (2016, July 7). *Youth 2000 summary report*. matesanddates.co.nz/assets/resources/synergia-youth2000-summary-report-2016.pdf

6 Clark et al., *Sexual and reproductive health and sexual violence among New Zealand secondary school students*.

7 Te Puni Kōkiri — Kāinga. (n.d.). *Māori family violence infographic*. tpk.govt.nz/ en/a-matou-mohiotanga/health/maori-family-violence-infographic

8 Appleton-Dyer et al., *Youth 2000 summary report*.

9 World Health Organization. (2012, July 11). *Violence against adults and children with disabilities*. who.int/disabilities/violence/en

10 Centers for Disease Control and Prevention. (2017, June 21). *LGBT youth*. cdc.gov/lgbthealth/youth.htm

11 UK Safer Internet Centre. (2017, December 6). *New research into sexual harassment of young people on the internet*. tinyurl.com/55kv7wtc

12 Warren, D., & Swami, N. (2019, November 1). Teenagers and sex. In Australian Institute of Family Studies, *Growing Up in Australia: The Longitudinal Study of Australian Children Annual Statistical Report 2018* (pp. 47–56) Melbourne: Australian Institute of Family Studies. growingupinaustralia.gov.au/research-findings/annual-statistical-reports-2018/teenagers-and-sex

13 Aspinall, G. (2018, September 25). 47% of people don't think you can withdraw consent if you're already naked. *Grazia*. graziadaily.co.uk/life/in-the-news/withdraw-consent-research-sexual-assault-rape

14 Basile, K. C., Clayton, H. B., DeGue, S., Gilford, J. W., Vagi, K. J., Suarez, N. A., Zwald, M. L., & Lowry, R. (2020). Interpersonal violence victimization among high school students — youth risk behavior survey, United States, 2019. *MMWR Supplements*, *69*(1), 28–37. doi:10.15585/mmwr.su6901a4

15 Smith, S. G., Zhang, X., Basile, K. C., Merrick, M. T., Wang, J., Kresnow, M., & Chen, J. (2018). *The national intimate partner and sexual violence survey (NISVS): 2015 data brief — updated release*. Atlanta, GA: National Center for Injury Prevention and Control, Centers for Disease Control and Prevention.

16 Singh, M. M., Parsekar, S. S., & Nair, S. N. (2014). An epidemiological overview of child sexual abuse. *Journal of Family Medicine and Primary Care*, *3*(4), 430. doi:10.4103/2249-4863.148139

17 Youth Law (n.d.). *Your rights: Consent.* youthlaw.co.nz/rights/sex-relationships/consent

18 Tots to Teens. (2019, July 11). *Teenagers and sexual consent — it's like a cup of tea.* totstoteens.co.nz/teens/teenagers-and-sexual-consent-its-like-a-cup-of-tea

19 Eve. (2018, September 25). Sexual health week 2018: Let's talk consent. *Never Settle.* evegreenow.com/2018/09/25/sexual-health-week-consent

20 Ibid.

21 Taub, A. (2014, December 15). *Rape culture isn't a myth. It's real, and it's dangerous.* Vox. vox.com/2014/12/15/7371737

22 UN Women. (2019, November 18). *16 ways you can stand against rape culture.* unwomen.org/en/news/stories/2019/11/compilation-ways-you-can-stand-against-rape-culture

23 Marshall University Women's & Gender Center. (n.d.). *Rape culture.* marshall.edu/wcenter/sexual-assault/rape-culture

24 Jancic, B. (2020, September 22). Only 6 per cent of sexual violence cases reported to police end in jail: Major government study. *New Zealand Herald.* tinyurl.com/y75dx36t

25 Ministry of Justice. (n.d.). *Latest crime survey reveals surprising high levels of unreported sexual violence.* justice.govt.nz/about/news-and-media/news/latest-crime-survey-reveals-surprising-high-levels-of-unreported-sexual-violence

26 Molyneux, V. (2020, February 26). *New Zealand rape survivors humiliated with 'irrelevant' questions during trials.* Newshub. newshub.co.nz/home/new-zealand/2020/02/new-zealand-rape-survivors-humilated-with-irrelevant-questions-during-trials-study.html

27 Joint Venture. (n.d.). *Te Aorerekura. National strategy to eliminate family violence and sexual violence.* violencefree.govt.nz/national-strategy

28 Walton, S. (2021, April 11). *'No means no': Christchurch students raise awareness about sexual violence.* Stuff. stuff.co.nz/national/124802878; Dooney, L. (2017, March 13). *Protest at Parliament against rape culture in schools.* Stuff. stuff.co.nz/national/education/90374283

29 Youthline. (n.d.). *Sexual harassment, abuse and violence.* youthline.co.nz/abuse.html#sexual

30 Aspinall, 47% of people don't think you can withdraw consent if you're already naked.

31 Valenzuela, F. (n.d.). *5 songs that 'get' consent, and 5 that don't.* The Lantern Project. thelanternproject.org/blog/2020/05/18/5-songs-that-get-consent-5-that-dont

12. SAFE RELATIONSHIPS

1 Raising Children Network. (2018, May 2). *Friends and friendships: Pre-teens and teenagers.* raisingchildren.net.au/pre-teens/behaviour/peers-friends-trends/teen-friendships

2 Netsafe. (2021, February 10). *Catfish or real?* netsafe.org.nz/catfish

3 Parent Zone. (2017, April 5). *Online dating — should you be worried?* tinyurl.com/4jencwsc

4   Department of Health WA. (n.d.). *Assertive communication*. healthywa.wa.gov.
    au/Articles/A_E/Assertive-communication
5   UN Women. (2019, May 15). *Gender equality starts at home: Seven tips for
    raising feminist kids*. Medium. medium.com/we-the-peoples/gender-equality-
    starts-at-home-seven-tips-for-raising-feminist-kids-75e1bf00b863
6   Teen Talk. (n.d.). *Relationships*. teentalk.ca/learn-about/relationships
7   Flood, M. (2021, July 7). *Australian study reveals the dangers of 'toxic masculinity'
    to men and those around them*. The Conversation. theconversation.com/
    australian-study-reveals-the-dangers-of-toxic-masculinity-to-men-and-those-
    around-them-104694
8   Ibid.
9   Ministry of Education. (2021, July 13). *Relationships and sexuality education*.
    parents.education.govt.nz/secondary-school/learning-at-school/sexuality-
    education
10 Cherry, K. (n.d.). *How to know if you are in a healthy relationship*. Verywell
    Mind. verywellmind.com/all-about-healthy-relationship-4774802
11 RAINN. (2017, February 6). *Early warning signs of dating violence*. rainn.org/
    news/early-warning-signs-dating-violence
12 Beres, M. (2017). *Preventing adolescent relationship abuse and promoting healthy
    relationships*. New Zealand Family Violence Clearinghouse. nzfvc.org.nz/
    issues-paper-12-preventing-adolescent-relationship-abuse
13 Domestic Abuse Intervention Programs. (2021, April 24). *Wheel information
    center*. theduluthmodel.org/wheels
14 Lohmann, R. C. (2017, August 31). Abusive teen dating relationships.
    Psychology Today. psychologytoday.com/nz/blog/teen-angst/201708/abusive-
    teen-dating-relationships
15 New Zealand Police. (n.d.). *Loves-me-not*. police.govt.nz/advice-services/
    personal-community-safety/school-portal/resources/successful-relationships/
    loves-me

13. THE PROBLEM WITH PORN

1   Office of Film and Literature Classification (OFLC). (2018). *NZ youth and
    porn: Research findings of a survey on how and why young New Zealanders view
    online pornography*. classificationoffice.govt.nz/assets/PDFs/NZYouthPorn-
    OFLC-December2018-PrintVersion.pdf
2   Lexico. (n.d.). *Pornography*. lexico.com/definition/pornography
3   Fritz, N., Malic, V., Paul, B., & Zhou, Y. (2020). A descriptive analysis of the
    types, targets, and relative frequency of aggression in mainstream pornography.
    Archives of Sexual Behavior, 49(8), 3041–3053. doi:10.1007/s10508-020-01773-0
4   Ibid.
5   Bentley, L. (2021, March 4). *Five things kids need parents to know about anime*.
    Parents Aware Info. parentsaware.info/index.php/2017/05/04
6   Boundy, A. (2021, June 14). *Advice on how to talk to your child about porn*.
    Netsafe. netsafe.org.nz/porn-advice-parents

7 OFLC, *NZ youth and porn.*

8 OFLC. (2019). *Breaking down porn: A Classification Office analysis of commonly viewed pornography in NZ.* classificationoffice.govt.nz/assets/PDFs/Breaking-Down-Porn.pdf

9 OFLC. (2020). *Growing up with porn: Insights from young New Zealanders.* classificationoffice.govt.nz/news/latest-news/growing-up-with-porn-insights

10 Ibid.

11 OFLC, *NZ youth and porn.*

12 Parker, I. (2014, August 27). *Young people, sex and relationships: The new norms.* IPPR. ippr.org/publications/young-people-sex-and-relationships-the-new-norms

13 Waterson, J. (2020, January 31). Porn survey reveals extent of UK teenagers' viewing habits. *The Guardian.* theguardian.com/culture/2020/jan/31/porn-survey-uk-teenagers-viewing-habits-bbfc

14 OFLC, *NZ youth and porn.*

15 Vera-Gray, F., McGlynn, C., Kureshi, I., & Butterby, K. (2021). Sexual violence as a sexual script in mainstream online pornography. *British Journal of Criminology, 61*(5), 1243–1260. doi:10.1093/bjc/azab035

16 OFLC, *NZ youth and porn.*

17 Vera-Gray et al., *Sexual violence as a sexual script.*

18 OFLC, *Breaking down porn.*

19 Parker, *Young people, sex and relationships.*

20 Girlguiding. (2015). *Girls' attitudes survey 2015.* girlguiding.org.uk/globalassets/docs-and-resources/research-and-campaigns/girls-attitudes-survey-2015.pdf

21 OFLC, *Growing up with porn.*

22 OFLC, *NZ youth and porn.*

23 Girlguiding, *Girls' attitudes survey.*

24 OFLC, *Growing up with porn.*

25 Wright, P. J., Tokunaga, R. S., & Kraus, A. (2015). A meta-analysis of pornography consumption and actual acts of sexual aggression in general population studies. *Journal of Communication, 66*(1), 183–205. doi:10.1111/jcom.12201

26 Quadara, A., El-Murr, A., & Latham, J. (2017, December 6). *Online pornography: Effects on children and young people. Research snapshot.* Melbourne: Australian Institute of Family Studies. aifs.gov.au/publications/effects-pornography-children-and-young-people-snapshot

27 Carey, T. (2019, August 31). 'Don't wait': How to talk to teenagers about porn. *The Guardian.* theguardian.com/lifeandstyle/2019/aug/31/how-to-talk-to-teenagers-about-porn

28 Boundy, *Advice on how to talk to your child about porn.*

29 British Board of Film Classification. (2019, September 27). *Children see pornography as young as seven, new report finds.* bbfc.co.uk/about-us/news/children-see-pornography-as-young-as-seven-new-report-finds

30 OFLC, *Growing up with porn.*

31 Chan, M. (2016, April 19). Utah governor declares pornography a public health crisis. *Time*. time.com/4299919/utah-porn-public-health-crisis

32 Mahan, B. (2021, December 13). Is my ADHD teen addicted to porn? *ADDitude*. additudemag.com/porn-addiction-adhd-teen-signs-help

33 OFLC, *Breaking down porn*.

34 OFLC, *Growing up with porn*.

35 OFLC, *NZ youth and porn*.

36 Parker, *Young people, sex and relationships*.

37 Isaacs, K. (2020, March 9). Pornhub needs to change — or shut down. *The Guardian*. theguardian.com/global-development/2020/mar/09/pornhub-needs-to-change-or-shut-down; Grant, H. (2020, December 10). Pornhub to ban unverified uploads after child abuse content claims. *The Guardian*. theguardian.com/global-development/2020/dec/10/pornhub-to-ban-unverified-uploads-after-child-abuse-content-claims

38 University of Auckland. (n.d.). *Youth2000 publications*. fmhs.auckland.ac.nz/en/faculty/adolescent-health-research-group/publications-and-reports.html

39 Netsafe (n.d.). *The bare facts*. netsafe.org.nz/barefacts

40 Carey, 'Don't wait'.

14. PREPARING YOUR TEEN FOR ADULTING

1 Education Counts. (n.d.). *School leaver destinations*. educationcounts.govt.nz/statistics/what-happens-to-school-leavers

2 Deakin University. (n.d.). *Happiness at a high in 21st century*. deakin.edu.au/research/research-news-and-publications/articles/happiness-at-a-high-in-21st-century

3 Parker, T. (2015, October 2). Kiwi kids expect to leave home at 27. *New Zealand Herald*. tinyurl.com/2wjrnajn

4 RNZ. (2020, September 27). *More millennials moving back in with mum and dad*. rnz.co.nz/national/programmes/sunday/audio/2018765783/more-millennials-moving-back-in-with-mum-and-dad

5 Parker, Kiwi kids expect to leave home at 27.

6 Chef's Pencil. (2020, October 23). *Top most popular countries and cities for vegans in 2020*. chefspencil.com/top-most-popular-countries-and-cities-for-vegans-in-2020

7 Ministry of Health (n.d.). *How much activity is recommended?* health.govt.nz/your-health/healthy-living/food-activity-and-sleep/physical-activity/how-much-activity-recommended

8 Health Navigator New Zealand. (n.d.). *Masculinity and men's health*. healthnavigator.org.nz/healthy-living/m/masculinity-and-mens-health

9 Health Quality & Safety Commission New Zealand. (n.d.). *Atlas of healthcare variation*. hqsc.govt.nz/our-programmes/health-quality-evaluation/projects/atlas-of-healthcare-variation

10 Better Homes & Gardens. (n.d.). *How to dry clothing the right way for wrinkle-free results*. bhg.com/homekeeping/laundry-linens/clothes/dry-clothes

11 Every Dollar Counts. (2020, September 24). *Saving money on transport.* everydollarcounts.org.nz/transport

12 New Zealand Automobile Association. (2015). *A guide to buying your teenager their first car.* aa.co.nz/cars/motoring-blog/a-guide-to-buying-your-teenager-their-first-car

13 Scanlon, J. (2021, February 10). *Life skills every teen needs before leaving home: Tweens to teens.* Kidspot. kidspot.co.nz/tweens-to-teens/life-skills-every-teen-needs-before-leaving-home

14 Ministry of Social Development. (n.d.). *Road casualties: The social report 2016 — Te pūrongo oranga tangata.* socialreport.msd.govt.nz/safety/road-casualties.html

15 Spaceships. (n.d.). *10 easy tips that will make driving in New Zealand safer.* spaceshipsrentals.co.nz/blog/driving-new-zealand/safe-driving-tips

16 New Zealand Police. (n.d.). *Keeping our teenagers safe.* police.govt.nz/advice/personal-community/keeping-safe/teenager-safe

17 No One Ever Stands Alone. (n.d.). *Drive sober and drug free and we will all get home safely.* nesa.org.nz/drunk-driving

18 CensusAtSchool New Zealand. (2017, February 26). *How much pocket money do Kiwi kids get? Censusatschool finds out.* new.censusatschool.org.nz/2017/02/28

19 Employment New Zealand. (n.d.). *Young employees.* employment.govt.nz/starting-employment/rights-and-responsibilities/young-employees

20 StudyLink. (n.d.). *Student Loan.* studylink.govt.nz/products/a-z-products/student-loan

21 Arnett, J. J. (2014). *Beyond emerging adulthood: What does it mean to become an adult?* In J. J. Arnett, *Emerging adulthood* (pp. 311–333). New York: Oxford University Press.

22 wikiHow. (2020, September 9). *How to change a duvet cover.* wikihow.com/change-a-duvet-cover

23 Careers.govt.nz. (n.d.). *Tips for answering interview questions.* careers.govt.nz/job-hunting/interviews/tips-for-answering-interview-questions

15. GLOBAL TOPICS FOR TEENS

1 International Development Education Association of Scotland. (n.d.). *What is global citizenship education?* ideas-forum.org.uk/what-is-global-citizenship-education

2 Cooks-Campbell, A. (2021, September 22). *Implicit bias: How unconscious attitudes affect everything.* BetterUp. betterup.com/blog/what-is-implicit-bias

3 *Storysellercomics.* (n.d.). Instagram. instagram.com/p/CR_v8QmJpP6

4 UN Women. (n.d.). *Gender equality starts at home: Seven tips for raising feminist kids.* unwomen.org/en/news/stories/2019/5/compilation-gender-equality-starts-at-home

5 Maguire, A. (2021). Figure 2. In S. Lynch, S. Sutherland, J. L. Walton-Fisette & J. Reyes, *The A–Z of Social Justice: Part 1.* researchgate.net/figure/The-difference-between-the-terms-equality-equity-and-liberation-illustrated-C_fig1_340777978

6 To create your pepeha, go to *Pepeha.* pepeha.nz

7   Toi Te Ora Public Health. (n.d.). *Calendar of events*. toiteora.govt.nz/
    publications-and-resources/calendar-of-events
8   International Women's Development Agency. (2020, January 27). *What does
    intersectional feminism actually mean?* iwda.org.au/what-does-intersectional-
    feminism-actually-mean
9   Dobson, M. (n.d.). *Intersectionality: A fun guide*. theavarnagroup.com/wp-
    content/uploads/2015/11/Intersectionality.pdf
10 Rani, S. (n.d.). *Listening: An essential tool for anti-racism work*. Taking Charge of
    Your Health & Wellbeing. takingcharge.csh.umn.edu/listening-essential-tool-
    anti-racism-work
11 Saady, M. (2021, June 15). *Explain intersectionality to kids with this simple
    metaphor*. ParentsTogether. parents-together.org/explain-intersectionality-to-
    kids-with-this-simple-metaphor
12 Black Lives Matter. (n.d.). *About*. blacklivesmatter.com/about
13 Hunt, R. (2020, June 8). Protests continue around the world. *Ryland's
    Newspaper*. rylandsnewspaper.wordpress.com/2020/06/08/protests-continue-
    around-the-world
14 Smith, C., Tinirau, R., Rattray-Te Mana, H., Tawaroa, M., Barnes, H. M.,
    Cormack, D., & Fitzgerald, E. (2021). *Whakatika: A survey of Māori experiences
    of racism*. Te Atawhai o Te Ao Charitable Trust. whakatika.teatawhai.maori.nz/
    wp-content/uploads/2021/03/Whakatika-Report-March-2021.pdf
15 SchoolNews. (2021, September 13). *Finalised Aotearoa New Zealand history
    curriculum nears*. schoolnews.co.nz/2021/09/finalised-aotearoa-new-zealand-
    history-curriculum-nears
16 Ministry of Education. (n.d.). *Treaty of Waitangi principle*. The NZ Curriculum
    Online. nzcurriculum.tki.org.nz/Principles/Treaty-of-Waitangi-principle
17 UNICEF. (2020, June 17). *Talking to your kids about racism*. unicef.org/lac/en/
    stories/talking-your-kids-about-racism
18 Kersten, C. (2020, October 14). 8 ways to be a (better) ally. *The Peel*. news.syr.
    edu/the-peel/2020/10/14/8-ways-to-be-a-better-ally
19 Bovell, S. (2020). *A template of responses to racist comments*, reproduced on
    Parkminster United Church Facebook page. tinyurl.com/2vpx4jpt
20 Pickles, K. (2021, May 11). *NZ was first to grant women the vote in 1893,
    but then took 26 years to let them stand for parliament*. The Conversation.
    theconversation.com/nz-was-first-to-grant-women-the-vote-in-1893-but-
    then-took-26-years-to-let-them-stand-for-parliament-123467
21 Gen Less. (2021, October 15). *On the right side of history on women's rights*. Gen
    Less. genless.govt.nz/stories/on-the-right-side-of-history-on-womens-rights
22 New Zealand History | Ngā korero a ipurangi o Aotearoa. (n.d.). *New Zealand
    women and the vote*. nzhistory.govt.nz/politics/womens-suffrage
23 New Zealand History | Ngā korero a ipurangi o Aotearoa. (n.d.). *Family
    Planning*. nzhistory.govt.nz/women-together/family-planning
24 Friedan, B. (1963). *The feminine mystique*. New York: W. W. Norton.
25 Crenshaw, K. (2017). *On intersectionality: Essential writings*. New York: The
    New Press.

26 Grady, C. (2018, March 20). *The waves of feminism, and why people keep fighting over them, explained.* Vox. vox.com/2018/3/20/16955588/feminism-waves-explained-first-second-third-fourth

27 Brown, H. G. (1983). *Having it all: Love-success-sex-money: Even if you're starting with nothing.* London: Sidgwick & Jackson.

28 Wolf, N. (1990). *The beauty myth: How images of beauty are used against women.* London: Chatto & Windus.

29 Gender Equal NZ. (n.d.). *Making equality, reality.* genderequal.nz

30 Wilkes, M. (2019, September 24). *The other gender gap: Who's doing the bulk of the housework in 2019?* Stuff. stuff.co.nz/life-style/homed/latest/116007357/the-other-gender-gap-whos-doing-the-bulk-of-the-housework-in-2019

31 Bachelet, M. (2019, September 16). *Women's empowerment, gender equality and social protection: Where next?* United Nations Office of the High Commissioner for Human Rights. tinyurl.com/3p7ywnsu

32 Delao, M. (2021, March 4), quoting Constance Grady. A brief look at the four waves of feminism. *The Humanist.* thehumanist.com/commentary/a-brief-look-at-the-four-waves-of-feminism

33 Criado Perez, C. (2019). *Invisible women: Data bias in a world designed for men.* London: Chatto & Windus.

34 XR Scientists. (n.d.). *Frequently asked questions.* scientistsforxr.earth/faq

35 Rinkesh. (2020, June 17). *20 current environmental problems that our world is facing.* Conserve Energy Future. conserve-energy-future.com/15-current-environmental-problems.php

36 Kennedy, C., & Lindsey, R. (n.d.). *What's the difference between global warming and climate change?* NOAA. climate.gov/news-features/climate-qa/whats-difference-between-global-warming-and-climate-change

37 Education Central | Pokapū Mātauranga. (2019, March 14). *Nearly half of Kiwi students believe climate change is an 'urgent problem'.* educationcentral.co.nz/nearly-half-of-kiwi-students-believe-climate-change-is-an-urgent-problem

38 Taylor, P. (2020, December 2). New Zealand declares a climate change emergency. *The Guardian.* theguardian.com/world/2020/dec/02/new-zealand-declares-a-climate-change-emergency

39 McFall-Johnsen, M. (2019). The fashion industry emits more carbon than international flights and maritime shipping combined. Here are the biggest ways it impacts the planet. *Business Insider Australia.* businessinsider.com.au/fast-fashion-environmental-impact-pollution-emissions-waste-water

40 Gen Less. (n.d.). *Everyday life.* tinyurl.com/3xp8ttu4

41 20 young people explain how they identify politically and why. (2019, October 17). *Teen Vogue.* teenvogue.com/story/teens-how-identify-politically

42 New Zealand History | Ngā korero a ipurangi o Aotearoa. (n.d.). *Māori and the vote.* nzhistory.govt.nz/politics/maori-and-the-vote

43 Green Party of Aotearoa New Zealand. (n.d.). *Chlöe Swarbrick.* greens.org.nz/chloe_swarbrick

44 Cooke, H. (2020, October 18). *Election 2020: How Chlöe Swarbrick won the*

campaign of a lifetime and turned a blue seat green. Stuff. stuff.co.nz/national/
politics/300135748

45 Family Lives. (n.d.). *Worried about extremism and radicalisation?* familylives.org.
uk/advice/teenagers/behaviour/worried-about-extremism-and-radicalisation

46 United Nations. (n.d.). *Universal Declaration of Human Rights.* un.org/en/
about-us/universal-declaration-of-human-rights

47 Di Mento, M. (2013, September 12). *90% of kids give to charity.* Philanthropy.
com. philanthropy.com/article/90-of-kids-give-to-charity

48 Charities Services. (n.d.). *Supporting charities in New Zealand for stronger
communities.* charities.govt.nz/view-data

49 Edens, J. (2017, July 10). *New Zealanders give generously — almost $3 billion a
year — but rarely talk about it.* Stuff. stuff.co.nz/business/94560462

50 Student Volunteer Army. (2021, August 27). *New Zealanders to give back to their
communities.* sva.org.nz/our-story

51 Citizens Advice Bureau. (n.d.). *Is there a way to find out whether or not an
organisation is a genuine non-profit charity?* cab.org.nz/article/KB00001917

52 The Global Goals. (n.d.). *The world's to-do list.* globalgoals.org/news/the-
worlds-to-do-list

53 The World's Largest Lesson. (2021, March 12). *Teaching the goals for the first
time.* worldslargestlesson.globalgoals.org/campaign/getting-started

54 Ministry of Foreign Affairs and Trade. (n.d.). *Sustainable Development Goals.*
mfat.govt.nz/en/peace-rights-and-security/our-work-with-the-un/sustainable-
development-goals

YOU'LL BE ALL RIGHT: AN OVERVIEW

1 Walus, Yvonne. (n.d.). Teens under pressure?! Here's how to build their
resilience. *Tots to Teens.* totstoteens.co.nz/child/teens/teens-under-pressure-
heres-how-to-build-their-resilience

INDEX

S